D1131984

# Systematic Theology

*VOLUME VI*

PNEUMATOLOGY

By

LEWIS SPERRY CHAFER, D.D., Litt.D., Th.D.

*President and Professor of Systematic Theology*
*Dallas Theological Seminary*

*PUBLISHED BY*

DALLAS SEMINARY PRESS

DALLAS, TEXAS

*First Printing, March, 1948, 2,500*
*Second Printing, November, 1948, 2,500*
*Third Printing, May, 1950, 2,500*
*Fourth Printing, December, 1953, 2,500*
*Fifth Printing, October, 1957, 2,500*
*Sixth Printing, January, 1962, 2,500*
*Seventh Printing, October, 1964, 2,500*

PRINTED IN THE UNITED STATES OF AMERICA
BY THE VAIL-BALLOU PRESS, INC., BINGHAMTON, N. Y.

# TABLE OF CONTENTS

## PNEUMATOLOGY

## THE HOLY SPIRIT IN RELATION TO THE CHRISTIAN

## THE BELIEVER'S RESPONSIBILITY

# PNEUMATOLOGY

# PNEUMATOLOGY

## PREFACE

(which every student should read)

PNEUMATOLOGY IS the scientific treatment of any or all facts related to spirit. In its larger ramifications it embraces a threefold division, namely, (1) its bearing on Theology Proper, or the general doctrines related to the divine Spirit—"God is a Spirit" (John 4:24); (2) the doctrine of angelic beings both unfallen and fallen; and (3) the specific study of the immaterial part of man, which division of the subject is now termed psychology. Since the second of these divisions—that of the angels—has had an earlier treatment under Angelology, and such portions of psychology as are germane to Systematic Theology have been examined in this work under Anthropology, the present volume will be restricted to what is generally recognized as the strictly theological aspects of Pneumatology. This calls for consideration of the Person and work of the Holy Spirit, the Third Person in the blessed Trinity. In the first four volumes of this work, where the general sevenfold outline of Systematic Theology has been set forth, the Holy Spirit has been accorded recognition according to His rightful place in the Godhead, in the whole redemptive undertaking, and in the life and service of those who are saved. However, as in the case of Christ and the later, more complete treatment of revelation respecting Him which has been attempted in Volume V under Christology, there is need at this point, if this work on theology is to serve its purpose, of an unabridged contemplation of the Person and work of the Holy Spirit. Such an unabridged treatment is the design of this volume.

Whatever is true of the triune God is true of the Holy Spirit. This averment may be made with equal justification of the Father or the Son, and, if heeded in regard to the Third Person, will go far toward the right understanding and estimation of the Person and work of the Holy Spirit. A strange neglect of the Holy Spirit's full identity is, and ever has been, abroad, which neglect is deplored by all attentive expositors. For want of extended and constructive teaching with respect to the Holy Spirit, the Christian church is, for the most part, in the same position as the twelve disciples of John the Baptist whom Paul found at Ephesus. Their statement—sincere and free from pretense—was, "We have not so much as heard whether there be any Holy Ghost" (Acts 19:2). Doubtless some natural causes lie behind the fact that Christians generally are so little informed regarding this great theme. (1) There is no lack of plain revelation regarding the Holy Spirit; yet neglect, ignorance, and error are transmitted from teacher to pupil as freely and effectively as is the truth. "Like people, like priest" (Hos. 4:9) is a principle which may be extended to read *Like teacher, like pupil.* Of this the wider range of its outworking as a principle Isaiah writes: "And it shall be, as with the people, so with the priest; as with the servant, so with his master; as with the maid, so with her mistress; as with the buyer, so with the seller; as with the lender, so with the borrower; as with the taker of usury, so with the giver of usury to him" (24:2). If the teacher is given to neglect, ignorance, and error respecting any point of doctrine, the pupil could hardly be expected to correct these impressions—excepting in rare instances when, having repudiated the narrow mold into which he has been run, the pupil reaches out for a larger understanding of the revelation God has given. Such, indeed, has been the experience of the men who, under God, have been accorded the high honor of adding something to the generally accepted body of recognized truth. Did not Christ refer to this when He said: "Therefore every scribe which is instructed unto the kingdom of heaven is like unto a man that is an householder, which bringeth forth out of his treasure things new and old" (Matt. 13:52)? Judging from the scant notice which the doctrine of the Holy Spirit has received at the hands of those who have assayed to write works on Systematic Theology, a reason is easily discovered to explain why their pupils give so little consideration to it. Almost every error or disproportionate emphasis upon some aspect of doctrine on the part of a few is caused by the neglect of that truth on the part of the many. The Pentecostal errors with their misuse of Biblical terms and their assumptions would never have developed to any extent had the full and right doctrine of the Holy Spirit been taught generally in its right proportions. Similarly, those cults which live solely by an emphasis upon healing of the body would not have arisen had the church recognized and defended that which is true in that field of doctrine. (2) Again, a reason for the general failure to recognize the Person and work of the Holy Spirit is due to the fact that, within the range of the usual comprehension of revealed truth, the Spirit is not set forth as an object of faith as are the Father and the Son. Salvation is not said to depend upon faith in the Holy Spirit as it is in the case of the Father (cf. Rom. 4:24), or the Son (cf. John 3:16). It is only as the deeper truths related to the power of the Holy Spirit within the believer are approached that the thought of dependence upon the Third Person of the Godhead is brought into view. Thus it has come about as a general effect that the Father and the Son are really esteemed the objects of saving faith and the Holy Spirit is lost somewhat from consideration. (3) Similarly, the Father and the Son are constantly associated with one another in the text of the New Testament. This is due to the fact that in a large portion of the Gospels, which four books occupy two-fifths of the whole New Testament, the Son is speaking and that as One sent out by the Father and doing the will of the Father (cf. John 14:10). Likewise, personal declarations are not recorded as directly proceeding from the Holy Spirit (John 16:13); nevertheless, a considered perusal of the Sacred Text yields an impression that the Holy Spirit is the mighty executive of the Godhead and by so much His relation to both Father and Son is a theme of great proportions. (4) Lastly, there is a reason for the general neglect of the doctrine of the Holy Spirit to be found in the fact that His work as executor of the Godhead is often attributed in a more or less impersonal way to God. Thus the precise truth that certain things are wrought specifically by the Holy Spirit are lost in a generalization. Of these four factors which together account, for the most part, for the failure to give due consideration to the Person and work of the Holy Spirit, the first—that of neglect, ignorance, and error all of which is passed down from teacher to pupil—is the most prolific source of the difficulty. Men in the pulpits would preach and teach this great line of doctrine had they themselves been so taught, and none can measure the loss in practical daily living on the part of the people of God that has come about by the withholding of these truths from them. The situation recognized by all who know these doctrines—that almost none of the limited number of hymns of the church which bear on the doctrine of the Holy Spirit are Scriptural—is to be explained by the fact that attention has not been given to this subject. Nothing much is gained by a mere deploring of unfortunate conditions. Constructive teaching is needed, and pastors and teachers would do well to measure the amount of emphasis that should be given to this theme in accord with the extent to which it appears in the New Testament text, rather than to fall into and become party to the prevailing neglect of these portions of vital truth. It is earnestly desired that this volume may serve to teach some who in turn may teach others also. This treatise in the course of its development will follow a fivefold division: (1) the Holy Spirit and the Trinity, (2) types and symbols of the Holy Spirit, (3) the Holy Spirit and prophecy, (4) the Holy Spirit in relation to Gentiles and Israel, i.e., in the Old Testament, (5) the Holy Spirit in relation to Christians. Because of its immediate bearing on the believer's life and service, the last division will receive the major consideration.

## CHAPTER I

# THE NAME OF THE HOLY SPIRIT

PROOF OF THE Deity and personality of the Holy Spirit is found alone in the divine attestation to be seen in the Word of God. No information is available elsewhere respecting the character and personality of any one of the Three who comprise the Godhead. Whatever conclusions may be drawn from an induction of the Bible witness respecting the Deity or the personality of either the Father or the Son, the same are to be drawn from an induction respecting the Holy Spirit. It is possible that the designation *Spirit* which He bears has influenced men in all generations to suppose He is no more than an influence emanating from God, or an attribute of God, or a periphrasis for Deity. Such suppositions, however, serve to reveal the fact that men either do not consider the Word of God, or, if considering it, are not amenable to it. Writers have employed many pages in proving the Deity and personality of the Holy Spirit. The task is not difficult, for every reference to Him is directly or indirectly a witness to His personality and essential Deity. It is sometimes asserted that the same arguments which demonstrate the Deity of Christ the Son serve to demonstrate the Deity of the Spirit, and that is true to a marked degree; but there is, nevertheless, a difference: for the Deity of the Second Person is involved with His assumption of humanity through the incarnation, while the Deity of the Holy Spirit is not thus involved. The Spirit ever sustains a mode of action which is altogether within the sphere of what belongs alone to God. Three lines of proof respecting the Deity and personality of the Holy Spirit are to be presented in this and the following chapter: (1) the Holy Spirit bears the names of Deity, (2) the Holy Spirit exhibits the attributes and perfections of Deity, and (3) the Holy Spirit accomplishes the works and exercises the prerogatives of Deity.

### I. THE THREEFOLD NAME OF DEITY

Right views of God—such as can be gained alone from the Holy Scriptures—are essential to every step in human life and progress. While it is true that God has revealed Himself through both the Written Word and the Living Word and that His essential character is reflected in all His words and works, He is also revealed through the appellations which He has published as distinctions of title representing Himself. It is important to recognize that God has revealed His own titles, that they are in no way mere human inventions or ideals; and to the satisfaction of Infinity these cognomens, though but partially comprehended by man, speak forth the truth respecting God. Neither a mortal man, nor combination of men, nor an angel has been called upon to select names for God. In the height of his unfallen state and while in closest relation to God, Adam was called upon to name the newly created things of earth; but never did he presume to confer a designation upon God. In Volume I of this work—when considering Theology Proper—the revealed names of Deity have been given extended consideration. It need be added that, while in the Old Testament various titles are recognized as pertaining to the Persons of the Godhead, the full and complete name—not, names—of God is revealed in the New Testament. He is there styled *The Father and the Son and the Holy Ghost.* At once the baffling truths related to God as One whose subsistence is threefold are confronted.

Writing in his *Principles of Theology* (p. 24), Dr. W. H. Griffith Thomas declares regarding the Trinity as taught in the New Testament:

When we have approached the doctrine by means of the personal experience of redemption, we are prepared to give full consideration to the two lines of teaching found in the New Testament. (*a*) One line of teaching insists on the unity of the Godhead (1 Cor. 8:4; James 2:19); and (*b*) the other reveals distinctions within the Godhead (Matt. 3:16, 17; 28:19; 2 Cor. 13:14). We see clearly that (1) the Father is God (Matt. 11:25; Rom. 15:6; Eph. 4:6); (2) the Son is God (John 1:1, 18; 20:28; Acts 20:28; Rom. 9:5; Heb. 1:8; Col. 2:9; Phil. 2:6; 2 Pet. 1:1); (3) the Holy Spirit is God (Acts 5:3, 4; 1 Cor. 2:10, 11; Eph. 2:22); (4) the Father, Son, and Holy Spirit are distinct from one another, sending and being sent, honouring and being honoured. The Father honours the Son, the Son honours the Father, and the Holy Spirit honours the Son (John 15:26; 16:13, 14; 17:1, 8, 18, 23). (5) Nevertheless, whatever relations of subordination there may be between the Persons in working out redemption, the Three are alike regarded as God. The doctrine of the Trinity is the correlation, embodiment, and synthesis of the teaching of these passages. In the Unity of the Godhead there is a Trinity of Persons working out Redemption. God the Father is the Creator and Ruler of man and the Provider of redemption through His love (John 3:16). God the Son is the Redeemer, Who became man for the purpose of our redemption. God the Holy Spirit is the "Executive of the Godhead," the "Vicar of Christ," Who applies to each believing soul the benefits of redemption. We see this very clearly in Heb. 10:7–17, where the Father wills, the Son works and the Spirit witnesses. The elements of the plan of redemption thus find their root, foundation, and spring in the nature of the Godhead; and the obvious reason why these distinctions which we express by the terms "Person" and "Trinity" were not revealed earlier than New Testament times is that not until then was redemption accomplished.

A renewed discussion of the right trinitarian views will not be introduced here. The objective in view at this point is to center conviction upon the truth that the Holy Spirit is a rightful and equal member of the Godhead Three. In that sense which is true of the Father and the Son, the Holy Spirit is a Person. It must be acknowledged, however, that the term *Person* (ὑπόστασις—cf. Heb. 1:3) as used of any one of the divine Three is employed under necessary and revealed limitations. These Persons are not three separate and independent Beings; rather, the thought of personal identity marks an indefinable distinction in the Godhead—indefinable because it is not fully defined by God in His Word. Attempts which have been made by men even to illustrate what is true in the trinitarian mode of God's Being have, in earlier pages, been repudiated and declared to be more conducive to confusion and the engendering of misunderstanding than to advantage.

In the great commission (Matt. 28:18–20), direction is given to baptize in the *name*—which name is *Father and Son and Holy Ghost*—not in the three names belonging respectively to three loosely related Persons, but the one name belonging to one God whose mode of subsistence is that of Three Persons who are identified as Father, Son, and Holy Ghost. If these distinctions do not seem to represent relationships familiar to men, it may be observed that these are not the relationships peculiar to men. They signify what is true of God. It is peculiar to God with no parallel in human affairs. The great commission pronouncement is one of the most exalted declarations of the divine designations, and the point to be observed and emphasized at this juncture is that the Holy Spirit is included in this name. The fact that His name is third in the order creates not the slightest suggestion of inferiority, since this sequence of titles does not aim to represent a decreasing degree of exaltation or worthiness. Naturally, if a series of appellations which are absolutely identical with respect to the character of those indicated is to be named—whatever may be the divine reason for the order in which the names appear, so far as dignity, power, authority, honor, and all divine attributes are concerned—the last could have been named first and the first could have been named last. Thus, also, the second could have exchanged places with either the first or the last. There is a reason for the order in which these names appear which is wholly apart from the idea of a descending scale of importance. In the eternal counsels of God, and but little revealed indeed to men, the same order is evidently sustained. The order reflects what has been termed the *doctrine of procession.* The idea of procession is based on what seems to be the uncomplicated teaching of the Bible with respect to the relation existing between the Persons of the Godhead. In recognition of the Scriptures the great creeds have made explicit averments. The Nicene Creed states: "And I believe in the Holy Ghost, the Lord and giver of life, who *proceedeth* from the Father and the Son, who, with the Father and Son together, is worshipped and glorified" (quoted by Watson, *Theological Institutes,* I, 628). So, also, the Athanasian Creed declares: "The Holy Ghost is of the Father and of the Son, neither made, nor created, nor begotten, but *proceeding*" (quoted by Watson, *loc. cit.*). Likewise the Thirty-Nine Articles state: "The Holy Ghost, *proceeding* from the Father and the Son, is of one substance, majesty, and glory, with the Father and the Son, very and eternal God" (quoted by Watson, *loc. cit.*). And the *Westminster Confession* asserts: "In the unity of the Godhead there be three persons of one substance, power, and eternity; God the Father, God the Son, and God the Holy Ghost. The Father is of none, neither begotten nor proceeding; the Son is eternally begotten of the Father; the Holy Ghost eternally proceeding from the Father and the Son" (II. III). Psalm 104:30, R.V. declares of Jehovah, "Thou sendest forth thy Spirit." Likewise Christ said: "But when the Comforter is come, whom I will send unto you from the Father, even the Spirit of truth, which proceedeth from the Father, he shall testify of me: . . . Nevertheless I tell you the truth; It is expedient for you that I go away: for if I go not away, the Comforter will not come unto you; but if I depart, I will send him unto you" (John 15:26; 16:7). The Holy Spirit is the Spirit of God and of Christ, not merely the spiritual presence of the Father or the Son; He is the Spirit of the Father because He is sent of the Father, and He is the Spirit of Christ in that He is sent of Christ. As the Son is ever the manifestation of the Father (John 1:18), so the Spirit is sent forth from both the Father and the Son. These are eternal facts of relationship which, though but little comprehended by men, represent mighty realities within the Godhead.

In an introduction to Dr. A. J. Gordon's book, *The Ministry of the Spirit,* Dr. F. B. Meyer writes:

Christianity is beset with three powerful currents, which insidiously operate to deflect her from her course. Materialism, which denies or ignores the supernatural, and concentrates its heed on ameliorating the outward conditions of human life; criticism, which is clever at analysis and dissection, but cannot construct a foundation on which the religious faculty may build and rest; and a fine literary taste, which has greatly developed of late, and is disposed to judge of power by force of words or by delicacy of expression. To all of these we have but one reply. And that is, not a system, a creed, a church, but the living Christ, who was dead, but is alive forevermore, and has the keys to unlock all perplexities, problems, and failures. Though society could be reconstituted, and material necessities be more evenly supplied, discontent would break out again in some other form, unless the heart were satisfied with his love. The truth which he reveals to the soul, and which is ensphered in him, is alone able to appease the consuming hunger of the mind for data on which to construct its answer to the questions of life and destiny and God, which are ever knocking at its door for solution. And men have yet to learn that the highest power is not in words or metaphors or bursts of eloquence, but in the in-dwelling and out-working of the Word, who is the wisdom and the power of God, and who deals with regions below those where the mind vainly labors. Jesus Christ, the ever-living Son of God, is the one supreme answer to the restlessness and travail of our day. But he cannot, he will not reveal himself. Each person in the Holy Trinity reveals another. The Son reveals the Father, but his own revelation awaits the testimony of the Holy Ghost, which, though often given directly, is largely through the church. What we need then, and what the world is waiting for, is the Son of God, borne witness to and revealed in all his radiant beauty of the ministry of the Holy Spirit, as he energizes with and through the saints that make up the holy and mystical body, the church. It is needful to emphasize this distinction. In some quarters it seems to be supposed that the Holy Spirit himself is the solution of the perplexities of our time. Now what we may witness in some coming age we know not, but in this it is clear that God in the person of Christ is the one only and divine answer. Here is God's yea and amen, the Alpha and Omega, sight for the blind, healing for the paralyzed, cleansing for the polluted, life for the dead, the gospel for the poor and sad and comfortless. Now we covet the gracious bestowal of the Spirit, that he may take more deeply of the things of Christ, and reveal them unto us. When the disciples sought to know the Father, the Lord said, He that hath seen me hath seen the Father. It is his glory that shines on my face, his will that molds my life, his purpose that is fulfilled in my ministry. So the blessed Paraclete would turn our thought and attention from himself to him, with whom he is One in the Holy Trinity, and whom he has come to reveal. Throughout the so-called Christian centuries the voice of the Holy Spirit has borne witness to the Lord, directly and mediately. Directly, in each widespread quickening of the human conscience, in each revival of religion, in each era of advance in the knowledge of divine truth, in each soul that has been regenerated, comforted, or taught. Mediately his work has been carried on through the church, the body of those that believe. But, alas! how sadly his witness has been weakened and hindered by the medium through which it has come. He has not been able to do many mighty works because of the unbelief which has kept closed and barred those avenues through which he would have poured his glad testimony to the unseen and glorified Lord. The divisions of the church, her strife about matters of comparative unimportance, her magnification of points of difference, her materialism, her love of pelf and place and power, her accounting herself rich and increased in goods and needing nothing, when she was poor, and miserable, and blind, and naked—these things have not only robbed her of her testimony, but have grieved and quenched the Holy Spirit, and nullified his testimony.—Pp. x–xiv

Again, a warning is timely lest the impression be entertained that the doctrine of Procession implies some variation between the divine Persons in exaltation or importance. In Theology Proper an effort has been made to defend the Second Person from the supposition that He, being the Manifester of the Father and having become incarnate in human form, is inferior to the Father. It is also important to note that the Holy Spirit—as His name appears in the full title of the Godhead—though ever sent by Father and Son, is eternally equal to the Father or to the Son. The great revelations that the Son is begotten of the Father and that the Spirit proceeds from the Father and the Son must be kept unconfused with human relationships; for, while the Scriptures assuredly present the doctrine of procession, these same Scriptures as certainly announce the absolute equality of the Persons within the Godhead. In the outworking of the divine interrelationships which are manifest in redemption, the Son comes into the world to do the Father's will (Heb. 10:4–7) and the Spirit is subject to both the Father and the Son; yet it will be remembered that Christ made Himself subject also to the Spirit. It is written: "And Jesus being full of the Holy Ghost returned from Jordan, and was led by the Spirit into the wilderness" (Luke 4:1). Thus the human notion that the greater must be served by the less is wholly foreign to the divine interrelationships. The Son is no less equal with the Father though He seeks the glory of the Father (cf. John 14:13), and the Spirit is no less equal with the Father and the Son though He seeks the glory of the Son (cf. John 16:14).

Dr. William Cooke has written in his *Christian Theology* effectively on the threefold name of God. A portion of his thesis is included here:

In the great commission to preach the Gospel to every creature, God speaks of himself under a threefold designation, saying, "Go ye therefore, and teach all nations, baptizing them in the name of the Father, and of the Son, and of the Holy Ghost." If in any part of our Lord's teaching special care was requisite in the use of words, in order to give men right views of God, it was here: for here is a declaration of God's Name; here is an authoritative mandate to make this

Name known to the whole world; and here is an injunction to perform a solemn ordinance in this Name, as one special means of publishing and perpetuating it among all mankind. This threefold Name, then, has no human origin; it is applied by our Lord himself to the Godhead, and applied by him as expressive of the Divine Nature; and because expressive of the Divine Nature, he commands it to be proclaimed to the whole world, as the Name by which the Deity should be acknowledged and worshipped by all mankind. To deny this Name is to deny the authority of Christ; to question its appropriateness is to question his wisdom; to withhold it from God is to rebel against the plainest injunction to make it known. Wherever the Gospel is preached, this threefold Name must be proclaimed as the Name of God; and wherever baptism is celebrated, it must be performed in this as the Name of Him whom we receive and acknowledge as our only God. The Gospel cannot be preached without its publication; for it is expressly specified as a part of the Gospel message. It stands out both as a first and fundamental proposition in the Gospel system. Other doctrines are doubtless included in the Divine message; but this is not only included, it is *expressed,* and expressed because it is the basis of all other truths, and must, therefore, be made the first element in all evangelic teaching. Such being the importance of this Threefold Name, it is satisfactory to know that the text which embodies it is admitted by men of all creeds to be authentic and genuine. Here there is no dispute, nor can there be even any diversity of opinion. The text expressing this Name is contained in all copies of the original Greek, ancient as well as modern, however high you ascend in antiquity. It is contained, also, in all the versions, ancient and modern; and the translation of this threefold Name of God in every version is the same. Nor, indeed, can a different translation be given; for the text consists of a few simple terms which admit of only one literal translation. This is so obvious, that no difference of which we are aware has ever been suggested, even by men of opposite creeds and opinions. Commentators, grammarians, theologians, and critics, though differing on some points wide as the poles are asunder, uniformly agree in the translation of this passage. Even in the Unitarian version of the New Testament, the Name of God as "the Father, and the Son, and the Holy Ghost," is in this passage rendered precisely as it is in our own version. This unanimity as to the genuineness and the translation of this passage is of the highest importance; for it narrows the ground of controversy, and gives an undisputed standard of appeal. We have, therefore, only to surrender our understanding to the teachings of acknowledged authority, in order to obtain clear and correct views of God. To this infallible standard, then, we come, and placing ourselves before the sacred oracle, we reverently inquire, "Who is the Christian's God, and what is his awful Name? Is he an absolute Unity, or a Duality, or a Trinity?" The text before us gives an answer, clear, decisive, and without the least ambiguity—"He is the Father, and the Son, and the Holy Ghost." Here, then, three appellations are applied to God; not more, not less. Each Name is distinct and separate from the other, yet connected by the copulative conjunction *"and."* We are sure these three appellations are appropriate; for they are applied to God by the Great Teacher and Saviour of mankind, who came to show men who God is. But if these three distinct appellations are appropriate, constituting together the Name of the Ever Blessed

God, they must be expressive of some distinctions in the Divine Nature. Yet in these distinctions there must, at the same time, be an essential union; for the three appellations constitute together but the Name of the One Living and True God. Guided by this important passage, and the general tenor of the Holy Scripture, we maintain that Jehovah, who is one in essence, has revealed himself to man as subsisting in a distinction of Three Persons, denominated Father, Son, and Holy Ghost. We do not profess to define or explain precisely the *nature* of this distinction, because God has not revealed it. It is probable, indeed, that the terms of human language are inadequate to express it; and that our capacities in this life are too limited and feeble to receive it. We use the word "person," therefore, under some limitation—not to express the existence of three separate and independent beings, but to mark the fact of a real threefold distinction existing in the Godhead. In this sense the word "person" has the sanction both of Holy Scripture and of a venerable ecclesiastical antiquity, being the translation of the word ὑπόστασις (*hypostasis*) as used by the Nicene Fathers, and by our own translators when they designate Christ the brightness of the Father's glory, and the express image of his person (Heb. 1:3). The distinction in the persons of the Godhead is such, we believe, as implies distinct consciousness, combined with united and co-equal participation of the Divine nature and attributes. Here, however, we are met by three opposing sentiments, which it is our duty to examine and refute—the Unitarian, the Sabellian, and the Tritheistic.

The *Unitarian* theory embraces two classes of opinion, both denying the doctrine of the Trinity, and contending for the absolute Unity of God. The high Arian maintains that the being called the Son is the chief of God's works, even higher than the angels; but the Socinian regards him as only a mere man. As to the Holy Spirit, the Unitarian sentiment is vague and diversified. Sometimes he is regarded as an attribute of God, or an influence proceeding from him; and sometimes as only another name for the Father himself. It is evident, at first sight, that these views of the Divine Nature are not derived from the threefold Name, which the Saviour applied to God in the great commission to preach the Gospel. There is nothing in these words to sanction the inferiority of the Son; nothing to sustain the notion that the Holy Spirit is an attribute or a mere influence proceeding from God; and nothing to countenance the idea of the Spirit being but another name for the Father himself. The natural and obvious meaning of the passage is decidedly against such notions. In the threefold Name of God we have evidently distinction and co-equality combined; for each one represented in that Name stands in the same relation to us as our God. As, however, the essential points of the Unitarian heresy are involved in the Sabellian creed, the same class of scriptural argumentation which overthrows the one will apply to the subversion of the other. . . .

*The Sabellian heresy* is somewhat diversified in its minor aspects, but in its substantial principles it maintains that the Deity is an absolute unity; that the distinctions indicated by the terms "Father, Son, and Holy Ghost" are not real and personal, but nominal or official; that the Father alone is the Deity in his paternal character; that the Son is the same Being or Person incarnate, or "God manifest in the flesh"; and that the Holy Ghost is also the same Being manifested in his spiritual influences. Now, this doctrine is equally repugnant to the threefold Name ascribed to Jehovah in the great Gospel commission, and in the formula of baptism. It is, indeed, directly contrary to the natural and obvious meaning of language. It is to assert that our Lord has used words without meaning; and not only so, but that he has used them in a sense *contrary* to their usual and proper signification. For in all languages the words Father and Son are *personal* and not nominal designations; and to say that our Lord intended these words to have merely a nominal signification, while in all languages they have a personal signification, is to say that he employed language more likely to deceive than to instruct; and not only so, but that he commanded others to perpetuate the same deception down to the end of time; and this on an occasion when his ostensible purpose was to make God known to mankind! Can we conceive a more revolting impeachment of the wisdom or sincerity of the Teacher and Saviour of mankind? Moreover, the appellations applied to God in the commission and formula of baptism are expressive of *relations;* and the relations are distinct, and personal as well as distinct; so personal, indeed, that they can be properly applied to none but persons; and so distinct that they are not interchangeable, but fixed and permanent in their personal application. For the relation of a father to his own son involves both a personality that cannot be resolved into a metaphor, and a distinction that cannot be commuted; both relations are grounded in the very nature of things, and are eternally immutable. A father cannot be identical with his own son, and a son cannot be identical with his own father. These terms, therefore, applied to the Deity necessarily involve both distinction and personality; and, consequently, the Sabellian theory is false. Equally clear is the distinction and personality of the Holy Ghost; for either to resolve him into an attribute of God, or into an influence proceeding from God, or into another name for the Father himself, would involve the grossest absurdities and contradictions. The Holy Ghost is not only here distinguished from the Father by a separate appellation, but he is associated with the Father and the Son in the ordinance of baptism; and hence the Sabellian and Unitarian heresies imply that "baptism is to be administered in the Name of the Father, and of a creature, and of an attribute"; or "in the Name of the Father, and of a creature, and of an influence"; or, "in the Name of the Father, and of a creature, and the Father." Can we conceive absurdities more glaring? Can we invent a grosser insult against the great Teacher and Redeemer of mankind? Would not the Scriptures, on this principle of interpretation, be the most absurd and deceptive volume ever written? We must either admit such follies and blasphemies, or reject the theories which involve them. Moreover, the fact that baptism is a *religious* ordinance implies the personality of the Holy Spirit, because it is to be performed in his Name, as well as in the Name of the Father and of the Son. Now, the Being in whose name a religious ordinance is performed, must be capable of approving and accepting the ordinance performed in his name: but to approve and accept imply intelligence, and intelligence implies consciousness; and intelligence and consciousness are the properties, not of an attribute, or of an influence, but of a real, personal existence. Thus, the fact that baptism is commanded to be performed in the Name of the Holy Spirit implies his personality, as much so as it implies the personality of the

Father and of the Son. Further evidence of the personality of the Holy Spirit, as displayed in his attributes, will be adduced when we come to discourse on his Godhead. The sublime facts recorded in connection with the Redeemer's baptism are striking evidences of the distinction and personality of each of the Glorious Three. When our Lord condescended to receive this ordinance at the hands of John, the heavens were opened, and the Holy Spirit descended like a Dove and abode upon him, and a voice proceeded from the parted sky, saying, "Thou art my beloved Son, in whom I am well pleased" (Mark 1:10, 11). Here was a visible and oracular demonstration of the distinction and personality of each of the Glorious Three. There was here the presence of the Incarnate Son, submitting to the rite of baptism; the presence of the Holy Spirit, descending in the form of a Dove, and filling his humanity with consecrating power; and the presence of the Father, bearing witness to his incarnation, and proclaiming his own complacency. The Father, therefore, is not the Son, the Son is not the Father, and the Holy Spirit is distinct from both; the distinction, therefore, is real, not nominal; personal, not official. This grand display of the Three Persons in the Saviour's baptism, is a practical illustration of the distinction and personalities intended in the formula of our *own* baptism, and it shivers both the Sabellian and the Unitarian heresy into a thousand fragments.

Another erroneous theory is that of the *Tritheist,* who maintains that there are not simply three personalities, but three separate and independent Beings; or, in other words, three Gods instead of One. It is no small homage to truth when it is assailed by sentiments directly opposite to each other; for in their opposition they mutually destroy each other; and in destroying each other they support the doctrine which is true. The Unitarian and Sabellian maintain the Divine Unity, but deny the Trinity; the Tritheist maintains, on the contrary, the Trinity is so evident, that he denies the Divine Unity, and asserts the existence of three Gods. The whole truth is held by neither party, but a portion of truth is held by both. The errors of each lie in what each denies, and the truth in what each maintains. The Scriptures maintain as clearly that God is One in one sense, as they do that he is Three in another sense; and as they maintain both, both must be true; and as all truths must harmonize, there is a sense in which a trinity is compatible with unity. Hence that doctrine alone is orthodox which denies neither the one nor the other, but combines and harmonizes both; which recognizes the Father, the Son, and the Holy Spirit as really and personally distinct, yet essentially united. This is the Trinitarian doctrine, which maintains a plurality, not of names only, but of persons having distinct consciousness, with mutual participation of the same attributes and essence.—5th ed., pp. 67–73

Obviously, the triune name—Father, Son, and Spirit—embodies, signifies, and exhibits about all that enters into the doctrine of the Trinity. That doctrine may for the moment be reconsidered with a view to the recognition of the equal position and honor which belong to the Third Person along with the First and Second. As already demonstrated under Theology Proper, when the discussion centered on the trinitarian mode of the existence of Deity, the Old Testament is the record concerning one God with little recognition of Three Persons, while the New Testament is the record concerning the character and achievements of the Three Persons with little recognition of their essential unity. No Jew of the early days or any student of either this or past generations could miss the significance of the plural form of the name *Elohim*. As Dr. Griffith Thomas has pointed out, when quoted above, it was not the purpose of God to unfold at the beginning all that was latent in the doctrine of the Trinity. In this revelation as in many others there is "first the blade, then the ear, after that the full corn in the ear" (Mark 4:28). Thus the essential revelation respecting God begins with the intimation which the plural form of *Elohim* presents. Without assigning a reason for rejecting this ancient belief that the name *Elohim* implies the Trinity and discovering any other reason for this plural ending that is worthy of the theme, modern theologians have sought to avoid the recognition of the Trinity to be seen in this one name *Elohim*. It is commonly accepted that the name *Jehovah*, being singular, is a representation of the unity in the Godhead. It is written, "Jehovah our God [*Elohim*] is one Jehovah" (Deut. 6:4, R.V.). However, in Genesis 11:6–9 it is recorded that Jehovah Himself said, "Let us go down, and there confound their language." As usual when great transformations are to be wrought, indeed, the accomplishment is secured by the Three Persons; that is, each may be accredited separately with doing what is done. Thus, while each Person is at different times and places in Scripture said to have created things that exist, the wise man has said, "Remember now thy Creators in the days of thy youth" (Eccl. 12:1, Heb.). The plural *Creators* is harmonious with the whole revelation of the Bible regarding creation.

Another recognition of plurality within the Godhead, as set forth in the Old Testament, is found in the threefold ascription of worship uttered by the heavenly beings and recorded in Isaiah 6:3: "Holy, holy, holy, is Jehovah of hosts: the whole earth is full of his glory" (R.V.). After Isaiah had testified, "Woe is me! for I am undone; because I am a man of unclean lips, and I dwell in the midst of a people of unclean lips: for mine eyes have seen the King, Jehovah of hosts," and the prophet's lips had been cleansed with a live coal from off the altar, it is then that Jehovah inquired: "Whom shall I send, and who will go for us?" The singular *Jehovah* is thus again coupled with the plural pronoun *us*. Then follows the prediction concerning Israel's blinding, which prediction is quoted several times in the New Testament. The record is all of one event from the threefold ascription of praise on to the judgment upon Israel. Since the context permits of no division, it is important to note that in John 12:41—when speaking of Christ the Son of God—it is said respecting this, Isaiah's vision of glory: "These things said Esaias, when he saw his glory, and spake of him"; and again in Acts 28:25, relative to the same vision, it is implied that it was the Holy Spirit who spoke to Isaiah. It is to be concluded, therefore, that it was the Father, the Son, and the Holy Spirit who spoke when Jehovah said, "Who will go for us?" The important issue being raised here is that the Holy Spirit is as essentially represented in all these disclosures of Isaiah as is the Father or the Son. Is He not the Objective when the third "holy" is uttered? Yet, again, the Old Testament benediction (Num. 6:24–26, R.V.) corresponds perfectly with the New Testament benediction of 2 Corinthians 13:14. When these two benedictions are read together the similarity is evident: "Jehovah [the Father] bless thee, and keep thee"—"The love of God . . . be with you all"; "Jehovah [the Son] make his face to shine upon thee, and be gracious unto thee"—"the grace of the Lord Jesus Christ [be with you]"; "Jehovah [the Spirit] lift up his countenance upon thee, and give thee peace"—"the communion of the Holy Ghost [be with you]." Lest the facts be overlooked, it is well to consider how definitely the Person and work of the Holy Spirit is referred to in the Old Testament. Only a few passages need be cited: "The Spirit of God moved upon the face of the waters" (Gen. 1:2); "My Spirit shall not strive with man for ever" (Gen. 6:3, R.V.); "Thy Spirit is good" (Ps. 143:10, R.V.); "Not by might, nor by power, but by my Spirit, saith Jehovah of hosts" (Zech. 4:6, R.V.); "The Spirit of God hath made me" (Job 33:4); "I will pour out my Spirit upon all flesh" (Joel 2:28, R.V.); "Take not thy holy Spirit from me" (Ps. 51:11).

Turning more specifically to the New Testament, it is discovered that the progress of trinitarian doctrine reaches its supreme and final revelation in the Acts, the Epistles, and the Revelation, where reference is made to the Third Person under the one title of *Spirit* at least 125 times; and in every reference He is seen to be acting with all divine authority, wisdom, and grace. In all of these passages He is seen quite apart from the Father or the Son. This immense body of truth and distinctive revelation will be considered more fully in later divisions of this volume.

## II. DESCRIPTIVE TITLES

In concluding at this place discussion of the Third Person as indicated by His place in the complete name of Deity, it may be said that all the appellations by which the Spirit is known besides are merely descriptive titles. He is styled *The Spirit* because He is a spirit; He is styled *Holy* because He is holy to the measure of infinity; He is identified as *The Spirit of God* because He belongs to the Godhead; He is called *The Spirit of Christ* because He is by Christ sent into the world. In his book *The Doctrine of the Holy Spirit,* Dr. John F. Walvoord presents a valuable study on the names of the Third Person. This may well be included here:

An examination of the Scriptural revelation on the Holy Spirit will indicate that He is nowhere given a formal name, such as we have for the Second Person, the Lord Jesus Christ, but is rather given descriptive titles, of which the most common in Scripture and in ordinary usage is *The Holy Spirit.* As His Person is pure spirit, to which no material is essential, He is revealed in the Scriptures as *the Spirit.* The descriptive adjective *holy* is used to distinguish Him from other spirits, which are creatures. A study of the references to the Holy Spirit by various titles in Scripture will reveal some significant facts. The basic words in the original are also used in reference to entities other than the Holy Spirit. In the Old Testament, however, *ruach* is used over one hundred times for the Holy Spirit. The matter of interpretation enters into the problem. Cummings lists eighty-eight references to the Holy Spirit in the Old Testment (*Through the Eternal Spirit,* p. 36). The American Standard Version of the Bible by means of initial capital letters indicates considerably more than this. In any case, the instances are numerous and well scattered throughout the Old Testament. Cummings notes that the Pentateuch has fourteen references, none in Leviticus, that Isaiah and Ezekiel have fifteen each, and that the references are scattered throughout twenty-two of the thirty-nine books of the Old Testament (*Loc. cit.*). The concise summary of Cummings on the significance of these references may well be quoted: "It is impossible to say that the passages increase in number, or in clearness, with any special characteristic of the books of Scripture. They seem to bear no special relation to chronology, as they appear chiefly in Isaiah (750 B.C.), in Ezekiel (590 B.C.), and in the books of Moses. Nor can we trace any relation to the comparative spirituality of the books, though Isaiah stands so high in the list; for whereas Ezekiel stands first, and Judges has seven, Psalms has only six, Deuteronomy only one, and 2nd Chronicles four. But it is possible to discern that each of the inspired writers has caught some special aspect of the Holy Spirit's person or work, which is reiterated in his pages. In Ezekiel, for instance, it is the action of the Holy Spirit in transporting the prophet bodily to the places where he is needed, which accounts for *six* of the passages out of fifteen. In Judges it is the in-breathing of courage or strength which is alluded to in every one of the seven passages. In Exodus it is as the

Spirit of wisdom that He is specially—and exclusively—regarded. It is His office as the Giver of prophetic inspiration which is most constantly spoken of in the books of Samuel and the Chronicles. In Isaiah, and in the Psalms, the twofold teaching concerning Him is His connection with the Messiah on the one hand, and what may be called His personal qualities, such as being grieved, or vexed, by ingratitude or rebellion, on the other" (*Ibid.*, pp. 37, 38). In the New Testament, the references to the Holy Spirit are even more numerous. The New Testament word for the Spirit, *πνεῦμα*, is found in two hundred and sixty-two passages, according to Cummings, scattered throughout all the major New Testament books (*Ibid.*, p. 44). To quote Cummings, "The Gospels contain fifty-six passages; the Acts of the Apostles, fifty-seven; St. Paul's Epistles, one hundred and thirteen; and the other books, thirty-six" (*Loc. cit.*). From these facts, it may be clearly seen that there is consistent reference to the Holy Spirit from Gen. 1:2 to Rev. 22:17, and the inference is plain that a constant ministry of the Holy Spirit is maintained suitable for each dispensation. The titles of the Holy Spirit as commonly translated are subject to significant classification which furnishes an interesting background for the doctrine.

Of the many titles and variations in reference to the Holy Spirit, sixteen reveal His relationship to the other Persons of the Trinity. Eleven titles are found relating the Holy Spirit to the Father: (1) *Spirit of God* (Gen. 1:2; Mt. 3:16); (2) *Spirit of the Lord* (Lk. 4:18); (3) *Spirit of Our God* (1 Cor. 6:11); (4) *His Spirit* (Num. 11:29); (5) *Spirit of Jehovah* (Jud. 3:10); (6) *Thy Spirit* (Psa. 139:7); (7) *Spirit of the Lord God* (Isa. 61:1); (8) *Spirit of your Father* (Mt. 10:20); (9) *Spirit of the living God* (2 Cor. 3:3); (10) *My Spirit* (Gen. 6:3); (11) *Spirit of Him* (Rom. 8:11). Five titles are found relating the Holy Spirit to the Son: (1) *Spirit of Christ* (Rom. 8:9; 1 Pet. 1:11); (2) *Spirit of Jesus Christ* (Phil. 1:19); (3) *Spirit of Jesus* (Acts 16:7, Revised Version); (4) *Spirit of His Son* (Gal. 4:6); (5) *Spirit of the Lord* (Acts 5:9; 8:39). While there is some distinction in meaning in the various titles, the chief significance is to bring out the relationship of the Holy Spirit as the Third Person of the Trinity, all affirming His deity and procession.

Abundant revelation is given in the titles of the Holy Spirit to disclose His attributes. At least seventeen of His titles indicate the divine attributes of His Person. (1) The unity of the Spirit is revealed in the title, *One Spirit* (Eph. 4:4). (2) Perfection is the implication of the title, *Seven Spirits* (Rev. 1:4; 3:1). (3) The identity of the Holy Spirit and the Essence of the Trinity is affirmed in the title, *the Lord the Spirit* (2 Cor. 3:18). (4) The eternity of the Spirit is seen in the title, *Eternal Spirit* (Heb. 9:14). (5) *Spirit of Glory* connotes His glory as being the same as the Father and the Son (1 Pet. 4:14). (6) *Spirit of Life* affirms the eternal life of the Spirit (Rom. 8:2). Three titles affirm the holiness of the Spirit: (7) *Spirit of Holiness* (Rom. 1:4), a possible reference to the holy human spirit of Christ; (8) *Holy Spirit* or *Holy Ghost* (Psa. 51:11; Mt. 1:20; Lk. 11:13), the most formal title of the Spirit and most frequently used; (9) *Holy One* (1 John 2:20). Five of the titles of the Holy Spirit refer to some extent to Him as the author of revelation and wisdom: (10) *Spirit of Wisdom* (Ex. 28:3; Eph. 1:17); (11) *Spirit of Wisdom and Understanding* (Isa. 11:2); (12) *Spirit of Counsel and Might* (Isa. 11:2); (13) *Spirit of Knowl-*

*edge and of the Fear of the Lord* (Isa. 11:2); (14) *Spirit of Truth* (John 14:17). The transcendence of the Spirit is indicated (15) in the title, *Free Spirit* (Psa. 51:12). The attribute of grace is found in two titles, (16) *Spirit of Grace* (Heb. 10:29), and (17) *Spirit of Grace and Supplication* (Zech. 12:10).

Many of the titles referred to as indicating His attributes also connote His works. In the discussion of the titles revealing His attributes, it may be noticed that the *Spirit of Glory* (1 Pet. 4:14) engages in a work to bring the saints to glory. The *Spirit of Life* (Rom. 8:2) is the agent of regeneration. The *Spirit of Holiness* (Rom. 1:14), the *Holy Spirit* (Mt. 1:20), and the *Holy One* (1 John 2:20) is our sanctifier. The *Spirit of wisdom* (Eph. 1:17), the *Spirit of Wisdom and Understanding,* the *Spirit of Counsel and Might,* the *Spirit of Knowledge and of the Fear of the Lord* (Isa. 11:2) speak of the several ministries of God in teaching, guiding and strengthening the saint. The *Spirit of Truth* (John 14:17) has a similar idea. The Spirit as one who manifests grace is revealed in the titles, *Spirit of Grace* (Heb. 10:29), and the *Spirit of Grace and Supplication* (Zech. 12:10). In addition to these, two other titles are given the Holy Spirit, affirming His works. (1) The *Spirit of Adoption* (Rom. 8:15) has reference to His revelation of our adoption as sons. (2) The *Spirit of Faith* (2 Cor. 4:13), while perhaps impersonal, and in this case not referring to the Holy Spirit as such, if admitted as a reference, indicates the ministry of the Spirit in producing faith in us. Another title of the Holy Spirit, which does not involve the name *spirit,* however, is that of *Comforter,* from παράκλητος, meaning, according to Thayer, when used in its widest sense, "*a helper, succorer, aider, assistant;* so of the Holy Spirit destined to take the place of Christ with the apostles" (*Greek-English Lexicon of the New Testament,* p. 483). It is found frequently in the New Testament (John 14:16, 26; 15:26; 16:7). It reveals the Holy Spirit as one who is always ready to help the Christian. The many titles of the Holy Spirit with their manifold meanings speak eloquently of the beauties of His Person and the wonders of His attributes. The many aspects revealed speak of His infinite Person, equal in power and glory with the Father and the Son.—Pp. 15–19

As many Scriptures in combination with one another, if cited, would prove that to the Holy Spirit the titles *God, Jehovah, the God of Israel, Jehovah God, Jehovah God of Hosts* are ascribed, it is certain that, in the divine reckoning, the Holy Spirit is One of the Glorious Three with the undiminished authority and exaltation which belong to Deity alone.

## CHAPTER II

# THE DEITY OF THE HOLY SPIRIT

IF PERCHANCE the personality and Deity of the Holy Spirit seem vague to a believer, it is not due to any failure of the Sacred Text to represent the Third Person as such. So far as the Scriptures are concerned, the Holy Spirit is set forth in connection with all the actions and characteristics which belong to a divine Person. According to the record presented in the Bible, the Holy Spirit, though constantly seen in action, never appears in any light other than that which must be construed of Deity. In this, as before observed, there is a wide range of distinctions to be noted between that which enters into Christology and that which enters into Pneumatology. A worthy treatment of the doctrine of Christ demands recognition of His human birth, His human body, soul, and spirit, certain human limitations, His death, His resurrection, His present session in a glorified body in heaven, and His return in visible form to the earth again. None of these features are ever related directly to the Father or to the Holy Spirit. Therefore, it is confidently asserted that the whole sphere of the Spirit's activities, like that of His own Person, is wholly within the sphere of that which pertains to Deity. In like manner, if actions and revealed characteristics can intimate personality, the Holy Spirit's personality is more sustained by evidence than that of the Father, since the Spirit is the Executive, the Creator of the universe, the divine Author of the Scriptures, the Generator of Christ's humanity, the Regenerator of those who believe, and the direct source of every vital factor in a spiritual Christian's life; yet, oddly enough, in all generations men have yielded to a strange uncertainty respecting the actuality of the Holy Spirit's Person. It would seem as though the Scriptures were not read at all, or, if being read, the human mind is incapable of itself to receive the simplest and most obvious truths respecting this Member of the Godhead. Since all men are affected to some degree with such an incapacity to receive the revealed truth on this subject, it becomes a worthy subject of prayer that He whose work it is to actualize to the believer the things of the Father and of the Son will actualize Himself also.

## I. DIVINE ATTRIBUTES

It is the burden of any work which purports to serve as a textbook that in so far as is possible it shall present all the facts involved, even those most obvious. It thus becomes imperative that at least some of the attributes of the Holy Spirit shall be listed as evidence respecting His divine perfection. If executed in full, the undertaking would involve a recounting of all the attributes of God—already named under Theology Proper—for every attribute of God is ascribed to the Holy Spirit as fully and freely as to the Father or the Son.

1. ETERNITY. " . . . Christ, who through the eternal Spirit offered himself without spot unto God" (Heb. 9:14).

It will be seen that in this one statement of but twelve words all three Persons of the Godhead are named, and it would be strained reasoning indeed to contend that in such a passage the identity of the Third Person is uncertain. The text could not—in conformity to human theories—read that Christ, through His own spirit, or through an attribute, or mere influence, offered Himself to God. The construction of the text, as well as the stupendous thing said to have been undertaken, demands as great a Person at the one point as is required at the other two. The Son is offering Himself; the Father is receiving; and all is executed by the Eternal Spirit. Could it possibly be demonstrated that the work of the Spirit in this vast undertaking is any less than that of the Son, or than the Father's responsibility in receiving? The term *eternal,* which with all propriety can also be assigned to God the Father or God the Son, is here assigned to the Holy Spirit. Since of God alone this attribute may be predicated, the Spirit is to be understood as God.

2. OMNIPOTENCE. "For Christ also hath once suffered for sins, the just for the unjust, that he might bring us to God, being put to death in the flesh, but quickened by the Spirit" (1 Pet. 3:18).

By this passage the resurrection of Christ is credited to the energizing power of the Holy Spirit. It is asserted no less than twenty-five times that Christ was raised by the power of the Father (cf. Acts 2:32; Gal. 1:1), and once that Christ said of His own life: "I have power to lay it down, and I have power to take it again" (John 10:18). Likewise, Christ said: "Destroy this temple [His own body], and in three days I will raise it up" (John 2:19). Nevertheless, the immeasurable omnipotence which can raise the dead is attributed also to the Holy Spirit. This is but one omnipotent achievement to which reference might be made. In truth, all the works of the Spirit, as will yet be indicated, are works which demand divine omnipotence.

3. OMNIPRESENCE. "Whither shall I go from thy spirit? or whither shall I flee from thy presence? If I ascend up into heaven, thou art there: if I make my bed in hell, behold, thou art there. If I take the wings of the morning, and dwell in the uttermost parts of the sea; even there shall thy hand lead me, and thy right hand shall hold me" (Ps. 139:7–10).

While not all of this context is quoted here, it is to be seen from the above portion that the reference is to the Holy Spirit, the Third Person. He is omnipresent. He has always been omnipresent in the whole of creation, but it is also true that He now, beginning with the Day of Pentecost and continuing until the removal of the Church, is *resident* in the world (Eph. 2:18–22).

4. OMNISCIENCE. "The Spirit searcheth all things, yea, the deep things of God. For what man knoweth the things of a man, save the spirit of man which is in him? even so the things of God knoweth no man, but the Spirit of God" (1 Cor. 2:10–11).

Nothing is ever hidden from the searching discernment of the Holy Spirit, not even "the deep things of God." Beyond what may be meant by the *deep things of God*, human imagination cannot function. The text definitely declares that unaided man cannot know the things of God (cf. vs. 14), but the Spirit knows all things. Reference is made to the outmost bounds of omniscience, and none can deny that, if the knowledge which the Spirit possesses reaches to the deep things of God, all else would likewise be comprehended by Him. He who thus plumbs the deepest ocean of truth and understanding is able as well to discern the thoughts and intents of the human heart. Those tempted to sin in secret may well remember that nothing is hidden from the Spirit of God. It is likewise a comfort to know that He as fully observes every sincere purpose, whether ability to execute it is found or not.

5. LOVE. "The fruit of the Spirit is love" (Gal. 5:22).

The attribute of love belongs to the Holy Spirit to the degree of infinity. Furthermore, He is the Executor of the things of God. So He literally loves with *divine* compassion through the one in whom He dwells. While this is a provision of priceless advantage to the Christian, the point to be recognized is that the Spirit exercises the full measure of divine love. He is its Source.

6. FAITHFULNESS. "The fruit of the Spirit is . . . faithfulness" (Gal. 5:22, R.V.).

Here is no reference to the attitude of *faith,* as suggested perhaps in the Authorized Version; but rather the Spirit is said to reproduce divine faithfulness in the believer. All the covenants of God, His promises, and His predictions speak of His faithfulness. "He abideth faithful." "Great is thy faithfulness." The Holy Spirit partakes fully of this attribute of God's.

7. TRUTHFULNESS. "And it is the Spirit that beareth witness, because the Spirit is truth" (1 John 5:6).

Christ earlier styled the Holy Spirit "the Spirit of truth." Thus it may be observed that the Spirit not only possesses the truth: He is the Faithful Witness to the truth. As such He is the divine Author of the Scriptures, and therein has He borne witness to the truth. A lie against the Spirit was instantly punished by death (Acts 5:1–11). Hence, infinitely vital is the truth as related to the Holy Spirit.

8. HOLINESS. "The Holy Spirit."

Whatever the underlying distinction inside the Trinity may be, there can be no doubt that the Scriptures place a peculiar emphasis upon the purity and sanctity of the Third Person. The very title "Holy Spirit" testifies to this solemn reality. Later in this volume it will be demonstrated that the Spirit is the One of the Three who copes directly with the sin nature in the believer and is the only existing power by which that nature is ever controlled. The truth that He is holy and that He, through that which Christ has wrought in bringing the sin nature into judgment, is Himself never tarnished by so much as a shadow of the evil He suppresses will also be made clear. It has been indicated above that instant death was inflicted upon two persons at the opening of this dispensation who presumed to lie to the Holy Spirit. Bearing on the same truth and with regard to the distinctive holiness of the Spirit, it will be remembered that there was a sin against the Holy Ghost which could never be forgiven. Of this Christ said: "Wherefore I say unto you, All manner of sin and blasphemy shall be forgiven unto men: but the blasphemy against the Holy Ghost shall not be forgiven unto men. And whosoever speaketh a word against the Son of man, it shall be forgiven him: but whosoever speaketh against the Holy Ghost, it shall not be forgiven him, neither in this world, neither in the world to come" (Matt. 12:31–32). It is impossible for the inner character of one Person in the Godhead to be more holy than that of Another; the distinction must lie somewhat within the sphere of that which is the official responsibility of the Spirit. Being the divine Executive, the Third Person may have an especial appointment to manifest as well as to defend the infinite holiness of God. It is with equal appropriateness, then, that the angelic beings ascribe to the Blessed Three the adoration: "Holy, holy, holy, is Jehovah of hosts."

## II. DIVINE WORKS

Introducing this theme in his *Christian Theology,* Dr. William Cooke writes:

> We have seen the works of creation ascribed to the Father and the Son, and the same authority ascribes them to the Holy Spirit. After the fiat which brought matter into being, the first agency we find employed in the construction of the universe is that of the Holy Spirit. Ere the heavens and the earth had received their form—when the chaotic mass was without form and void, and darkness was upon the face of the deep, the Spirit of God *was moving* or brooding over the inert and confused mass, penetrating it with his omnipotent and vivifying energy, impregnating the congeries with their appropriate qualities, affinities, and laws; arranging and disposing the whole according to his unerring wisdom and sovereign pleasure. In each successive act of creating energy the blessed Spirit participated, for, says Job, "by his Spirit he hath garnished the heavens" (26:13), and Elihu says, "The Spirit of God hath made me, and the breath of the Almighty hath given me life." Thus, if the glorious work of creation be challenged as a proof of the existence and Deity of the Father and the Son, it is equally a proof of the Deity of the Holy Spirit. The wonderful economy of Providence implies the same omnipotent agency and all-pervading presence as the work of creation. It is, indeed, a continued creation—a perpetual renovation and reproduction. The pious Psalmist acknowledges this fact, and ascribes the work to the Holy Spirit. Speaking of the absolute dependence of all creatures upon God, he says, "Thou hidest thy face, they are troubled: thou takest away their breath, they die, and return to their dust. Thou sendest forth thy Spirit, they are created: and thou renewest the face of the earth" (Ps. 104:29, 30). Thus each reviving spring, and each successive generation of men and inferior animals, like a new creation, is declaratory of the Spirit's presence and omnipotent energy. In the economy of grace the Holy Spirit performs a benign and conspicuous part. He begins, carries forward, and completes the work of salvation in the hearts of his people. It is impossible to estimate the immense amount of moral and spiritual good resulting from his holy influence upon the human heart. He is the great source of light and grace to the world—the fountain of holiness, love, and joy; and, excepting the gift of Christ, the bestowment of his agency is the greatest and most important blessing ever conferred upon our fallen world.—Pp. 154–155

Though much has been intimated earlier in these volumes on the work of the Holy Spirit and much that will yet appear will bear on this same theme, it is essential to an analysis of the present aspect of the truth to indicate in order some of the works of the Spirit which supply evidence respecting His Deity. These works now to be listed are approached with this one purpose in view. Later, they will be listed again and classified when the essential character of each must be considered.

1. CREATION. It is significant indeed that in the first two verses of the Bible two Persons of the Godhead are mentioned—God and the Spirit of God. The combination of the First and Third Persons is far less frequent than the combination of the First and Second Persons, as in Psalm 2:2 and constantly in the New Testament. God is said to have created while "the Spirit of God moved [brooded as in incubation] upon the face of the waters." What division in creative work, if any, is implied is not clear. It is written in Psalm 33:6: "By the word of the LORD were the heavens made; and all the host of them by the breath of his mouth." Likewise, in Psalm 104:30: "Thou sendest forth thy spirit, they are created: and thou renewest the face of the earth," and Job declares: "By his spirit he hath garnished the heavens; his hand hath formed the crooked serpent" (26:13). It has been indicated earlier that each Person of the Godhead is credited with creating all things; consequently, since the Holy Spirit is the Executor of the divine purpose, His part in creation is to be expected. By His incubation, He brought forth every living thing. Of this specific work of the Holy Spirit, Matthew Henry in his *Commentary* writes, "The Spirit of God was the first mover: He *moved upon the face of the waters.* When we consider the earth without form and void, methinks it is like the valley full of dead and dry bones. Can these live? Can this confused mass of matter be formed into a beautiful world? Yes, if a spirit of life from God enter into it (Ezek. 37:9). Now there is hope concerning this thing; for the Spirit of God begins to work, and, if he work, who or what shall hinder? God is said to make the world by his Spirit (Ps. 33:6; Job 26:13), and by the same mighty worker the new creation is effected. He moved upon the face of the deep, as Elijah stretched himself upon the dead child,—as the *hen gathers her chickens under her wings,* and hovers over them, to warm and cherish them (Matt. 23:37),—as the eagle stirs up her nest, and *flutters* over her young (it is the same word that is here used, Deut. 32:11). Learn hence, That God is not only the author of all being, but the fountain of life and spring of motion" (at Gen. 1:2). A parallel is here suggested with the Spirit's work in bringing into existence the present spiritual, new creation. Of the three creative acts—that of Genesis, that of the present spiritual, New Creation, and that of the creation of the new heaven and the new earth—the

Spirit is seen to work mightily in the first two, but no record is given of His participation in the last. Dwelling on the contrast between creation and evolution, *The Companion Bible* states:

> The introduction to Genesis (and to the whole Bible), Genesis 1:1—2:3, ascribes everything to the living God, creating, making, acting, moving, and speaking. There is no room for evolution without a flat denial of divine revelation. One must be true, the other false. All God's works were pronounced "good" seven times (Gen. 1:4, 10, 12, 18, 21, 25, 31). They are "great" (Ps. 111:2; Rev. 15:3). They are "wondrous" (Job 37:14). They are "perfect" (Deut. 32:4). Man starts from nothing. He begins in helplessness, ignorance, and inexperience. All his works, therefore, proceed on the principle of *evolution.* This principle is seen *only in human* affairs; from the hut to the palace; from the canoe to the ocean liner; from the spade and ploughshare to machines for drilling, reaping, and binding, etc. But the birds build their nests today as at the beginning. The moment we pass the boundary line, and enter the divine sphere, no trace or vestige of evolution is seen. There is growth and development *within,* but no passing, change, or evolution out from one into another. On the other hand, *all* God's works are *perfect.* . . . Evolution is only one of several theories invented to explain the phenomena of created things. It is admitted by all scientists that no one of these theories covers all the ground; and the greatest claim made for Evolution, or Darwinism, is that "it covers more ground than any of the others." The Word of God claims *to cover all the ground:* and the only way in which this claim is met, is by a denial of the inspiration of the Scriptures, in order to weaken it. This is the special work undertaken by the so-called "Higher Criticism," which bases its conclusions on human assumptions and reasoning, instead of on the documentary evidence of manuscripts, as Textual Criticism does.—Volume I, Appendix 5

He who creates has declared how it was done and His testimony commands attention.

2. STRIVING. Jehovah said: "My spirit shall not always strive with man, for that he also is flesh" (Gen. 6:3). The wickedness of the antediluvian days and the unwillingness of men to heed the preaching of Noah prompted this prediction on Jehovah's part. It looks on for complete fulfillment to a future time when God's offers of mercy and grace and His restraining power are withdrawn from the earth (2 Thess. 2:7–8). This striving of the Spirit is closely related to His convicting work (John 16:7–11).

3. INSPIRATION. There are certain divine undertakings which are said to be wrought by the three Persons of the Godhead, notably, creation, the death of Christ, and the resurrection of Christ; and there are divine undertakings which belong specifically to One or Another of

the members of the Godhead. The Father gives the Son—it could not be said that the Son gives the Father, or that the Spirit gives the Son or the Father. The Son becomes incarnate, dies, is raised from the dead, ascends into heaven, and will come again. Though they cooperate in that which belongs to the Son, there is no intimation that the Father or the Spirit become incarnate, that they die, are raised, ascend into heaven, or will return to the earth again. There are achievements the doing of which belongs only to God the Holy Spirit. It is the purpose of this chapter of this volume to enumerate at least seventeen of these specific works of the Holy Spirit. Three of those to be named are of the greatest importance since they are in the sphere of generation or production, namely, the inspiring of the Scriptures, the generating of the humanity of Christ, and the regenerating of those from among the lost who believe. It seems probable that the part the Spirit takes in the production of the Living Word and the part He takes in the production of the Written Word are above the level of that creative act by which a soul is regenerated. Human estimations in the sphere of such values may be submitted only as a finite opinion. Since in the production of the Living Word the Spirit adds the humanity and in the production of the Written Word the Spirit adds the divinity, it would follow—from the same course of finite reasoning—that the inspiration of the Scriptures is the greatest of all the Spirit's undertakings which are specifically His own. Since truth is from God and is so finally contained in the Oracles of God, the character, authority, and dependability of those Oracles become a fundamental issue. Naturally the whole problem relating to the inspiration of the Scriptures is raised again at this point; but it is the purpose of this division of the general theme only to point out that which is the peculiar work of the Holy Spirit and to observe in that work the evidence of His Deity. That the Scriptures are perfect, being, in the original languages, the very words of God, has been asserted and defended in Volume I under Bibliology; the present purpose is to demonstrate that the Holy Spirit is the divine Author of those Oracles. An impartial mind, sufficiently instructed to be able to place a relative value on any work of God, would normally expect that production of the Scriptures, like that of all other works of God, must result in what is perfect to infinity. That the Scriptures in their original writings are the inerrant Word of God—a master work of the Holy Spirit—is usually demonstrated, when defended, from an examination of the text itself. That effort has been made by many faithful men, and by none more conclusively than S. R. L. Gaussen in a volume published in 1842 (in English) entitled *Theopneusty.* In his introductory definition of the word *Theopneusty,* he declares:

It is thus that God, who would make known to his elect, in an eternal book, the spiritual principles of the divine philosophy; has dictated its pages, during sixteen centuries, to priests, kings, warriors, shepherds, tax-gatherers, boatmen, scribes, tent-makers. Its first line, its last line, all its instructions, understood or not understood, are from the same author, and that is sufficient for us. Whoever the writers may have been, and whatever their understanding of the book; they have all written with a faithful, superintended hand, on the same scroll, under the dictation of the same master, to whom a thousand years are as one day; such is the origin of the Bible. I will not waste my time in vain questions; I will study the book. It is the word of Moses, the word of Amos, the word of John, the word of Paul; but it is the mind of God and the word of God. We should then deem it a very erroneous statement to say; certain passages in the Bible are from men, and certain others from God. No; every verse, without exception, is from men; and every verse, without exception, is from God; whether he speaks directly in his own name, or whether he employs all the individuality of the sacred writer. And as St. Bernard says of the living works of the regenerated man, "that our will performs none of them without grace; but that grace too performs none of them without our will"; so must we say, that in the scriptures, God has done nothing but by man, and man has done nothing but by God. There is, in fact, a perfect parallel between Theopneusty and efficacious grace. In the operations of the Holy Spirit in inditing the sacred books, and in those of the same Spirit converting a soul, and causing it to walk in the paths of holiness, man is in some respects entirely passive, in others entirely active. God there does everything; man there does all; and we may say of all these works, as St. Paul said of one of them to the Philippians; "it is God who worketh in you both *to will and to do.*" And we see that in the Scriptures, the same work is attributed alternately to God and to man; God converts, and it is man who converts himself; God circumcises the heart, God gives a new heart, and it is man who must circumcise his own heart and make to himself a new heart. "Not only because we must employ the means of obtaining such an effect," says the famous Pres. Edwards, in his admirable remarks against the Arminians, "but because this effect itself is our act, as well as our duty; God producing all, and we acting all." . . . In theory, we might say that a religion could be divine, without the miraculous inspiration of its books. It might be possible, for example, to conceive of a Christianity without Theopneusty; and it might perhaps, be conceived that every other miracle of our religion, except that, was a fact. In this supposition (which is totally unauthorized), the eternal Father would have given his Son to the world; the all-creating Word, made flesh, would have undergone the death of the cross for us, and have sent down upon the Apostles the spirit of wisdom and miraculous powers; but, all these mysteries of redemption once accomplished, he would have abandoned to these men of God the work of writing our Sacred books, according to their own wisdom; and their writings would have presented to us only the natural language of their supernatural illuminations, of their convictions and their charity. Such an order of things is undoubtedly a vain supposition, directly contrary to the testimony of the Scriptures as to their own nature; but, without remarking here, that it explains nothing; and that, miracle for miracle, that of illumination is not less inexplicable than Theopneusty; without further saying that the word of God possesses a divine power peculiar to itself: such an order of things, if it were realized, would have exposed us to innumerable errors, and plunged us into the most ruinous uncertainty. With no security against the imprudence of the writers, we should not have been able to give their writings even the authority which the Church now concedes to those of Augustine, Bernard, Luther, Calvin, or of a multitude of other men enlightened in the truth by the Holy Spirit. We are sufficiently aware how many imprudent words and erroneous propositions mar the most beautiful pages of these admirable writers. And yet the Apostles (on the supposition we have just made), would have been subjected still more than they, to serious errors; since they could not have had, like the doctors of the Church, a word of God, by which to correct their writings; and since they would have been compelled to invent the entire language of religious science; for a science, we know, is more than half formed, when its language is made. What fatal errors, what grievous ignorance, what inevitable imprudence had necessarily accompanied, in them, a revelation without Theopneusty; and in what deplorable doubts had the Church then been left!—errors in the selection of facts, errors in estimating them, errors in stating them, errors in the conception of the relations which they hold to doctrines, errors in the expression of these doctrines themselves, errors of omission, errors of language, errors of exaggeration, errors in the adoption of national, provincial or party prejudices, errors in the anticipations of the future and in the estimate of the past. But, thanks to God, it is not so with our sacred books. They contain no errors, all their writing is inspired of God. "Holy men of God spake as they were moved by the Holy Ghost; not in the words which man's wisdom teacheth, but which the Holy Ghost teacheth"; so that none of these words ought to be neglected, and we are called to respect them and to study them even to their least iota and to their least tittle; for this "scripture is purified, as silver seven times tried in the fire; it is perfect." These assertions, themselves testimonies of the word of God, contain precisely our last definition of Theopneusty, and lead us to characterize it finally, as "that inexplicable power which the Divine Spirit formerly exercised over the authors of the Holy Scriptures, to guide them even in the employment of the words they were to use, and to preserve them from all error, as well as from every omission."— Pp. 36–39

More determining and impressive than this argument for inspiration, which is based on the obvious divine character of the Sacred Text itself, is the fact that the Scriptures are the product of God the Holy Spirit. The works of God are infinitely perfect and worthy of Him, of course. It is therefore to be assumed that the Bible, being a work of God, is no exception, being, as it is, the Holy Spirit's literary monument. When error or imperfections are thought to exist, it would be the first impulse of a truly devout mind to investigate whether the difficulty does not arise in the sphere of the finite understanding. No more does the human element in the Written Word jeopardize the infinite excellency of the divine element therein than does the humanity of Christ, the Living Word, jeopardize the Deity which He is. To believe the Bible to be an inerrant document is to honor its Author the Holy Spirit, to respect the Bible's own claim for itself, and to agree with the conclusions of devout scholars of all generations. It has been pointed out that the Sadducees denied the resurrection, which denial indeed did not alter the fact of the resurrection, but only prompted Christ to say to them: "Ye do err, not knowing the scriptures, nor the power of God."

All Scripture is *theopneustos* (θεόπνευστος), which declaration is made in 2 Timothy 3:16 and which includes all the Bible. The Scriptures originate with God and are His very breath. In the preceding verse the statement is made by Paul that, from a child, Timothy has known the sacred letters (γράμματα). All Scripture (γραφή), composed, as it is, of sacred letters, is God-breathed. Accordingly Peter states: "Knowing this first, that no prophecy of the scripture is of any private interpretation. For the prophecy came not in old time by the will of man: but holy men of God spake as they were moved by the Holy Ghost" (2 Pet. 1:20–21). The word *prophecy* as used by Peter in this passage reaches out to all utterance which is inspired by God; that is, it is not restricted to prediction. It includes forthtelling as well as foretelling. It comprehends all Scripture. Likewise, the declaration which the Scriptures set forth must be interpreted as related to, and in the light of, all other Scriptures. Prophecy did not in old time, or in any other time, arise from the volition of man. Holy men of God spake as they were *borne along* by the Spirit of God. The testimony of the prophets to themselves is most revealing and convincing. They said: "The mouth of Jehovah hath spoken it." "The Spirit of Jehovah spake by me, and his word was upon my tongue." "Hear this word that Jehovah hath spoken." "The word of the LORD came unto me." He "put a word in Balaam's mouth." "Who by the mouth of thy servant David hast said . . ." "Which the Holy Spirit spake before by the mouth of David." "Those things, which God before had shewed by the mouth of all his prophets." It is clearly the testimony of the Bible respecting itself that it is a work of the Holy Spirit, its words are the inerrant words of God, and it is therefore in its perfection as suitable for heaven as it is for the earth.

4. GENERATING CHRIST. What may have been the Spirit's work in the impartation of life when creation took place is not revealed. Further-

more, the phase of the Spirit's work now under consideration is quite removed from His work in regeneration. The one great generating act of the Holy Spirit occurred when He brought the humanity of Christ into being. It is too often assumed that Mary the mother of Christ contributed His humanity and that the Holy Spirit contributed His Deity; but a moment's reflection would disclose that the Deity of Christ was His own from all eternity and therefore was not originated at the time of His birth. He became incarnate when His eternal Person took on the human form. It is also true that in this instance, as in any other human gestation, Mary could contribute no more than that assigned to the woman in childbearing; she nurtured and developed the life committed to her. The Spirit caused the humanity of Christ to originate and that is His act of generation. Thus the Scripture declares: "And the angel answered and said unto her, The Holy Ghost shall come upon thee, and the power of the Highest shall overshadow thee: therefore also that holy thing which shall be born of thee shall be called the Son of God" (Luke 1:35).

5. CONVINCING. The convincing work of the Holy Spirit is threefold —of sin, of righteousness, and of judgment—and much light falls upon the character of this essential ministry of the Holy Spirit when it is observed that the end which He accomplishes is the impartation of an understanding of facts, which understanding results in an enlightenment essential to an intelligent acceptance of Christ as Savior. The declaration on this point made by Christ in the Upper Room Discourse reads: "Nevertheless I tell you the truth; It is expedient for you that I go away: for if I go not away, the Comforter will not come unto you; but if I depart, I will send him unto you. And when he is come, he will reprove the world of sin, and of righteousness, and of judgment: of sin, because they believe not on me; of righteousness, because I go to my Father, and ye see me no more; of judgment, because the prince of this world is judged" (John 16:7–11). This unfolding of truth is not addressed to the unsaved, though it describes a work of the Holy Spirit in their behalf; it is addressed to those who are saved and provides priceless instruction concerning the most vital factor in all evangelizing efforts. Much has been presented earlier respecting this ministry of the Spirit and the same theme must again come into consideration at a later time. Enough will have been said here if it is pointed out that this threefold convincing is the divine method of overcoming the veil which Satan has cast over the mind of each unregenerate person. Of this blindness it is written: "But if our gospel be hid, it is hid to them that

are lost: in whom the god of this world hath blinded the minds of them which believe not, lest the light of the glorious gospel of Christ, who is the image of God, should shine unto them" (2 Cor. 4:3–4). In the act of lifting this veil from the unsaved person's mind, a clear vision is gained of the one sin of rejecting Christ, of a righteousness which is derived from the invisible Christ in glory, and of the completed judgment of the cross. That this judgment is wholly achieved in the interests of the unsaved constitutes a challenge for faith. It becomes thereby, not something to persuade God to do, but something to believe that He has done. In fact, the only human responsibility indicated in all of this determining Scripture is *belief*. It is something to believe when the statement is made respecting imputed righteousness, which righteousness is the portion of all who are saved. It is likewise a demand upon faith to accept and rest in the revelation that Christ has borne all the individual's sin. The one remaining sin is that "they believe not on me," i.e., Christ. This convincing ministry of the Holy Spirit is not one of condemnation or of impressing the sinner with his sinfulness; it is distinctly a message of good news saying that Christ has died, "the just for the unjust," and that a perfect standing and acceptance before God are provided in the resurrected Son of God. Due warning of the necessary consequences if this message should not be believed is part of the Spirit's convincing work.

6. RESTRAINING. In the present age there are two ministries of the Holy Spirit to the unsaved, namely, that of convincing and that of restraining. The ministry of convincing, just considered, is directed to the individual and is the only hope that he will turn intelligently and sufficiently to Christ as Savior, while the ministry of restraining is directed to the whole *cosmos* world in mass. As the word *restrain* implies, it has to do with the impeding of the evil that is possible in the world. Evidently this curbing is not with a view to discontinuing all evil, else that would be accomplished without delay; it is rather a ministry by which evil is held within certain divinely predetermined bounds. The Restrainer will be removed in due time—and then follows an unprecedented tribulation, a period of seven years, before the King returns to exercise absolute authority over the earth. During these seven years the true character of evil will be demonstrated. It is clearly asserted that the restraint is to the end that the man of sin should not be revealed until his divinely appointed time, which time is that of the great tribulation. That time of distress is not something imposed upon humanity from without; it is simply the reaction of wickedness when the present

divine restraint is removed. It is impossible to estimate what the church on earth, governments, and society in general owe to this unceasing inhibiting influence of the Holy Spirit. The Scripture bearing on this theme reads: "And now ye know what withholdeth that he [the man of sin] might be revealed in his time. For the mystery of iniquity [lawlessness] doth already work: only he [the Spirit] who now letteth [restraineth] will let [go on restraining], until he [the Restrainer] be taken out of the way. And then shall that Wicked be revealed, whom the Lord shall consume with the spirit [breath] of his mouth, and shall destroy with the brightness of his coming" (2 Thess. 2:6–8).

7. REGENERATION. The word παλιγγενεσία, translated *regeneration*, is used but twice in the New Testament. In the first instance—Matthew 19:28—the Lord speaks of the restoration of all things unto God which He Himself shall yet accomplish (cf. 1 Cor. 15:24–28). This is not said to be a work of the Holy Spirit, but rather a work of the Son. The second instance is found in Titus 3:5, which reads: "Not by works of righteousness which we have done, but according to his mercy he saved us, by the washing of regeneration, and renewing of the Holy Ghost." To be sure, the truth which this term expresses is set forth in many Scriptures and under various terms, but then always as a work of the Holy Spirit. The background of the doctrine of regeneration is its necessity springing from the universal fallen estate of man. Since the need is world-wide, the demand for regeneration is imperative in the case of every person born into the world. None can be excepted other than the Christ of God. In His conversation with Nicodemus by night (John 3:1–21), Christ recognized as acceptable to God nothing of the model character and attainments in Judaism on the part of this ruler in Israel. It was to such a one that Christ said: "Marvel not that I said unto thee, Ye must be born again" (or, from above); and to the same purpose Christ said: "That which is born of the flesh is flesh; and that which is born of the Spirit is spirit." As human generation begets a life "after its kind," so divine regeneration means the impartation of a life from God which is wholly foreign to that of fallen man. It is the divine nature. It is "Christ in you, the hope of glory" (Col. 1:27). The Lord said: "The thief cometh not, but for to steal, and to kill, and to destroy: I am come that they might have life, and that they might have it more abundantly" (John 10:10). Upwards of eighty-five New Testament passages bear on this fact of an imparted divine life. No change in the human estate could be conceived which is as far-reaching and effective as that of an actual birth into a legitimate and actual, filial relationship

with God. This provision constitutes God's supreme message to man. Individual regeneration, so far as the testimony of Scripture is concerned, is a New Testament provision. Though Israelites were rightly related to God as such by physical birth, they anticipated in time to come the reception of eternal life as an "inheritance" (cf. Matt. 19:29; Luke 10:25–29; 18:18–30). Of Israel's relation to personal regeneration by the Holy Spirit, John L. Nuelsen writes in the *International Standard Bible Encyclopaedia:* "Whether the Divine promises refer to the Messianic end of times, or are to be realized at an earlier date, they all refer to the nation of Israel as such, and to individuals only as far as they are partakers in the benefits bestowed upon the commonwealth. This is even true where the blessings prophesied are only spiritual, as in Isa. 60:21, 22. The mass of the people of Israel are therefore as yet scarcely aware of the fact that the conditions on which these Divine promises are to be attained are more than ceremonial and ritual ones" (*s.v.*, "Regeneration," IV, 2547). The Gospel written by John in its opening chapter states that a new thing has come into the range of human experience. This Scripture declares: "But as many as received him, to them gave he power to become the sons of God, even to them that believe on his name: which were born, not of blood, nor of the will of the flesh, nor of the will of man, but of God" (vss. 12–13); and Peter describes a Christian thus: "Being born again, not of corruptible seed, but of incorruptible, by the word of God, which liveth and abideth for ever" (1 Pet. 1:23). As for the human responsibility in regeneration, Christ said to Nicodemus: "For God so loved the world, that he gave his only begotten Son, that whosoever believeth in him should not perish, but have everlasting life" (John 3:16). As this subject is to be reconsidered later in another connection, however, it will suffice to add that to be born of God means an induction into the order of heavenly beings. None, of a surety, are now able to comprehend the reality in which God becomes the regenerating and therefore legitimate Father for all eternity and the one who believes becomes a regenerated legitimate son for all eternity. Salvation includes a new creation (2 Cor. 5:17, R.V. marg.), which is wrought by the Holy Spirit as the Executor of the Godhead.

8. ILLUMINATION. Lying back of the Holy Spirit's illumination of the believer is the threefold condition of need calling for it, seeing that all members of the human family are dulled in their natural powers of understanding by sin, likewise by a specific veiling of their minds from

Satan (cf. 2 Cor. 4:3–4), and that the truth to be comprehended, being of a celestial character, is not apprehended apart from a personal revelation of the truth wrought in the mind and heart by the Holy Spirit. The whole divinely arranged provision whereby the believer may come to know the things of God and all that enters into relationship with God is a system of pedagogy quite unlike anything of which this world knows and wholly outside the range of experience into which the natural man could enter. Much has already been made of this aspect of the Holy Spirit's ministry under Bibliology and the same theme will yet be considered more exhaustively in a later section of this volume. Illumination is specifically a work which is wrought by the Third Person, and, in so far as He opens the understanding to the Scriptures, He unveils that which He Himself has originated; yet when Christ declared that the Spirit would guide the believer into all truth, He made clear that the Spirit does not originate the message which He imparts, for He, the Spirit, does not speak from Himself, but whatsoever He shall hear that shall He speak (John 16:13). In this instance it is Christ who originates the message. Christ opened this particular declaration with the words: "I have yet many things to say unto you, but ye cannot bear them now." Thus in the sphere of "all truth," "things to come," and "all things that the Father hath," the message arises with the Son and is delivered to the mind and heart of the believer by the Spirit who indwells him. To this end the Apostle declares, "We have received . . . the spirit which is of God" (1 Cor. 2:12). The position within the heart of the believer which the Holy Spirit now occupies secures the closest relationship, so that He, the Spirit Himself, is thus able to create impressions within the Christian's consciousness which seem to have occurred only to his own finite mind. All spiritual truth must be imparted by the indwelling Spirit in this way. This particular body of truth, or threefold group of "things," will be known by the believer only through the revelation which the Holy Spirit accomplishes. Of this the Apostle states: "But as it is written, Eye hath not seen, nor ear heard, neither have entered into the heart of man, the things which God hath prepared for them that love him. But God hath revealed them unto us by his Spirit: for the Spirit searcheth all things, yea, the deep things of God" (1 Cor. 2:9–10). Using earlier the same term as here, namely, "things," Christ implied that "all truth" must be *shown* to the believer by the Holy Spirit (John 16:12–15). The practical appeal which is here confronted by Christians reveals the necessity for adjustment of heart and life to the mind and will of the Holy Spirit lest all progress in learning spiritual things be hindered.

9. AS A PARACLETE. When translators turn from translating to interpreting the result may easily be misleading. In His Upper Room Discourse (John 13:1—17:26), for example, Christ refers to the Holy Spirit as the Paraclete (παράκλητος) several times. The Authorized Version translation of the word *Comforter* is the result of interpretation; that is, Paraclete means *helper* or one called to one's side as an aid—and in this case an all-sufficient One. This includes the idea of comforting, but to restrict it to comforting is wholly inadequate. In the breadth of the meaning of this descriptive title almost all of the Spirit's activities as presented in this section of Chapter II could be included. For three and a half years Christ had been to the disciples to whom He was speaking their Paraclete, their all-sufficient One. When leaving them He promised another Paraclete. It follows, accordingly, that whatever Christ had been to them, the Holy Spirit would continue. In his *Word Studies,* Dr. M. R. Vincent discusses this title *Paraclete* as follows:

Only [used] in John's Gospel and First Epistle (14:16, 26; 15:26; 16:7; 1 Ep. 2:1). From παρά, *to the side of,* and καλέω, *to summon.* Hence, originally, *one who is called to another's side to aid him,* as an advocate in a court of justice. The later, Hellenistic use of παρακαλεῖν and παράκλησις, to denote *the act of consoling* and *consolation,* gave rise to the rendering *Comforter,* which is given in every instance in the Gospel, but is changed to *advocate* in 1 John 2:1, agreeably to its uniform signification in classical Greek. The argument in favor of this rendering *throughout* is conclusive. It is urged that the rendering *Comforter* is justified by the fact that, in its original sense, it means more than a mere *consoler,* being derived from the Latin *confortare,* to *strengthen,* and that the Comforter is therefore one who strengthens the cause and the courage of his client at the bar: but, as Bishop Lightfoot observes, the history of this interpretation shows that it is not reached by this process, but grew out of a grammatical error, and that therefore this account can only be accepted as an apology after the fact, and not as an explanation of the fact. The Holy Spirit is, therefore, by the word παράκλητος, of which *Paraclete* is a transcription, represented as our *Advocate* or *Counsel,* "who suggests true reasonings to our minds, and true courses of action for our lives, who convicts our adversary, the world, of wrong, and pleads our cause before God our Father." It is to be noted that *Jesus* as well as the Holy *Spirit* is represented as Paraclete. The Holy Spirit is to be *another* Paraclete, and this falls in with the statement in the First Epistle, "we have an *advocate* with God, even *Jesus Christ.*" Compare Romans 8:26. See on Luke 6:24. Note also that the word *another* is ἄλλον, and not ἕτερον, which means *different.* The advocate who is to be sent is not *different* from Christ, but *another* similar to Himself.—II, 243–44

In the title *Paraclete* there is abundant evidence both for the Personality and the Deity of the Holy Spirit. In his *Lectures on the Doctrine of the Holy Spirit,* therefore, William Kelly writes:

> But I apprehend the word "Comforter" sometimes fails (perhaps to most fails) to give an adequate notion of what it is that our Lord Jesus really meant us to gather from thus speaking of the Holy Ghost. We might very naturally draw from it, that the term was in relation to sorrow, that it intimated a person who would console us in the midst of the distresses of this lower world. And, indeed, the Holy Ghost does console us and comfort us. But this is only a very small part of the functions here conveyed by the word "Paraclete." This is the expression, if one would give an English reproduction of that which is in point of fact the very word our Lord employed. But the meaning of that word "Paraclete" is not merely "Comforter," but one who is identified with our interests, one who undertakes all our cause, one who engages to see us through our difficulties, one who in every way becomes both our representative and the great personal agent that transacts all our business for us. This is the meaning of the Advocate or Paraclete or Comforter, whatever equivalent may be preferred. Manifestly, then, it has an incomparably larger bearing than either "advocate" on the one hand, or "comforter" on the other: it includes both, but takes in a great deal more than either. In point of fact, it is One who is absolutely and infinitely competent to undertake for us whatever He could do in our favour, whatever was or might be the limit of our need, whatever our want in any difficulty, whatever the exigencies of God's grace for the blessing of our souls. Such the Holy Ghost is now; and how blessed it is to have such an One! But remark here, that it never was known before. I have already hinted, and indeed plainly expressed the conviction, that it will never be known again, fully allowing that there will be, as to extent, a larger outpouring of blessing in the world to come. But the personal presence of the Spirit here below as an answer to the glory of Christ at the right hand of God!—such a state of things never can be repeated. While the High Priest is above, the Spirit sent down gives a heavenly entrance into His glory as well as redemption; when the High Priest comes out for the earthly throne, the Spirit then poured out will give a testimony suited to the earth over which the Lord will reign.—Pp. 87–88

10. WITNESSING. "The Spirit itself beareth witness with our spirit, that we are the children of God" (Rom. 8:16). In this distinctive work the Holy Spirit actualizes to the believer that which has been taken by faith. It is not, therefore, regeneration or the Spirit's work in generating the believer, but the consciousness of this new reality, the Christian's recognition of that which the Spirit has wrought in regeneration. Those who believe on Christ become in their own right the sons of God (John 1:12), and the Spirit Himself witnesseth that this great reality has been accomplished. John declares it in 1 John 5:10, "He that believeth on the Son of God hath the witness in himself." The advantage and bless-

ing of this work of the Holy Spirit cannot be estimated. The whole field of experimental evidence for regeneration is important, though also fraught with danger lest confidence should be made to rest in changeable experience rather than in the unchanging Word of God. One truth needs ever to be considered, namely, that the Spirit's witness, like all His ministries which relate to life experience, will be hindered and, to that extent, imperfect for the Christian who is not in right spiritual relation to God. Thus the richest witness of the Holy Spirit regarding sonship is not experienced fully by all who are saved and simply because the witness is hindered. There are those in the world who are saved, but who lack this form of assurance. In a much larger sphere the Spirit, being *the Spirit of Truth* and the divine Author of the Holy Scriptures, is God's special witness. As the Son manifests God both by a life on earth and a ministry now in heaven, so the Spirit manifests God both by a written testimony and by the illumination through which the testimony may be comprehended.

11. ANOINTING. Indwelling and anointing are synonymous terms in Pneumatology and therefore depend on the same body of Scripture for their exact meaning. As certainly as every believer is indwelt by the Holy Spirit, thus to become a temple of the Holy Spirit, so certainly every believer is anointed by the Holy Spirit. Without reference to any special class of Christians whatsoever, the Apostle John writes: "But the anointing which ye have received of him abideth in you, and ye need not that any man teach you: but as the same anointing teacheth you of all things, and is truth, and is no lie, and even as it hath taught you, ye shall abide in him" (1 John 2:27). There could not be such a thing as a Christian who has not been anointed by receiving the Holy Spirit and thus made to partake of the divine nature, being born of the Spirit. The doctrine of the indwelling and anointing of the Holy Spirit calls for unprejudiced study, and will be treated quite at length in a later chapter.

12. BAPTISM. While tragic confusion obtains relative to various activities of the Holy Spirit—due, in the main, to a failure to consider all that the Scriptures declare on a given theme—no aspect of His work for the Christian is as perverted, if considered at all, as His baptism. The word *baptize*—more distorted by religious prejudice than any other term—is itself in need of careful definition. This is undertaken in other places in this work on theology. It may well be added here, however, that the word *βαπτίζω* in its various forms presents a primary and a secondary usage. The primary usage, which carries with it no

implication that it is more often used or is of greater importance, indicates a literal envelopment within an element and so to become subject to that element. This word is to be distinguished from βάπτω, the primary meaning of which is to dip whereby two actions are involved —that of putting in and that of taking out. Over against this, βαπτίζω, which it has just been shown means to immerse or submerge, implies only the putting in with no reference to the removal. Its secondary meaning has doubtless evolved from the primary meaning, since it represents an object being brought under the influence of another quite apart from any physical envelopment or intusposition. Such, indeed, is the baptism into repentance, the baptism into the remission of sins, the baptism into the name of the Father, the Son, and the Holy Ghost, the baptism by the cup into suffering, the baptism of Israel into Moses by the cloud and the sea, and the baptism by the Spirit into Christ. In none of these is there the remotest suggestion of a momentary dipping and removal. That which is most desired and fully assured respecting the union formed by the baptism into Christ is that there shall be no removal either in time or eternity; yet it is not a physical envelopment or an intusposition, but must be classified as the secondary use of the word βαπτίζω in which one thing is brought under the power and influence of another. By the Spirit's baptism into Christ the believer is joined permanently unto the Lord; he has put on Christ, and therefore, being in Christ, partakes of all that Christ is. This vital union is the ground of every position and possession into which the child of God has entered. It is obviously a grave error to confuse the baptism which the Spirit accomplishes when He joins the believer to Christ with any other experience, or to confound it with the filling of the Spirit, by which ministry Christian experience and power for life and service are secured. Since all that is vital in the Christian's relation to God depends upon this union with Christ, it is ever a point of satanic attack so as to hinder any right apprehension of it. Apart from this union which secures the imputation of the merit of Christ, there could be no standing before God and no entrance into heaven.

13. SEALING. The presence of the Holy Spirit within the believer becomes a distinguishing identification, not observable or useful as such in human spheres, but rather a mark of divine discrimination which God sees. "The Lord knoweth them that are his" (2 Tim. 2:19), and what greater mark of recognition could any individual bear in the sight of God than that he is a temple of the Holy Spirit? Thus, being indwelt, the believer is sealed. Similarly, the seal speaks of a completed under-

taking. Sealing belongs to those who are justified and perfected forever in Christ. So, also, sealing indicates security. The one who seals becomes responsible for the object upon which the seal is imposed. In the case of the believer, he is "sealed unto the day of redemption." Much that is suggested by the function of the seal is presented in Jeremiah 32:9–12. The Apostle Paul declares: "Who hath also sealed us, and given the earnest of the Spirit in our hearts" (2 Cor. 1:22); "In whom ye also trusted, after that ye heard the word of truth, the gospel of your salvation: in whom also after that ye believed, ye were sealed with that holy Spirit of promise" (Eph. 1:13); "And grieve not the holy Spirit of God, whereby ye are sealed unto the day of redemption" (4:30).

14. FILLING. That ministry of the Holy Spirit which is termed His *filling* is the very center of the entire theme of the spiritual life. It is the Spirit fulfilling in the believer all that He came into that heart to do. This ministry represents two quite different spheres of achievement. On its negative side, the spiritual life calls for a deliverance from the power of the three great enemies—the *cosmos* world, the flesh, and the devil. On its constructive or positive side, the spiritual life calls for the manifestation of every divine grace—no less than the showing forth of the virtues of Him who called the believer out of darkness into His marvelous light. In a later chapter of this volume these two features of the spiritual life will be investigated and due consideration be given to the great body of Scripture involved. It will be disclosed that there is a divine plan and provision whereby the believer may be saved from the reigning power of sin and also from the habit and practice of sinning, as there is a divine arrangement whereby the unsaved may be saved from the penalty of sin and from their lost estate. The life that is delivered is not to be explained by human traits or dispositions of character, nor is it accidental when the change comes. It rests completely on the sufficient power of the Holy Spirit, which power is available to those who follow the precise plan which God has revealed. Few will question the statement that there is a precise plan for the salvation of the lost; yet, on the other hand, but few have been awakened to the equally evident truth that God has a specific procedure whereby the power of the Holy Spirit may be realized in the individual believer's daily life. Though so much neglected, the way of life in dependence upon the Spirit is vital beyond measure.

15. INTERCESSION. One central passage bears upon the intercession of the Spirit, namely, Romans 8:26–27: "Likewise the Spirit also helpeth

our infirmities: for we know not what we should pray for as we ought: but the Spirit itself maketh intercession for us with groanings which cannot be uttered. And he that searcheth the hearts knoweth what is the mind of the Spirit, because he maketh intercession for the saints according to the will of God." On this passage Dean Alford writes:

> The Holy Spirit of God dwelling in us, knowing our wants better than we, Himself pleads in our prayers, raising us to higher and holier desires than we can express in words, which can only find utterance in sighings and aspirations: see next verse. Chrysostom interprets the words of the spiritual gift of prayer, and adds, "For the man who is granted this grace, standing praying in great earnestness, supplicating God with many mental groanings, asks what is good for all." Calvin understands, that the Spirit suggests to us the proper words of acceptable prayer, which would *otherwise have been unutterable by us.* Macedonius gathered from this verse that the Holy Spirit is *a creature,* and *inferior to God,* because He *prays to God for us.* But as Augustine remarks, "The Holy Spirit groans not in Himself, with Himself, in the Holy Trinity, but *in us,* in that He makes us to groan." No *intercession in heaven* is here spoken of, but a *pleading in us* by the indwelling Spirit, of a nature above our comprehension and utterance. **But** [opposed to the words *"which cannot be uttered:"* the groanings are indeed unutterable by us, but . . . ] **He that searcheth the hearts** [God] **knoweth what is the mind** [*intent,* or *bent,* as hidden in those sighs] **of the Spirit.** A difficulty presents itself in the rendering of the next clause. The particle with which it opens may mean either **because,** or **that.** If it is to be *causal,* **because He** [the Spirit] **pleads for the saints according to the will of God,** it would seem that **knows** must bear the meaning *"approves,"* otherwise the connection will not be apparent; and so Calvin and others have rendered it. Hence many render it **that**—*"knows what is the mind of the Spirit, that He pleads, etc. with* [or, according to] *God."* But I must confess that the other rendering seems to me better to suit the context: and I do not see that the ordinary meaning of the word **knoweth** need be changed. The assurance which we have that God the Heart-Searcher interprets the inarticulate sighings of the Spirit in us,—is not, strictly speaking, His Omniscience,—but *the fact that the very Spirit who thus pleads, does it* according to God,—in pursuance of the divine purposes and in conformity with God's good pleasure.—All these pleadings of the Spirit are heard and answered, even when *inarticulately uttered:* we may extend the same comforting assurance to the *imperfect and mistaken verbal utterances* of our prayers, which are not themselves answered to our hurt, but the answer is given to the voice of the Spirit which speaks through them, which we *would* express, but *cannot.* Compare 2 Corinthians 12:7–10 for an instance in the Apostle's own case.—*New Testament for English Readers,* new ed., at Rom. 8:27

This divine provision for the right and effective exercise of prayer should be apprehended and claimed as a new-birth privilege by every child of God. So important is the Holy Spirit's part in prevailing prayer that one further quotation which expounds this Scripture is added here, taken from W. R. Newell:

**And in like manner also—** We have just read that "we that have the first-fruits of the Spirit groan within ourselves," waiting for that blessed day of "the liberty of the glory of the sons of God." These words "in like manner," refer to that operation within us of the Spirit, which makes us, in real sympathy, one with the groaning creation about us. "In like manner," then, with this truly wonderful help, the Spirit "helps our infirmity,"—in its ignorant and infirm dealing with God. Note, the word "infirmity" is singular number: for we have nothing but infirmity! **We know not how to pray as we ought.** Oh, beware of the glib and intimate chatter of the "Modernist" preacher in his *prayers!* He would flatter both the Almighty and his hearers, and most of all, himself, in his "beautiful" and "eloquent" addresses to God! Not so with Paul, and the real saints of God, who have the Holy Ghost. There is with them the sense of utter and boundless *need,* and along with this the sense of *ignorance* and *inability.* Yet, still, bless God! there is, with all this, the sense of limitless help of the Holy Spirit! **The Spirit Himself maketh intercession for us with groanings which cannot be uttered—** We know that Christ maketh intercession for us at the right hand of God, but here the Spirit is making intercession within us: The Spirit, who knows the vast abysmal need of every one of us, knows that need to the least possible particular. **Groanings which cannot be uttered**—expresses at once the vastness of our need, our utter ignorance and inability, and the infinite concern of the blessed indwelling Spirit for us. "Groanings"—what a word! and to be used of the Spirit of the Almighty Himself! How shallow is our appreciation of what is done, both by Christ for us, and by the Spirit within us! **Which cannot be uttered—** Here, then, are needs of ours, of which our minds know nothing, and which our speech could not utter if we could perceive those needs. But it is part of God's great plan in our salvation that this effectual praying should have its place—praying, the very meaning of which we cannot grasp. Men of God have testified to the spirit of prayer prostrating them into deep and often long-continued "groanings." We believe that such consciousness of the Spirit's praying within us is included in this verse, but the chief or principal part of the Spirit's groaning within us, perhaps never reaches our spirit's consciousness. **And He that searcheth the hearts knoweth what is in the mind of the Spirit, because He maketh intercession for the saints according to God.** It is God the Father here that is "searching the hearts." How we used to shrink from the thought of such Divine searching! But here God is "searching hearts" to know what is the mind of the indwelling, holy Spirit concerning a saint, to know what the Spirit groans for, for that saint; in order that He may supply it. For in the plan of salvation, God the Father is the Source, Christ the Channel, and the Spirit the Agent. **Because He maketh intercession for the saints according to God—** We feel that the introduction of the words "the will of" before the word *God* merely obscures the meaning. "According to God"—what an all-inclusive, blessed expression, enwrapping us as to our salvation and blessing, wholly in Divine love and power. We know not how to pray as we ought; but the Spirit makes intercession in us, "according to God," according to His nature (of which we are partakers); according to our needs, which He discerns; according to our dangers, which He foresees—according to all the desires He has toward us.—*Romans Verse by Verse,* pp. 326–27

16. SANCTIFICATION. The root meaning of *sanctification* is to be set apart, to be classified, and specifically qualified unto the realization of some particular end. As presented in the Scriptures, sanctification is threefold: (a) that which is positional, or the setting apart which occurs when by the Holy Spirit the one who believes is joined unto Christ and thus comes to be in Christ. Of this it is written: "For by one offering he hath perfected for ever them that are sanctified. Whereof the Holy Ghost also is a witness to us" (Heb. 10:14–15). No classification known in heaven or on earth is more distinctive, far-reaching, or true than that wrought by the Spirit when He joins the individual to Christ. This same positional aspect of sanctification is also set forth in three other passages: "But of him are ye in Christ Jesus, who of God is made unto us wisdom, and righteousness, and sanctification, and redemption" (1 Cor. 1:30); "But we are bound to give thanks alway to God for you, brethren beloved of the Lord, because God hath from the beginning chosen you to salvation through sanctification of the Spirit and belief of the truth" (2 Thess. 2:13); "Elect according to the foreknowledge of God the Father, through sanctification of the Spirit, unto obedience and sprinkling of the blood of Jesus Christ" (1 Pet. 1:2). (b) Sanctification is also experimental, in that by the power of the Holy Spirit operating inside the child of God that one is energized both to be delivered from sin and to be effective in every right attitude and service. Progressive, or experimental, sanctification is said to be God's will for each believer and this is reasonable. It is written: "For this is the will of God, even your sanctification, that ye should abstain from fornication: that every one of you should know how to possess his vessel in sanctification and honour" (1 Thess. 4:3–4). Progress in the maturing of Spirit-wrought character can be attained only by and through the Third Person in the Godhead. (c) Sanctification will yet be achieved in its third or ultimate form; that is, the Christian will be presented faultless before the presence of God (cf. Eph. 1:4; Jude 1:24) and conformed to the image of Christ (cf. Rom. 8:29; 1 John 3:1–3). Thus it is revealed that sanctification is a work of the Holy Spirit. Other Scriptures reveal that the Holy Spirit, though infinitely holy, is free

to undertake all His ministries in the believer—even in spite of his fallen nature and his failures—since Christ has died not only *for* his sins, but *unto* sin.

17. As an Earnest. This, the concluding theme in this list, presents the engaging thought that all these limitless blessings together which are secured by the presence and power of the Holy Spirit in the believer are as an earnest or token, a pre-experience of the heavenly glory which will be. An earnest is a down payment—alike in kind, but the merest fraction in quantity though an exact specimen of the whole—of the believer's assured experience in heaven. It is written: "Who hath also sealed us, and given the earnest of the Spirit in our hearts" (2 Cor. 1:22); "Now he that hath wrought us for the selfsame thing is God, who also hath given unto us the earnest of the Spirit" (5:5); "Ye were sealed with that holy Spirit of promise, which is the earnest of our inheritance until the redemption of the purchased possession, unto the praise of his glory" (Eph. 1:13–14).

## CONCLUSION

This list of the activities of the Holy Spirit has been presented at this point with a view to demonstrating His Personality and Deity. None of the above-named undertakings could be wrought to the least degree by any other power than that of God. It is thus evidenced that the Holy Spirit is a Person and One of the Godhead Three.

## Chapter III

# TYPES AND SYMBOLS OF THE HOLY SPIRIT

Though the Bible abounds with metaphors, similes, symbols, types, parables, allegories, and emblems—a sevenfold classification of its figures of speech—it is needful to remember that behind every form of utterance there is a reality of truth, which truth must not be underestimated because of the form in which it is presented. All these varied forms of speech which the Bible employs are directly chosen and utilized by God the Holy Spirit. They in no way represent mere literary notions of men. It is of more than passing interest that the Holy Spirit Himself is presented under various types and symbols. The types and symbols which anticipate and describe the Second Person have been realized or fulfilled in concrete, visible form through His incarnation; but the Person and work of the Third Person remains in that obscurity which the invisible and therefore intangible ever involves. Since acquaintance with the Holy Spirit must depend so largely on what is said rather than upon what is seen or felt, attention should be given to every intimation. Though a number of secondary symbols obtain in Scripture, the listing given here will be restricted to the following which are well-marked or major unveilings of the Holy Spirit.

### I. OIL

As oil was used for healing, for comfort, for illumination, and for anointing unto specific purposes, so the Holy Spirit heals, comforts, illuminates, and consecrates. In the meal offering of Leviticus 2:1–16 in which Christ is foreshadowed in His human perfections, oil appears, first as mingled with the fine flour, and second as poured upon it. All this anticipates in type the life and ministry of Christ in His unique relation to the Holy Spirit, which relationship He maintained while here on earth—a relationship in which Christ's humanity was sustained and His actions empowered by the Holy Spirit. It was altogether possible, and it would have been natural, for Christ to have sustained His humanity by the power of His own Deity; yet, as man must be sustained by the Holy Spirit and not by the Second Person, and since Christ is the pattern man and God's ideal man, it is required that He, too, shall be cast upon the Holy Spirit respecting every need and limitation which His humanity presented. In type (cf. Lev. 2:4–5, 7) the fine flour is mingled with oil, suggesting that, with regard to His humanity, Christ was generated by the Holy Spirit; and, again (cf. Lev. 2:1, 6, 15), the oil poured over the meal foresees the Spirit coming upon Christ, as was true at His baptism. There is real significance in the requirement that the priest, when cleansing the leper (Lev. 14:10–32), should apply oil in the specific manner prescribed. The work of Christ in physical healing, as in spiritual transformation, was wrought by the power of the Holy Spirit. The cleansing of the leper is one of the most evident types of Christ since it foreviews salvation from sin. C. H. Mackintosh presents here the following:

"And the priest shall take some of the log of oil, and pour it into the palm of his own left hand: and the priest shall dip his right finger in the oil that is in his left hand, and shall sprinkle of the oil with his finger seven times before the Lord. And of the rest of the oil that is in his hand shall the priest put upon the tip of the right ear of him that is to be cleansed, and upon the thumb of his right hand, and upon the great toe of his right foot, upon the blood of the trespass-offering; and the remnant of the oil that is in the priest's hand he shall pour upon the head of him that is to be cleansed; and the priest shall make an atonement for him before the Lord" (vss. 15–18). Thus, not only are our members cleansed by the blood of Christ, but also consecrated to God in the power of the Spirit. God's work is not only negative, but positive. The ear is no longer to be the vehicle for communicating defilement, but to be "swift to hear" the voice of the Good Shepherd; the hand is no longer to be used as the instrument of unrighteousness, but to be stretched forth in acts of righteousness, grace, and true holiness; the foot is no longer to tread in folly's paths, but to run in the way of God's holy commandments: and, finally, the whole man is to be dedicated to God in the energy of the Holy Ghost. It is deeply interesting to see that "the oil" was put "upon the blood of the trespass-offering." The blood of Christ is the divine basis of the operations of the Holy Ghost. The blood and the oil go together. As sinners, we could know nothing of the latter save on the ground of the former. The oil could not have been put upon the leper until the blood of the trespass-offering had first been applied. "In whom also, after that ye believed, ye were sealed with that Holy Spirit of promise." The divine accuracy of the type evokes the admiration of the renewed mind. The more closely we scrutinize it, the more of the light of Scripture we concentrate upon it, the more its beauty, force, and precision are perceived and enjoyed. All, as might justly be expected, is in the most lovely harmony with the entire analogy of the Word of God.—*Notes on Leviticus*, Amer. ed., pp. 258–59

Again, Exodus 40:10, 13, 15 records the requirement respecting three particular anointings, namely, that of the altar, which speaks of

Christ's death through the eternal Spirit, that of Aaron as the high priest, which speaks of the Spirit being upon Christ (Isa. 61:1), and that of the sons of Aaron, who are the type of the believer of this age and whose anointing contemplates the Holy Spirit's present relation to the Christian. In the theocracy of old, kings were anointed (cf. 1 Sam. 16:12), as were officers (cf. 1 Sam. 10:1); and all this indicates the direct authority of God over His people in that form of His government.

An equally beautiful type of the Holy Spirit is to be seen in the fact that oil served as the source of light. The Israelites were directed to provide oil for the lights in the tabernacle (cf. Ex. 25:6). Two vital truths are implied in this particular typology, namely, that God the Holy Spirit is the essential light and the believer is to walk in the light which the Holy Spirit sheds upon his mind and heart, and that by so doing believers are themselves "as lights in the world." The light which the Christian may display is a manifestation of the presence and power of the Holy Spirit in his life. In the light of old there was oil, flame, and the wick which served as a medium between the oil and the flame. There must be contact between the oil and the wick, and so the wick must be kept free from charred portions; it must be snuffed. This truth, so essential to all spiritual effectiveness, is obvious. The ten virgins of Matthew 25:1–13 were either wise or foolish according to their spiritual preparation, which fact oil symbolizes in the parable. Five are to be excluded from the King's palace when He returns to the earth, and five are to meet Him with right preparation and enter the palace with Him. The virgins represent Israel on the earth awaiting the return of Messiah with His Bride (cf. Luke 12:35–36; Ps. 45:8–15).

Yet three other themes appear in connection with the typology which oil represents. In Psalm 45:7 there is reference to "the oil of gladness" —"the fruit of the Spirit is . . . joy"—while in Psalm 104:15 oil is prescribed to make the face shine and in Psalm 23:5 David gives praise to God who has anointed his head with oil, all of which is a presage of the Spirit's presence and power in the believer.

Writing of oil as a symbol of the Spirit, Dr. John F. Walvoord declares:

> In both the Old and New Testaments, the Holy Spirit is frequently found in this type. In the tabernacle, the pure olive oil which kept the lamp burning continually in the holy place speaks eloquently of the ministry of the Holy Spirit in revelation and illumination, without which the showbread (Christ) would be unseen in the darkness, and the way into the holiest of all would not

be made plain (Ex. 27:20, 21). Oil played an important part in the sacrifices (Lev. 1–7). It was used in the anointing of the priests and the consecration of the tabernacle (Lev. 8). It was used to induct kings into office (1 Sam. 10:1; 16:13; 1 Ki. 1:39; etc.). In addition to these sacred uses, it was used as food (Rev. 6:6), medicine (Mk. 6:13), and even as a means of commodity exchange (1 Ki. 5:11; cf. *International Standard Bible Encyclopaedia, s.v., Oil*). The instances of reference to oil in the Old Testament outnumber those to the Holy Spirit. According to Young's Concordance, there are one hundred and seventy-five references to oil in the Old Testament and a dozen instances in the New Testament, the most notable being Matthew 25:3–8; Hebrews 1:9; James 5:14. An interesting reference is John 3:34, speaking of the Spirit as not being poured out "by measure" on Christ. From the various uses of oil in the Bible, we may conclude that oil speaks of holiness, sanctification, revelation, illumination, dedication, and healing.—*The Doctrine of the Holy Spirit*, pp. 22–23

## II. WATER

This so common and so vast an element in the world serves as a type of judgment (cf. the flood, the destruction at the Red Sea, and the floods described by Christ in Matthew 7:25), of the Word of God (cf. John 3:5; Titus 3:5; 1 John 5:6, 8), and of the Holy Spirit. In His conversation with the woman of Samaria, Christ spoke of the water He would give as "living water," which living water is foreshadowed in the type as *running water*. The Holy Spirit is typified by water and this body of truth is indeed extensive. As water is essential for cleansing, satisfying, reviving, and refreshing, so the Holy Spirit is vital to the child of God. This general theme may be divided in a threefold manner: (a) the Spirit applies the blood of Christ for all cleansing, (b) the Spirit dwells within, and (c) the Spirit's manifestations flow out. These three divisions are here considered more at length. (a) The cleansing aspect is typified by the bathing of the priests in connection with their induction into the priestly office. They were then wholly and once-for-all bathed by the high priest (cf. Ex. 29:4; Lev. 8:6), which bathing prefigures the once-for-all washing of regeneration wrought for the believer-priest upon his entrance into both the saved estate and his service for God as a priest. So, also, there is a constant cleansing for the Christian in his walk which is anticipated in type by the cleansing provided by the sacrifice and ashes of the red heifer (Num. 19:2 ff.). The New Testament antitype is declared in 1 John 1:9: "If we confess our sins, he is faithful and just to forgive us our sins, and to cleanse us from all unrighteousness" (cf. Eph. 5:26). It is the Holy Spirit who applies the blood of cleansing. As a symbolic act, Christ bathed the disciples' feet

(John 13:1–17). (b) As for the Holy Spirit within, Christ said to the woman of Samaria: "But whosoever drinketh of the water that I shall give him shall never thirst; but the water that I shall give him shall be in him a well of water springing up into everlasting life" (John 4:14). The Holy Spirit indwelling the believer is a reality and His presence a measureless blessing, in all of which He is ever active. Like an artesian well, He is "springing up" unto everlasting life. Eternal life is not only gained and attained by the operation of the Holy Spirit, but is maintained—as are all its manifestations—by the Spirit. (c) With reference to the Spirit flowing out, the promise by Christ as recorded in John 7:37–39 is central. There it is written: "In the last day, that great day of the feast, Jesus stood and cried, saying, If any man thirst, let him come unto me, and drink. He that believeth on me, as the scripture hath said, out of his belly shall flow rivers of living water. (But this spake he of the Spirit, which they that believe on him should receive: for the Holy Ghost was not yet given; because that Jesus was not yet glorified.)" The river itself is by some interpreted as a separate type of the Holy Spirit, and in such a case much is made of the river which Ezekiel predicts will flow out from the very presence of Jehovah in the age to come (cf. Ezek. 47:1–12), symbolical of the vast increase of the Spirit's blessing and power in that day.

The majority of Christians interpret water, or ritual, baptism as an outward sign or symbol of the inward working of the Holy Spirit in the believer. To some, therefore, this type—water—represents all aspects of the Holy Spirit's work in the Christian; to others, it is more specifically related to the Spirit's baptism. It is believed among the latter that the "one baptism" of Ephesians 4:5 refers to the baptism by the Holy Spirit but includes also its outward sign or symbol—the two, the real and the ritual, together combining to form the "one baptism." The Spirit's approach to the believer with all that His gracious presence secures is signified, it is believed, by the application of water in baptism; and this, in turn, corresponds completely with the typical use of water throughout the Old Testament (cf. Isa. 52:15; Ezek. 36:25). One commendable feature of this interpretation of ritual baptism is seen in the fact that no separate, independent, and diverse baptism has been set up apart from the all-important baptism by the Holy Spirit which would compel the recognition of two baptisms—that of the Spirit and that which is ritual—in the face of the Scripture assertion that there is "one baptism." In all this truth respecting baptism, for those who so interpret it water becomes, again, an emblem of the Holy Spirit.

## III. FIRE

With reference to fire as a symbol of the Holy Spirit, the late F. E. Marsh of London writes:

> We often find that one symbol may represent two or more things. Lion, for instance, is used as a metaphor of Christ and Satan, and yet with a difference, for while it is used to express the boldness and achievements of our Lord, it symbolizes the cruelty and ferociousness of Satan (Rev. 5:5; 1 Pet. 5:8). Fire, also, is used of several things. It is a symbol of the Lord's presence, hence, Jehovah appeared to Moses "in a flame of fire" (Ex. 3:2). Fire is a sign of the Lord's approval. Thus in connection with the Tabernacle (Lev. 9:24), at the dedication of the temple (2 Chron. 7:1), and on Mount Carmel, fire came down from heaven and consumed the sacrifice, as a sign of God's approval and acceptance (1 Kings 18:38). Fire is associated with the protection of God's presence, hence, He was as a "pillar of fire" to the children of Israel for illumination and defence (Ex. 13:21), and He promises to be a "wall of fire" about His people (Zech. 2:5). Fire is a simile of His discipline and testing. When the Lord purifies the sons of Levi, He does it as a refiner purifies gold, by the action of fire (Mal. 3:3); and when Christ searched the seven churches, His eyes are described as "a flame of fire" (Rev. 1:14); and when believers are tried, they are reminded "the trial of your faith" is "much more precious than of gold that perisheth, though it be tried with fire" (1 Pet. 1:7); and we are also reminded, "Our God is a consuming fire" (Heb. 12:29). Fire is an emblem of God's Word, igniting and warming. Jehovah's declaration to Jeremiah was, "Behold I will make my words in thy mouth, fire"; and later, when the prophet resolved not to speak the Word, he had to confess, "Then I said, I will not make mention of him, nor speak any more in his name. But his word was in mine heart as a burning fire shut up in my bones . . . . and I could not stay" (Jer. 5:14; 20:9). Fire speaks of God's judgment. When Aaron's sons brought the strange fire in their self-willed effrontery, "there went out fire from the LORD, and devoured them" (Lev. 10:2); and fire is also an emblem of the Holy Spirit, for He is compared to "seven lamps of fire burning before the throne" (Rev. 4:5), and His gifts at Pentecost are compared to "cloven tongues like as of fire" (Acts 2:3). . . . Directly and indirectly the Spirit's might and ministry may be compared to fire. The zeal of service, the flame of love, the fervour of prayer, the earnestness of testimony, the devotion of consecration, the sacrifice of worship, and the igniting-power of influence are attributable to the Spirit.—*Emblems of the Holy Spirit,* 2nd ed., pp. 114–15

## IV. WIND

The breath of God is likened to wind, and it may be as a judgment (cf. Isa. 40:24) or as a blessing. The Scriptures, for instance, are the breath of God. After His resurrection, Christ breathed on His disciples and said, "Receive ye the Holy Ghost" (John 20:22). Thus, also, when man was created, God breathed into the lifeless form the breath of life and man became a living soul. Christ compared the working of the Spirit to the action of the wind when to Nicodemus He said: "The wind bloweth where it listeth, and thou hearest the sound thereof, but canst not tell whence it cometh, and whither it goeth: so is every one that is born of the Spirit" (John 3:8). Thus, also, the Spirit moved the holy men of old in the writing of the Sacred Text. They were *borne along* as a ship is driven by the wind. Peter states, "For the prophecy came not in old time by the will of man: but holy men of God spake as they were moved by the Holy Ghost" (2 Pet. 1:21). The Spirit came on Pentecost as a "rushing mighty wind," and thus He comes as a quickening and reviving power to save the lost.

## V. DOVE

It was at Christ's baptism that the Holy Spirit descended upon Him in a bodily shape like a dove. Of this important moment in the life of Christ on earth John the Baptist asserted: "This is he of whom I said, After me cometh a man which is preferred before me: for he was before me. And I knew him not: but that he should be made manifest to Israel, therefore am I come baptizing with water. And John bare record, saying, I saw the Spirit descending from heaven like a dove, and it abode upon him. And I knew him not: but he that sent me to baptize with water, the same said unto me, Upon whom thou shalt see the Spirit descending, and remaining on him, the same is he which baptizeth with the Holy Ghost. And I saw, and bare record that this is the Son of God" (John 1:30–34). There are many particulars in which the Holy Spirit may be likened to a dove. As for the character of a dove, C. H. Mackintosh in his *Notes on Genesis* writes of the dove which Noah released from the ark:

"And it came to pass, at the end of forty days, that Noah opened the window of the ark which he had made: and he sent forth a raven, which went forth, to and fro, until the waters were dried up from off the earth." The unclean bird made its escape, and found, no doubt, a resting-place on some floating carcass. It sought not the ark again. Not so the dove,—"She found no rest for the sole of her foot, and she returned unto him into the ark . . . and again he sent forth the dove out of the ark: and the dove came in to him in the evening; and, lo, in her mouth was an olive leaf, plucked off." Sweet emblem of the renewed mind, which, amid the surrounding desolation, seeks and finds its rest and portion in Christ; and not only so, but also lays hold of the earnest of the inheritance, and furnishes the blessed proof that judgment has passed away, and that a renewed earth is coming fully into view. The carnal mind, on the contrary, can rest in anything and everything but Christ. It can feed upon all uncleanness. "The olive leaf" has no attraction for it. It can find all it needs in a scene of death, and hence is not occupied with the thought of a new world and its glories; but the heart that is taught and exercised by the Spirit of God, can only rest and rejoice in that in which He rests and rejoices. It rests in the Ark of His salvation "until the times of the restitution of all things." May it be thus with you and me, beloved reader,—may Jesus be the abiding rest and portion of our hearts, that so we may not seek them in a world which is under the judgment of God. The dove went back to Noah, and waited for his time of rest: and we should ever find our place with Christ, until the time of His exaltation and glory in the ages to come. "He that shall come will come, and will not tarry." All we want, as to this, is a little patience. May God direct our hearts into His love, and into "the patience of Christ."—4th ed., pp. 104–5

This emblem, as all others found in the Scriptures, is directly chosen, appointed, and employed as such by God the Holy Spirit.

## VI. EARNEST

Looking toward that eternal estate in glory which awaits every child of God, there is some foretaste of it accorded the believer. Those immeasurable gifts and graces of the Holy Spirit into which the Christian may enter now are but an earnest of that blessedness, that incomparable fullness, which awaits the hour of release from this sphere of life. The fruit which the spies brought from the promised land was an earnest of all that the land held in store for the covenant people. The jewels which Isaac's servant placed on Rebekah were an earnest of all of Isaac's wealth and honor. Nothing can be added to that already promised, when it is said that "all things are your's" and that ye are "joint-heirs with Christ." It is essential to note, however, that the gifts and the blessings are not the earnest; it is the Holy Spirit Himself that secures these who is the earnest. Again, as in the relation which the believer sustains to Christ, the attention is centered not on things, however glorious, but on a Person.

## VII. SEAL

This theme, which speaks of the ownership and the authority of the Spirit over the believer, and of his security and portion unto the day of redemption, has been considered earlier and will yet be contemplated more at length in another chapter of this volume.

## VIII. ABRAHAM'S SERVANT

There remains one outstanding type of the Holy Spirit, which is presented in Genesis 24:1–67. It is the part of the trusted servant whom Abraham sent to secure a bride for Isaac. Since no real name is given in the Scriptures to the Holy Spirit, but He is known only by descriptive titles, no name has been assigned this servant. Doubtless, it was Eliezer of Damascus, steward of Abraham's household (cf. Gen. 15:2); but still no name is given, that the type may be complete. Abraham is a type of God the Father in many respects, here and elsewhere, as Isaac is the type of the Son of God. The servant is sent to a distant place to secure a bride for the son. Every step of this journey and all that was accomplished is fragrant with rich suggestion relative to the Holy Spirit's present mission in the world and the outcalling of the Bride of Christ. The late Dr. George E. Guille in a pamphlet entitled *Isaac and Rebecca* writes, "Three persons are prominent in this twenty-fourth chapter of Genesis: a father, his son, and their servant. The father and son are hidden in the father's house in Canaan, while the servant journeys after the bride. Canaan is the well-known picture of heaven, whither Christ has gone to prepare for the coming of His bride, for whom the Father has sent the Holy Spirit into the scene of His Son's rejection. The length of our chapter (67 verses) shows how much God's heart is occupied with the story,—how He is absorbed in the work of His Spirit: wooing and winning souls to Himself." Continuing with a description of the journey that Rebekah took with the servant, Dr. Guille writes: "Camel-riding is not pleasant, and the desert has no charm, but one thing made every hour of the journey a delight: the servant, who was under oath to bring the bride, was there, leading the way to Isaac, and refreshing the heart of Rebekah by telling her of him. Over and over again did he tell the story of his miraculous birth, of his willing sacrifice on Mt. Moriah, of his position and honor and wealth, as Abraham's beloved son and heir, and of his personal loveliness and dignity. . . . Oh, soul, do you know the spiritual experience of which this is a figure? The Holy Spirit, who won you for Christ, is dwelling in your heart, and is leading the way to the true Isaac. And at each step of the journey, He has a blessed ministry to perform. He would take the things of Christ and show them unto you" (pp. 15, 26–27).

### CONCLUSION

He who is not seen, who has never been "made manifest" as was Christ—excepting as He was identified to John the Baptist by the symbolism of a bodily shape like a dove—is, nevertheless, presented under types and symbols or emblems to the end that He may become real to the child of God and that His many characteristics may be disclosed.

# CHAPTER IV

# THE HOLY SPIRIT AND PROPHECY

IN THE BROADEST sense of this theme, the Holy Spirit is (1) the Author of all prophecy and (2) He is Himself the subject of prediction. These two aspects of truth may well be considered separately.

## I. THE AUTHOR OF PROPHECY

At once it should be observed that the word *prophecy* as here used is contemplated in its larger meaning which includes both forthtelling and foretelling. In the former idea is included the entire revelation from God, while in the latter is included only that which is predictive in its character. This distinction demands full recognition of the former as well as the latter.

God has spoken. His Word is recorded and His message forms the text of Scripture. The forming of the Bible is distinctly a task committed to the Holy Spirit of God. It was the Holy Spirit who caused the words of the Father and the words of the Son to be written down; for the Spirit is the Recorder of all that is written. In the unity which obtains in the Godhead, the Father may speak of the Scriptures as "my word" (Isa. 55:11) and, likewise, the word of the Son may be thus indicated (Col. 3:16); but the Holy Spirit remains the Author of the Sacred Text which records these words.

An extended and somewhat replete treatment of the authorship of the Scriptures has been included in this work under Bibliology. A repetition of this general thesis is not called for. Dr. John F. Walvoord's approach to this subject is such as may well be incorporated here. He states:

Of the many ministries of the Holy Spirit in the Old Testament, few are of more immediate concern to Christians than the work of the inspiration of Old Testament Scriptures. While the peculiar doctrines of Christianity to a large extent are based on New Testament revelation, it is clear to even a casual observer that the New Testament is based on the Old Testament, and one without the other does not constitute a complete or satisfying revelation. The doctrine of inspiration, having to do with the formation of the Scriptures, does not differ to a great extent in the two Testaments. The doctrine of the inspiration of the Scriptures has been the historic position of most Protestant churches, as their creeds bear abundant testimony. Whatever the degrees of unbelief latent in either the clergy or the laity, and whatever disagreements there may be between denominational groups on other doctrines, Protestant churches have officially held the doctrine of the inspiration of the Scriptures. This has been subject to extended discussion and argument, however, as various views of inspiration have been proffered. A complete discussion of the doctrine of inspiration cannot be undertaken here. The importance of the inspiration of the Scriptures, while tacitly denied by some in modern times, is easily sustained. It is a matter of tremendous import whether the Scriptures are a supernaturally produced Word of God, or whether they are a collection of the works of men, containing the errors one must expect in any human work. As Boettner writes: "That the question of inspiration is of vital importance for the Christian Church is easily seen. If she has a definite and authoritative body of Scripture to which she can go, it is a comparatively easy task to formulate her doctrines. All she has to do is to search out the teachings of Scripture and embody them in her creed. But if the Scriptures are not authoritative, if they are to be corrected and edited and some parts are to be openly rejected, the Church has a much more serious problem, and there can be no end of conflicting opinions concerning either the purpose of the Church or the system of doctrine which she is to set forth" (*The Inspiration of the Scriptures,* p. 10). It is not the purpose of the present discussion to attempt the display of the arguments supporting the inspiration of the Scriptures. The arguments from sources external to the Scriptures will not be considered at all, and the Biblical evidences discussed only as they illustrate the work of the Holy Spirit. What the Bible says on the subject is far more conclusive and plain to the eye of faith than all the high-flown arguments of unbelievers. . . .

The technical meaning of *inspiration* is quite apart from its common usage in reference to non-Biblical concepts. As B. B. Warfield points out, "The word 'inspire' and its derivatives seem to have come into Middle Eng. from the Fr., and have been employed from the first (early in the 14th cent.) in a considerable number of significations, physical and metaphorical, secular and religious" (*International Standard Bible Encyclopaedia, s.v. Inspiration,* p. 1473). We still speak of being inspired by a beautiful sunset, or of hearing an inspiring sermon. Such common usages, however, are not parallel to *inspiration* in a doctrinal sense. Even in ordinary speech, we conceive of inspiration as something that constitutes an influence from without. As Warfield says, "Underlying all their use, however, is the constant implication of an influence from without, producing in its object movements and effects beyond its native, or at least its ordinary, powers" (*loc. cit.*). Turning to the Scriptures, we observe a paucity of reference to the word *inspiration* as far as the term itself is concerned. In Job 32:8, Elihu is quoted, "But there is a spirit in man: and the inspiration of the Almighty giveth them understanding." This can hardly be referred to the inspiration of Scripture, however, as it is doubtful if any of the Bible, in its present form at least, was in existence at that time. The only other reference is found in 2 Timothy 3:16, where the Authorized Version gives this translation, "All scripture is given by inspiration of God, and is profitable for doctrine, for reproof, for correction, for instruction in righteousness." Even here, in the American revision, the translation is changed to read, "Every scripture inspired of God is also profitable for teaching, for reproof, for correction, for instruction which is in righteousness." The revised translation, while attempting to solve the problem created by the absence of the copula, not at all unusual in the Greek, has greatly weakened the passage, and that, unjustly. The noun *inspiration* would disappear entirely from the English New Testament if this translation were allowed, and a misleading impression is created that some Scripture is not inspired. The difficulty lies chiefly in the word *inspiration* itself. The Greek, θεόπνευστος, really does not mean *inspiring* at all. As Warfield notes, "The Gr. term has, however, nothing to say of *in*-spiring or of *in*spiration: it speaks only of a 'spiring' or 'spiration.' What it says of Scripture is, not that it is 'breathed into by God' or is the product of the Divine 'in-breathing' into its human authors, but that it is breathed out by God, 'God-breathed,' the product of the creative breath of God. In a word, what is declared by this fundamental passage is simply that the Scriptures are a Divine product, without any indication of how God has operated in producing them" (*Ibid.*, p. 1474). From 2 Timothy 3:16, we may conclude that inspiration is the work of God by which or through which the Scriptures are given. After stating the fact of inspiration, however, the same verse draws a most interesting and significant conclusion. Because the Scriptures are inspired, they are, therefore, profitable for doctrine, reproof, correction, and instruction in righteousness. In other words, inspiration guarantees accuracy, and gives divine authority to the record. It is hardly necessary here to review the abundant testimony of the Scriptures to this very fact. Christ Himself frequently quoted the Old Testament as the Word of God. The writers claimed inspiration for their own works. The content of Scripture is such that its prophecies must have been the product of divine revelation and its accurate recording the work of inspiration. The witness to inspiration is all the more conclusive because the Scriptures never attempt to prove inspiration; they merely state it and assume it, in the same manner as the Scriptures assume the existence of God. A matter of further observation is that the Scriptures are not only divine, but also human. The words used were those within the vocabulary of the writers. Their own emotions, human knowledge, experiences, and hopes entered into the Scriptures which they wrote, without compromising in the least their inspiration. Without doubt, some portions of Scripture are dictated, as the Scriptures themselves indicate, but most of the Scriptures do not have this characteristic. Regardless of the degree of human or divine influence in the Scriptures, the resultant is equally inspired and equally suited to God's purpose. The examination of the work of the Holy Spirit in inspiration will sustain these evidences for the dual authorship, divine and human, of the Scriptures.

A proper statement of the meaning of inspiration must contend that God so supernaturally directed the writers of Scripture that without waiving their human intelligence, their individuality, their literary style, their personal feelings, or any other human factor, His own complete and coherent message to man was recorded in perfect accuracy, the very words of Scripture bearing the authority of divine authorship. Nothing less than a plenary and verbal inspiration will satisfy the demands of the Scriptures themselves and give to faith the confidence in the Word of God which is essential to faith and life.—*The Doctrine of the Holy Spirit*, pp. 56–60

Within the range of his own competency, no human being could write Scripture. The subject matter must be harmonized with the eternal plan and purpose of God. It must comprehend all that characterizes God and eternity to come. It must recognize the divine intent in the whole field of permitted evil and provide a redemption. It must be not only a revelation of God, but be worthy of Him. A moment's consideration of these stupendous requirements would convince a thoughtful mind of the absolute necessity that there be a dual authorship respecting every word of the Bible—one of the Holy Spirit and one of human agency—and that the Scriptures be a divine product as definitely as were the tables of stone written with the finger of God.

## II. THE SUBJECT OF PREDICTION

Again, Dr. Walvoord may well be quoted. On the Eschatology respecting the Holy Spirit he writes:

The doctrine of the future work of the Holy Spirit has attracted practically no attention in existing works on theology and in books on the Holy Spirit. We search in vain for an exposition of this doctrine in standard theologies such as those of Hodge, Strong, Shedd, Alexander, Watson, Wardlaw, Dorner, Dick, Miley, Gerhart, Valentine, Buel, and the recent work of Berkhof. In works on the Holy Spirit such as those of Kuyper, Smeaton, Moule, Cummings, and Simpson there is practically no mention of the doctrine. The chief factor causing this defect is the three-way division in the treatment of eschatology itself. The postmillennial theory holds that the prophesied millennium will be fulfilled in the present age through preaching the Gospel or a "spiritual" return of Christ. If this theory be held, of course, the present ministries of the Spirit will continue through the age and culminate in the conclusion of all things in the final judgment. There is, in this theory, no need of treating the eschatology of the Holy Spirit. A similar situation is found among the writings of the so-called amillennialist view, i.e., that the present age will continue and issue into the eternal state without any millennium. Only the premillennialist, who anticipates a millennium on earth after Christ returns to set up His kingdom, can be expected to consider the doctrine and furnish an exposition of it. In the writing of premillennial teachers and theologians there is also, however, a surprising neglect of this doctrine. Among the older premillennialists, such as Van Oosterzee, there is little exposition and defense of the premillennial position, and practically no attention is given the prophesied ministries of the Spirit in the millennial period. More attention has been given to the other great themes of prophecy. The result has been that there has been little understanding of the nature of the ministries of the Spirit in the prophesied period of tribulation and in the millennium which follows. It is to this task that we now turn.

The usual premillennial position is assumed as the basis for the discussion. The Scriptures prophesy that after the return of Christ for the Church a period of unprecedented trouble will follow, a period of approximately seven years according to Daniel 9:27, shortened a little (Mt. 24:22), and divided into two halves of three and one-half years each. The latter half is known as the great tribulation and in it is an unprecedented display of sin and of divine judgment upon sin. The return of Christ to set up His kingdom abruptly closes the tribulation, and the millennium follows in which Christ will rule and establish universal righteousness and peace. The millennium itself closes with another outbreak of sin and the final judgment of the wicked, and the establishment of the new heavens and new earth brings in the eternal state. It is amidst these stirring events that the Holy Spirit ministers in fulfillment of prophecy. It is clear that in the nature of the circumstances His work will be quite different than His present undertaking for the Church. While the body of Scripture is not large, it does speak with certain voice on important points.

One of the popular misconceptions of the prophesied period of tribulation is that all who enter this period are irrevocably lost. It is true that individuals who have had opportunity to hear the Gospel and receive Christ during this present dispensation of grace are unlikely to accept Christ in the difficult days of tribulation. On the other hand, it is obvious that many will be saved, some of them surviving the horrors of the tribulation to enter the millennium, and others to die the death of martyrs. The rapture of the Church before the seven-year period of tribulation removes every Christian from the world. Immediately, however, Israel's blindness is removed (Rom. 11:25), and thousands among Israel turn to their long-neglected Messiah. Among Gentiles, too, there will be conversions from every nation and tongue (Rev. 7:9–17). While the tribulation period is characterized by wickedness and apostasy, it will be a period attended by a great harvest of souls. In the light of these facts, one might expect to find the Holy Spirit ministering during this period. . . .

The millennium will undoubtedly be the most glorious of all the dispensations. There will be the fullest display of righteousness, and universal peace and prosperity will characterize the period. Christ will rule all the earth, and every nation will acknowledge Him. The knowledge of the Lord will be from sea to sea. Throughout the millennium, Satan will be bound, and there will be no demonic activity. Man will continue to possess a sin nature with its inherent weakness, but there will be no outside temptation to arouse it. The ministry of resurrected saints in the earth will add its distinctive touch to the unusual situation. It is manifest that in such a period the Holy Spirit will have a ministry which exceeds previous dispensations in its fullness and power, even though the millennium will be legal in its government instead of gracious as in the present dispensation. . . .

The prophecies picturing the millennium, to which reference has already been made, unite in their testimony that the work of the Holy Spirit in believers will be more abundant and have greater manifestation in the millennium than in any previous dispensation. It is evident from the Scriptures that all believers will be indwelt by the Holy Spirit in the millennium even as they are in the present age (Ezk. 36:27; 37:14, cf. Jer. 31:33).

The filling of the Holy Spirit will be common in the millennium, in contrast to the infrequency of it in other ages, and it will be manifested in worship and praise of the Lord and in willing obedience to Him as well as in spiritual power and inner transformation (Isa. 32:15; 44:3; Ezk. 39:29; Joel 2:28, 29). In contrast to present-day spiritual apathy, coldness, and worldliness, there will be spiritual fervor, love of God, holy joy, universal understanding of spiritual truth, and a wonderful fellowship of the saints. The spiritual unity and blessings which characterized the early church assemblies are a foreview of the fellowship of saints throughout the world in the millennium. The emphasis will be on righteousness in life and on joy of spirit.

The fullness of the Spirit will also rest upon Christ (Isa. 11:2) and will be manifest in His Person and in His righteous rule of the earth. The millennium will be the final display of the heart of God before the bringing in of the eternal state. In it God is revealed again as loving and righteous, the source of all joy and peace; and in the period also, at its close, man is revealed as at heart in rebellion against God and unwilling to bow even before such glorious evidence of His power.

From such revelation as is found in the Scriptures, all the ministries of the Spirit known to us in the present age will be found in the millennium except the baptism of the Spirit—which has already been shown to be peculiar to the dispensation of grace, from the day of Pentecost to the rapture. Though ourselves in the midst of growing apostasy in the world and indifference to the Spirit even among those in whom He dwells, we can envision the coming day; and as we wait for Him whose right it is to reign, we can by yieldedness and by dependence on the indwelling Spirit find in our hearts and manifest in our own lives the fragrance of the fruit of the Spirit.—*Ibid.*, pp. 255–57, 262, 264–65

The outstanding prediction respecting the Holy Spirit is found in Joel 2:28–32. The passage reads: "And it shall come to pass afterward, that I will pour out my spirit upon all flesh; and your sons and your daughters shall prophesy, your old men shall dream dreams, your young men shall see visions: and also upon the servants and upon the handmaids in those days will I pour out my spirit. And I will shew wonders in the heavens and in the earth, blood, and fire, and pillars of smoke. The sun shall be turned into darkness, and the moon into blood, before the great and the terrible day of the LORD come. And it shall come to pass, that whosoever shall call on the name of the LORD shall be delivered: for in mount Zion and in Jerusalem shall be deliverance, as the LORD hath said, and in the remnant whom the LORD shall call."

On this important anticipation, which has been too often misunderstood, William Kelly writes:

It is the very scripture, as we know, which the apostle Peter quotes on the day of Pentecost to shew that the immense blessing of that day was in accordance with the highest favour promised for the kingdom, not that human excitement or moral folly which mistaken or deluded men were quick to impute to those who surpassed others in spiritual power. But, observe, the apostle did not affirm that this scripture was fulfilled. He says, "It is that thing which was spoken by the prophet Joel"; and so it is. What was promised was the outpouring of the Holy Ghost. Without saying that the present fact was the fulfilment of the prophecy (which men have assumed, to the great misunderstanding of scripture and lowering of Christianity), he shewed that it was of that nature, and such therefore as to be vindicated by the prophecy before their conscience; but the apostle's language is guarded, while commentators are not. They go too far. We do well always to hold fast to scripture. As to the promise that the Spirit should be poured upon "all flesh," we must bear in mind that "all flesh" is in contrast with restriction to the Jew. This is another feature which made the Pentecostal gift so admirably illustrate the scripture. For the patent fact that God caused those who received the Holy Ghost to speak in the different tongues distributed over the Gentile world, not causing all the converts to speak the Jewish language (a poor thing if true, which it is not, but a mere dream of superficial paradox), but causing the Jews gathered from their dispersion among all nations to speak the tongues of the Gentiles was a magnificent witness of the grace that was going out to the Gentiles to meet them where they were. The judgment of God had inflicted these various tongues upon them, and completely broken up the ambitious project of joining together to establish an unity of their own through the tower of Babel. But the grace of God went out exactly where His judgment had placed them. If a crushing blow laid their pride in ever so many separate ditches, the grace of God went out to these ditches, and blessed them where they lay, raising them out of their fallen estate. Such then is the first interruption, and really the beginning of a new strain, which is sufficiently plain from the way in which it is introduced. "It shall come to pass *afterward,* that I will pour out my Spirit"—makes therefore a break with what goes before, and thus again most admirably suits it to the use to which the apostle Peter applies it. But then we must remember that when the day comes for the Holy Spirit to be poured out afresh, not for the gathering out of a people for heaven, but for the earthly purposes of God's grace (for that is the difference), it will be manifest that the Holy Spirit will be given to men altogether apart from their being Jews. So on the day of Pentecost, when they were exclusively Jews, it was yet shewn by the miracle of Gentile tongues that God did not mean to stop there, but to go out towards all the nations. God will never give up that principle. He does not mean to be limited to the children of Israel again. He will bless the children of Israel once more, and will take up Judah also as such, and will accomplish every word He has promised to their united joy.

There is no good that He has annexed to them in His word which He will not bestow; but He will never more restrict Himself to the Jew in the day that is coming. And therefore, when the Holy Ghost is poured out at that time, it will be strictly upon "all flesh," not meaning that every individual in the millennium will have the Holy Ghost; but that no race left after that great day will be excluded from the gift of the Spirit. No class of persons, no age, no sex will be forgotten in God's grace. But it may be desirable to remark here that there is no thought of healing or improving the flesh, as the fathers and the theologians say. The light of the New Testament shews us the fallacy of such a view. The old nature is judged; our old man is crucified, not renovated. To our Adam state we have died, and enter a new position in Christ, and are called to walk accordingly as dead and risen with Christ. The external signs here named will precede the day which is still unfulfilled. It is vain to apply verses 30, 31 to the first advent. "I will shew wonders in the heavens and in the earth" is evidently another character of things. "And I will shew wonders in the heavens and in the earth, blood, and fire, and pillars of smoke. The sun shall be turned into darkness, and the moon into blood, before the great and the terrible day of Jehovah come." There will be a remarkable outward manifestation of divine power before the judgment is executed. God always sends a testimony before the thing itself. He does not strike before He warns. It is so in His dealings with us every day. What Christian has a chastening upon him before he is admonished of the Spirit of God? There is always a sense of wrong, and a lack of communion sensible to the spirit before the Lord inflicts the blow which tells of His watchful love over our careless ways. He gives the opportunity, if one may say so, of setting ourselves morally right; and if we do not heed the teaching, then comes the sorrow. And so it is here. These wonders cannot but attract the mind and attention of men, but they will not really be heeded. Infatuated and under judicial hardness, they will turn a deaf ear to all, and so the great and terrible day of Jehovah will overtake them like a thief. But God at least will not fail. He had foretold that so it should be, and His people will take heed. There will be a remnant enabled to see, and pre-eminently, as we know, from among the Jews, though by no means limited to them, as we learn from the second half of Revelation 7 and the end of Matthew 25. There will be still the witness of "all flesh" prepared for the glory of Jehovah about to be revealed. "Whosoever will call upon the name of Jehovah shall be delivered" shews that the blessing is by faith, and hence by grace. "All flesh" does not necessarily mean every individual, but, as we know from other scriptures, blessing here goes forth largely toward all classes—that is, toward all nations and even all divisions among nations. But all this is of great importance, because the Jewish system naturally tended to limit God as well as to make classes within the Jews. Only the family of Aaron could go into the sanctuary; only Levites could touch the holy vessels with impunity; whereas this greatest blessing of God will go out with the most indiscriminate character of grace. "And it shall come to pass, that whosoever shall call on the name of Jehovah shall be delivered: for in mount Zion and in Jerusalem shall be deliverance, as Jehovah hath said, and in the remnant whom Jehovah shall call." Hence it is plain that, although it is blessing for

Israel, still our prophet Joel keeps true to his purpose. The city of Jerusalem abides the great and royal centre; mount Zion reappears, the sign of grace for the kingdom which Jehovah will establish in that day.—*Lectures Introductory to the Study of the Minor Prophets,* 5th ed., *in loc.*

In an article in *Bibliotheca Sacra* (CI:374) on "The Baptism with the Spirit," Dr. Merrill Frederick Unger writes: "The whole context of Joel's prophecy, which forms the basis of Peter's quotation in Acts 2:17–21, emphasizes (apart from any consideration of the events of Pentecost) that these words quoted by Peter have never been fulfilled. The Spirit was outpoured at Pentecost, but not in the full sense of Joel's prophecy. His special coming to form the Church was unrevealed in the Old Testament (Eph. 3:1–9). Joel knew nothing of the baptism with the Spirit, or the formation of the Church. Indeed, the fulfilment of this graphic passage, in the time of Israel's restoration, will consist, not in the baptism with the Spirit, which is strictly confined to the Church age, but in the indwelling of, and especially the filling with, the Spirit, which Joel describes as the 'pouring out upon all flesh' (2:28). Before ever it is fulfilled, however, the great invasion from the North must occur (Joel 2:1–10), the tribulation take place (Acts 2:19–21), Armageddon be fought (Joel 2:11), Israel be regathered and converted (Joel 2:12–17), and the Lord's second advent come about, issuing in a great deliverance (Joel 2:18–27)."

### CONCLUSION

The Holy Spirit is the Author of prophecy in its widest form and to its last and least detail. This is the doctrine of inspiration which is advanced in the Sacred Text itself and which has been defended in this theological work. The Holy Spirit is likewise the subject of prediction. His Person and work are so extensive and so vital to the whole program of God that any scheme of prediction which essays to forecast the plan and purpose of God from its beginning would hardly fail to contemplate features which pertain to the Holy Spirit.

# CHAPTER V

# THE HOLY SPIRIT IN THE OLD TESTAMENT

PNEUMATOLOGY has more to do with New Testament truth than with Old Testament. Still, in any consideration of the theme that covers the whole field more or less completely, some of the time must be devoted to revelation given before Christ and the Church.

## I. FROM ADAM TO ABRAHAM

Since the work of the Holy Spirit as related to Gentiles in the present age will be considered later in this volume (Chapter VII) and in connection with the outcalling of the Church, and since all other history from Abraham to the end of the kingdom age is centered in Israel, the present discussion is necessarily restricted to Gentiles and the first two thousand years or more of human history, i.e., the period from Adam to Abraham. It is recognized that the Holy Spirit, being the active divine agency in the world, exercises a constant sovereignty over the affairs of men of all classes and of all dispensations. The stupendous program of God which includes the birth, rise, character, and end of nations, extending down to the least conception of God which ever originates in the most obscure individual's mind, is all the sovereign work of the Holy Spirit. What a mainspring is to a timepiece the Holy Spirit has been and is and ever must be to all that enter into this mundane enterprise. The period from Adam to Moses which is specifically contemplated in this section will be discussed under a twofold division: (1) the direct references to the Holy Spirit and (2) the Holy Spirit as the Revealer of truth.

1. DIRECT REFERENCES. Only five direct references to the Holy Spirit are found in the history of that long period which precedes the call of Abraham. These Scriptures are full of significance and freighted with suggestive truth.

*Genesis 1:2.* "And the earth was without form, and void; and darkness was upon the face of the deep. And the Spirit of God moved upon the face of the waters."

This work of the Holy Spirit is one of reconstruction following the cataclysm which is indicated here. Dr. James M. Gray declares:

> What was the condition of inert matter as represented in verse 2? The first verb "was" has sometimes been translated "became." Read it thus and you get the idea that originally the earth was otherwise than void and waste, but that some catastrophe took place resulting in that state. This means, if true, that a period elapsed between verses 1 and 2, long enough to account for the geological formations of which some scientists speak, and a race of pre-Adamite men of which others speculate. It suggests too that the earth as we now know it may not be much older than tradition places it. The word "earth" in this verse, however, must not be understood to mean our globe with its land and seas, which was not made till the third day, but simply matter in general, that is, the cosmic material out of which the Holy Spirit organized the whole universe, including the earth of today. "And the Spirit of God moved upon the face of the waters." "Moved upon" means brooded over as a bird on its nest. "Waters" means not the oceans and seas as we know them, but the gaseous condition of the matter before spoken of. The Spirit of God moved "upon" the waters, and not "inside of" them, showing that God is a personal Being separate from His work. As the result of this brooding, what appeared? We need not suppose that God spake just as a human being speaks, but the coming forth of light out of thick darkness would have seemed to a spectator as the effect of a divine command (Ps. 33:6–9). On the natural plane of things vibration is light or produces light, which illustrates the relation between the moving of the Spirit upon inert matter and the effect it produced.—*Christian Workers' Commentary,* 6th ed., at Gen. 1:2–5

Jamieson, Fausset, and Brown may well be quoted also: "the Spirit of God moved—*lit.,* continued brooding over it, as a fowl does, when hatching eggs. The immediate agency of the Spirit, by working on the dead and discordant elements, combined, arranged, and ripened them into a state adapted for being the scene of a new creation. The account of this new creation properly begins at the end of this second verse; and the details of the process are described in the natural way an onlooker would have done, who beheld the changes that successively took place" (*The Critical and Explanatory Commentary,* at Gen. 1:2). So, also, C. H. Mackintosh states: " 'The Spirit of God moved upon the face of the waters.' He sat brooding over the scene of His future operations. A dark scene, truly; and one in which there was ample room for the God of light and life to act. He alone could enlighten the darkness, cause life to spring up, substitute order for chaos, open an expanse between the waters, where life might display itself without fear of death. These were operations worthy of God" (*Notes on Genesis,* 4th Amer. ed., p. 4).

*Job 26:13.* "By his spirit he hath garnished the heavens; his hand hath formed the crooked serpent."

The three references to the Holy Spirit in the book of Job are included in the pre-Abrahamic period both because of the probable dating of that book within that period and because of the fact that in this earliest book no mention is made of any other than the general purpose of God with the undivided human stock, which stock obtained before the call of Abraham. The reference quoted above is of creation by the Holy Spirit and contains the record that by His hand the Holy Spirit formed the "crooked serpent." This is usually taken to refer to the Milky Way with its unnumbered constellations. The direct intimation of the passage is that God the Holy Spirit served as the Creator of the material universe.

*Genesis 6:3.* "And the LORD said, My spirit shall not always strive with man, for that he also is flesh: yet his days shall be an hundred and twenty years."

On this divine warning Matthew Henry comments: "God's resolution not always to strive with man by his Spirit. The Spirit then strove by Noah's preaching (1 Pet. 3:19, 20) and by inward checks, but it was in vain with the most of men; therefore, says God, *He shall not always strive.* Note, 1. The blessed Spirit strives with sinners, by the convictions and admonitions of conscience, to turn them from sin to God. 2. If the Spirit be resisted, quenched, and striven against, though he strive long, he will not strive always (Hos. 4:17). 3. Those are ripening apace for ruin whom the Spirit of grace has left off striving with. The reason of this resolution: *For that he also is flesh,* that is, incurably corrupt, and carnal, and sensual, so that it is labour lost to strive with him. Can the Ethiopian change his skin? *He also,* that is, All, one as well as another, they have all sunk into the mire of flesh" (*Commentary,* at Gen. 6:3). The whole theme of divine judgment is introduced here. That judgment was to fall upon the immediate situation described in the context; but the passage also serves as a warning that God's time of grace is restricted in its duration. "Sons of God"—so termed here (vs. 2) and in Job 1:6; 2:1—may be angelic beings, probably those who kept not their first estate. Of the judgment upon them it is written: "For if God spared not the angels that sinned, but cast them down to hell, and delivered them unto chains of darkness, to be reserved unto judgment" (2 Pet. 2:4); "And the angels which kept not their first estate, but left their own habitation, he hath reserved in everlasting chains under darkness unto the judgment of the great day" (Jude 1:6).

*Job 27:3; 33:4.* "All the while my breath is in me, and the spirit of God is in my nostrils. . . . The Spirit of God hath made me, and the breath of the Almighty hath given me life."

Both of these Scriptures present human life as utterly dependent upon the Holy Spirit of God. In the former Job likens his own breath and life to the immediate presence of the Holy Spirit; and in the latter, Elihu, expressing the convictions of godly men of his time, asserts that he is made by the Holy Spirit.

All these five passages serve to construct an indication of what men believed and what was true of the Holy Spirit from the beginning of the race.

2. THE REVEALER OF TRUTH. The Spirit who produces and provides the written word likewise produces and provides all communications from God to men. In the days preceding the Jewish age God spoke to men and doubtless more freely and more often than would be implied from the text of Scripture. A notable instance is the truth revealed to Enoch as recorded in the next to the last book of the Bible—a revelation given to Enoch which finds no expression in the Old Testament as being given to him. The passage reads: "And Enoch also, the seventh from Adam, prophesied of these, saying, Behold, the Lord cometh with ten thousands of his saints, to execute judgment upon all, and to convince all that are ungodly among them of all their ungodly deeds which they have ungodly committed, and of all their hard speeches which ungodly sinners have spoken against him" (Jude 1:14–15). A distinction should be made between a thing revealed from God which calls for no proclamation of it and a revelation from God which anticipates its publication. God spoke to Adam, to Cain, and to Noah, but with no instruction that it be transmitted to others and preserved as revelatory truth. But to the prophets He spoke with the expectation that the message would be conveyed somehow to others. Of this distinction Kuyper writes: "God spoke also to others than prophets, *e.g.*, to Eve, Cain, Hagar, etc. To receive a revelation or a vision does not make one a prophet, unless it be accompanied by the command to communicate the revelation to others. The word 'nabi,' the Scriptural term for prophet, does not indicate a person who receives something of God, but one who brings something to the people. Hence it is a mistake to confine divine revelation to the prophetic office" (*The Work of the Holy Spirit,* p. 70, as cited by Walvoord, *The Doctrine of the Holy Spirit,* p. 46).

In view of the evidence at hand it would seem reasonable to assume that a very full revelation was given to the early members of the race.

Much was said directly to Adam. The difference between the sacrifice offered by Cain and that offered by Abel implies not only the knowledge relative to sacrifice on their part, but indicates that peculiar features were included in the divine instructions. The antediluvians had sufficient light to serve as a basis upon which the world that then was could be judged for its sinfulness. The book of Job is rich with doctrine. Recently, R. R. Hawthorne has identified over a hundred doctrines in the book of Job and collected the various passages under their doctrinal heads (*Bibliotheca Sacra,* CI:64 ff.). All that Job had on which to live for God was wholly apart from even a verse of written Scripture. From whence came Melchizedek with the bread and wine which he served to Abraham? And to what is reference made in Genesis 26:5 when it says: "Because that Abraham obeyed my voice, and kept my charge, my commandments, my statutes, and my laws"? How extensive was the knowledge of God's purpose and of the future consummation of all things if the prophecy by Enoch is to be considered as an indication of the knowledge possessed in the day in which he lived? Noah was deeply taught of God both with regard to the building of the ark as Moses was taught regarding the tabernacle, and with regard to a message to preach—one not his own, but come from God—for he was a preacher of righteousness (2 Pet. 2:5). All that characterizes the first two thousand or more years of human history is compressed into the first eleven chapters of the Bible, so that every feature of that time has but meager recognition in the Sacred Text; but from that which is revealed and that which may be deduced, it is to be concluded that the Holy Spirit was active then in the furtherance of those relationships which exist between God and men. The Gentiles, or the original human stock, were favored by the ministries of the Holy Spirit.

## II. FROM ABRAHAM TO CHRIST

This division of the Spirit's work is extensive since it embraces the entire history of Jewry as recorded in the Scriptures, reaching all the way from Abraham to Christ. It properly contemplates the whole Bible relative to its inspiration, owing to the truth that these Oracles are, with slight exception, given through members of the Jewish race (in the case of the New Testament, however, the writers were Christians, strictly speaking). It is to be noted, also, that the great company of prophets spoke as they were "moved" by the Holy Spirit, and that often officers and rulers were under the guiding power of the Spirit of God.

The Spirit came upon men for the accomplishment of divinely appointed undertakings reaching even to mechanical tasks and to works of art. Especially to be observed is the fact that there was no provision for, and no promise of, an abiding presence of the Holy Spirit in the life of any Old Testament saint. In this truth is to be seen one of the most differentiating features of the Spirit's relationship in the Mosaic age, as compared to the present age. The term *sovereign* best describes the Spirit's relation to men of old. He came upon them and departed according to His sovereign good pleasure. In no instance did the faith of men determine the Spirit's actions. Two passages may be cited in this connection. (1) There is the request of Elisha when Elijah was about to be taken from him. The account presents the old prophet Elijah accompanied by the young prophet Elisha as they moved on together to the place where the former was to be translated. The description as it is given follows: "And it came to pass, when they were gone over, that Elijah said unto Elisha, Ask what I shall do for thee, before I be taken away from thee. And Elisha said, I pray thee, let a double portion of thy spirit be upon me. And he said, Thou hast asked a hard thing: nevertheless, if thou see me when I am taken from thee, it shall be so unto thee; but if not, it shall not be so. And it came to pass, as they still went on, and talked, that, behold, there appeared a chariot of fire, and horses of fire, and parted them both asunder; and Elijah went up by a whirlwind into heaven. And Elisha saw it, and he cried, My father, my father, the chariot of Israel, and the horsemen thereof. And he saw him no more: and he took hold of his own clothes, and rent them in two pieces. He took up also the mantle of Elijah that fell from him, and went back, and stood by the bank of Jordan; and he took the mantle of Elijah that fell from him, and smote the waters, and said, Where is the LORD God of Elijah? and when he also had smitten the waters, they parted hither and thither: and Elisha went over" (2 Kings 2:9–14). In this account Elisha makes a request of Elijah that "a double portion" of Elijah's spirit may be upon himself. It is not at all determined by this text that the young prophet recognized and requested for himself the Holy Spirit of God. If he did so recognize the Holy Spirit, his request is forthwith treated as a "hard thing," which would indicate the exceptional character of it. It still stands as a characteristic of that age that as a rule men did not expect to receive the Spirit by asking for Him. (2) The second passage is found in Psalm 51:11, R.V. where David prays, "And take not thy holy Spirit from me." Two things are at once evident—the Holy Spirit might be taken from David, and David desired that the presence and power of the Holy Spirit might be his portion for a longer period so that he might serve Israel well as her king. The evidence is well sustained that, in contrast to the present-age provision whereby every believer is indwelt by the Holy Spirit and quite apart from asking for that Presence, in the past dispensation the Spirit's relation to men was sovereign. The force of this truth is seen in the fact that, when at the beginning of His three and a half years' ministry Christ promised the Holy Spirit to those who would ask—He said: "If ye then, being evil, know how to give good gifts unto your children: how much more shall your heavenly Father give the Holy Spirit to them that ask him?" (Luke 11:13)—so far as the record reveals, none of the disciples ever made this request. The offer and all it implies evidently was too much of an innovation for that which was the age-condition relative to the Spirit and that to which they were adjusted. Later, at the end of His ministry, Christ said: "And I will pray the Father, and he shall give you another Comforter, that he may abide with you for ever; even the Spirit of truth; whom the world cannot receive, because it seeth him not, neither knoweth him: but ye know him; for he dwelleth with you, and shall be in you" (John 14:16–17). Why, indeed, should Christ pray thus for the Spirit if the Spirit had been the portion of the saints of that dispensation already? It will be observed that the issue here under consideration has only to do with the fact that the Spirit's relation to the saints of old was *sovereign*. The men of that age who were Christ's disciples did not act as if prepared for so great a privilege, namely, that the Holy Spirit could be claimed by merely asking. Note, also, that the present immeasurable blessing of the interminable indwelling of the Holy Spirit is due to Christ's asking and not to the request of any person on earth. Every reference to the Spirit's presence and work in this age, especially those references related to its introduction which publish and disclose the new order and character thereof, imply a wholly new plan for the Christian which provides the very presence and power of the Holy Spirit in each believer's life. These implications constitute a very important indication of the relation that the Spirit sustained to the saints of old. That interpretation—far too common—which assumes that the Old Testament saints were on the same ground of privilege as the believers of this age, is rendered possible only through unpardonable inattention to the revelation which has been given on this point.

Of the present ministries of the Holy Spirit in relation to the believer—regeneration, indwelling or anointing, baptizing, sealing, and filling—nothing indeed is said with respect to these having been experienced by the Old Testament saints, excepting a few well-defined instances where individuals were said to be filled with the Spirit. Old Testament saints are invested with these blessings only theoretically, and without the support of the Bible, by those who read New Testament blessings back into the Old Testament—an error equalled in point of the danger to sound doctrine only by its counterpart, which reads Old Testament limitations forward into the New Testament portions designed to present the new divine purpose in grace.

With respect to regeneration, the Old Testament saints were evidently renewed; but as there is no definite doctrinal teaching relative to the extent and character of that renewal, no positive declaration can be made. In its New Testament aspect, regeneration provides for the impartation of the divine nature; the regenerated person becomes thus the very offspring of God, an heir of God and a joint heir with Jesus Christ. It results in membership in the household and family of God. If the first law of interpretation is to be observed—that which restricts every doctrinal truth to the exact body of Scripture which pertains to it—it cannot be demonstrated that this spiritual renewal known to the Old Testament, whatever its character may have been, resulted in the impartation of the divine nature, in an actual sonship, a joint heirship with Christ, or a placing in the household and family of God. So the case of Nicodemus—a perfected saint under Judaism—was duplicated in the experience of every Jew who passed from the old order into the new. To Nicodemus Christ said, "Ye must be born again," and it is significant that this imperative was not addressed to the lowest member of Jewish society but to one of its rulers who could serve as the supreme example of all that entered into the reality which Judaism provided. Nicodemus, like Saul of Tarsus, could have been classed as a "just man" before the Mosaic Law; but to claim for him that he was justified on the ground of imputed righteousness through a placing in Christ by the Holy Spirit is to assert that which could have no foundation in fact, otherwise he would have had no need or occasion to be born "from above." The silence of God must be respected relative to what constituted one a *just man* according to the Mosaic demands. He naturally stood "touching the righteousness which is in the law blameless" if, perchance, he had provided the sacrifices required; but his actual standing with God was largely determined by the fact that he was born into a covenant relation with Him. The Old Testament will be searched in vain for record of Jews passing from an unsaved to a saved state, or for any declaration about the terms upon which such a change would be secured. In other words, their national covenant standing was a tremendous spiritual advantage; but it cannot rightfully be compared with the estate of the believer today who is justified and perfected forever, having received the *plērōma* of the Godhead through vital union with Christ.

1. INDWELLING. Regarding the indwelling of the Holy Spirit in Old Testament saints, it has been stated already that the Spirit came and went, in accord with His sovereign relation to men of old. His coming to them was for a specific purpose, as in the case of Bezaleel merely to give skill in his work as an artisan and that restricted to the construction of the tabernacle. The conception of an abiding indwelling of the Holy Spirit by which every believer now becomes an unalterable temple of the Holy Spirit belongs only to this age of the Church, and has no place in the provisions of Judaism.

2. BAPTIZING. Of all the present functions of the Holy Spirit, none is more completely foreign to the Old Testament than the Spirit's baptism. The Old Testament knows nothing of the Body of Christ, nor of the New Creation Headship in the resurrected Christ. Men were *just* and *righteous* as related to the Mosaic Law, but none had the righteousness of God imputed to them on the ground of simple faith except Abraham, he who was so evidently marked out and raised up of God to anticipate and illustrate (cf. Romans and Galatians) the New Testament doctrine of imputed righteousness; so of Abraham alone Christ said, "Abraham rejoiced to see my day: and he saw it, and was glad" (John 8:56).

3. SEALING. Again, no similar idea is discovered in the Old Testament. The "bond of the covenant" was that which bound the Jew to Jehovah and those bonds were perfectly recognized by Jehovah Himself; but that is far removed from the sealing of the Spirit unto the day of redemption (cf. Eph. 4:30).

4. FILLING. The filling of the Holy Spirit is common to both Testaments; likewise, its equivalent expression, *the Spirit came upon:* but as the filling of the Holy Spirit is unto the end that the whole purpose of God in something may be fulfilled, it is important to discover in every instance precisely what that filling was designed to accomplish. In the case of the men of Old Testament times, the Holy Spirit came upon them or filled them that they might accomplish some particular work, which objective may have comprehended all the field of their activity or have been restricted to some one feature. Over against this, it will be seen that the divine purpose in filling as set forth in the New Testament is the larger and unlimited ministry of the Spirit manifest in every

aspect of the believer's life—its conflicts, its victories and achievements. As before indicated, the Holy Spirit is said to have come upon Bezaleel. He came also upon Balaam, Samson, Saul, the prophet Azariah, and Ezekiel; and, by a consideration of the things wrought through this relationship, it will be seen that the Spirit's presence was not determined by moral or spiritual qualities in the one thus blessed, whereas, as is so clearly taught in the New Testament, the Spirit's filling depends now upon a complete adjustment to His mind and will.

In every consideration of the problem of the salvation of Old Testament saints, it should be remembered that, in its complete form, all Israel shall yet be saved when the Deliverer comes out of Zion (cf. Rom. 11:26–27) and this includes men of the Abrahamic and Mosaic dispensations who will be raised for Israel's specific judgment and, if accepted, to enter into their earthly kingdom, but excludes those who are rejected and condemned at that specific judgment. Whatever salvation was wrought in Old Testament times was wrought by the Holy Spirit, as in the New Testament the Spirit is the Executor of all the works of God.

The "holy men of God" who wrote the Old Testament Scriptures were moved by the Holy Spirit (2 Pet. 1:21). That influence upon these holy men represents a very distinct divine undertaking and forms a large part of the doctrine respecting the Holy Spirit as found in the Old Testament. The prophets spoke by divine power whether their message was recorded in written form or not. The prophet was God's messenger to the people and his declarations, if appointed of God, were accomplished by the power of the Holy Spirit. Thus the fact of revelation by the Spirit and its kindred doctrine of inspiration are included in the listing of the works of the Holy Spirit in His relation to the Jewish people. The assertion that "all scripture is given by inspiration of God" refers primarily to the Old Testament and these Oracles of God are given almost wholly through Jewish authors. Israel gave to the world both the written Word and the Living Word. On the extent of inspiration, Dr. John F. Walvoord has written:

> An examination into the records of the Old Testament will reveal literature of all types: history, poetry, drama, sermons, love stories, and insight into the innermost devotional thoughts of the writers. It is a matter of great significance that inspiration extends to all of these kinds of literature, without regard as to form or style, without concern as to the origin or the knowledge embodied in writing. The question naturally presents itself concerning the relation of inspiration to various portions of Scripture. Every attempt to fathom

the supernatural is doomed to a measure of failure. Man has no criterion by which to judge that which transcends our experience. Without trying to explain inspiration, an examination of its application may be undertaken. At least seven types of operation may be observed in the work of inspiration.

(1) *The Unknown Past.* Scripture occasionally speaks with authority concerning the past in such detail and upon such themes as would be unknown to man. In the early chapters of Genesis, for instance, Moses portrays events occurring before the creation of man, therefore beyond all possible bounds of tradition. In Isaiah and Ezekiel, reference is made to events in heaven outside the sphere of man's knowledge and prior to his creation. It is clear that these narratives demand both a revelation concerning the facts and the work of the Holy Spirit in inspiration to guarantee their accurate statement. Some have advanced the idea in relation to the accounts of creation that these are similar in many details to pagan accounts of creation. It is possible that revelation was given prior to the writing of Scripture on the subject of creation, and that men had added to and altered this revelation in the formation of non-scriptural accounts of creation. The existence of other records of creation and points of similarity of these with the Scriptures in no wise affects the inspiration of Genesis. Whether Moses used documents or not has no bearing on the writing of the Scriptures. Whether documents were used, whether there was knowledge of pagan ideas of creation, or whether tradition had contributed some truth on the subject, the work of inspiration was necessary in any event to distinguish truth from error and to incorporate in the record all that was true and to omit all that was false. Without doubt, the primary source of information was direct revelation, and the documents if any and such traditional accounts as may have been known by Moses were quite incidental.

(2) *History.* A large portion of the Old Testament conforms to the pattern of history. In such sections, the writer is speaking about events known to many and concerning which other documents not inspired may have been written. In many cases, the writer is dealing with contemporary events in which the element of revelation is practically absent. How may inspiration be said to operate in such Scripture? As in all Scripture, inspiration is not concerned with the source of the facts but only with their accurate statement. In the record of history, the Holy Spirit guided the writers in the selection of events to be noted, the proper statement of the history of these events, and the omission of all that should not be included. The result is an infallibly accurate account of what happened with the emphasis on the events important to the mind of God.

(3) *Law.* Certain portions of the Old Testament consist in laws governing various phases of individual and national life. This kind of Scripture is found chiefly in the Pentateuch, where the law is revealed in three major divisions: the commandments, governing the moral life of the people; the ordinances, governing the religious life of the people; and the judgments, dealing with the social life of the people. In some cases, the law consisted in commandments given by means of dictation, the laws retaining in every particular the character of being spoken by God. In other cases, Moses charges the people as God's prophet and gives commandments which can hardly be construed to

have been committed to him by way of dictation; yet the commandments have equal force with other commandments. Inspiration operates in the writing of all law in the Scriptures to the end that the laws perfectly express the mind of God for the people to whom they are given; the laws are kept from error and include all that God desires to command at that time; the laws are authoritative and are a proper basis for all matters to which they pertain.

(4) *Dictation.* As previously intimated, some portions of God's Word consist in direct quotation of God's commands and revelation. How does inspiration operate under these circumstances? Inspiration guarantees that commands and revelation received from God are properly recorded in the exact way in which God wills. On His part, God speaks in the language of the one writing, using his vocabulary and speaking His message in such a way that naturally or supernaturally the writer can receive and record the message from God. In such portions, the writer's peculiarities are probably noticed least. Dictation, however, should not be regarded as more authoritative than other portions of Scripture. Inspiration extends freely and equally to all portions of Scripture, even in the faithful record of human sin and the repetition of human speech which may be untruth. Inspiration adds to the account the stamp of an infallible record, justifying the reader in accepting the Scriptures in all confidence.

(5) *Devotional Literature.* One of the intricate problems of inspiration is to relate its operation to the writing of the devotional literature of the Old Testament, of which the Psalms are the major portion. Does inspiration merely guarantee an accurate picture of what the writers felt and thought, or does it do more than this? In the case of the recording of human speech, inspiration does not necessarily vouch for the truth of what is said. For instance, in the record of the temptation, Satan is recorded to have said, "Ye shall not surely die" (Gen. 3:4). Inspiration guarantees the accuracy of this quotation of the words of Satan, but does not make these words true. In the case of the Psalmists, then, who were men subject to sin and mistake, whose experiences and thoughts were not necessarily accurate, does inspiration do more than merely give a faithful record? The answer to the problem is found in the Psalms themselves. An examination of their content will reveal that God not only caused an inspired record of their thoughts to be written, but worked in their thoughts and their experiences with the result that they revealed God, portrayed the true worship of the heart, the hearing ear of God to prayer, the joy of the Spirit, the burden of sin, and even prophesied of future events. Thus David, in his own experience realizing the preservation of God, speaks of the goodness of God, his praise transcending the bounds of his own experience to that of Christ's, the greater David. He exults, "Therefore my heart is glad, and my glory rejoiceth: my flesh also shall rest in hope. For thou wilt not leave my soul in hell; neither wilt thou suffer thine Holy One to see corruption" (Psa. 16:9, 10). Much that David said would apply to himself. David could say that his heart was glad, that his flesh rested in hope. David knew that his soul would not remain forever in hell. But when David said that his body would not see corruption, he was clearly beyond his own experience and was revealing that of Christ. Peter states this fact in his sermon at Pentecost

(Acts 2:25–31), and points out the difference between David and Christ. Inspiration can, therefore, be said to result in more than a record of devotional thoughts. While the process is inscrutable, inspiration so wrought that an accurate record was made of the thoughts of the writers, these thoughts being prepared by the providence of God. All that the writers experienced was not incorporated in Scripture. Inspiration was selective. As Warfield so well describes: "Or consider how a psalmist would be prepared to put into moving verse a piece of normative religious experience: how he would be born with just the right quality of religious sensibility, of parents through whom he should receive just the right hereditary bent, and from whom he should get precisely the right religious example and training, in circumstances of life in which his religious tendencies should be developed precisely on right lines; how he would be brought through just the right experiences to quicken in him the precise emotions he would be called upon to express, and finally would be placed in precisely the exigencies which would call out their expression" (*International Standard Bible Encyclopaedia, s.v.* "Inspiration," p. 1481). While providential preparation should not be confused with inspiration, it can be seen that *with* providential preparation, inspiration of the devotional literature of the Old Testament takes on the nature of the recording of revelation, not revelation by the voice of God, but revelation by the workings of God in the human heart.

(6) *The Contemporary Prophetic Message.* Much that is recorded as a message from a prophet concerned the immediate needs of his own generation. To them he would bring God's messages of warning; he would exhort; he would direct their armies; he would choose their leaders; in the manifold needs of the people for the wisdom of God, the prophet would be God's instrument of revelation. In this aspect of prophetic ministry, the Scripture doubtless records only a small portion. The record is given for the sake of its historic importance and to constitute a living example to later generations. How is inspiration related to this aspect of Scripture? As in the case of other types of Scripture, inspiration is first of all selective. In the writing of the Scripture, the writer is guided to include and exclude according to the mind of God. Inspiration assures that the record is an accurate one, giving the message of the prophet the character of infallibility. This was true even in the case of the few ungodly men who gave voice to prophecy and were guided in it by God. The work of inspiration in this particular type of Scripture is similar to that operative in recording history in the larger sense, in the writing of history, guiding in the selection and statement of the history, and in the case of prophecy, guiding in the selection and statement of the message and deeds of God through His prophets.

(7) *Prophecy of the Future.* In the nature of prophecy, it frequently took the aspect of predicting future events. It would warn of impending judgment, and in the midst of chastening experiences, it would portray the glory and deliverance that would come with the Messiah. Approximately a fourth of the Old Testament is in the form of prediction. Does inspiration have a peculiar relation to this form of prophecy? Most of the Old Testament Scripture was comprehended by the writers. They could understand to a large degree the

events of history. They could appreciate much of the Psalms. What they wrote was in a large measure passing through their own thoughts and was subject to their understanding. The introduction of predictive prophecy, however, brings to the foreground the statement of future events which were not understood. The prophets themselves confessed that they did not always understand what they wrote. As Peter writes, "Of which salvation the prophets have inquired and searched diligently, who phophesied of the grace that should come unto you: searching what, or what manner of time the Spirit of Christ which was in them did signify, when it testified beforehand the sufferings of Christ, and the glory that should follow" (1 Pet. 1:10, 11). The work of inspiration in predictive prophecy is probably more evident than in the other types of Scripture. Here indeed human wisdom was of no avail, and accuracy of the finest kind was demanded. Here inspiration can be tested more severely than in any other field, and the testimony of fulfilled prophecy gives its conclusive voice to the work of the Holy Spirit which caused it to be written. Predictive prophecy required revelation from God in such form that inspiration could cause it to be written revealing the eternal purposes and sovereign will of God. Visions and trances play an important part in some revelation of future events, and the power of God through the Holy Spirit was especially evident.

While distinctive aspects of the operation of the Holy Spirit may be seen, corresponding to the various types of Scripture, it can be concluded that in the main inspiration bears the same characteristics in all kinds of Old Testament Scripture. In it all the Spirit guided, excluding the false, including all that the mind of God directed, giving to revelation accurate statement, to history purposeful selection and authentic facts, to providentially guided experience its intimate record of God dealing with the hearts of His servants, to prophecy, whether a contemporary message or predictive, the unfailing accuracy that made it the proper standard for faith to apprehend. The work of inspiration was not accomplished by an impersonal force, by a law of nature, or by providence alone; but the immanent Holy Spirit, working in the hearts and affairs of men, not only revealed the truth of God, but caused the Old Testament to be written, the most amazing document ever to see the light of day, bearing in its pages the unmistakable evidences that the hands which inscribed them were guided by the unwavering, infinitely wise, unfailing Holy Spirit.—*The Doctrine of the Holy Spirit*, pp. 64–70

## CHAPTER VI

# THE DISTINCTIVE CHARACTER OF THE PRESENT AGE

AS AN INTRODUCTION to the vast theme of the Holy Spirit's relation to the present age—which subject takes up the remainder of this volume—it would be well to indicate the four time-periods which mark off the Holy Spirit's activities throughout the whole of human history: (1) The Old Testament. As indicated before, the Spirit's relation in the former ages was sovereign. He came upon whom he would and for such purposes as God determined; He left them as freely as He came, when His designs were realized. If He abode with a king or a prophet, it was only because of the fact that such abiding was the immediate purpose of God, hence not in conformity to some age-characteristic of universal and unbroken indwelling of either good or useful men. In this first period, as previously stated, the Holy Spirit is seen as Creator, as the energizing power working in certain men who fulfilled a specific purpose of God's, and as Author of the Scriptures. (2) The period of transition. From the beginning of Christ's ministry upon earth as incarnate to the first preaching of the Gospel to Gentiles in Cornelius' house (Acts 10:44), there is indicated a period of transition: the Holy Spirit was offered by Christ to all who asked for Him (Luke 11:13), Christ promised to pray that the Spirit might come and be an abiding, indwelling presence within His own (cf. John 14:16–17), after His resurrection He breathed upon them the Spirit (John 20:22), they were to tarry in Jerusalem until endued with power by the Spirit (Luke 24:49), the Spirit came on Pentecost as prophesied, at which time Jewish believers (the gospel was still restricted to Jews at that time) were joined into one spiritual Body (Acts 2:47), the giving of the Holy Spirit was preceded by the laying on of apostolic hands in Samaria (Acts 8:14–17; cf. Heb. 6:2), and the Spirit "fell on" Gentile believers in the house of Cornelius (Acts 10:44). Much in this transitional situation became permanent; but the final age-condition of receiving the Holy Spirit, as Christ had indicated it in John 7:37–39, was not established until Gentiles were received into the same spiritual Body with the believing Jews. There is no record respecting the laying on of any hands in Cornelius' house. Undoubtedly, this experience marked the beginning of a new and permanent order for the present age. (3) The present age. Since this time is the theme of the greater portion of this volume and the major Biblical revelation respecting the Holy Spirit's undertakings, it will not be outlined here more than to state that in this period are unfolded the whole new reality which the Christian is as well as his daily-life responsibility and service, which life and service are to be wrought by the Holy Spirit in answer to a continuing faith. (4) The kingdom age. Again, to the end that repetition may be avoided, this theme which has constituted the subject of earlier pages in this volume (Chapter IV) will not be developed here. It should be recalled, however, that there yet remains an entire age of specific undertakings and benefits on the part of the Holy Spirit, which age is yet future.

The present age, which extends from the first advent of Christ onward to His return to receive His own, is distinct in several particulars from the other time-periods listed above.

## I. AN INTERCALATION

The age itself is an intercalation which is unaccounted for in all predictions of the Old Testament. These Old Testament predictions trace the course and final destiny of Israel, the nations, the angels, and the promised land; but each of these lines of prophecy passes over the present age of the outcalling of the Church as though it did not exist. It is restated as fundamental to a right understanding of all Biblical prophecy, then, that the present dispensation is not only unforeseen by prophets of old (cf. 1 Pet. 1:10–11), but is wholly unrelated to that which went before and as wholly unrelated to that which follows.

## II. A NEW DIVINE PURPOSE

This age is distinctive also, being, as it is, the outworking of a wholly new divine purpose, namely, the gathering out (*ἐκκλησία*) from both Jews and Gentiles of a heavenly people, the Body and Bride of the glorified, resurrected Christ, which by divine transforming power will not only be qualified for residence in the highest heaven, but be qualified as well for everlasting association with the Members of the blessed Trinity. That Bride will satisfy every ideal of the Bridegroom throughout all eternity. Naught but an infinite, divine undertaking could accomplish this. This incomprehensible age-purpose marks off this dispensation as being unique and unrelated to any other era in human history that has been or ever will be. In their attempt to unify the ages about one supposed covenant of divine grace and to blend the present dispensation into one unbroken sequence with the rest, theologians have lost the characterizing features of this period and by so much have failed to see the surpassing and historically unrelated position and glory of the Church, the Body and Bride of Christ.

## III. AN AGE OF WITNESSING

This age is peculiarly an age of witnessing. Israel as a nation bore a testimony concerning the one God, Jehovah, to the people of the earth; but they had no gospel to proclaim, no great commission like the Church's, nor did they sustain a missionary enterprise. Even Christ, when restricted to His Israelitish ministry (cf. Rom. 15:8) as He was throughout His precross days, said of Himself: "I am not sent but unto the lost sheep of the house of Israel" (Matt. 15:24); and when sending His disciples forth with their specific message to their own people, He commanded that they should *not* go to the Gentiles nor enter into any city of the Samaritans, but "go rather to the lost sheep of the house of Israel" (Matt. 10:5–6). Respecting that ministry to Israel alone, Christ gave no instructions on the meaning of the message they were to impart, well understood as it was from the Old Testament, though He entered into minute details relative to the manner of their going unto a still rebellious people (cf. Matt. 10:1–42). Over against this is the later command that these same disciples should go into all the world and preach such an innovation as the gospel to every creature, as a witness unto Himself in His new character of a crucified and risen Savior. This striking and far-reaching contrast should not be passed over lightly. He had likened the enterprise of this age to a sower going forth to sow, not a reaper. Similarly, the Apostle declares that the word of reconciliation "is committed unto us" (2 Cor. 5:18–19). In the future age there will be no need of an evangel, at least to Israel, saying to them "Know the LORD," for all shall know Him from the least unto the greatest (Jer. 31:34). It therefore becomes evident that the present age, bounded as it is by the two advents of Christ, is distinctive in that it is an age of witnessing to the ends of the earth of the saving grace provided through the death and resurrection of Christ.

## IV. ISRAEL DORMANT

Now Israel is dormant and all that is related to her covenants and promises is in abeyance. To them—not as a nation, but as individuals—the privilege of being saved unto heavenly glory along with individual Gentiles is extended in this day of God's heavenly purpose. No Jewish covenants are now being fulfilled; they are "scattered," "peeled," "broken off," and yet to be "hated of all nations" for Christ's name's sake. This is the one peculiar age in which there is "no difference" between Jew and Gentile, though in former times God Himself had instituted the most drastic distinction between these two classes of people.

## V. SPECIAL CHARACTER OF EVIL

Evil attains a special character in the present time. Several reasons account for the fact that the Apostle writes of this as an "evil age" (Gal. 1:4, R.V. marg.). (1) Christ describes the evil character of this period in connection with the seven parables of Matthew, chapter 13. In this description He speaks of the influence of evil in relation to the falling of the seed, the darnel, the birds in the mustard tree, the leaven in the meal, and the bad fish. It is evident that His purpose was to assign a new and hitherto unexperienced character to evil as it appears in this age. (2) Likewise, the Apostle states that there is a mystery form of evil in this age which had already begun to work in his own day (2 Thess. 2:7). (3) Believers are said to maintain a warfare against the *cosmos* world, the flesh, and the devil. Doubtless the *cosmos* and the flesh exercised an evil influence in past ages. A special revelation is given in Ephesians 6:10–12, however, in which a conflict peculiar to this age has been shown to exist between the believer and Satan. (4) Satan himself bears the title of "god of this age" (2 Cor. 4:3–4, R.V. marg.). (5) So, also, the specific conflict of the "last days" of the Church on the earth presents a new form of evil in the world. And (6) the claim of Christ upon man's faith through His death and resurrection obliges all people to make a reasonable response and by so much creates the possibility of a new and unprecedented sin—the sin of unbelief in the Savior.

## VI. AN AGE OF GENTILE PRIVILEGE

According to a truth wholly peculiar to this age, the Gentiles are privileged to enter into the highest divine purpose and glory. Their estate before God in past ages is described in Ephesians 2:12: "That at that time ye were without Christ, being aliens from the commonwealth of Israel, and strangers from the covenants of promise, having no hope, and without God in the world." Their estate before God in the coming kingdom age is likewise clearly and fully predicted, as found in Isaiah 14:1–2; 60:12. These passages read: "For the LORD will have mercy on Jacob, and will yet choose Israel, and set them in their own land: and the strangers shall be joined with them, and they shall cleave to the house of Jacob. And the people shall take them, and bring them to their place: and the house of Israel shall possess them in the land of the LORD for servants and handmaids: and they shall take them captives, whose captives they were; and they shall rule over their oppressors. . . . For the nation and kingdom that will not serve thee shall perish; yea, those nations shall be utterly wasted." At the judgment of the nations as described in Matthew 25:31–46, certain nations are to enter the kingdom prepared for them from the foundation of the world; but in this relation and position they must conform to the restrictions set forth in the Scripture quoted above from Isaiah. From such a comparison with past and future ages it is made certain that the present age has been marked off as one of peculiar privilege and benefit for Gentile peoples.

## VII. THE WORK OF THE SPIRIT WORLD-WIDE

Even more evident than what has preceded is the truth that the present age is one in which the Holy Spirit exercises an influence over the whole human family, and especially over those who are saved and those who according to the eternal purpose of God are yet to be saved. As for this latter company, the Apostle writes that they are those "who are the called according to his purpose" (Rom. 8:28–30). This the seventh characteristic of the present age not only concludes the summarization set forth in this chapter, but points to the major feature of the whole doctrine of the Holy Spirit.

# CHAPTER VII

## THE WORK OF THE HOLY SPIRIT IN THE WORLD

THE PRESENT AGE, because of the extensive activities of the Holy Spirit, has rightfully been styled *the dispensation of the Spirit.* A proportionate treatment of the Person and work of the Holy Spirit as His Person and work are exhibited in the Bible will disclose the fact that at least ninety percent of the material which enters into Pneumatology is found in those portions of the Scripture which relate to the age of grace. This same proportion is of necessity reflected to some extent in the pages of this volume. This extended treatment will be pursued under three general divisions: (1) the Spirit as the Restrainer of the *cosmos* world, (2) the Spirit as the One who convicts the unsaved, and (3) the Spirit in relation to the Christian. The first two divisions are to be considered in this chapter.

### I. THE RESTRAINER OF THE *COSMOS* WORLD

Though but one passage is found bearing upon the restraining work of the Holy Spirit, the scope of the issues involved is such as to command the utmost consideration. It contemplates the divine government over the forces of evil at work in the world throughout the present age. The passage, being somewhat veiled, has not received a uniform interpretation. It reads: "Let no man deceive you by any means: for that day shall not come, except there come a falling away first, and that man of sin be revealed, the son of perdition; who opposeth and exalteth himself above all that is called God, or that is worshipped; so that he as God sitteth in the temple of God, shewing himself that he is God. Remember ye not, that, when I was yet with you, I told you these things? And now ye know what withholdeth that he might be revealed in his time. For the mystery of iniquity doth already work: only he who now letteth will let, until he be taken out of the way. And then shall that Wicked be revealed, whom the Lord shall consume with the spirit of his mouth, and shall destroy with the brightness of his coming: even him, whose coming is after the working of Satan with all power and signs and lying wonders, and with all deceivableness of unrighteousness in them that perish; because they received not the love of the truth, that they might be saved" (2 Thess. 2:3–10). Few passages present more vital truth concerning the future than this. After having declared the fact that the Day of the Lord (R.V.)—the thousand-year kingdom with all its introductory judgments (not, the Day of Christ, as in the A.V.)—cannot come until the final apostasy has been experienced and the man of sin has appeared, that man of sin is identified, here as elsewhere, by his wicked assumption of the prerogatives of Deity (cf. Ezek. 28:1–10). He is the lawless one (R.V.). The mystery of that lawlessness which he consummates was begun in the Apostle's day and would have been completed at an earlier time had not that lawlessness, promoted by Satan, been restrained. The Restrainer will go on restraining until He, the Restrainer, is taken out of the way. Then shall "that Wicked" one be revealed, and not before. But who is the Restrainer? The notion it is the church herself is corrected at once by the disclosure that the Restrainer is a Person, for the identification is of one who may be designated with the masculine gender. Likewise, the claim that this Person is Satan is as untenable, since Satan cannot be said to restrain himself. That the Restrainer is accomplishing a stupendous, supernatural task classes Him at once as one of the Godhead Three; and since the Holy Spirit is the active agency of the Trinity in the world throughout this age, it is a well-established conclusion that the Restrainer is the Holy Spirit of God. Some portion of this restraint is, no doubt, wrought through the Church, which is the temple of the Spirit (cf. 1 Cor. 6:19; Eph. 2:19–22). Of this notable passage, Dr. C. I. Scofield states, "The order of events is: (1) The working of the mystery of lawlessness under divine restraint which had already begun in the apostle's time (v. 7); (2) the apostasy of the professing church (v. 3; Lk. 18:8; 2 Tim 3:1–8); (3) the removal of that which restrains the mystery of lawlessness (vs. 6, 7). The restrainer is a person—'he,' and since a 'mystery' always implies a supernatural element (Mt. 13:11, *note*), this Person can be no other than the Holy Spirit in the church, to be 'taken out of the way' (v. 7; 1 Thes. 4:14–17); (4) the manifestation of the lawless one (vs. 8–10; Dan. 7:8; 9:27; Mt. 24:15; Rev. 13:2–10); (5) the coming of Christ in glory and the destruction of the lawless one (v. 8; Rev. 19:11–21); (6) the day of Jehovah (vs. 9–12; Isa. 2:12, *refs.*)" (*The Scofield Reference Bible*, p. 1272).

It is clearly implied that were there no restraint in the world the tide of evil would rise to incomprehensible heights. This conclusion accords with the Biblical declaration that the human heart is not only "desperately wicked" in itself, but is under the dominion of Satan (Jer. 17:9; Eph. 2:2–3). Over against this evidence, man has contended that he is fundamentally right and needs only to attain to culture, education, and refinement. The hour in which the present restraint is removed from the earth will demonstrate the truthfulness of the Word of God respecting the corruption of the human heart. Nothing needs to be imposed upon fallen humanity to set up the great tribulation in the earth: that tribulation will automatically result when the Spirit's restraint is removed. The removal of the Holy Spirit is the reversing of Pentecost. On the Day of Pentecost He who had been omnipresent in relation to the world became resident in the world, and when He is removed He who is now resident will be again omnipresent in His relation to the world. This explains the seeming paradox that He who was already here on earth because infinite came on the Day of Pentecost, and He who is removed will still be present. So far as its being a mere inference that the Church—the Spirit's present abode in the world—will remain here after the Spirit is removed, her departure with the Holy Spirit, though that departure is not expressly mentioned in this context, is a necessity. The most vital unifying fact respecting the Church is the truth that her members are possessed of the divine nature which is imparted through the operation of the Holy Spirit of God. Christians are, every one, indwelt by the Holy Spirit and His presence constitutes their sealing, which sealing, so far from being intermittent or temporary, is "unto the day of redemption." It is an absurdity to contemplate the idea of a Christian who has not received the Holy Spirit, since the presence of the Spirit in the Christian is his most distinguishing feature. Should the Holy Spirit depart from the Church, she would instantly cease to be what she is; and should any church members, thus void of the Spirit, pass into the great tribulation, that company, being no longer the Church, would not involve the true Church in the hour of testing. In other words, since there can be no separation between the Holy Spirit and the Church, when the great tribulation is reached either the Holy Spirit must remain here with the Church, which is an unscriptural notion, or the Church must be removed with the Spirit from this world. Hidden in one of the Savior's most precious promises is the assurance that the Spirit will abide forever with those in whom He dwells (John 14:16–17), and John himself writes in 1 John 2:27: "But the anointing which ye have received of him abideth in you, and ye need not that any man teach you: but as the same anointing teacheth you of all things, and is truth, and is no lie, and even as it hath taught you, ye shall abide in him." From these declarations it must be concluded that any separation now or ever between the Holy Spirit and the believer is divinely prohibited. When the Spirit is removed, the Church will be removed with Him. She cannot be left behind.

The extent of the Spirit's restraint of the *cosmos* world has not been revealed. As implied above, the extent of the Spirit's restraint may be measured by comparing the world in its present more or less civilized relationships, its recognition and defense of human rights, and its patronizing attitude toward God and His Word, with the picture of the oncoming tribulation as seen in Revelation. A slight indication of the Spirit's present restraining power is to be seen in the fact that of all the profanity uttered by human lips, there is never a cursing in the name of the Holy Spirit. This restraint is not due to any conscious sentiment on the part of God-hating and God-defying men; it is due to a supernatural restraint wrought by the Holy Spirit Himself against whom man must not blaspheme. It is thus demonstrated that the Holy Spirit restrains the corruption of the world-system until that corruption has run its course (cf. Gen. 15:16), that He will go on restraining until He be taken out of the way, and that, when He is taken away, the unrestrained powers of darkness will constitute the trial and terror of the great tribulation. It is further indicated that of necessity the Church must depart with the Holy Spirit when He is removed from His place of residence in the world.

## II. THE ONE WHO CONVICTS THE UNSAVED

Within the whole divine enterprise of winning the lost, there is no factor more vital than the work of the Holy Spirit in which He convinces or reproves the *cosmos* world respecting sin, righteousness, and judgment. The wholly unscriptural and untenable Arminian notion of common grace, which asserts that all men at birth are so wrought upon by the Holy Spirit that they are rendered capable of an unhindered response to the gospel invitation, has, with the aid of human vanity which owns no limitations in human ability, so disseminated its misleading errors that little recognition is given to the utter incapacity of the unsaved, natural man to respond to the gospel appeal. Inattentive or uninstructed evangelists and zealous soul-winners too often go forth assuming that all persons anywhere and everywhere are able at any time to comply with the terms of the gospel, whereas the Scriptures teach that no man is able to make an intelligent decision for Christ apart from the enlightening work of the Holy Spirit. Evangelists and preachers are called upon to face, if they will, a supernatural factor in this program of winning the lost. Because of failure to understand this factor or because of unwillingness to be restricted thus to the sovereign working of the Spirit, men invent methods which prescribe human action as the terms upon which a soul may be saved, not recognizing the truth that the lost are to be saved, not when they do some prescribed action, but only when they believe on Christ as Savior. The evangelist's problem is not one of coaxing individuals to make some public demonstration; it is rather that of creating a clear conception of the saving grace of God. No individual is capable in himself of believing on Christ to the saving of his soul, apart from the enlightening work of the Holy Spirit by which he receives the vision of Christ as Savior and is inclined to receive Him by faith. Every sincere preacher senses this supernatural factor more or less, but not many are aware of its significant meaning. It becomes disconcerting to the evangelist's program of methods in soul-winning to confront an arbitrary supernatural situation over which he or the unsaved to whom he appeals has not the slightest control. The work of the Spirit in this particular sphere of influence is sovereign. It is the point where divine election is exercised and where it makes its demonstration. It is true that only the elect will be saved. It is true, also, that God may indite within the Christian that prayer which shall be an essential factor in the great work of inclining the lost to accept the Savior; but prayer does not determine the election of men: rather, prayer will itself be subject to the same sovereign Spirit, if prayed in the will of God. It is quite evident that human response to the gospel may be secured where there is no divinely wrought vision of Christ. Most emphatic, nevertheless, are the words of Christ when He said: "And this is the will of him that sent me, that every one which seeth the Son, and believeth on him, may have everlasting life: and I will raise him up at the last day" (John 6:40), for there is no small implication here that only those believe who have by Spirit-wrought vision seen the Son as their Savior. It is clearly asserted, too, that there can be no salvation apart from a preliminary, preparatory enlightenment of the unsaved by the Holy Spirit. That such a work by the Spirit is required becomes evident from certain Scriptures which set forth the inability of the unsaved. Some of these are here presented.

*1 Corinthians 2:14.* "But the natural man receiveth not the things of the Spirit of God: for they are foolishness unto him: neither can he know them, because they are spiritually discerned."

This, the natural (ψυχικός) man—one in the Apostle's threefold division of humanity as presented in this context—is definitely the unregenerate person, and his incapacity is constitutional. Over this incapacity he has no control, nor can any human instruction apart from the Holy Spirit alter this inability. The unsaved in himself cannot receive the things of the Spirit of God. To him they are foolishness. He is incapable of even comprehending them. He remains thus impotent until he is wrought upon by the Holy Spirit.

*2 Corinthians 4:3–4.* "But if our gospel be hid, it is hid to them that are lost: in whom the god of this world hath blinded the minds of them which believe not, lest the light of the glorious gospel of Christ, who is the image of God, should shine unto them."

Not only are the unsaved here said to be blinded with respect to the very gospel by which they might be saved, but that blindness is imposed upon their minds by Satan because he purposely would hinder the gospel from reaching them. No human appeal of itself may hope to lift this veil from the mind of the one who does not believe. It is a great misconception to speak of a "common grace" upon all men, in the light of such a revelation as this. Only inattention to the Word of God can account for this strange perversion of the truth.

*John 14:16–17.* "And I will pray the Father, and he shall give you another Comforter, that he may abide with you for ever; even the Spirit of truth; whom the world cannot receive, because it seeth him not, neither knoweth him: but ye know him; for he dwelleth with you, and shall be in you."

One of the important facts regarding the Holy Spirit in relation to men in this age is that all that He accomplishes as well as any recognition of Himself is wholly outside the observation of the unsaved. With such limitations upon them, it is as unreasonable as it is unscriptural to suppose that they, unaided by the Spirit, are able to turn to God in saving faith. This word of Christ plainly asserts that the world cannot receive the Spirit because it knoweth Him not.

*Ephesians 2:1.* "And you hath he quickened, who were dead in trespasses and sins."

The unsaved are declared to be spiritually dead, and truly from such there can come no living recognition of Christ.

*John 6:39–40.* "And this is the Father's will which hath sent me, that of all which he hath given me I should lose nothing, but should raise it up again at the last day. And this is the will of him that sent me, that every one which seeth the Son, and believeth on him, may have everlasting life: and I will raise him up at the last day."

There is an election of the Father's and not one of these will ever be lost. It is equally true that not every person "seeth the Son" (cf. John 6:40) by that vision which the Holy Spirit engenders; but immediately upon seeing Him as the Answer to every need they will have in time or eternity, the individual whom God thus calls is able to receive Christ as Savior.

*John 6:44.* "No man can come to me, except the Father which hath sent me draw him: and I will raise him up at the last day."

As presented in this passage, the restrictions which rest upon the unsaved are as complete as can be. Only those can come to Christ whom the Father by His Spirit draws. Recognition should be made of a general or universal drawing which accompanies the preaching of the cross of Christ. This universal drawing is described by Christ in the following words: "And I, if I be lifted up from the earth, will draw all men unto me" (John 12:32); but the Savior does not say of any thus drawn, "And I will raise him up at the last day," for He will raise up just those whom the Father specifically designates and draws.

*1 Corinthians 1:23–24.* "But we preach Christ crucified, unto the Jews a stumblingblock, and unto the Greeks foolishness; but unto them which are called, both Jews and Greeks, Christ the power of God, and the wisdom of God."

Again the incapacity in the direction of the saving power of the cross of Christ for the unregenerate Gentile and the unregenerate Jew is asserted. The cross by which they alone might be saved avails for nothing to them, being to the Gentile "foolishness" and to the Jew a "stumblingblock." Over against this is the evidence of the work of the Holy Spirit in those who are called of God. To them that same cross of Christ, which before was meaningless, at once becomes the ground of all the wisdom and power of God—wisdom, since by the cross God solved His greatest problem of how He could be just and yet be the justifier of the ungodly, and power, since by the cross all the infinite ability of God to save the lost is released from those restrictions which the sin of man imposed.

*Romans 8:28–30.* "And we know that all things work together for good to them that love God, to them who are the called according to his purpose. For whom he did foreknow, he also did predestinate to be conformed to the image of his Son, that he might be the firstborn among many brethren. Moreover whom he did predestinate, them he also called: and whom he called, them he also justified: and whom he justified, them he also glorified."

This vital Scripture may well be considered the central New Testament passage related to the doctrine of an efficacious call, but the deeper implication to be discovered in this context is the truth that only those thus called are able to respond. That is, apart from this call none will turn to God. Every sincere believer is conscious of the fact that had he not been moved in that direction by the Holy Spirit he would never of himself have turned to God for salvation through Christ. This passage asserts that those who are "the called according to his purpose" are the objects of an all-inclusive providence. Specifically, certain divine undertakings are here itemized as "working together" for the good of those thus called, namely, divine foreknowledge, divine predestination, divine calling, divine justification, and divine glorification. It should be observed that the divine call is here listed along with the most determining and far-reaching of all the divine achievements. In fact, the truth set forth in this context, it will be seen, is centered specifically upon the fact of the divine call. In the first instance, believers are designated as "the called according to his purpose," and, in the second instance, they are said to be called by God. The title, *the called according to His purpose,* may well include all of the elect, even those who are yet to be saved; for such a description applies to them and they are identified perfectly in the mind of God (cf. Eph. 1:4–5). However, the elect who are yet unsaved are blinded—equally with the rest—by Satan respecting the gospel until they are enlightened by the Holy Spirit. Foreknowledge and predestination are related to eternity past; glorification, being perfectly assured through the faithfulness of God, is related to eternity to come. Thus the two remaining divine undertakings of this list—calling and justification—are left as the representation of that which God accomplishes in the present earthly experience of the one who believes. At once it will be noted that these two undertakings are exalted to the highest importance as the representation of all that God executes when He saves a soul here and now. Justification is easily the consummating act of God's saving grace in this world for the one who believes, though not because it follows other features of salvation in point of time. It consummates logically, but not chronologically, all other aspects of salvation in its first tense of the sinner's actual contact with God. On the other hand, the call of God marks the initial step in the actual process accomplishing the salvation of a soul.

Thus the Apostle employs the alpha and the omega of the divine effort in applying salvation as a representation of all that lies in between. Now, finally, what is wrought when the divine call is issued? Is it merely the extending of an invitation which may or may not—as the Arminian supposes—be accepted according to the caprice of the human will? The text itself supplies the answer. *All* that are predestinated are called, and all who are called are justified. The language breathes out the absolute sovereignty of God and by so much might suggest that a divine call is no less than coercion; but the thought expressed in the word *call* is not one of coercion but invitation, and the use of the term here is no exception, unless it be thought different in that both divine sovereignty and human free will coalesce in this particular instance. That which God the Holy Spirit undertakes is to enlighten the mind with regard to Christ as Savior, and to create in the innermost consciousness of the unsaved individual a desire for that salvation which Christ provides and to a degree that the individual thus impressed will certainly act in receiving Christ as Savior; but it will be observed that when so acting the individual exercises his free will to the last degree. It still remains true that "whosoever will may come," and it is equally true that apart from this divinely wrought inclination no lost person ever wills to come. God is thus declared in the Scripture to be One who, apart from any degree of coercion yet nonetheless with sovereign certainty and with the complete freedom of the human will unimpaired, is able to guarantee that, without the exception of one in all generations of humanity in this age, all who are predestinated will be called, all who are called will be justified, and all who are justified will be glorified. The experience of the one thus called is such as to bring a new consciousness of the desirability of Christ and a supreme longing to claim Him as Savior. The degree to which this divinely wrought experience may develop, though doubtless varying with different individuals, will in every instance be abundantly sufficient to secure a perfect response and hearty cooperation of the individual's own will. The objective in this discussion is to demonstrate again that no unregenerate person unaided by the Holy Spirit will turn to Christ as Savior. Some preparation may thus be made in the direction of a right understanding of the one central passage bearing upon this work of the Holy Spirit in the innermost consciousness of the unregenerate person, namely,

*John 16:7–11*. "Nevertheless I tell you the truth; It is expedient for you that I go away: for if I go not away, the Comforter will not come unto you; but if I depart, I will send him unto you. And when he is come, he will reprove the world of sin, and of righteousness, and of judgment: of sin, because they believe not on me; of righteousness, because I go to my Father, and ye see me no more; of judgment, because the prince of this world is judged."

It may first be noted that no such work of the Holy Spirit was, so far as the records go, undertaken in other ages of human history; and as Christ is the One who speaks with direct and absolute authority, it is significant that this crucial declaration falls from the lips of Christ Himself and in a context which, above any other wherein His words are recorded, is characterized as instruction to Christians. These words of Christ's are not addressed as instruction to the unsaved, they rather impart the most vital information to the child of God who would be intelligent and effective in his soul-winning service. With great clarity and emphasis the Savior asserts that the Holy Spirit, having come as now He is present in the world, will undertake a threefold, indivisible work in the mind and heart of the unsaved. Though reference is made to the *cosmos* world as the objective toward which the Holy Spirit's work is directed, the conviction that the Spirit accomplishes is of necessity individual and, according to all related Scriptures, is restricted to those whom "the Lord our God shall call." The determining word is ἐλέγχω, since it defines what it is that the Holy Spirit does in the mind and heart of the unsaved individual respecting sin, righteousness, and judgment. The A.V. translates this word by *reprove*, the R.V. translates it *convict*, and still other scholars have translated it *convince*. In every instance in which this word appears, the word connotes the impartation of understanding regarding the subject in question. With this in view the translation by the word *enlighten* is perhaps the most satisfactory. It is not implied that this work of the Holy Spirit in the individual's heart is one of creating sorrow or remorse. So far from pointing the attention of the unsaved to themselves and their sinfulness over which they might mourn, the Spirit directs attention to Christ and to the truth that Christ has borne their judgments, that they need but to believe on Him to be saved. Such, indeed, is the good news which the gospel announces. The Scriptures never assert that the unsaved are hindered from being saved by failing to be sorry for their sins. The notion—wholly of human origin—that a due sense of one's sinfulness with its corresponding depression must precede the exultation which salvation secures is due, no doubt, to the supposition that the impelling motive in the unsaved is a consciousness of their wickedness, whereas the true motive which the Holy Spirit engenders is that, since all condemnation rightfully ours because of sin has been laid on Christ, the way is open to absolute forgiveness and to celestial peace. It is a manifestation of human perverseness when would-be gospel preachers stress the sinner's unworthiness in the hope that it will lead to salvation. It is possible for the whole doctrine of repentance to be misunderstood and perverted, supposing that repentance is a sorrow for sin rather than a change of mind about it. Basing their message upon this error, men have substituted a plea for depression of spirit in the place of the "glorious gospel of Christ."

The threefold ministry of the Holy Spirit to the unsaved as revealed by Christ is indivisible in the sense that the Spirit does not undertake one of the aspects of it and omit two, nor does He undertake two and omit one. If the Spirit works at all in the heart of the unsaved, He will do all that this threefold operation of the Spirit connotes. The need of this enlightening work of the Holy Spirit in the mind and heart of the unsaved is clearly indicated in the Word of God. Attention has been called above to the passages which aver that the unsaved are wholly incapable within themselves of turning intelligently to Christ as Savior. In 2 Corinthians 4:3–4 it is said that the mind—not the eyes—of those who are lost is blinded by Satan. This veil must be lifted else the light of "the glorious gospel of Christ" will not reach them. Similarly, in 1 Corinthians 2:14 it is written that the unregenerate, natural man does not receive the things of the Spirit of God, nor can he receive them. In John 14:17 Christ is recorded to have said of the *cosmos* world that it receiveth not the Spirit because it seeth Him not, neither knoweth Him. Again, it is recorded in Acts 26:18 that the first effect of the ministry of the Apostle to the Gentiles would be to "open their eyes," and Christ declared to Nicodemus that unless born from above he could not "see the kingdom of God" (John 3:3). This total incapacity of the unsaved to understand, to see, to receive, or to believe the things of God is by divine provision overcome when the Holy Spirit enlightens with respect to sin, righteousness, and judgment. These divine undertakings may well be considered separately and more specifically.

1. OF SIN. This enlightenment is not of *sins*. Were it of personal sins it could accomplish no more than a deepening of remorse and shame, and would provide no cure. The Spirit's enlightenment is respecting one sin, and that is the failure to receive Christ and His salvation. This implies that the way of life through faith in Christ has been made clear unto those who are thus enlightened, and with that disclosure there was revelation of the new sin—a sin which before the death of Christ could

not have been committed—namely, unbelief in Christ and the salvation He has secured. The student should concern himself with the implications as well as the direct declarations which are found in this passage. If it be inquired why the Spirit does not enlighten the unsaved with respect to his sins, the answer is that Christ has borne those sins and that God recognizes this perfectly. It seems all but impossible for men to accept the truth that all sin has been laid on Christ and that Christ has already endured their judgments in a manner which satisfies God even to infinity. Evidently, it is the Spirit's work to create this consciousness in the mind of the individual unregenerate person. It is this message which the Holy Spirit would promote and which He could use on the lips of the preacher; but too often the obligation of the unsaved is presented to them as though it were needful for them to persuade God to be good enough to do something regarding their sins. The gospel of good news declares that God *has* done everything, leaving the individual with but the one issue of belief or unbelief in what He has done. The gospel does not present something for the unsaved to do, it rather presents something for them to believe; and needful, indeed, is the work of the Holy Spirit in enlightening those who are lost about the character and extent of the sin that "they believe not on me."

2. OF RIGHTEOUSNESS. This passage presents the one and only instance in all of Christ's teachings when He speaks directly of imputed righteousness—that righteousness which so far from being a product of human effort and attention is the gift of God (cf. Rom. 5:17), in which the believer is now alone accepted of God (Eph. 1:6), and by which alone any person from this earthly sphere will enter heaven. It is wholly on the ground of this imputed righteousness that God justifies the ungodly. It is legitimately and actually the portion of every believer and on the all-sufficient ground that he is in Christ. Being a member in the Body of Christ, the believer becomes by absolute necessity all that Christ is, even the righteousness of God (cf. Rom. 3:22; 1 Cor. 1:30; 2 Cor. 5:21; Phil. 3:9). It is not contended that the unsaved must comprehend the difficult doctrine of imputed righteousness; it is evident, however, that to put his trust in Christ he must abandon all confidence in self as being able to commend himself to God, and count that all that a condemned sinner will ever need before God is provided and awaiting him in Christ Jesus, who is the very righteousness of God. Since such a confidence is so foreign to the life, limitations, and experience of the natural man, it is essential that this vital truth be revealed to the unsaved by the Holy Spirit. This the Spirit does when He enlightens

with respect to righteousness. Imputed righteousness is the major theme of the letter to the Romans, which letter is the central and exhaustive declaration of the gospel of the grace of God. It therefore follows that the fact of imputed righteousness is the central factor in the gospel of grace. Christ, too, has given the theme of imputed righteousness the central place according to this context. It follows that one who would so preach that this work of the Spirit may be accomplished will not only include the theme of imputed righteousness in his message, but give it the central place. The obvious fact that gospel preachers have almost wholly neglected this central truth forms no valid excuse for its continued neglect. As before indicated, no intelligent acceptance of Christ can be secured apart from some apprehension of this vital truth. It is precisely that understanding of Him, however, which the Holy Spirit imparts to the unsaved. In the sweet-savor aspect of His death, Christ offered Himself without spot to God (cf. Heb. 9:14). This offering of Himself became a perfect and efficacious substitution for those who have no merit or virtue of their own. By His death on the cross Christ released His own *plērōma* and perfection, and so when the Father would clothe the one who believes with the fullness of Christ, that fullness is bestowed in perfect equity on the ground of the truth that it is provided and made available in the death of Christ. The death of Christ in its sweet savor aspect is as efficacious in the direction of securing merit as the non-sweet savor aspect of His death is efficacious in disposing of demerit. The sweet savor aspect of Christ's death is not some mere sentimental incident between the Father and the Son with no achievement in behalf of those for whom Christ died. Yet, as almost universally treated, there is no recognition of the value of this aspect of the saving grace of God. How very essential is the securing of merit for those who have none! And how complete is the provision in the sweet savor feature of Christ's offering of Himself without spot to God!

3. Of Judgment. Since this feature of the Holy Spirit's work in the mind of the unsaved is so closely related to His enlightening work respecting sin—already considered—the enlightenment respecting judgment has been anticipated. While this ministry of the Spirit is said to bear directly on the judgment of Satan, it is something already accomplished by Christ in His death. It is not a warning regarding some future disposal of evil, but refers to the greatest of all judgments that ever was or will be undertaken, namely, when Christ became the Substitute for man in bearing the condemnation which the Father must impose upon those who are fallen and sinful. The individual may well conceive

of himself as having been apprehended and drawn before the tribunal of divine judgment, as having been justly sentenced to death, and as having been taken out and executed—except for Another who stepped in and was executed in the sinner's room and stead. The execution belonged completely and only to the individuals who sinned. By the death of Christ, then, the sinner is placed on the other side of his own execution. Though alive and uninjured, the believing sinner may look back upon his own execution as accomplished (cf. 2 Cor. 5:14). Having believed upon Christ and having thus by faith entered into the value of His death, that judgment once borne by Christ can never be returned upon the one for whom Christ died. "There is therefore now no condemnation to them which are in Christ Jesus" (Rom. 8:1). It is of this complete substitution that the Holy Spirit, in the first instance of these three ministries, enlightens, when it is said: "of sin, because they believe not on me." Again, it is to be observed that the gospel which the Spirit indites is a setting forth of something to be believed. It is now asserted in this third and final declaration that Satan, the prince of this *cosmos,* has been judged. The ground upon which Satan has held his authority over fallen men was the fact that divine condemnation rests upon them because of sin. In his claim over them, they were as his prisoners (Isa. 14:17), but the same Old Testament prophet, when anticipating what Christ would accomplish, stated—in words which later on Christ directly applied to Himself (cf. Luke 4:18–19)—that He would "proclaim liberty to the captives, and the opening of the prison to them that are bound" (Isa. 61:1). It is probable that in this sense Christ triumphed over principalities and powers through the cross, as recorded in Colossians 2:15. The passage reads: "And having spoiled principalities and powers, he made a shew of them openly, triumphing over them in it."

## CONCLUSION

Thus it is seen that the Holy Spirit reveals to the unsaved whom He calls the very essentials of the gospel of divine grace—the substitutionary death of Christ as that which has been accomplished, along with the all-condemning sin of not believing on the One who thus died, also the perfect standing provided in the same cross, which standing is no less than the righteousness of God imputed. Apart from this enlightenment, the individual unsaved person does not respond though confronted with all the persuasion human sincerity and eloquence may devise. It hardly need be pointed out again that any form of evangelism which ignores this work of the Holy Spirit and which assumes that the unsaved are capable within themselves of receiving the gospel and turning in intelligent, saving faith to Christ—though it may be that through human influence outward actions may be secured—is doomed to superficial results and in great danger of hindering rather than helping those to whom it appeals. Christ must be received as the choice of the individual heart and this must be actuated by the innermost conviction of His Saviorhood—an understanding and choice which could never be secured apart from the Spirit's enlightenment respecting sin, righteousness, and judgment.

# THE HOLY SPIRIT IN RELATION TO THE CHRISTIAN

## Chapter VIII

## INTRODUCTION TO THE WORK OF THE HOLY SPIRIT IN THE BELIEVER

When considering the amount of Scripture pertaining to it, the Spirit's relation to the Christian is seen to be the major feature of the entire doctrine respecting the Holy Spirit. In the New Testament alone, where the truth regarding the Holy Spirit is given its fullest presentation, there is set forth, as noted above, both the fact that the Spirit restrains the world (which is largely disclosed in one passage) and the fact that He enlightens the unsaved (also a limited body of truth); but the whole unfolding revelation of the New Testament regarding the Holy Spirit occupies a great portion of the New Testament, insomuch that this age of the Church is also properly styled the dispensation of the Holy Spirit. The divisions of the doctrine of the Holy Spirit as related to Christians contemplate two general features, namely, (a) the Holy Spirit's work in and through the believer (Chapters IX–XI) and (b) the believer's corresponding responsibility (Chapters XII–XVII). Before these major aspects of this truth are given constructive treatment, attention is called to the fact that at this point this thesis enters upon ground which is exceedingly vital, but which is as foreign to works on theology as though it did not exist. In fact, as the fountain source from which educated ministers have gained their knowledge of Biblical doctrine Systematic Theology is reprehensible because of its neglect of the doctrine of the Holy Spirit, and especially that vital feature of this doctrine which pertains to the believer's life and service by the enabling power of the Holy Spirit. There has been no recognition of the patent truth that the Bible contains three major rules of life which are addressed respectively to different peoples and applicable in different ages—no mention being made at this point, to be sure, of the divine government in those ages that came before the giving of the law by Moses (cf. Gen. 26:5), which ages could not have been benefited by Scripture records because they were not yet written. The three ages under consideration began with the age of the law, which was followed by the present age of grace, and this age, in turn, is to be followed by the thousand-year kingdom age. The Mosaic age obtained until the death of Christ (John 1:17), and the system of divine government for that age was in every respect adapted to Israel to whom alone it was addressed, who were contemplated as not yet of age and subject to tutors and governors (Gal. 4:1–3). The Mosaic system, though perfect in itself (cf. Rom. 7:12), is, in contrast to the high calling of the present age, termed the "weak and beggarly elements" into which a believer of today reverting to this system may be plunged (cf. Gal. 4:9) and to the loss, not of his salvation but, of his liberty in Christ (Gal. 5:1–4). To revert to the law is to fail to obey the truth (Gal. 5:7). Such error never comes forth from God (cf. Gal. 5:8), but from Judaizing teachers who "zealously affect" the child of God (Gal. 4:17). Though they encourage each other in so doing, theologians have no excuse for ignoring the change both in position and in the requisite corresponding manner of life which stupendous intervening events interposed between the Mosaic age and this age of the Church have wrought. These events are: (a) the introduction of a new and unforeseen age with its specific revelation concerning its character, (b) the death of Christ with all the new realities and relationships which it secures, (c) the resurrection of Christ with its New Creation Headship, (d) the present session of Christ with its limitless provisions, (e) the coming of the Spirit on Pentecost with His limitless blessings for all those in whom He dwells, (f) the inauguration of a new divine purpose in the calling out of a heavenly people from both Jews and Gentiles into one Body, and (g) the introduction of a new ethic or governing code adapted to a people who are perfected in Christ, clothed in divine righteousness, justified forever, and filled with the *plērōma* of the Godhead. The thoughtless, though zealous, imposition of a merit system of law upon a perfected people is most erroneous and is done only because theologians have suffered themselves to be bound by an indefensible covenant theory imposing upon God's right divisions of Scripture a man-made notion of unity throughout the Word of God.

Likewise, great intervening events will form a drastic cleavage between the human responsibility in this present age and the responsibility of the people in the age to come. These events are: (a) the removal of the Church and the termination in the earth of all that pertains to her, (b) the regathering and reinstating of Israel with the completion of her unfulfilled covenants, (c) the termination of Gentile times with their judgments, (d) the glorious return of Christ to judge both Jews and Gentiles and to set up His predicted Messianic, Davidic, earthly kingdom, (e) the binding of Satan, (f) the Church as Bride and Consort of the King in her reign with Him over all realms wherein He exercises authority, and (g) the application of a new rule of life adapted to conditions created by these mighty changes. Again, theologians, though generally they make no recognition of a kingdom age or of the covenants and promises of God—sealed by His oath—which demand a realization of that coming age, seek to blend this vast body of Scripture into the one idea of a redeemed people embracing men of all ages. The Covenant theory can make no place for different divine purposes and corresponding ages of time. According to this teaching, Israel must merge into the Church and the Church must be the consummation of all previous earthly purposes. Regardless of misunderstandings in doctrine, however, it still remains true that there are new undertakings being consummated by the Holy Spirit, a new and divinely perfected people being called out today, a new obligation in life and service being announced for those called out, which responsibility can be discharged only by the enabling power of the indwelling Spirit. Turning, then, to the two main divisions of this theme as indicated above, consideration will be given to the Holy Spirit's work in and through the believer, first of all.

In addition to the two ministries of the Holy Spirit already attended (Chapter VII), there are still five more and they constitute the Spirit's relation to the Christian, these with the two presented above making a total of seven ministries of the Holy Spirit in this age. Of the five now in view, the first four may be classed in one group (as suggested earlier) since they represent the Spirit's undertakings in behalf of all who are saved. These are vital features of salvation, being wrought to infinite perfection for each believer at the moment he is saved. Likewise, these four ministries represent aspects of the Spirit's work which are never repeated, being accomplished once for all. The fifth in this series, which is also seventh when all the Spirit's ministries are contemplated, is that of the Spirit's filling—itself unique in that it is not a feature of salvation, for not all Christians experience it and it must be renewed constantly. In no particular are the distinctions between these seven ministries to be treated lightly. It is at this point, and for want of accuracy in the analysis of these truths, that sincere yet misinformed groups of Christians have separated themselves over questions of holiness and certain manifestations of the Spirit's presence. Extreme claims among Christians and heretical religious professions are usually traceable to the neglect of some truth among Christian leaders, and it is especially evident that the present confusion among less instructed believers respecting the work of the Spirit in this age is due in large measure to the complete default of Christian leaders and instructors to give even elementary teaching regarding these vital and extended themes. Bible teachers and expositors generally have sought to overcome the effects of the neglect of the doctrine of the Holy Spirit in usual theological disciplines by special emphasis upon these themes. The church of the present generation owes much to the Keswick movement of England and its extensive testimony in this and other lands. The inclusion of these subjects in modern Bible study conventions and by men able to speak with authority has done much to give these doctrines their rightful emphasis. A great theologian who has written massive treatises on the Person and work of Christ but who practically never ventures into the field of the Person and work of the Holy Spirit may be credited with such testimony as he has given, but must, at the same time, suffer discredit for the encouragement he has given to neglect of such vital truth on the part of all who follow him. That this presentation of Systematic Theology may not be thus challenged, the remainder of this volume is incorporated in this extended work. The five distinctive ministries of the Holy Spirit to the believer are now to be considered in the following order: (a) regeneration, (b) the indwelling of the Holy Spirit, (c) the baptism with the Holy Spirit, (d) the sealing of the Holy Spirit, and (e) the filling with the Holy Spirit.

## CHAPTER IX

# REGENERATION AND THE HOLY SPIRIT

IN THE INCOMPARABLE purpose of God by which He is bringing "many sons unto glory" (Heb. 2:10) and to the end that Christ may be the first-born among many brethren (Rom. 8:29)—no less an undertaking than that of populating the third and highest heaven (hitherto the abode only of the triune God) with beings suited to that holy and exalted sphere and, indeed, sufficiently perfected to be the all-satisfying Bride of the Second Person—one vital step is that of constituting these beings partakers of the very nature of God. Such a structural change as this is essential in the very nature of the case. The new birth, then, is not a mere remedy for human failures: it is a creation by divine generation, a constituting of believers inherent, innate, legitimate sons of God. The human mind cannot approach the comprehension of that which is involved in the immeasurable realities of an actual sonship relation to God, which makes the Christian an heir of God and a joint heir with Jesus Christ (Rom. 8:17). In every feature of it, this is a work of God and is wrought as an expression of His sublime purpose and the satisfying of His infinite love for those He thus saves. Pursuing these intimations more fully, several facts may be observed:

## I. THE NECESSITY

Before the kingdom of God may be entered by a fallen individual from this human sphere, there must be a God-wrought metamorphosis in the form of a birth from above. Such a birth is specifically indicated by Christ in His words to Nicodemus: "That which is born of the flesh is flesh; and that which is born of the Spirit is spirit" (John 3:6). In announcing these great truths about flesh and spirit, Christ did not address them to the lowest in the social order—such as obviously need to be improved; He chose to speak these words to a ruler and teacher in Israel who was without doubt the very flower of Judaism. At this point the question of what constituted the right relation of a Jew to God within the scope and purpose of Judaism might be asked.

It is the Covenant theologian who advances at this point the assumption that the saints of the old order were regenerated and on the same basis of relationship to Jehovah as is accorded the saints of the New Testament. Such an assumption is needful if their theory is to be sustained. But pertinent questions are in order: Why the direct and unconditional demand of a new birth upon one of the character that Nicodemus represented? Why the oft-repeated and emphasized account of the salvation of Saul of Tarsus who had lived in all good conscience before the law (Acts 9; 22; 26, etc.)? And why the salvation of the apostles, of three thousand Jews on the Day of Pentecost, and of the many priests who were obedient to the faith? Is it contended that not one of all these thus saved had answered before to the spiritual ideals of Judaism? Is it true that all these might have been as perfectly saved under Judaism as they later were under Christianity, but that everyone only accidentally declared his adjustment to God after the Christian faith was established? What, indeed, does the Apostle mean when he says: "But before faith came, we were kept under the law, shut up unto the faith which should afterwards be revealed. Wherefore the law was our schoolmaster to bring us unto Christ, that we might be justified by faith. But after that faith is come, we are no longer under a schoolmaster" (Gal. 3:23–25)? Why, also, should he pray for Israel and define their spiritual failure as he did when he said: "Brethren, my heart's desire and prayer to God for Israel is, that they might be saved. For I bear them record that they have a zeal of God, but not according to knowledge. For they being ignorant of God's righteousness, and going about to establish their own righteousness, have not submitted themselves unto the righteousness of God. For Christ is the end of the law for righteousness to every one that believeth" (Rom. 10:1–4)? And what did the same Apostle mean when in referring to the motives which actuated him at the moment of his own choice of Christ as Savior he said: "Though I might also have confidence in the flesh. If any other man thinketh that he hath whereof he might trust in the flesh, I more: circumcised the eighth day, of the stock of Israel, of the tribe of Benjamin, an Hebrew of the Hebrews; as touching the law, a Pharisee; concerning zeal, persecuting the church; touching the righteousness which is in the law, blameless. But what things were gain to me, those I counted loss for Christ. Yea doubtless, and I count all things but loss for the excellency of the knowledge of Christ Jesus my Lord: for whom I have suffered the loss of all things, and do count them but dung, that I may win Christ, and be found in him, not having mine own righteousness, which is of the law, but that which is through the faith of Christ, the righteousness which is of God by faith" (Phil. 3:4–9)? Why in every contrast between any of the features of Judaism and the features of Christianity is the former represented as insufficient from which the individual must be saved by adherence to the latter? The answer to all such questions will be found when it is determined that God was not doing precisely the same thing in Judaism as He is now doing in Christianity. God never said to Israel, "I will present you faultless before the presence of my glory." It is doubtless in accord with humility to state that one assumes no higher place in God's purpose than that accorded the Old Testament saints. But none of this is according to man's election: it is a matter of God's revealed and unalterable plan. God so emphasizes the difference between Israel and the Church that, when receiving Jews along with Gentiles into the Church, He recognizes no specific superior qualities in the Jew over the Gentile, but declares "there is no difference" (cf. Rom. 3:9; 10:12). However, if the Jew were already upon Christian ground, it is a most unreasonable procedure to lower him to the level of the Gentile position only to exalt him back to his original position again. Though in the Jewish age that people had covenant relations with Jehovah, it cannot be demonstrated that they were in any particular upon Christian ground. Regeneration, accordingly, is as much a necessity for Jew as for Gentile. Apart from it even Nicodemus could not see the kingdom of God.

## II. THE IMPARTATION OF LIFE

In the stupendous task of preparing and qualifying fallen, earthly beings for the company of the Father, the Son, and the Holy Spirit—even to be a suitable Bride for the Lamb—in the highest heaven and glory, the partaking of the divine nature by the impartation of the very life of God is one of the most important features of the whole transforming undertaking. The receiving of the divine nature means that the individual thus blessed has been born of God. God has become his legitimate Father and he is the Father's legitimate son. This is a change so radical and so complete that there is thus achieved a passing from one order of being into another. Eventually in this great change the Adamic nature will be dismissed and the ego as a separate entity will represent little else than the stupendous fact of being a son of God and a rightful member in the family and household of God. The saved one will have become precisely what his new position in glory requires him to be. The basic metamorphosis which is achieved by a birth from above—a generating wrought by the Holy Spirit—though actually now entered by all who are saved, is too often and for want of due consideration almost wholly misapprehended. The conception that regeneration by the Holy Spirit is an indefinite influence for good in the individual's present life is far below the conception set forth in the New Testament. There it is taught that a new and eternal order of being is created with indissoluble filial relations to the Creator of all things. The fact of the new birth, whether comprehended or not, is the basic and distinguishing feature of the Christian. The life of God which is eternal and which therefore Christ is has been imparted as definitely as the breath of natural life was breathed by God into Adam at the first creation. At least eighty-five New Testament passages aver that a Christian is a changed person by virtue of the fact that he has received the very life of God. Through infinite love, the Son of God was given by the Father that sinful men should not perish but have everlasting life (John 3:16). Christ said, "I am the way, the truth, and the life" (John 14:6) and "I am come that they might have life" (John 10:10). So, also, "the gift of God is eternal life" (Rom. 6:23). That imparted life is said to be "Christ in you, the hope of glory" (Col. 1:27). Though some slight evidence of this great change should be recognized while yet in this sphere, the full-orbed experience of the divine nature awaits the "manifestation of the sons of God." Certain present evidences of the abiding in the heart of the life of God may well be noted.

1. A KNOWLEDGE OF GOD. From the heart with definite consciousness of His reality, the saved one will be able to say, "Abba, Father." Such a recognition of God as Father is wrought in the heart by Christ. Of this He said, "All things are delivered unto me of my Father: and no man knoweth the Son, but the Father; neither knoweth any man the Father, save the Son, and he to whomsoever the Son will reveal him. Come unto me, all ye that labour and are heavy laden, and I will give you rest" (Matt. 11:27–28). The rest here promised is that of the soul and is the result of coming to know God as Father. It is one thing to know about God, but quite another thing to know God. According to this great invitation, it is possible to come to know the Father by the gracious offices and effective working of the Son, and no soul has ever found true rest apart from this intimacy with God.

2. A NEW REALITY IN PRAYER. Prayer is communion with God that has been based on confidence born of the knowledge of God. It is not natural to speak to one who is unknown and unknowable as is the case

with the unsaved trying to pray; but when God is recognized and real to the heart, there is definiteness in every form of prayer and then, as at no other time or under no other conditions, the praying soul finds rest.

3. A NEW REALITY IN THE READING OF GOD'S WORD. The Word of God is food only to those who have received the nature of God. As a new-born child cries for food, so will a normal Christian desire the Word of God. That Word is milk to such as are "babes" and "strong meat" to those prepared in heart to receive it.

4. A RECOGNITION OF GOD'S FAMILY. John places this to the front as a very dependable test of whether an individual is a child of God. He writes: "We know that we have passed from death unto life, because we love the brethren" (1 John 3:14). The Christian naturally delights in the fellowship of those who are saved. His love for them will be manifested in loving sacrifice for them. This is not human love, but an out-working of the love of God shed abroad in believing hearts from the indwelling Spirit (Rom. 5:5). In the same context mentioned above John states: "Hereby perceive we the love of God, because he laid down his life for us: and we ought to lay down our lives for the brethren. But whoso hath this world's good, and seeth his brother have need, and shutteth up his bowels of compassion from him, how dwelleth the love of God in him? My little children, let us not love in word, neither in tongue; but in deed and in truth" (1 John 3:16–18).

5. A DIVINE COMPASSION FOR A LOST WORLD. The objects of the divine love are unchanged respecting their identity even when that love is reproduced in or is passing through the Christian. He will love, therefore, what God loves. This is indeed an extensive field of contemplation. Above all, the love of God for a lost world—that love which spared not His Son in consequence—will be wrought in the child of God as an unceasing burden for those who are unsaved. This constitutes a suffering in company with Christ, and for it there is great reward. "If we suffer [with Him], we shall also reign with him."

All of these experiences which have been indicated are naturally the expression of the new divine nature; but, like all Christian experience, it may be hindered and all but unobserved owing to some unspiritual condition that is allowed to exist in the heart of the believer. If the indwelling Holy Spirit who is the Reproducer of Christ in the believer is grieved, the power of His presence will not be made manifest. At this point, the danger should be recognized of judging anyone according to that one's experience or conduct. Even though every normal experience is enjoyed, yet how limitless is that which awaits the day of His manifestation!

## III. ACQUISITION OF THE NATURE OF GOD

The basic fact of having a new divine nature imparted is of such a character that it must be recognized at once as a change that God alone may effect. Human effort is utterly foreign to the entire undertaking. Where would Nicodemus begin were he to attempt the achievement of his own birth from above? That alone which is born of the Spirit is spirit. Closely allied to the gift of eternal life is the impartation of the divine nature. Probably distinctions cannot be drawn between them. The child of God, receiving these realities, enters upon a career thereby in a realm of relationship which belongs to another order of existence. In truth, it is the highest form of existence—the vast reality and eternity of God. No comparison may be drawn between the acquiring of a human nature and the acquiring of the divine nature. The fundamental distinction, beyond that of their dissimilarity respecting inherent character, is the fact that the one has a beginning though no ending, while the other, being related to God, can have no beginning or ending. Relative to consciousness, the human nature is now an active reality to varying degrees, but the conscious experience of the divine nature, though something fully possessed, awaits the time of entrance into the heavenly life and abode. The increase of experimental consciousness that will break upon the child of God when removed from earth to heaven, when passing from a time mode of existence to an eternal mode, when "the power of an endless life" supplants all human limitations, is too vast for any present comprehension of it. In this earthly sphere, men are affected by prejudices, opinions, and estimations which constitute but a mere shadow of that which is true. In the coming sphere and position, all things will be seen, and then not merely as added information may expand human capacity to understand but as God sees them, as God understands. It is then that the saved one will know even as also he is known (1 Cor. 13:12); that is, he will then know as God now knows. The phrase *as also I am known* must refer to God's present knowledge. By the enabling power of the Holy Spirit some measure of the experience of divine love, divine joy, and divine peace yet to come may be secured now. So, likewise, the knowledge of God and especially that part which He has caused to be written down in Scripture may be entered into by the same Spirit. But when the heavenly sphere is entered, there will be an entrance into unbroken and undiminished divine love, joy, and peace, and a larger understanding which is comparable to that of God Himself. All this will arise from the nature of God which is possessed and will be as unrestricted, within finite limits, as God is unrestricted. Herein lies a basis for the companionship of saints with God and with each other. Nothing can be hidden and nothing can be misunderstood. Motives will be as pure as God is pure and even the history of earth's sins, failures, and doubts will be seen only in that retrospect and understanding which belongs to God. The Christian's life in glory in all its outreach will be in the mold and pattern of that which is now deemed supernatural, namely, the *experience* to the full of the divine nature. Those who are saved are to be adapted to the sphere which is God's.

## IV. INDUCTION INTO THE FAMILY AND HOUSEHOLD OF GOD

No earthly relation so unites members of the human race as does the family, and so this human kinship is the best available illustration of the heavenly association together of believers. Both the fact of father and son relationship and the fact of brotherhood appear. As indicated above, the Fatherhood of God is due to an absolute divine generation: though, as in the case of the birth of Christ, the generating is wrought by the Third Person, still the First Person is universally addressed as the Father of all who believe. The placing of an individual into the family and household of God is no mere adoption, though a believer is adopted in the sense that when born of God as His child he is at once advanced to the position of an adult son with all the privileges and responsibilities attendant on full maturity. The human practice of adoption, which merely establishes legal responsibility over an otherwise unrelated child, imparts no parental nature and creates no actual oneness with the new parent. In human relationships, indeed, a father may by legal action repudiate his son and withdraw all responsibility toward his son, although he cannot prevent the son resembling himself in appearance, in disposition, or salient characteristics. In other words, the basic nature which generation imparts cannot be extinguished even in human spheres, just as it cannot be extinguished in divine spheres. Once a son of God always a son of God is a truth not only taught in the Scriptures, but sustained by every sonship experience known whether it be here on earth or in heaven. The family and household of God is composed of the actual and legitimate offspring of God. No such relationship is intimated between Jehovah and the Israelites. The whole nation Israel is likened to a son, but wholly as an expression describing Jehovah's care over them. The styling of a nation as a son is far removed from the generating of individuals into eternal, unalterable offspring of God. Membership in the household and family of God implies fitness for the position. For a brief time—the period of the Christian's life on earth after he is saved—the Father does get on with imperfections in His child and administers discipline; but in an eternity of reality which follows, the members of His family will demonstrate how to all infinity the saved ones have been "made meet to be partakers of the inheritance of the saints in light" (Col. 1:12).

## V. INHERITANCE OF A SON'S PORTION

Based on the actuality of sonship through the generating power of the Holy Spirit is the unavoidable fact of possession of a son's portion. The extent of that portion is indicated by the Apostle when he avers: "The Spirit itself beareth witness with our spirit, that we are the children of God: and if children, then heirs; heirs of God, and joint-heirs with Christ" (Rom. 8:16–17). The eternal sonship of Christ is in view here and into this heirship in which are included all the treasures of the universe, all the πλήρωμα of wisdom, and the infinity of authority and power, the newly constituted sons are brought as "joint-heirs with Christ." So long as the believer is detained in this world as a witness, but little use can be made of these heavenly riches. They belong to another realm, and their enjoyment awaits the time of entrance upon the sphere to which these riches belong.

## VI. GOD'S OWN PURPOSE TO HIS ETERNAL GLORY

Most arresting and encouraging is the revealed truth that all that enters into constituting a Christian what he is and what he will be in glory is wrought of God. The Apostle declares: "For we are his workmanship, created in Christ Jesus unto good works, which God hath before ordained that we should walk in them" (Eph. 2:10). By so much every uncertainty about the ultimate outcome of regeneration is dismissed forever. Life's varying experience may present immediate problems; but the essential factors of salvation, preservation, and eternal glory are His to accomplish and are never made to depend upon human success, achievement, or merit. The Christian learns after he is saved—

not before—that he has been "chosen in him [Christ] before the foundation of the world," that in due time and by the power of God alone he came into a saved relationship to God on the principle of grace, and that by the same divine power he will appear in glory—all in the unchangeable faithfulness of God. It is written of believers: "Being confident of this very thing, that he which hath begun a good work in you will perform it until the day of Jesus Christ" (Phil. 1:6). Great significance is to be seen in the description of a believer as one "called according to his purpose" (Rom. 8:28). That purpose of God is immediately defined in the context, which reads: "For whom he did foreknow, he also did predestinate to be conformed to the image of his Son, that he might be the firstborn among many brethren. Moreover whom he did predestinate, them he also called: and whom he called, them he also justified: and whom he justified, them he also glorified" (vss. 29–30). To be "conformed to the image of his Son" indicates that divine sonship is to be realized on the part of the one who is saved—a sonship patterned after the very *image* of the Son of God. No word of God ever disclosed a higher estate and destiny than this; but it is yet added, "that he might be the firstborn among many brethren." Christ will indeed be First-Born in point of time and in character, the Source of all that enters into the Christian's eternal reality and glory; but the emphasis indicated here is rather on the fact that all those thus saved are His *brethren,* being begotten of God as such and constituted actually and immutably the sons of God. Too often it is assumed that Christ came into the world so that men might have a new ideal for daily living, an example of an exalted character, or a new rule of life. When Christ said, however: "The thief cometh not, but for to steal, and to kill, and to destroy: I am come that they might have life, and that they might have it more abundantly" (John 10:10)—but one of about eighty-five passages bearing on this essential factor in the Christian's new being—He was speaking of an imparted life which no human being has ever received or possessed apart from the regenerating power of the Holy Spirit. With all reason, God appeals to the saved one for a daily life which is in accord with this high calling in Christ; but the need for holy living must ever be disassociated from "the gift of God [which] is eternal life through Jesus Christ our Lord" (Rom. 6:23). The possession of eternal life creates the true motive for holy living; certainly holy living will never impart divine life or substitute for a birth from above by the Spirit. A commendable daily life represents the purpose of the one who lives it; the gift of eternal life represents the eternal provision of God for man which He purposed in Christ Jesus. From this sublime truth the spiritual mind naturally advances to the contemplation of the fact that the divine purpose, like all the works of God, will yet be so realized and completed to infinity that God will be satisfied with it and be glorified by it. Thus it is concluded properly that salvation from its beginning in the eternal counsels of God, down through the provision of and exercise of redeeming grace, and on to its consummation in glory is wrought only by God and with the same purpose ever in view, namely, that it should redound to His eternal glory. He will of a certainty be glorified thus.

## VII. THE BASIS IN FAITH

Reason alone would dictate the truth that, since salvation is altogether wrought of God, the individual who cares to be saved can sustain no other relation to it than to receive it in simple faith. Every aspect of salvation in its completed, past tense—release from sin's penalty, in its present tense—release from sin's power, and in its future tense—release from sin's presence, calls for dependence upon God. The great realities, namely, *forgiveness*, the *gift of eternal life*, and the *gift of righteousness* which is the ground of justification (Rom. 3:22, 26; 4:5; 10:4), are the portion of those who do no more than to believe in Jesus as Savior. Two passages bearing upon this essential truth will suffice here: (a) John 1:12–13: "But as many as received him, to them gave he power to become the sons of God, even to them that believe on his name: which were born, not of blood, nor of the will of the flesh, nor of the will of man, but of God." It is to them that receive Christ, or believe on Him, that right both to become and to be the sons of God is accorded. This means that God's answer to an individual's faith in Christ is such that by the power of God he is born of God and thus becomes an actual son of His. The knowledge of the Savior upon whom faith must rest is gained from the word of God through the Spirit, hence Christ said that such are born of the Word which is symbolized by water and the Spirit (John 3:5) and the Apostle declares: "Not by works of righteousness which we have done, but according to his mercy he saved us, by the washing of regeneration, and renewing of the Holy Ghost" (Titus 3:5). (b) John 3:16: "For God so loved the world, that he gave his only begotten Son, that whosoever believeth in him should not perish, but have everlasting life." What statement could be more direct or conclusive than this? It is asserted that "whosoever believeth in him should not perish, but have everlasting life." Thus without exception all that enters into salvation, including the gift of eternal life, depends only on the one human requirement of believing on the Savior.

An excellent treatment of the doctrine of regeneration is included in Dr. John F. Walvoord's book cited previously. Since this is so well stated and since the theme is so vitally important, these pages, though extended, are reproduced here.

In his introduction Dr. Walvoord states: "Few doctrines are more fundamental to effective preaching than the doctrine of regeneration. Failure to comprehend its nature and to understand clearly its necessity will cripple the efficacy of Gospel preaching. Both for the Bible teacher and the evangelist an accurate knowledge of the doctrine of regeneration is indispensable. The Biblical concept of regeneration is comparatively simple, and a study of its theological history is not entirely necessary to accurate preaching. The history of the doctrine, however, reveals its natural pitfalls and may warn the unwary of the dangers of a shallow understanding of regeneration. The doctrine of regeneration offers a rich reward to those who contemplate its treasures and live in the light of its reality" (*The Doctrine of the Holy Spirit,* p. 140).

On the meaning of regeneration Dr. Walvoord writes:

The word *regeneration* is found only twice in the New Testament (Mt. 19:28; Tit. 3:5), but it has been appropriated as the general term designating the impartation of eternal life. Only one of the two instances in the New Testament is used in this sense (Tit. 3:5), where reference is made to "the washing of regeneration, and renewing of the Holy Ghost." The Greek word παλιγγενεσία is properly translated *"new birth, reproduction, renewal, re-creation"* (Thayer). It is applied not only to human beings but also to the renewed heaven and earth of the millennium (Mt. 19:28). In relation to the nature of man, it includes the various expressions used for eternal life such as *new life, new birth, spiritual resurrection, new creation, new mind, "made alive," sons of God,* and *translation into the kingdom.* In simple language, regeneration consists of all that is represented by eternal life in a human being. Theological usage of the word *regeneration* has tended to confuse rather than enrich the word. Other words such as *conversion, sanctification,* and *justification* have been either identified or included in the concept of regeneration. Roman Catholic theologians have regarded *regeneration* as including all that is embraced in salvation, not only justification and sanctification, but even glorification. Regeneration is taken to include the means, the act, the process, and the ultimate conclusion of salvation. Protestant theologians have been more cautious in extending the meaning of regeneration. The early Lutheran theologians used *regeneration* to include the whole process by which a sinner passed from his lost estate into salvation, including justification. Later Lutherans attempted a clarification of the doctrine by holding that justification did not include a transformation of life, thereby excluding sanctification from the doctrine of regeneration. The Lutheran Church continues to hold that infants are regenerated at the moment of water baptism, however, at the same time affirming that this regeneration signifies only their entrance into the visible church, not their certain salvation. Regeneration becomes then merely a preparatory work of salvation. On the subject of infant regeneration, the Lutheran theologian Valentine writes: "May the child be said to be *regenerated* by the act of Baptism? We may properly answer, Yes; but only in the sense that the established vital and grace-conveying relation, under imputed righteousness and the Holy Spirit, may be said to hold, in its provisions and forces, the final covenanted development" (*Christian Theology,* Vol. II, pp. 329–30). Valentine objects, however, to the statement that baptism regenerates children. Elsewhere, Valentine writes, "Justification *precedes* regeneration and sanctification" (*Ibid*, p. 237). It is clear that Lutheran theology does not use the term in the Biblical sense of impartation of eternal life. The Lutheran theology does, however, exclude sanctification from the doctrine of regeneration. Reformed theologians have failed to be consistent in usage also, and have shared to some extent the errors embraced by others. During the seventeenth century, conversion was used commonly as a synonym for regeneration. This usage ignored a most important fact, however—that conversion is the human act and regeneration is an act of God. Further, conversion, while usually related to regeneration, is not always so, as demonstrated by its use in connection with Peter's repentance and restoration (Lk. 22:32), as prophesied by Christ. Even Calvin failed to make a proper distinction between regeneration and conversion. Charles Hodge, however, argues effectively for the necessary distinction in the meaning of these terms (*Systematic Theology,* Vol. III, pp. 3–5). Shedd agrees with Hodge and cites the following contrasts: "Regeneration, accordingly, is an act; conversion is an activity, or a process. Regeneration is the origination of life; conversion is the evolution and manifestation of life. Regeneration is wholly an act of God; conversion is wholly an activity of man. Regeneration is a cause; conversion is an effect. Regeneration is instantaneous; conversion is continuous" (*Dogmatic Theology,* Vol. II, p. 494). For the last century, Reformed theologians have agreed that regeneration properly designates the act of impartation of eternal life. As Charles Hodge states it: "By a consent almost universal the word *regeneration* is now used to designate, not the whole work of sanctification, nor the first states of that work comprehended in conversion, much less justification or any mere external change of state, but the instantaneous change from spiritual death to spiritual life" (*Op. cit.,* Vol. III, p. 5). In a study of the doctrine of regeneration, then, the inquirer is concerned only with the aspect of salvation related to the impartation of eternal life. Other important works which may attend it, be antecedent to it, or immediately follow it, must be considered as distinct works of God.—*Ibid.,* pp. 140–43

So, also, of regeneration as an act of the Holy Spirit, Dr. Walvoord declares:

Regeneration by its nature is solely a work of God. While sometimes considered as a result, every instance presumes or states that the act of regeneration was an act of God. A number of important Scriptures bear on the subject of regeneration (John 1:13; 3:3–7; 5:21; Rom. 6:13; 2 Cor. 5:17; Eph. 2:5, 10; 4:24; Tit. 3:5; Jas. 1:18; 1 Pet. 2:9). It is explicitly stated that the one regenerated is "born, not of blood, nor of the will of the flesh, nor of the will of man, but of God" (John 1:13). Regeneration is likened unto resurrection, which by its nature is wholly of God (John 5:21; Rom. 6:13; Eph. 2:5). In other instances regeneration is declared to be a creative act, the nature of which assumes it to be the act of God (Eph. 2:10; 4:24; 2 Cor. 5:17). It may be seen clearly, then, that regeneration is always revealed as an act of God accomplished by His own supernatural power apart from all other agencies. The work of regeneration is properly ascribed to the Holy Spirit. Like the work of efficacious grace, regeneration is often ascribed to God without distinction as to Persons, and in several instances is ascribed to the Father, to the Son, and to the Holy Spirit severally. The First Person is declared to be the source of regeneration in at least one instance (Jas. 1:17, 18). Christ Himself is linked with regeneration several times in Scripture (John 5:21; 2 Cor. 5:17; 1 John 5:12). Again, the Holy Spirit is declared the agent of regeneration (John 3:3–7; Tit. 3:5). As in other great undertakings of the Godhead, each Person has an important part, in keeping with Their one essence. As in the birth of Christ, where all the Persons of the Godhead were related to the conception of Christ, so in the new birth of the Christian the First Person becomes the Father of the believer, the Second Person imparts His own eternal life (1 John 5:12), and the Holy Spirit, the Third Person, acts as the efficient agent of regeneration. The work of regeneration can be assigned to the Holy Spirit as definitely as the work of salvation can be assigned to Christ.—*Ibid.*, pp. 143–44.

On the important truth that eternal life is imparted by regeneration, the same writer asserts:

As the word itself implies, the central thought in the doctrine of regeneration is that eternal life is imparted. Regeneration meets the need created by the presence of spiritual death. The method of impartation is, of course, inscrutable. There is no visible method or process discernible. By its nature it is supernatural and therefore its explanation is beyond human understanding. The Scriptures in presenting the impartation of eternal life use three figures to describe it. Regeneration is sometimes presented in the figure of new birth. As Christ told Nicodemus, "Ye must be born again" (John 3:7). In contrast to human birth of human parentage, one must be born "of God" (John 1:13) in order to become a child of God. According to James 1:18, "Of his own will begat he us with the word of truth, that we should be a kind of firstfruits of his creatures." The figure is eloquent in portraying the intimate relation of the child of God to his heavenly Father and in relating the kind of life the believer in Christ receives to the eternal life which is in God. Frequently in Scripture, regeneration is portrayed as spiritual resurrection. The Christian is revealed to be "alive from the dead" (Rom. 6:13), and God "even when we were dead in sins, hath quickened us together with Christ" (Eph. 2:5). Christ Himself said, "Verily, verily, I say unto you, The hour is coming, and now is, when the dead shall hear the voice of the Son of God: and they that hear shall live" (John 5:25). The fact of our resurrection is made the basis for frequent exhortation to live as those raised from the dead (Rom. 6:13; Eph. 2:5, 6; Col. 2:12; 3:1, 2). Regeneration is also presented in the figure of creation or re-creation. We are "created in Christ Jesus unto good works" (Eph. 2:10), and exhorted to "put on the new man, which after God is created in righteousness and true holiness" (Eph. 4:24). The revelation of 2 Corinthians 5:17 is explicit, "Therefore if any man be in Christ, he is a new creature: old things are passed away; behold, all things are become new." The figure of creation indicates that regeneration is creative in its nature and results in a fundamental change in the individual, a new nature being added with its new capacities. The individual becomes a part of the New Creation which includes all the regenerated ones of this dispensation and Christ its Head. The new life given to the Christian is manifested in the new capacities and activities found only in those regenerated, forming the source and foundation of all other divine ministry to the saved. The important fact, never to be forgotten in the doctrine of regeneration, is that the believer in Christ has received eternal life. This fact must be kept free from all confusion of thought arising from the concept of regeneration which makes it merely an antecedent of salvation, or a preliminary quickening to enable the soul to believe. It is rather the very heart of salvation. It reaches the essential problem of absence of eternal life without which no soul can spend eternity in the presence of God. Regeneration supplies this lack of eternal life as justification and sanctification deal with the problem of sin specifically. It is a smashing blow to all philosophies which hold that man has inherent capacities of saving himself. Regeneration is wholly of God. No possible human effort however noble can supply eternal life. The proper doctrine of regeneration gives to God all glory and power due His name, and at the same time it displays His abundant provision for a race dead in sin.—*Ibid.*, pp. 144–45

Again, that regeneration is not accomplished by means is well expressed by Dr. Walvoord as follows:

Reformed theology has definitely opposed the introduction of any means in accomplishing the divine act of regeneration. The question of whether means are used to effect regeneration is determined largely by the attitude taken toward efficacious grace. Pelagian and Arminian theologians, holding as they do to the cooperation of the human will and the partial ability of the will through common grace or natural powers, recognize to some extent the presence of means in the work of regeneration. If the total inability of man be recognized, and the doctrine of efficacious grace believed, it naturally follows that regeneration is accomplished apart from means. Reformed theology in keeping with its doctrine of efficacious grace has held that the human will in itself is ineffectual in bringing about any of the changes incident to salvation of the soul. As related to faith, the human will can act by means of efficacious grace. The human will can act even apart from efficacious grace in hearing the Gospel. In the act of regeneration, however, the human will is entirely passive. There is no cooperation possible. The nature of the work of regeneration forbids any possible human assistance. As a child in natural birth is conceived and born without any volition on his part, so the child of God receives the new birth apart from any volition on his part. In the new birth, of course, the human will is not opposed to regeneration and wills by divine grace to believe, but this act in itself does not produce new birth. As in the resurrection of the human body from physical death, the body in no way assists the work of resurrection, so in the work of regeneration, the human will is entirely passive. It is not that the human will is ruled aside, nor does it waive the human responsibility to believe. It is rather that regeneration is wholly a work of God in a believing heart. All other means are likewise excluded in the work of regeneration. While regeneration is often preceded by various antecedents such as the work of common grace and accompanying influences, these must be sharply distinguished from regeneration. Even the work of efficacious grace, though simultaneous with regeneration, and indispensable to it, does not in itself effect regeneration. Efficacious grace only makes regeneration possible and certain. Regeneration in its very nature is instantaneous, an immediate act of God, and in the nature of an instantaneous act, no means are possible. The fact that regeneration is consistently revealed as an act of God and the Scriptural revelation of the doctrine of efficacious grace are sufficient evidence for excluding the possibility of the use of means in effecting regeneration.—*Ibid.*, pp. 145–47

Of great import, especially to all evangelistic effort, is the word by Dr. Walvoord respecting the nonexperimental character of regeneration, which reads:

Until the matter has been considered carefully, it is a striking thought that regeneration is not experimental. In Christian testimony, much has been said of the experience of regeneration. If regeneration is instantaneous and an act of divine will, it follows that regeneration in itself is not experimental. It may be conceded freely that abundant experimental phenomena follow the act of new birth. The experiences of a normal Spirit-filled Christian may immediately ensue upon new birth. This fact does not alter the non-experimental character of regeneration. If it be admitted that regeneration is an instantaneous act of God, it is logically impossible for it to be experimental, in that experience involves time and sequence of experience. It may be concluded, therefore, that no sensation attends the act of new birth, all experience proceeding rather from the accomplished regeneration and springing from the new life as its source. In the nature of the case, we cannot experience what is not true, and regeneration must be entirely wrought before experience can be found. While the regenerated soul may become immediately conscious of new life, the act of regeneration itself is not subject to experience or analysis, being the supernatural instantaneous act of God. The non-experimental nature of regeneration if comprehended would do much to deliver the unsaved from the notion that an experience of some sort is antecedent to salvation, and, in turn, it would prevent those seeking to win souls of expecting in partial form the fruits of salvation before regeneration takes place. The popular notion that one must *feel* different *before* being saved has prevented many from the simplicity of faith in Christ and the genuine regeneration that God alone can effect. The non-experimental nature of regeneration has also, unfortunately, opened the door for the teaching of infant regeneration as held by the Lutheran Church. It is argued that if regeneration is not experimental, there is no valid reason why infants cannot be regenerated. Even Shedd approves the idea of infant regeneration on the ground that regeneration is not experimental in the following statement: "Regeneration is a work of God in the human soul that is below consciousness. There is no internal sensation caused by it. No man was ever conscious of that instantaneous act of the Holy Spirit by which he was made a new creature in Christ Jesus. And since the work is that of God alone, there is no necessity that man should be conscious of it. This fact places the infant and the adult upon the same footing, and makes infant regeneration as possible as that of adults. Infant regeneration is taught in Scripture. Luke 1:15, 'He shall be filled with the Holy Spirit, even from his mother's womb.' Luke 18:15, 16, 'Suffer little children to come unto me; for of such is the kingdom of God.' Acts 2:39, 'The promise is unto your children.' 1 Cor. 7:14, 'Now are your children holy.' Infant regeneration is also taught symbolically. (*a*) By infant circumcision in the Old Testament; (*b*) By infant baptism in the New Testament" (*Op. cit.*, Vol. II, pp. 505–6). It is doubtful if any of the proof texts offered by Shedd really prove infant regeneration. While it is true that many Christians never know a crisis-experience to which the act of new birth may be traced, there is no certain Scripture warrant for affirming infant regeneration, at least in the present age. The normal pattern for regeneration is that it occurs at the moment of saving faith. No appeal is ever addressed to men that they should believe because they are already regenerated. It is rather that they should believe and receive eternal life. Christians are definitely told that before they accepted Christ they were "dead in trespasses and sins" (Eph. 2:1). The case of those who die before reaching the age of responsibility is a different problem. The proper position seems to be that infants are regenerated at the moment of their death, not before, and if they live to maturity, they are regenerated at the moment they accept Christ. Infant baptism, certainly, is not efficacious in effecting regeneration, and the Reformed position is in contrast to the Lutheran on this point. The doctrine of infant regeneration, if believed, so confuses the doctrine as to rob it of all its decisive character. No one should be declared regenerated who cannot be declared saved for all eternity.—*Ibid.*, pp. 147–49

In concluding his thesis on regeneration, Dr. Walvoord writes of the *effect* of regeneration and indicates truth respecting a new nature, a new experience, and a new security. Of all this he says:

The work of regeneration is tremendous in its implications. A soul once dead has received the eternal life which characterizes the being of God. The effect of regeneration is summed up in the fact of possession of eternal life. All other results of regeneration are actually an enlargement of the fact of eternal life. While life itself is difficult to define, and eternal life is immaterial, certain qualities belong to anyone who is regenerated in virtue of the fact that eternal life abides in him.

In the nature of eternal life, it involves first of all the creation of a divine nature in the regenerated person. Without eradicating the old nature with its capacity and will for sin, the new nature has in it the longing for God and His will that we could expect would ensue from eternal life. The presence of the new nature constitutes a fundamental change in the person which is denominated "creation" (2 Cor. 5:17; Gal. 6:15) and "new man" (Eph. 4:24). A drastic change in manner of life, attitude toward God and to the things of God, and in the desires of the human heart may be expected in one receiving the new nature. The new nature which is a part of regeneration should not be confused with the sinless nature of Adam before the fall. Adam's nature was a human nature untried and innocent of sin. It did not have as its source and determining its nature the eternal life which is bestowed on a regenerated person. The human nature of Adam was open to sin and temptation and was peccable. It is doubtful whether the divine nature bestowed in connection with regeneration is ever involved directly in sin. While the Scriptures are clear that a regenerated person can sin, and does sin, the lapse is traced to the sin nature, even though the act is that of the whole person. This must not be confused with various statements to the effect that a Christian can be sinless or unable to sin. The state of sinless perfection can never be reached until the sin nature is cast out, and this is accomplished only through the death of the physical body or the transformation of the body without death at the rapture. Even the new nature, though never the origin of sin, does not have the ability sufficient to conquer the old nature. The power for victory lies in the indwelling presence of God. The new nature provides a will to do the will of God, and the power of God provides the enablement to accomplish this end in spite of the innate sinfulness of the sin nature. The state of being in the will of God is reached when the will of the new nature is fully realized. Eternal life and the new nature are inseparably united, the nature corresponding to the life which brings it into being.

While regeneration in itself is not experimental, it is the fountain of experience. The act of impartation of eternal life being instantaneous cannot be experienced, but the presence of eternal life after regeneration is the source of the new spiritual experience which might be expected. New life brings with it new capacity. The person who before regeneration was dead spiritually and blind to spiritual truth now becomes alive to a new world of reality. As a blind man for the first time contemplates the beauties of color and perspective when sight is restored, so the new-born soul contemplates new revelation of spiritual truth. For the first time he is able to understand the teaching ministry of the Holy Spirit. He is able now to enjoy the intimacies of fellowship with God and freedom in prayer. As his life is under the control of the Holy

Spirit, he is able to manifest the fruit of the Spirit, utterly foreign to the natural man. His whole being has new capacities for joy and sorrow, love, peace, guidance, and all the host of realities in the spiritual world. While regeneration is not an experience, it is the foundation for all Christian experience. This at once demands that regeneration be inseparable from salvation, and that regeneration manifest itself in the normal experiences of a yielded Christian life. Regeneration that does not issue into Christian experience may be questioned.

One of the many reasons for confusion in the doctrine of regeneration is the attempt to avoid the inevitable conclusion that a soul once genuinely regenerated is saved forever. The bestowal of eternal life cannot be revoked. It declares the unchangeable purpose of God to bring the regenerated person to glory. Never in the Scriptures do we find anyone regenerated a second time. While Christians may lose much of a normal spiritual experience through sin, and desperately need confession and restoration, the fact of regeneration does not change. In the last analysis, the experiences of this life are only antecedent to the larger experiences the regenerated person will have after deliverance from the presence and temptation of sin. Regeneration will have its ultimate display when the person regenerated is completely sanctified and glorified. Our present experiences, limited as they are by the presence of a sinful nature and sinful body, are only a partial portrayal of the glories of eternal life. Through the experiences of life, however, the fact of regeneration should be a source of constant hope and abiding confidence "that he which hath begun a good work . . . will perform it until the day of Jesus Christ" (Phil. 1:16).—*Ibid.*, pp. 149–51

## CONCLUSION

Regeneration is a most essential step in that preparation which must be made if individuals from this fallen race are to be constituted worthy dwellers within that highest of all spheres and made associates there with the Father, the Son, and the Holy Spirit. It becomes one of the greatest facts in the whole universe. Its full extent and value will be seen not on earth or in time, but in glory and for all eternity.

# Chapter X

## THE INDWELLING OF THE HOLY SPIRIT

From the doctrinal viewpoint or as a foundation for all truth respecting the relation between the Holy Spirit and the believer in the present age, there is no more characterizing or determining fact than that the Holy Spirit indwells every regenerated person. To fail to recognize the body of Scripture upon which this distinction in doctrine rests is to misapprehend one of the most essential factors in the Christian's being, to conceive of the Christian as totally unprepared for the high and holy requirements which are laid upon him, to open the door for the promotion of unscriptural assumptions relative to personal holiness, and to create unwarranted divisions in the Body of Christ. No student should pass over this aspect of truth lightly. No progress can be made in the knowledge of the Holy Spirit's relation to the believer until this feature in the doctrine of the Spirit is recognized and accepted as declared by the Sacred Text. The failure to discern that the Holy Spirit indwells every believer was the common and all but universal error of men two generations ago. That error was promoted in the early Keswick conferences and received and taught generally throughout Great Britain and America. However, American expositors of the last two generations have done much to recover this important doctrine from this and other similar misconceptions. The notion that the Holy Spirit is received as a second work of grace is now defended only by extreme holiness groups. In other words, it is more clearly understood than it was earlier that there can be no such a thing as a Christian who is not indwelt by the Holy Spirit. This truth is so emphatically declared in the New Testament that it seems almost impossible that any other view could ever have been entertained. It will be remembered that the ministry of the Spirit as One who indwells is but one of His present benefits and is not to be confused with His baptism, His sealing, or His filling. Of these other works, more will yet be presented. Though, as has been observed, the presence of the Holy Spirit in the believer may not be indicated by any corresponding revolutionary experience, His indwelling is nonetheless one of the most characterizing of all the features which constitute a Christian what he is (cf. Rom. 8:8–9). The same indwelling of the

Holy Spirit becomes, as well, an age-characterization. This is a dispensation of the Spirit, a period of time in which the Holy Spirit is the believer's all-sufficient Resource both for power and guidance. In this age the Christian is appointed to live by a new life-principle (cf. Rom. 6:4). The realization of the Spirit's presence, power, and guidance constitutes a wholly new method of daily living and is in contrast to that dominance and authority which the Mosaic Law exercised over Israel in the age that is past. In Romans 7:6 it is written: "But now we are delivered from the law, that being dead wherein we were held; that we should serve in newness of spirit, and not in the oldness of the letter." The phrase *newness of Spirit* is in contrast to the phrase *oldness of the letter*. These do not refer to spiritualizing and literal methods for interpretation of the truth; they rather indicate different divine economies which characterize two different dispensations. The age now past is marked off by the letter of the law, in which age no provision for enablement was ever made. The present age is distinguished as a period of the indwelling Spirit, whose presence provides every resource for the realization of a God-honoring daily life. The same distinction is presented in 2 Corinthians 3:6, which reads: "Who also hath made us able ministers of the new testament; not of the letter, but of the spirit: for the letter killeth, but the spirit giveth life." So far from enabling, the law was a ministry of condemnation and death (cf. Rom. 7:4, 6, 10–11). Over against this, the indwelling Spirit is now an unlimited Resource who sustains in every aspect of human life. Recognizing the same contrast in principles by which men's lives in two different dispensations have been guided, the Apostle avers in Galatians 5:18: "But if ye be led of the Spirit, ye are not under the law." Thus it is to be seen that because of the new provision made available every Christian from the least unto the greatest has been equipped with the needed sufficiency whereby every supernatural responsibility may be fully discharged to the glory of God. The Christian does face problems of adjustment, but his is never the problem of acquiring the Spirit or enablement. To walk by means of the Holy Spirit is a wholly new technique; since every child of God is charged with a life which is superhuman, however, each one without exception has received the Spirit and each one is therefore confronted with the necessity, if he would fulfill the divine ideal, of living his life in the enabling power of the Spirit, new technique though it is.

The fact of the Holy Spirit's indwelling should be recognized in its own uncomplicated features. This ministry must be distinguished from other ministries which are His, regardless of the dependence which other ministries sustain to this one. Confusion arises more often than otherwise between the truth respecting the indwelling of the Spirit and that respecting His filling. The filling depends upon personal adjustments, which adjustments will be set forth in a later chapter of this volume; and because of this dependence upon adjustments human weakness may be manifested and thus the experience of the filling with the Spirit may not be secured at all, while in other cases the filling may be characterized as partial, variable, or complete. No imperfect filling with the Spirit is satisfactory to God, for He commands all Christians without any allowances to be filled with the Spirit (Eph. 5:18). The indwelling, being a feature of salvation and secured by saving faith, is common to all regenerate persons alike. The Holy Spirit is received but once and He never departs; but there are many fillings as need for them arise. The Spirit indwells without necessarily engendering an experience; but the filling is directed unto love, joy, peace, and the full measure of life and service. That the Spirit indwells every Christian is asserted by revelation and is demanded by reason. Consideration of these two widely different approaches to this truth is now in order, besides which there must be notice in due course of two related ministries of the Spirit, namely, anointing and sealing.

## I. ACCORDING TO REVELATION

The contemplation of the truth relative to the Holy Spirit's indwelling should be with due recognition of His other ministries to the believer, for not one of them is complete within itself, but hinges of course upon the Spirit's presence. However, in the interest of a true evaluation, an analysis of each ministry is required separately. Each must be considered in its own peculiar and individual character. The Scriptures abundantly sustain the truth of the Spirit's indwelling, which ministry is to be examined here. The major passages are now to be taken up in their order by books, every one in its context.

*John 7:37–39.* "In the last day, that great day of the feast, Jesus stood and cried, saying, If any man thirst, let him come unto me, and drink. He that believeth on me, as the scripture hath said, out of his belly shall flow rivers of living water. (But this spake he of the Spirit, which they that believe on him should receive: for the Holy Ghost was not yet given; because that Jesus was not yet glorified.)"

This prediction spoken by Christ before His death anticipates the present age and asserts that in this age all who *believe* receive the Holy Spirit when they believe. In other words, the Spirit is received on precisely the same condition and at the same moment as salvation is achieved. Two operations of faith are not implied; the sole human instrumentality in salvation is believing and that complete salvation which is thus secured includes the coming of the Spirit to indwell the one who is saved. Being an essential feature of salvation, the human condition for indwelling, when that aspect of soteriological truth is considered separately, is believing and only believing. It therefore follows from this passage that the Holy Spirit is given to all who believe and when they believe. The Spirit was not yet given when Christ spoke, nor could He be given until Christ was glorified (cf. John 16:7). Incidentally, a very clear distinction is drawn here between the saints of the former dispensation and those of the present. New and far-reaching realities certainly belong to those who are identified with the glorified Christ.

*John 14:16–17; 1 John 2:27.* "And I will pray the Father, and he shall give you another Comforter, that he may abide with you for ever; even the Spirit of truth; whom the world cannot receive, because it seeth him not, neither knoweth him: but ye know him; for he dwelleth with you, and shall be in you. . . . But the anointing which ye have received of him abideth in you, and ye need not that any man teach you: but as the same anointing teacheth you of all things, and is truth, and is no lie, and even as it hath taught you, ye shall abide in him."

Here the same implication, which under due consideration cannot be misconstrued, is present, to the effect that each Christian has received the Holy Spirit; but an added truth is advanced which is of immeasurable import to doctrine of the Spirit's indwelling, namely, that, having taken up His abode in the believer, His presence is never removed. He abides there forever. As important as it is in itself, a correct manner of life does not enter into the terms upon which the Spirit indwells, any more than it enters into the terms of salvation. However, a holy life does enter into the terms upon which the child of God may be filled with the Spirit. It is the very presence of the Holy Spirit, to be sure, which calls for a holy life. When correcting the Corinthian believers respecting their unspiritual practices, the Apostle said: "What? know ye not that your body is the temple of the Holy Ghost which is in you, which ye have of God, and ye are not your own? For ye are bought with a price: therefore glorify God in your body, and in your spirit, which are God's" (1 Cor. 6:19–20). The dread lest the Holy Spirit might depart from the heart has been a deep sorrow to multitudes in past generations. Their unwarranted exercise of soul was well expressed in a verse of a hymn by William Cowper often sung:

> Return, O Holy Dove, return,
> Sweet Messenger of rest:
> I hate the sins that made Thee mourn,
> And drove Thee from my breast.

It is doubtful whether the passages under consideration could be more positively denied than they are by this bit of poetry.

*Acts 11:17.* "Forasmuch then as God gave them the like gift as he did unto us, who believed on the Lord Jesus Christ; what was I, that I could withstand God?"

This passage records Peter's account of the first preaching of the gospel to the Gentiles. That which arrested the Apostle's attention on that memorable occasion of which he speaks is that the Gentiles, as had the Jews at Pentecost, received the Holy Spirit when they believed on Christ. That reception was and is a part of salvation itself. The indwelling presence of the Spirit is God's gift to those who believe.

*Romans 5:5.* "And hope maketh not ashamed; because the love of God is shed abroad in our hearts by the Holy Ghost which is given unto us."

A more literal rendering of this Scripture is to the effect that the love of God gushes forth from the believer's heart, and that divine love proceeds from the Holy Spirit who is given unto him to dwell within. This text is the first in order out of several which declare specifically that the Spirit is given alike to all who are saved. The universality of the gift of the Spirit is asserted here in the use of the pronoun *us,* which word cannot by any right interpretation be made to represent a select or particular group of Christians. If it be contended, as too often it is, that there are saved ones who have not received the Holy Spirit, the answer found here, as likewise in other passages yet to be considered, is that the pronoun *us* cannot be limited, for it represents *all* who are saved.

*Romans 8:9.* "But ye are not in the flesh, but in the Spirit, if so be that the Spirit of God dwell in you. Now if any man have not the Spirit of Christ, he is none of his."

This declaration is dogmatic and final. If any man have not, which means as an indwelling presence, the Spirit of Christ—distinctly a title of the Holy Spirit, as the Spirit come from Christ and sent into the world (cf. John 16:7)—he is none of His. The ground of this statement is most reasonable. Among other things and quite above many things, the Christian is characterized by the fact that he has received the divine nature. No such being could exist as a Christian who does not possess the divine life which is essential to his newly created self. That new life is often declared to be none other than the Holy Spirit.

*Romans 8:23.* "And not only they, but ourselves also, which have the firstfruits of the Spirit, even we ourselves groan within ourselves, waiting for the adoption, to wit, the redemption of our body."

Again a universal meaning inheres in the word *ourselves.* This term can refer to no class or group within the Christian fellowship; it reaches to all. And the positive averment is that all have the first-fruits which only the presence of the Holy Spirit secures.

*1 Corinthians 2:12.* "Now we have received, not the spirit of the world, but the spirit which is of God; that we might know the things that are freely given to us of God."

Similarly, as above, the pronoun *we* attests an all-inclusive company of believers. It is God's purpose that everyone of all who are saved shall be instructed relative to those truths which can enter the human understanding only by divine revelation. No consideration could be given even for a moment to the assumption that the Spirit's ministry of teaching, which is set forth in this context (cf. vss. 9–16), is intended only for a restricted company within all those who are saved. It follows that, if it is God's purpose for all His children alike to know the glorious revelations He has in store for them, they must alike be in close and vital relation to the Holy Spirit their Teacher. God could not expect any believer to make progress in the knowledge of Himself or to be informed about His will for them if, perchance, that believer were not in possession of the Spirit, the divine Teacher who alone reveals the things of God. This great provision and necessity is declared in no uncertain terms when it is said: "Now we have received . . . the spirit which is of God; that we might know the things that are freely given to us of God."

*1 Corinthians 6:19–20.* "What? know ye not that your body is the temple of the Holy Ghost which is in you, which ye have of God, and ye are not your own? For ye are bought with a price: therefore glorify God in your body, and in your spirit, which are God's."

This passage serves again to answer completely those who contend that the Spirit is given only to a favored group, and especially does it answer the claim that He is given only to those who are yielded and faithful in their lives. This appeal, cited above, is to believers in criticism of whom the Apostle has declared that they are carnal (cf. 3:1–4), fornicators (cf. 5:1), disregarding their right relation to God and to each other (cf. 6:1–8); yet they are, all the same, intreated to turn from these unholy ways on the ground of the fact that their bodies are temples of the Holy Spirit. It will not do to reverse this appeal, as some do, and assert that Christians like the Corinthians, if they turned from their sins, would be rewarded by the presence of the indwelling Holy Spirit. The direct reason for invoking a holy life is that believers are already temples of the Spirit. Therefore, it is not a question of securing the Spirit by a holy life, but rather of a holy life being expected from one who has received the Spirit. This is the fundamental order of the grace relationship to God. The Mosaic merit system would say, "Be good so that ye may become the temples of the Holy Spirit"; grace says, "Ye are the temples of the Holy Spirit, therefore be good."

*1 Corinthians 12:13.* "For by one Spirit are we all baptized into one body, whether we be Jews or Gentiles, whether we be bond or free; and have been all made to drink into one Spirit."

The same unworthy Corinthians are again said to have all been "made to drink into one Spirit"—not some of them, but *all* of them. In this same verse it is also declared that these same carnal believers have, every one, been joined to the Lord by the baptism of the Holy Spirit. It is not more difficult to believe that all believers are indwelt by the Spirit than it is to believe that all have been baptized by the Spirit into the Body of Christ. Both truths are clearly taught in the New Testament and in neither case is the work wrought because of personal worthiness in the child of God, but simply in answer to the faith which results in salvation—that gracious work of which both the indwelling and the baptism of the Spirit are integral parts.

*2 Corinthians 5:5.* "Now he that hath wrought us for the selfsame thing is God, who also hath given unto us the earnest of the Spirit."

An earnest is a partial payment which is given in advance and which guarantees the final payment of the whole. The divine blessing which the presence and power of the indwelling Spirit secures, being an earnest, guarantees the full and final realization of all God's measureless provisions for the believer in glory. In business transactions, similarly, a down payment binds the whole with assurance that it will be paid in full and that it will be paid in the same kind. Not only does the gift of the Spirit assure the fulfillment of every promise which God has made, but it indicates the character of that which is yet to come. The Spirit is designated an *earnest* in three New Testament passages—2 Corinthians 1:22; 5:5; Ephesians 1:14—and it would be unwarranted indeed to assume that this foretaste of all of heaven's glories is withheld from even one of the least of all saints. His abiding presence is assured the Christian, since He Himself must indwell to be the Earnest which He is.

*Galatians 3:2.* "This only would I learn of you, Received ye the Spirit by the works of the law, or by the hearing of faith?"

The assurance given in this text is that the Galatians had received the Spirit in answer to saving faith, that is, as a feature of their salvation. Thus it is taught again that the Spirit becomes the indwelling presence in every individual who is saved and at the moment he is saved.

*Galatians 4:6.* "And because ye are sons, God hath sent forth the Spirit of his Son into your hearts, crying, Abba, Father."

This determining Scripture is wholly contradicted by the theory that the Spirit is given in answer to personal sanctification. Rather it is because of the fact that believers are *sons* that the Spirit is given unto them, and this procedure of necessity must include every son.

*1 John 3:24; 4:13.* "And he that keepeth his commandments dwelleth in him, and he in him. And hereby we know that he abideth in us, by the Spirit which he hath given us. . . . Hereby know we that we dwell in him, and he in us, because he hath given us of his Spirit."

These passages serve to seal and confirm the truth that the Holy Spirit being given unto *us* is given to all who are saved. Not a single one born of God could be excluded.

The conclusion to be drawn from this clear and extended body of Scripture is that the Holy Spirit is a living presence in every Christian; on the basis of this determining fact other relationships between the Spirit and the believer are built. It is evident that once a misinterpretation of this basic truth arises there will also come misconceptions of those other ministries of the Spirit which are built thereon.

Certain passages, because of their dispensational setting or because of their wording, have been assumed by some to contradict the body of Scripture which declares that the Holy Spirit indwells and is a permanent presence in every Christian. A discussion of the doctrine of the indwelling of the Spirit would be incomplete apart from a consideration of these passages.

*1 Samuel 16:14.* "But the Spirit of the LORD departed from Saul, and an evil spirit from the LORD troubled him."

In an age when the Holy Spirit did not indwell the saints universally and when He exercised sovereign freedom in entering and leaving those upon whom He came, it was wholly in order for the Spirit to leave King Saul and especially as a judgment upon him.

*Psalm 51:11.* "Cast me not away from thy presence; and take not thy holy spirit from me."

Thus within the same dispensation as that of King Saul and doubtless remembering God's judgments upon the former king, David prays that he may be spared the same judgment. He knows that the Spirit might in complete freedom—so far as any promise to the contrary was concerned—leave him never to return. Evidently, David was conscious to some extent of the advantage and blessing which the presence of the Spirit meant to him.

*Luke 11:13.* "If ye then, being evil, know how to give good gifts unto your children: how much more shall your heavenly Father give the Holy Spirit to them that ask him?"

Because it is located in the New Testament and because it was spoken by Christ, many have concluded that this passage must be incorporated into the general doctrine of the Spirit's relation to the Christian. Great error and misunderstanding have thus been engendered. There are two widely separated provisions with no reconciliation between them at this point in Pneumatology and there is no occasion to attempt their reconciliation. The passage under consideration conditions reception of the Holy Spirit upon asking, whereas the Christian, as has been seen, receives the Holy Spirit without any asking as a part of his salvation and when he believes. The Spirit, consequently, is now given to those who do no more than believe. In the dispensational divisions of the doctrine of the Holy Spirit, which were declared at the beginning of this volume, it was pointed out that the period between the baptism of Christ and the Day of Pentecost was characterized by transition, and in that period Christ offered the Spirit to those who would ask for Him. This provision of His was so in advance of the relation which the Spirit sustained to the saints in Old Testament times, to which relationship the apostles were in some measure adjusted, that there is no record they ever ventured on to this new ground; accordingly at the end of His earth-ministry, Christ said : "I will pray the Father, and he shall give you another Comforter, that he may abide with you for ever" (John 14:16). This introduces an entirely different relationship to the Spirit. The disciples were not now to receive the Holy Spirit in answer to their own petition, but in answer to the petition of Christ. Thus it is indicated that the Holy Spirit has now been given because of Christ's prayer and to all who believe. As 1 Samuel 16:14 and Psalm 51:11 serve to demonstrate that the experience of the Old Testament saints cannot be made the norm of Christian experience, in like manner Luke 11:13, which was for the disciples between Christ's baptism and the Day of Pentecost, cannot be made the norm of present experience.

Four passages yet remain to be considered which are often supposed to teach that the Spirit is received as a step or experience subsequent to salvation. These Scriptures fall within the present divine relationship of the Spirit. They are:

*Acts 5:32.* "And we are his witnesses of these things; and so is also the Holy Ghost, whom God hath given to them that obey him."

The use of this text to prove the Holy Spirit is given only to those who are obedient to the will of God in their daily lives is possible only when there is failure to recognize that the adherence here indicated is that of the unsaved to the gospel of their salvation. The context clearly sustains that interpretation and, besides, obedience to the gospel as a requirement for salvation is enjoined in other New Testament passages. The Apostle writes of the vengeance that shall fall on them that know not God and obey not the gospel of our Lord Jesus Christ (2 Thess. 1:8). To make the reception of the Holy Spirit to depend on obedience in daily life is to ignore the whole body of Scripture already presented in which He is seen to be present in every believer, and then to assign to the Christian the ability to be obedient within his own strength, whereas the faithful life is lived only through the power that the indwelling Spirit provides. Who, indeed, would ever comply with the requirement of obedience if that adherence were exalted, as it would have to be, to the last demand of infinite righteousness?

*Acts 8:14–20.* "Now when the apostles which were at Jerusalem heard that Samaria had received the word of God, they sent unto them Peter and John: who, when they were come down, prayed for them, that they might receive the Holy Ghost: (for as yet he was fallen upon none of them: only they were baptized in the name of the Lord Jesus.) Then laid they their hands on them, and they received the Holy Ghost. And when Simon saw that through laying on of the apostles' hands the Holy Ghost was given, he offered them money, saying, Give me also this power, that on whomsoever I lay hands, he may receive the Holy Ghost. But Peter said unto him, Thy money perish with thee, because thou hast thought that the gift of God may be purchased with money."

There is introduced by this passage what would seem to be an exception to all other direct teachings by which it is established that the Holy Spirit is bestowed in this age as a gift upon all who believe and when they believe. An exception of such a character would, because of its contradictory nature, be most serious. That the passage records an exception to the present order, indeed, is freely admitted. It is well to note, however, that, as before indicated, the final order for this age and for people other than the Jews was not established until the experience in Cornelius' house as recorded in Acts 10:44–46. The introduction of the Spirit's relation to Jews who received Christ was accomplished on the Day of Pentecost, and intimations in various passages suggest the importance which the Spirit assigns to this event. As certainly as the Spirit was to be given in due time to Samaritans and to Gentiles, as certainly as they had no part in Pentecost, and as surely as it was important in the gift of the Spirit to avoid a superior attitude on the part of Jews over Samaritans and Gentiles, it was necessary to mark the initial reception of the gospel by each of these groups with a distinctive emphasis on the ministry of the Spirit in their behalf. There is no claim made whatever that here in Samaria was a repetition of Pentecost; it is merely to point out that no ground was allowed believing Jews—altogether prone to look askance at Gentiles—for the assumption that they, having had the experience of Pentecost, were superior to all others. It is of significance when Peter declares that the manifestation of the Spirit in Cornelius' house was a reminder to him of Pentecost (Acts 11:15). The record respecting Samaria as given in the above passage, then, is of a special demonstration of the Holy Spirit and to the end that the gospel might be sealed to the Samaritans with undiminished power. A notable and much needed exception to the order of this age was thereby introduced.

*Acts 19:1–6.* "And it came to pass, that, while Apollos was at Corinth, Paul having passed through the upper coasts came to Ephesus: and finding certain disciples, he said unto them, Have ye received the Holy Ghost since ye believed? And they said unto him, We have not so much as heard whether there be any Holy Ghost. And he said unto them, Unto what then were ye baptized? And they said, Unto John's baptism. Then said Paul, John verily baptized with the baptism of repentance, saying unto the people, that they should believe on him which should come after him, that is, on Christ Jesus. When they heard this, they were baptized in the name of the Lord Jesus. And when Paul had laid his hands upon them, the Holy Ghost came on them; and they spake with tongues, and prophesied."

In the first place, the term *disciple* is not synonymous with the term *Christian*. A disciple is a follower or learner, and furthermore to be a disciple of John the Baptist was far removed from being saved through faith in Christ, crucified and risen. The Apostle, having missed certain realities in these twelve men, which realities belong to regenerated persons, inquired, *Upon believing* did ye receive the Holy Spirit? This is a more accurate rendering (cf. R.V.; also Eph. 1:13), and this question drew out the answer which at once revealed their unsaved condition. Thereupon the Apostle turned their attention to Christ as the one to trust, and having believed they were baptized in the name of the Lord Jesus, signs following this exceptional case too as in the previous ones cited and for the same reasons.

*Ephesians 1:13*. "In whom ye also trusted, after that ye heard the word of truth, the gospel of your salvation: in whom also after that ye believed, ye were sealed with that holy Spirit of promise."

All the difficulty which this passage seems to present is due to a misleading translation. The passage can be read, *Upon believing ye were sealed* (cf. R.V.). Believing is the logical, but not the chronological, cause of the sealing. Believers are sealed when they believe and because they believe.

## II. IN RELATION TO ANOINTING

Since the Spirit's indwelling and His anointing are in reality the same, the three references to the Holy Spirit as an anointing should be included in this chapter. By the same conclusive arguments from revelation as given above, the anointing is seen to be, like the indwelling, a present fact in every believer's life. These passages include:

*2 Corinthians 1:21–22*. "Now he which stablisheth us with you in Christ, and hath anointed us, is God; who hath also sealed us, and given the earnest of the Spirit in our hearts."

Four immediate results of the Spirit's indwelling are herewith suggested: (a) The baptism with the Spirit places the believer in Christ; thus each child of God is said now to be "stablished . . . in Christ" (1 Cor. 12:13; 6:17; Gal. 3:27). (b) Likewise, by giving us the Spirit, God hath anointed us. (c) Again, God through the Spirit hath sealed us (Eph. 4:30), and the Spirit Himself is the seal. (d) So, also, God is here said to have given us the Spirit as an "earnest," and since an earnest is a part of the purchase money, or property, given in advance as security for the remainder, the Spirit is seen to be the earnest of the whole heavenly inheritance which belongs to every believer through infinite grace (2 Cor. 5:5; Eph. 1:14; 1 Pet. 1:4).

*1 John 2:20* (*R.V.*). "And ye have an anointing from the Holy One, and ye know all things."

Here, again, it is implied that every Christian, being anointed, is indwelt by the Spirit and therefore is in the way of knowing those "deep things" of God which are alone imparted by the indwelling Spirit (1 Cor. 2:10, 12, 15; John 16:12–15).

*1 John 2:27*. "But the anointing which ye have received of him abideth in you, and ye need not that any man teach you: but as the same anointing teacheth you of all things, and is truth, and is no lie, and even as it hath taught you, ye shall abide in him."

In this passage, the important truth disclosed is that the anointing abides. The Spirit actually may be grieved (Eph. 4:30), but He is never grieved away. He may be quenched, or resisted (1 Thess. 5:19), but He never departs (John 14:16).

By all this it is demonstrated that there is no Scripture which contradicts the clear witness of the New Testament to the truth that all believers are permanently indwelt by the Holy Spirit once they believe.

## III. ACCORDING TO REASON

As certainly as it is urged upon all who are saved to live a supernatural life, so certainly are all in need of that enabling power which the Holy Spirit supplies. God has not mocked even one of His redeemed ones by placing a superhuman task upon him without at the same time providing the resources whereby he may do all His will. It may therefore be the testimony of reason that every believer has received the Holy Spirit. It is not claimed that every believer is filled with the Spirit, thereby to attain all of God's will for him. The filling depends upon human adjustments to the Spirit within and these too often fail. On the other hand, the indwelling of the Holy Spirit is God's responsibility toward His child with no human condition involved other than that faith shall be exercised which secures salvation with all of its features. Since it is so completely His undertaking and since He is ever faithful in all that is His to do, there could be no such thing as a Christian who is not provided with all the resources by which he may do God's will. Again, a protest is registered against the notion that by self-strength and effort the believer is ever able to make himself fit for the receiving of the Holy Spirit. This could not be true since the strength to do the will of God is available only by the new plan for daily living under grace derived from the fact of the indwelling Spirit. Christ declared, "Apart from me ye can do nothing," but a merit system ever contends that quite apart from Christ the individual must do everything in order to merit His presence and blessing.

Reason, therefore, dictates that since a holy life is as much demanded of one Christian as another and since there are not two standards for daily life—one for those who have the Spirit and one for those who have not—and also since every requirement addressed to the believer is supernatural in its scope, the Holy Spirit must be given to all alike. The fact that God addresses all Christians as though they possessed the Spirit is sufficient evidence that all have the Spirit.

A summarization of the teachings of the Bible on the fact of the indwelling Spirit is made by Dr. John F. Walvoord as follows:

While the indwelling of the Holy Spirit begins at the same moment as other tremendous undertakings by God for the newly saved soul, a careful distinction must be maintained between these various works of God. Indwelling is not synonymous with regeneration. While the new life of the believer is divine and by its nature identified with God's life, the possession of divine life and divine presence are distinct. The work of baptism by the Spirit is also to be distinguished from indwelling. Baptism occurs once and for all and relates to separation from the world and union with Christ. Indwelling, while beginning at the same moment as baptism, is continuous. As will be indicated in the ensuing material, the indwelling presence of the Holy Spirit does have a most intimate relation to the sealing of the Holy Spirit, the presence of the Holy Spirit constituting the seal. Probably the most difficult distinction is that of the indwelling and filling of the Spirit. The two doctrines are closely related, yet are not synonymous. Filling relates wholly to experience, while indwelling is not experimental, in itself. In the Old Testament period, a few saints were filled temporarily without being permanently indwelt by the Spirit. While filled with the Spirit, Old Testament saints could in one sense be considered also indwelt, but not in the permanent unchanging way revealed in the New Testament. In the Church age, it is impossible for anyone to be filled with the Spirit who is not indwelt. Indwelling is the abiding presence of the Spirit, while the filling of the Spirit indicates the ministry and extent of control of the Spirit over the individual. Indwelling is not active. All the ministry of the Spirit and experience related to fellowship and fruit issues from the filling of the Spirit. Hence, while we are never exhorted to be indwelt, we are urged to be filled with the Spirit (Eph. 5:18). The importance of the abiding presence of the Holy Spirit in the life of the Christian cannot be overestimated. It constitutes a significant proof of grace, and of divine purpose in connection with fruitfulness and sanctification. The presence of the Holy Spirit is our "earnest" of the blessing ahead (2 Cor. 1:22; 5:5; Eph. 1:14). The presence of the Spirit not only brings all assurance of God's constant care and ministry in this life, but the unfailing purpose of God to fulfill all His promises to us. The presence of the Holy Spirit makes the body of the believer a temple of God (1 Cor. 6:19). It reveals the purpose of God that the Spirit be resident in the earth during the present age. To surrender this doctrine or to allow its certainty to be questioned strikes a major blow at the whole system of Christian doctrine. The blessed fact that God has made the earthly bodies of Christians His present earthly temple renders to life and service a power and significance which is at the heart of all Christian experience.—*The Doctrine of the Holy Spirit,* pp. 173–75

## IV. IN RELATION TO SEALING

Much truth which pertains to the Christian's salvation presents that which in its essential character is more an advantage to God than it is to the one who is saved. This is especially true of the fact of the Spirit's sealing, which sealing serves as a classification and an identification peculiar to heaven and the outworking of the divine purpose. It is the very presence of the Holy Spirit in the believer which constitutes the seal. Thus this aspect of truth is closely related to the doctrine of the Spirit's indwelling. Reference is made to the Spirit's sealing in three New Testament passages—2 Corinthians 1:22; Ephesians 1:13 and 4:30. These passages read: "Who hath also sealed us, and given the earnest of the Spirit in our hearts. . . . In whom ye also trusted, after that ye heard the word of truth, the gospel of your salvation: in whom also after that ye believed, ye were sealed with that holy Spirit of promise. . . . And grieve not the holy Spirit of God, whereby ye are sealed unto the day of redemption." It will be observed that this is a work of God since there is no appeal to any person, saved or unsaved, to pray for or to strive for this reality. Since it belongs to all believers, it is evidently wrought by God at the moment one is saved and as an essential factor in salvation. The rendering of Ephesians 1:13 by the words "After that ye believed, ye were sealed" is misleading. The more correct translation (cf. R.V.) would be: "When ye believed, ye were sealed." Naturally only those who believe are sealed and thus the act of believing becomes logically, though not chronologically, the cause of the sealing. There is a very vital assurance in Ephesians 4:30 relative to the eternal character of the sealing and thus of the salvation of which it forms a part. The future consummation of salvation when the body is redeemed is in view. Based as it is upon the merit and worthiness of Christ, salvation is as secure and as enduring as it is because of the foundation on which it stands. It is therefore no new or incredible idea that the sealing of the Spirit would mark off the full measure and intent of God with respect to those who are saved according to His purpose (cf. Rom. 8:28). Though there is no corresponding experience connected with the sealing of the Spirit, this peculiar ministry is, nevertheless, real and should call forth ceaseless praise to God as faith lays hold of that which God has revealed.

# CHAPTER XI

# THE BAPTISM OF THE HOLY SPIRIT

SINCE BY THE Spirit's baptism the greatest transformations are wrought in behalf of the believer, it is to be expected that Satan, the enemy of God, will do all within his power to distract, misdirect, and confuse investigation respecting this specific ministry of the Holy Spirit. This harm Satan has been permitted to do. Not only is there need that all the false conceptions be corrected which have reached the masses of unsuspecting people, but special attention is demanded on the part of those who would be instructed lest they themselves fail to comprehend the precise truth which the doctrine embraces. No further explanation than the influence of Satan is needed for the otherwise inexplicable disarrangement and ignorance of, together with a corresponding prejudice toward, this specific doctrine. It is the strategic point at which Satan can accomplish most in obliterating the effect of the present truth. This nullifying of the truth is seen in at least three most important fields of doctrine, namely, the believer's positions and standing in Christ, his eternal security, and the ground of the only effective motive for a God-honoring daily life.

In attempting to arrive at a right understanding of the essential character of this ministry of the Holy Spirit, four general divisions of the subject will be considered: (1) the meaning of the word *βαπτίζω*, (2) the determining Scriptures, (3) the thing accomplished, and (4) its distinctive character.

## I. THE WORD ΒΑΠΤΙΖΩ

More than passing significance should be attached to the fact that the same word *βαπτίζω* is used in the New Testament both for real and ritual baptism, thus signifying a bond of relationship between these two aspects of truth. The word would hardly be employed properly had it a separate unrelated meaning in the one instance. The basic word of this root, *Βάπτω*, in its primary import connotes a dipping and occurs but three times in the New Testament—Luke 16:24; John 13:26; and Revelation 19:13. In its secondary meaning, which is to dye or stain—

that usually accomplished by dipping, but not always so—the word appears but once and that in the third passage cited above, which reads, "And he was clothed with a vesture dipped in blood: and his name is called The Word of God." The same event and situation are presented in Isaiah 63:1–6 wherein among other details it is written: "Wherefore art thou red in thine apparel, and thy garments like him that treadeth in the winefat? I have trodden the winepress alone; and of the people there was none with me: for I will tread them in mine anger, and trample them in my fury; and their blood shall be sprinkled upon my garments, and I will stain all my raiment" (vss. 2–3). The garments of the returning Messiah are not dipped in a vat of blood, rather they have been sprinkled and stained with blood; yet this is still described by *βάπτω* in the LXX. In like manner, the word *βαπτίζω* has both a primary and secondary meaning. In its primary sense it indicates an intusposition, a physical envelopment in an element, which element has power to influence or change that which it envelops. In its secondary meaning, however, *βαπτίζω*, as in the case of the secondary meaning of *βάπτω*, departs somewhat from the original physical aspect and refers to one thing being brought under the transforming power or influence of another thing. None could speak with more authority respecting the precise meaning of *βαπτίζω* than Dr. James W. Dale because of his extensive research. He defines this word in its secondary meaning thus: "Whatever is capable of thoroughly changing the character, state, or condition of any object, is capable of baptizing that object; and by such change of character, state, or condition does, in fact, baptize it" (*Classic Baptism,* 2nd ed., p. 354). Such a definition is most important since the great majority of New Testament usages of this word are wholly within its secondary meaning. In the course of his great works on the subject of baptism, Dr. Dale asserts that the word is, in his opinion, never used in the New Testament in any other than its secondary meaning. Here it should be noted that the same distinction obtains between the Greek words *βάπτω* and *βαπτίζω* as between their English equivalents, namely, to *dip* and to *immerse.* A dipping is a momentary contact involving two actions, the putting in and the taking out, while immersing implies but one action, that of putting in. In the strict and proper use of the words, regardless of the all but universal careless way in which they are employed, ritual baptism is never an immersion, which immersion would result in death by drowning. What has commonly been termed an immersion is better described by *βάπτω* in the primary meaning of that word. No physical intusposition certainly is in view when the

Scriptures speak of a baptism unto repentance (Matt. 3:11), a baptism unto the remission of sins (Mark 1:4), a baptism unto the name of the Father, the Son, and the Holy Spirit (Matt. 28:19), Christ's own being baptized by drinking the cup of suffering (Matt. 20:23; Luke 12:50), a baptism of Israel unto Moses (1 Cor. 10:2), a baptism wrought by the presence and influence of the Holy Spirit in the believer's heart, that is, the baptism of a believer into the Body of Christ (1 Cor. 12:13). These baptisms, let it be repeated, represent no physical intusposition and must be classed as belonging to the secondary use of *βαπτίζω*. Not one could be properly classed as a use of *βάπτω*, either in its primary or secondary meaning. They could not be merely a dipping into an element for they all present the estate as permanent. When a believer is by the Spirit baptized into Christ, the thing most to be desired is that he shall never be taken out again. To be baptized unto repentance is to be brought under the influence of repentance—not for a moment, but abidingly; to be baptized unto the remission of sins is to be brought under the power or value of the remission of sins—not for a moment, but abidingly; to be baptized unto the name of the triune God is to come under the power of God—not for a moment, but abidingly; to be baptized unto Moses as Israel was by the agency of the cloud and the sea was to be brought under the leadership of Moses, which leadership had not been accorded him before—not for a moment, but abidingly; to be baptized unto Christ's death and resurrection is to become so identified with Him in that death and resurrection that all their values are secured—not for a moment, but eternally. Christ's suffering of anguish was not a momentary dipping down into suffering. That baptism which results from the advent of the Spirit into the heart with His heavenly influences is not for a moment, but endures forever. To be baptized into Christ's Body is to come under the power and Headship of Christ; it is to be joined unto the Lord, to be identified with Him, to partake of what He is and what He has done —not for a moment, but unalterably.

It may be said in concluding this portion of the chapter that to be placed in Christ by the baptizing agency of the Holy Spirit results in a new reality of relationship in which the one thus blessed comes under the power and Headship of Christ, which position supplants the relationship to the first Adam and is itself a new organic union with the Last Adam, the resurrected Christ. In this instance, as in other baptisms, the word *βαπτίζω* is used only in its secondary meaning apart from a physical intusposition, for it secures the merit, the dominating influence, and Headship of Christ.

## II. THE DETERMINING SCRIPTURES

Those Scriptures in which the Holy Spirit is related to baptism are to be classified in two divisions. In the one group, Christ is the baptizing agent, yet the Holy Spirit is the blessed influence which characterizes the baptism. In the other group of passages, the Holy Spirit is the baptizing agent and Christ as the Head of His mystical Body is the receiving element and by so much that blessed influence which characterizes the baptism. Six passages are to be identified as belonging to the first group, namely, Matthew 3:11; Mark 1:8; Luke 3:16; John 1:33; Acts 1:5 and 11:16. Though there is repetition involved, these passages—all of which happen to present the testimony of John the Baptist respecting Christ—are quoted in full: "I indeed baptize you with water unto repentance: but he that cometh after me is mightier than I, whose shoes I am not worthy to bear: he shall baptize you with the Holy Ghost, and with fire" (Matt. 3:11); "I indeed have baptized you with water: but he shall baptize you with the Holy Ghost" (Mark 1:8); "John answered, saying unto them all, I indeed baptize you with water; but one mightier than I cometh, the latchet of whose shoes I am not worthy to unloose: he shall baptize you with the Holy Ghost and with fire" (Luke 3:16); "And I knew him not: but he that sent me to baptize with water, the same said unto me, Upon whom thou shalt see the Spirit descending, and remaining on him, the same is he which baptizeth with the Holy Ghost" (John 1:33); "For John truly baptized with water; but ye shall be baptized with the Holy Ghost not many days hence" (Acts 1:5); "Then remembered I the word of the Lord, how that he said, John indeed baptized with water; but ye shall be baptized with the Holy Ghost" (11:16). By the authority of Christ the Holy Spirit is given to all those who believe, and to come under the Spirit's power and influence, as every Christian does when he believes, is to have been baptized by that influence. However, this universal blessing of the indwelling Spirit is to be distinguished from some supposed second work of grace subsequent to salvation, which experience, as claimed by extreme holiness groups, is accompanied by manifestations which are supernatural. It has already been demonstrated from the New Testament that the Holy Spirit is received as Christ's gift by all who believe and when they believe. This gift is the new birthright and, being possessed by all, indicates that all who are saved are under the power of the Holy Spirit, which fact is, according to the strict meaning of the word *βαπτίζω*, a baptism. It could be said on the ground of this meaning of the word that any person coming under the influence of Satan is by so much baptized by Satan. This particular baptism related so closely to the Holy Spirit is quite removed from the baptism wrought by Him when bringing believers into the Body of Christ, which reality is now to be considered.

The second classification of passages presents the Holy Spirit as baptizing agent and the Body of Christ or Christ Himself as the receiving element. These passages constitute a distinct testimony by themselves, which is to the effect that by the operation of the Holy Spirit the believer is organically and vitally joined to the Lord and thus has become a partaker of the standing, merit, and perfect worthiness of Christ. Since these passages bear on the baptizing ministry of the Holy Spirit or real baptism as over against ritual, they should be given specific consideration. Doubtless some disagreement might arise over what passages should be included in this list; but where the results of the baptism are such as could never be accomplished by a mere ritual baptism, it is evident that reference is being made to a real or Spirit baptism: indeed, aside from those Scriptures already considered which assert that the presence of the Spirit in the believer is a special baptism wrought by Christ in bestowing the Spirit, the remaining passages must refer either to a real or a ritual baptism. As a general rule, it will be found that no Scripture refers to both real and ritual baptism. An exception will be indicated later when Ephesians 4:5 is considered. These passages are:

*1 Corinthians 12:12–13*. "For as the body is one, and hath many members, and all the members of that one body, being many, are one body: so also is Christ. For by one Spirit are we all baptized into one body, whether we be Jews or Gentiles, whether we be bond or free; and have been all made to drink into one Spirit."

As nearly as any Scripture will be found to present didactic definitions, this passage defines the Spirit's baptism. It is a joining of the believer to, the bringing into, the Body of Christ—in other words, the forming of that organic relation between Christ and the believer which is expressed by the words *in Christ* and which is the ground of all the Christian's positions and possessions. The context of this passage sets forth the absolute unity or identity which obtains between Christ and the members of His Body. The members are a unity, being in one Body, and in its larger meaning this Body when joined to its Head is also one unity—the Christ. This revelation, which is a vital feature in the Pauline doctrine of the one Body, is most illuminating, emphatic, and convincing. However, this emphasis upon unity which verse 12 deposes is only to prepare the way for the revelation of how members are joined to this Body. They are said to be *baptized* into this Body by one Spirit. The reference to one Spirit is but the continuation of that which has been declared time and again through the preceding portion of this chapter, namely, that it is by the one and selfsame Spirit the varied gifts are wrought. Thus, also, though many are baptized into the Body of Christ, it is wrought by the one Spirit in every instance. The central truth is that the one Spirit baptizes all—every believer—into the one Body. What is thus accomplished for every believer is a part of his very salvation, else it could not include each one. The investigation into that which this baptism accomplishes is reserved for the next part of the chapter. That believers are all made to drink into one Spirit is an added testimony to the fact of the indwelling of the Spirit, which indwelling, as has been seen, is a matter of baptism. The universality of both the baptism into the Body and the indwelling is asserted by the repeated use of the word *all,* which term is inclusive of both Jews and Gentiles who believe.

*Galatians 3:27.* "For as many of you as have been baptized into Christ have put on Christ."

According to this revealing declaration the baptism which is into Christ has resulted in the vital union which is here described by the phraseology *have put on Christ.* On this passage Dean Alford writes, along with a quotation from Chrysostom: "Not '*have been baptized,*' and '*have put on,*' as A.V., which leaves the two actions only concomitant: the past tenses make them identical: as many as were baptized into Christ, did in that very act, put on, clothe yourselves with, Christ. The force of the argument is well given by Chrysostom: 'Why did he not say, "As many of you as were baptized into Christ, were born of God?" for this would naturally follow from having shewn that they were sons. Because he lays down a far more startling proposition. For if Christ is the Son of God, and thou hast put Him on, having the Son in thee, and fashioned after His likeness, thou wert brought into one family with Him and one type' " (*New Testament for English Readers,* new ed., at Gal. 3:27). It is important to note that in the preceding verse—"For ye are all the children of God by faith in Christ Jesus"—the fact of sonship is declared and it is this precise numerical company that by baptism into Christ have put on Christ. The phrase *as many of you* is properly a reference to *all of you* who have been begotten of God. These have been joined to Christ thus. It is clear from other Scriptures that this baptism is wrought by the Holy Spirit and that Christ's Body, or Christ Himself, is the receiving element. It is impossible for one who is joined to Christ not to have *put on Christ* with all His merit and standing. The error of such as make this effect to stem from ritual baptism is exceeded only by those who make it merely an emotional or energizing experience. This baptism is wrought by the Holy Spirit and is altogether positional and therefore vital.

*Romans 6:1–4.* "What shall we say then? Shall we continue in sin, that grace may abound? God forbid. How shall we that are dead to sin, live any longer therein? Know ye not, that so many of us as were baptized into Jesus Christ were baptized into his death? Therefore we are buried with him by baptism into death: that like as Christ was raised up from the dead by the glory of the Father, even so we also should walk in newness of life."

Having declared that the believer is eternally justified—for justification is as enduring as the merit of Christ on which it stands—the Apostle enters the question of whether anyone thus saved and secure should continue in sin, thereby yielding to the sin nature, that grace may abound. The answer of inspiration to this question will be the reply of every regenerate person, namely, "God forbid." It is not consistent nor is it necessary to go on bearing fruit unto the sin nature. Respecting the point of its necessity, the truth revealed is to the effect that in the death of Christ the believer's sin nature has been judged. "How shall we that are dead to sin [that is, who died in Christ's death], live any longer therein?" It is true that Christ died "for our sins," that He was buried, and that He rose from the dead that men might be saved (cf. 1 Cor. 15:3–4); but it is equally true—and Romans 6:1–10 now under consideration has only to do with this added fact—that Christ died *unto sin,* meaning the nature (cf. Rom. 6:10; Col. 2:11–12). In this context the judgment of the sin nature on the cross is indicated by various phrases or statements—"dead to sin" (vs. 2), "planted [or, conjoined] together [with Him] in the likeness of his death" (vs. 5), "our old man is [better, following R.V., was] crucified with him" (vs. 6), "if we be dead with Christ" (vs. 8), "he died unto sin [that is, the sin nature] once" (vs. 10). By all of this it is not implied that the death of Christ resulted in the destruction or termination of this nature (the word καταργέω of verse 6, translated *destroyed,* is better rendered *annulled*—cf. R.V.); it is rather that the death of Christ unto sin has wrought a judgment against the sin nature in the sight of God, to the end that the Holy Spirit who indwells the believer may be made free to deal with the judged nature, restraining or nullifying it in response to the believer's dependence upon the One indwelling to interpose and control that nature. This aspect of the death of Christ and the believer's identification with it is all to the one end that "we should walk in newness of life." "Like as Christ was raised up from the dead by the glory of the Father, even so we also should walk in newness [meaning the new power of Christ's resurrected] life" (vs. 4), which is the new provision for a walk in and by the enabling Holy Spirit, He Himself being set free to render aid because of Christ's judgment death unto sin. The Christian's union with Christ, achieved by the Spirit's baptism unto Him, is the ground of the perfect identification with Christ in all that His death unto sin accomplished. Coming thus into the value and under the power of Christ's crucifixion, death, burial, and resurrection is a baptism in the secondary meaning of that word. Those baptized into Christ are baptized into His death, are buried with Christ by their baptism into the Savior's death. No ordinance is intimated by these expressions, nor is there any obligation being imposed that justifies an attempt to enact what is here set forth. This passage, with that which follows in the context, presents the central statement respecting the basis of the Christian's victory in daily life over the sin nature. This is its objective and its meaning. To discover in it only the outward form of a ritual ordinance, as many have done, is to surrender one of the most priceless assets in the whole field of Christian doctrine and by so much (for many) to abandon the hope of any life well-pleasing to God; for if this context means the one thing it cannot mean the other.

*Colossians 2:9–13.* "For in him dwelleth all the fulness of the Godhead bodily. And ye are complete in him, which is the head of all principality and power: in whom also ye are circumcised with the circumcision made without hands, in putting off the body of the sins of the flesh by the circumcision of Christ: buried with him in baptism, wherein also ye are risen with him through the faith of the operation of God, who hath raised him from the dead. And you, being dead in your sins and the uncircumcision of your flesh, hath he quickened together with him, having forgiven you all trespasses."

The passing reference to baptism which this Scripture presents will not be understood apart from the entire context. As related to the rite of circumcision, the Apostle divides the human family into three classes, namely, the "Uncircumcision"—the Gentiles, "the Circumcision in the flesh made by hands"—the Jews, and "the circumcision made without hands"—the Christians (cf. Eph. 2:11; Col. 2:11). That circumcision which characterizes the Jew and which the Gentile lacks is "made by hands," while the circumcision which the Christian has received is "made without hands" and is a spiritual reality. Four times the Bible speaks of circumcision in connection with the heart—Deuteronomy 10:16; 30:6; Ezekiel 44:7; Acts 7:51—before mention of the blessing brought to Christians when the body of the sins of the flesh was put off and that by the circumcision of Christ. As the human body manifests the life which is in it, in like manner the sin nature manifests itself by "sins of the flesh." Christ's circumcision, here referred to, is not that which was made with hands when He was eight days old, but His death unto the sin nature. There is a striking similarity to Romans 6:1–10 to be found in the passage just considered, and this similarity concerns the reference to Christ's burial and resurrection as factors providing immeasurable value for, and influence over, the believer. Securing the results which they do, the death, burial, and resurrection of Christ are in their most absolute sense a baptism. The transformations which are here indicated, as they were also in Romans 6:1–10, could never be produced by any ritual baptism and to read ritual baptism into this passage is again to ignore the limitless realities for which Christ died, was buried, and rose again. It is to substitute a human effort for one of God's most glorious achievements. Doubtless, it is easier for those who comprehend but little of these great realities to substitute a tangible, physical undertaking such as ritual baptism for the deeper, unseen, and spiritual values of the real baptism. However, regardless of human limitations, the significance of this passage does not descend to the level of an impotent ritual.

*Ephesians 4:4–6*. "There is one body, and one Spirit, even as ye are called in one hope of your calling; one Lord, one faith, one baptism, one God and Father of all, who is above all, and through all, and in you all."

In the midst of these seven unifying agencies, and not the least of them, is "one baptism." At once the question may arise in many minds whether reference in this instance is to real baptism by the Spirit placing believers into the Body of Christ or to ritual water baptism. Some contend that the latter baptism is in view and that the passage teaches there is but one right mode of such baptism. To impose such limitations on the text is deplorable. There is nothing in the passage to support a mode of baptism. The unqualified statement that there is but *one* baptism becomes a very demanding problem to those who have elevated water baptism to the place where it must be a separate, independent, and diverse baptism—something, therefore, which is wholly unrelated to the Spirit's baptism. Some contend that, since real baptism so outweighs the ritual in importance, the ritual baptism is not to be mentioned at all in comparison with real baptism, here or elsewhere. Still others claim that the Apostle does not here contemplate ritual baptism, reckoning he only asserts that in the realm of spiritual forces which unify there is but one baptism and this of necessity would be the baptism with the Spirit. Yet further to be considered is a class of interpreters who hold that the Spirit's baptism occurred once for all and in behalf of all the Church on the Day of Pentecost, and that it is not a thing wrought at the time someone is saved. This conception, which so little articulates with the New Testament Scripture bearing on the theme, does not challenge the *fact,* though it attempts to change the time, of the Spirit's baptism so plainly mentioned here in Ephesians. The larger portion of the Christian church, however, in so far as they consider the subject at all, assert that ritual baptism is a sign or outward symbol of the Spirit's work and thus the two combine to form what is called here *one* baptism. Among the arguments advanced in support of the conviction that the one baptism is that of the Spirit by which believers are joined to the Lord and by which they gain all possessions and positions, the one most effective observes that this reference to one baptism is given as one of seven unifying agencies. It is easily discerned that the baptism by the Holy Spirit into one Body engenders the most vital and perfect union that could be formed among men; on the other hand, if the history of the church on earth bears a testimony to the course of events at all, it is to the effect that ritual baptism has served more than any other one issue to shatter that manifestation of organic union which Christian fellowship is intended to exhibit. On the right interpretation of Ephesians 4:5, Dr. John W. Bradbury, Editor of the *Watchman-Examiner,* the leading Baptist journal of this day in America, writes the following as a special contribution to the present discussion of Ephesians 4: "The corporate concept of the Church is as essential as the individual one. The 'body' of Christ is held together 'in the bond of peace' by keeping the 'unity of the Spirit' (v. 3). The thought that the Church is a 'body' whose life is uniformly identified with the Holy Spirit is illustrated by what we know of an organism such as the human body having the human spirit as a sign of life. We have, therefore, in the *ecclesia* a body having God's Spirit, evidencing such through professing 'one hope . . . one Lord, one faith, one baptism, one God . . . in all.' The emphasis on 'one' is in opposition to corporate diversity in the 'body' of Christ. As to 'hope,' 'Lord,' 'faith,' 'God,' there will be little, if any, difference among true believers. But in regard to the word 'baptism' there is a difference, because most people have only one viewpoint as to baptism and that is, an ordinance. But in this passage, where ordinances are not before us but the truth concerning the organism called 'the body of Christ,' we have baptism mentioned in equal terms with 'hope,' 'Lord,' 'faith,' 'God.' This signifies that the 'baptism' referred to is that of I Corinthians 12:13—'For by one Spirit are we all baptized into one body, whether we be Jews or Gentiles, whether we be bond or free; and have been all made to drink into one Spirit.' " Likewise, on the belief that the one baptism of Ephesians 4 is not ritual baptism, Dr. Merrill Frederick Unger writes:

> Erroneously, Spirit baptism is made a once-for-all operation at Pentecost (Acts 2), and in Cornelius' house (Acts 10), and then said to have ceased. During this present age, it is maintained, there is no baptism with the Holy Spirit. 1 Corinthians 12:13 is construed as referring back to those events. Such Scriptures as Romans 6:3, 4; Colossians 2:12; Galatians 3:27; 1 Peter 3:21 are made to refer exclusively to water baptism. The "one baptism" of Ephesians 4:5 is also strongly asserted to be water baptism, and that alone. Dr. I. M. Haldeman,[1] adopting this position, comments thus on Ephesians 4:5: "If it be Holy Ghost baptism, water baptism is excluded. There is no authority, no place for it. No minister has a right to perform it; no one is under obligation to submit to it. To perform it, or submit to it, would be not only without authority, but useless, utterly meaningless. If it be water baptism, Holy Ghost baptism is no longer operative. Baptism must be either the one or the other, Holy Ghost or water. It cannot be both. Two are no longer permissible" (*Holy Ghost Or Water?*, p. 4). Others, adopting the opposite extreme position, while rightly insisting that Ephesians 4:5 refers to Spirit baptism, drastically rule out any practice of water baptism for the Church Age. Although they find ritual baptism, of course, regularly practised in the early church (Acts 2:38; 8:12, 13, 16, 36; 9:18; 10:47, 48; 16:15, 33; 18:8; 19:3, 5) and mentioned in 1 Corinthians 1:13–17, this practice is thought of as confined to the early "Jewish" church, and discontinued by the Apostle Paul, when the "real" New Testament church was begun late in the book of Acts. This position must be rejected. The basic fact, which is ignored, is that the Church actually began

[1] Author's note: Dr. Haldeman was one of the clearest thinkers and logicians of his generation. It is therefore strange that he did not recognize the necessary confusion to which his interpretation would lead at last. Logic or no, here Dr. Haldeman is admitting the perplexity which arises when it is assumed that there are two unrelated and independent baptisms in the Church—the one with water related to the death of Christ and the other related to the Holy Spirit. Apparently Dr. Haldeman held with others of this school of exegesis that the Spirit's baptism was wrought for all and once for all at Pentecost, that it anticipated the elect company who would be saved, and that, being undertaken at the beginning of the history of the Church, it does not come into conflict with ritual baptism. But surely the mere question of time, to determine when the Spirit's baptism is wrought, does not change the *fact* of that particular baptism. It is doubtless still in force and so may well be, even if wrought at Pentecost, the one baptism of Ephesians 4:5.

with the baptism with the Spirit on the Day of Pentecost (Acts 1:4; 2:4, 47 with 11:16; 1 Cor. 12:13), and that water baptism was regularly administered, not only in the early so-called "Jewish" church, but also long after in fully established "Gentile" churches (Acts 18:8; 1 Cor. 1:13–17).

The Apostle, in speaking of the "one baptism" in Ephesians 4:5, to be sure, is speaking of Spirit baptism, which is likewise the case in Romans 6:3, 4; Colossians 2:12; Galatians 3:27. But when he describes this momentous operation of the Spirit as the "one baptism," and as one of the seven essential unities to be recognized and kept in maintaining Christian oneness and concord, does he necessarily imply that water baptism is no longer to be administered? Did he not mean merely to say, "There is only one [spiritual] baptism"? His theme is no more water baptism in Romans 6:3, 4; Colossians 2:12; Galatians 3:27 than in Ephesians 4:5. In these passages the holy Apostle is not considering ritual baptism at all. The sublimity of the thought, the context of the argument, the exalted nature of the spiritual verities taught are strongly in support of this position. He is speaking of something infinitely higher—not of a mere symbolic ordinance that is powerless to effect intrinsic change, but of a divine operation which places us eternally in Christ, and into His experiences of crucifixion, death, burial, and resurrection. It is to be feared that man, in reading water baptism into these sublime passages, has put them into ecclesiastical "stocks" and tortured and twisted until they screamed out some confession never written in them. To be sure, this tortuous, corrupting process began very early, perhaps even within the lifetime of the great Apostle. But it seems evident, if historical and philological facts are but allowed to speak, that a first-century reader, uncorrupted as to the truth, would never have thought of reading water baptism into these passages. To him they meant Spirit baptism, and that alone. Their very mold would have hindered him from associating them with any ritual use of water. His whole concept of the meaning and mode of baptism would have been utterly foreign to the Apostle's words concerning "death," "burial," and "resurrection." It would never have occurred to him to connect these figures with water baptism.

Baptism, referring to the Levitical ceremonies of the Old Testament (Heb. 9:10), had come to have a wide meaning of "ceremonial cleansing, or ritual purification by water, and that by sprinkling or pouring," centuries before the Christian era. Fairchild, with full array of facts, and unanswerable logic, conclusively proves this established usage of *βαπτίζω* from the Septuagint, the Apocrypha, Josephus, and the Greek New Testament (Edmund B. Fairchild, *Letters on Baptism,* pp. 32–122). Dale, with brilliant and exhaustive scholarship, employed with consummate skill in minute, scientific examination of every phase of this subject, thus concludes his monumental work on the study of baptism among the ancient Jews: "Judaic baptism is a condition of Ceremonial Purification effected by washing . . . sprinkling . . . pouring . . . dependent in no wise, on any form of act, or on the covering of the object" (James W. Dale, *Judaic Baptism,* p. 400). Dale concludes his great work on the study of John the Baptist's baptism with these words: "This same *βάπτισμα* is declared by word and exhibited in symbol, by the application of pure water to the person in the ritual ordinance. This is Johannic Baptism in its shadow. . . . Dipping or immersing into water is phraseology utterly unknown to John's baptism" (*Johannic Baptism,* p. 417). Biblical, historical, and philological proofs abound, therefore, that John the Baptist "ceremonially purified" (baptized) by sprinkling or pouring, that Jesus was so baptized (consecrated) unto His Priesthood (Ex. 29:4; Ps. 110:1; Matt. 3:15; Heb. 7:9, E. E. Hawes, *Baptism Mode Studies,* pp. 81–109), and that early Jewish and Christian baptisms knew no other mode (James W. Dale, *Christic and Patristic Baptism,* pp. 162–240). With all of this great weight of established usage of the word βαπτίζω behind him, made crystal-clear as a result of his intimate knowledge of Judaism, as a trained Rabbi, how unthinkable it is that the great Apostle would have so violated every principle of established usage of language and custom of centuries, as to have made βαπτίζω in such passages as Romans 6:3, 4; Colossians 2:12; Galatians 3:27; Ephesians 4:5 refer to any mode of water baptism, indeed, to water baptism at all!—"The Baptism with the Holy Spirit," *Bibliotheca Sacra,* CI, 244–47

*1 Peter 3:21.* "The like figure whereunto even baptism doth also now save us (not the putting away of the filth of the flesh, but the answer of a good conscience toward God,) by the resurrection of Jesus Christ."

The peculiar tendency with many to assume that ritual baptism is implied whenever the word βαπτίζω occurs has led to much confusion. In the light of its relative importance, it would be more reasonable to imply that real baptism is in view until it is made certain that ritual baptism is indicated. Two points are to be noted in this passage: (1) that the baptism mentioned is saving in its effect and (2) that it is related to the resurrection of Christ, which is vitally true of real baptism but not directly true of ritual baptism.

*Mark 16:16.* "He that believeth and is baptized shall be saved; but he that believeth not shall be damned."

Again baptism is mentioned as though it had saving power. The reference evidently is to real baptism. On this passage Dr. G. Campbell Morgan writes: "*He that believeth* (that is the human condition) *and is baptized* (that is the divine miracle) *shall be saved.* When the negative side is stated, baptism is omitted, as being unnecessary; for he that disbelieveth cannot be baptized. If it is water baptism, he can; but if it is the baptism of the Spirit, he cannot" (*The Spirit of God,* pp. 181–82).

As a summarization of these seven passages bearing on the Spirit's baptism, it may be observed that 1 Corinthians 12:13—which is not only the first of them chronologically but also the central testimony regarding the Spirit's baptism—declares directly what that baptism accomplishes. In the second—Galatians 3:27—the Spirit's baptism is said to result in the putting on of Christ. In the third—Romans 6:1–10—identification with Christ in His crucifixion, death, burial, and resurrection as a judgment of the sin nature is in view, and to the end that the believer may walk in resurrection power in spite of the sin nature. In the fourth passage—Colossians 2:9–13—the same influence of Christ's death (contemplated now as a spiritual circumcision), burial, and resurrection is again said to be a baptism. In the fifth passage—Ephesians 4:4–6—the Spirit's baptism is set forth as one of the unifying elements in the Body of Christ. In the sixth and seventh passages—1 Peter 3:21; Mark 16:16—this baptism is related to salvation as a most vital feature of it. Since by the baptism with the Spirit the believer is joined to Christ, more than a hundred passages which include the phrases *in Christ* or *in him* (that is, Christ) should be added to this list for exhaustiveness.

It may prove advantageous to call attention again at this point to the secondary meaning of βαπτίζω—the meaning which so largely obtains in the New Testament—which signifies that apart from a physical intusposition one thing baptizes another thing when its power and influence are exerted over that other thing. Christ gives the Holy Spirit to all believers to indwell them, to comfort them, and to enable them; thus the believer comes under the power and influence of the Holy Spirit. Such a gift is not a baptism into anything physical, but is that form of baptism which a dominating power and influence secures. To be joined to Christ by the Spirit's baptism is not a physical envelopment in Christ or in His Body; it is nevertheless a true baptism in that the one thus joined to the Lord has not only been wrought upon by the Spirit who baptizes, but that he comes under the immeasurable values of all Christ is and all He has done, being in Christ. The importance of a due recognition of all that enters into the secondary meaning of βαπτίζω can hardly be overestimated. The larger portion of theologians have more or less definitely related ritual baptism to the work of the Holy Spirit as a shadow or symbol is related to substance and reality. Other theologians, it would seem, have all but lost the secondary meaning of this great word in a sectarian effort to defend a mode of ritual baptism.

## III. THE THING ACCOMPLISHED

One of the greatest disclosures in the New Testament is confronted at this point in the discussion: no less a theme than the whole Pauline doctrine of the Church, the New Creation, with its Headship in the resurrected Christ. Though this great line of truth has had an extended treatment under Ecclesiology, it must be introduced again, being, as it is, so vital a feature in the doctrine of the Spirit's baptism. Regardless of its fundamental place in Pauline theology, this phase of Ecclesiology is almost wholly neglected by Covenant theologians, and for the obvious reason that their ideal of one covenant which unifies the whole Bible is shattered by revelation of a new Headship and its New Creation. The indictment, before mentioned, which is to the effect that the entire doctrinal aspect of Christ's resurrection—central in Pauline theology—is neglected, is most serious and damaging. The scope and importance of the doctrine of the Spirit's baptism, then, is to be seen from the thing it accomplishes.

1. ORGANIC UNION. The divine illustrations of this union engendered between Christ and the believer include that of the branch grafted into the vine (Rom. 11:17) and that of the joining of a member to a human body. It is readily recognized that human surgery does not attempt such an achievement as the latter, but then this determines nothing in the value of the figure as a setting forth of the union which the Spirit forms. An intensity of *inness* is secured when the believer is joined to Christ which, though wholly superhuman, is, nevertheless, feebly illustrated by these human figures. Both the branch and the body's member become living, organic parts of that to which they are joined. This new relationship as established in the case of the branch and the member results in the life of the vine or of the body being run *into* the branch and the member; it also results in the branch and the member being *in* the vine and the body. This twofold result is expressed by Christ in seven of the smallest yet most meaningful words ever uttered. They afford a miniature expression of one of infinity's masterpieces. The seven words are: "Ye in me, and I in you" (John 14:20). As before indicated, two mighty ministries of the Holy Spirit are here recognized—that of forming Christ in the believer or the regenerating work ("I in you") and that of placing the believer in Christ or the baptizing work He performs ("Ye in me"). No human language can describe these two realities, either with respect to the heaven-high character of these blessings or with respect to their eternal duration.

2. THE FOURFOLD PRAYER OF CHRIST. No little wonder is created when it is observed for the first time that Christ made the same declaration twice in His last priestly prayer. Twice He said, "They are not of the world, even as I am not of the world" (John 17:14, 16). Why, indeed, should any word of the Son to the Father be repeated? The answer is that by so doing there is recorded an emphasis, in this case one which exalts the truth of the believer's separation from the *cosmos*

world system. If, however, the Savior should repeat the same request four times, as actually happened here in the same priestly prayer, the emphasis exceeds all bounds and demands attention to an incomparable degree. These are the four similar petitions He offered in this one prayer: "That they may be one, as we are" (vs. 11), "That they all may be one; as thou, Father, art in me, and I in thee, that they also may be one in us" (vs. 21); "That they may be one, even as we are one" (vs. 22); "That they may be made perfect in one" (vs. 23). This fourfold stress exalts the thing for which He prayed above other features of this prayer regardless of their all having a supernatural character. The Lord is asking the Father to accomplish a very definite thing. In spite of notions to the effect that men have the responsibility of answering this prayer, the request is for the Father to do this very thing; and when the nature and the scope of the thing are considered, there is complete evidence that God alone could answer this prayer. There are three vast unities set forth in the Bible—the unity between the Persons of the Godhead; the unity between the Persons of the Godhead and the believer, in which unity each Person is said to be in the believer and the believer to be in each Person; and the unity between believers themselves. All three of these unities are referred to by Christ in this priestly prayer as recorded in verses 21 to 23. However, the unity of believers is the basic request of this portion of His prayer. He presents the oneness between the Persons of the Godhead and the believer as the grounds for the unity between believers. They will be one, therefore, when this prayer is answered because they are "in us," that is, the Persons of the Godhead. It would be impossible for believers to be in the Persons of the one Godhead and not thereby be constituted one in themselves; but still the realms of infinity are reached when the Savior prays that the believers may be one in relation to each other "as thou, Father, art in me, and I in thee" (vs. 21). What mind can conceive or what language can express the reality declared when it is prayed by the Son, whose prayer cannot go unanswered, that the Father create a unity between believers which is on the plane of the unity existing between the Persons of the Godhead! The truth of the triune existence of God is a sublime mystery, so its exaltation is a reality which lies wholly within the sphere of infinity. In the light of this fact, the conclusion must be reached that, as measured by God Himself, there is achieved through His creative power a supernatural union between Christians which is similar to that which unites the Persons of the Godhead. How tragic that for want of due instruction Christians in the main have never heard of such a relationship! And how deplorable the misunderstanding which conceives of this unity as mere membership in human ecclesiastical organizations!

This fourfold prayer of the Son of God was first answered on the Day of Pentecost when all believers then living were baptized by the Holy Spirit into one Body—the Body of Christ—and were all made to drink into one Spirit, to the end that a unity might exist between the Persons of the Godhead and the believers. To this original company and by the same operation of the Holy Spirit, all who have been saved from that day until now have been joined to Christ when they believed and as a feature of their salvation. Thus and only thus is the prayer of Christ being answered.

3. THE ONLY GROUND FOR IMPUTED RIGHTEOUSNESS. That there is a righteousness which the believer may possess wholly apart from any works or effort of his own and as a gift from God (cf. Rom. 5:17) is pure revelation and devoid of any confirmatory experience; besides, this bestowed righteousness is the only righteousness which God accepts in time or eternity. He Himself, being infinitely righteous, can receive nothing less than that which He is personally. Since present salvation is unto eternal and intimate association with God in His abode up in the highest glory, the necessity of being qualified for that sphere with a perfection which goes beyond human ability to provide is obvious. Thus the Apostle writes: "Giving thanks unto the Father, which hath made us meet to be partakers of the inheritance of the saints in light" (Col. 1:12). Respecting that righteousness which is God's gift through His Son, Abraham is the divinely ordered pattern. Though the head of the Jewish race, he does not represent the Jew under the Mosaic Law since the law was not then given; he rather depicts a believer of the present age under the grace relationship as himself under a similar relationship. Practically every illustration employed by the Apostle to set forth the grace of God as that is now exercised toward those who have no merit is drawn from the life and experience of Abraham. In response to God's promise about a son, Abraham believed, or amened, God and his faith became the ground of imputed righteousness. That righteousness which was bestowed on Abraham in answer to his faith is bestowed now upon all who exercise the same belief in the Word or promise of God. It is written: "Now it was not written for his sake alone, that it was imputed to him; but for us also, to whom it shall be imputed, if we believe on him that raised up Jesus our Lord from the dead" (Rom. 4:23–24). Of Israel it is said that they failed to secure this righteousness

since they sought it by the works of the law and not by faith; but some Gentiles who followed not after the righteousness which is of the law, or a basis in personal merit, found the perfect righteousness of God through believing on Christ. Israel's failure—as that of uncounted members of churches today—is to be found in the fact that they are "ignorant" respecting the whole provision of imputed righteousness and are going about to establish their own personal righteousness as a ground for God's acceptance of them, not knowing that Christ answers every need of the meritless and is Himself the "end of the law for righteousness to every one that believeth" (Rom. 9:30—10:4). To be in Christ is to be possessed with the righteousness of God which Christ is and which answers every need for such a character both in this life and in that which is to come. The unsaved are not in Christ, nor is Christ in them; but when one of these believes on Christ as Savior, he instantly comes to be in Christ by the baptizing ministry of the Holy Spirit and Christ comes to be in that one by the regenerating ministry of the Holy Spirit. This great twofold operation of the Holy Spirit fulfills the prediction of Christ given in His farewell to the disciples in the upper room, namely: "At that day ye shall know that I am in my Father, and ye in me, and I in you" (John 14:20). The determining words of this operation are *in Christ,* or the synonymous *in Him, in the Beloved,* and it is just that incomparable position in Christ which is secured by the baptism of the Spirit into Christ; for it is impossible that any should be in Christ and not partake of what Christ is, He who is the righteousness of God. Because of their apparently insignificant character, the words *in Christ* or *in Him* are passed by unnoticed; yet, as in the following passages, all that is declared of the Christian is made to depend solely on the fact that the one so blessed is in Christ: "There is therefore now no condemnation to them which are in Christ Jesus" (Rom. 8:1); "But of him are ye in Christ Jesus, who of God is made unto us wisdom, and righteousness, and sanctification, and redemption" (1 Cor. 1:30); "Therefore if any man be in Christ, he is a new creature: old things are passed away; behold, all things are become new. . . . For he hath made him to be sin for us, who knew no sin; that we might be made the righteousness of God in him" (2 Cor. 5:17, 21); "Blessed be the God and Father of our Lord Jesus Christ, who hath blessed us with all spiritual blessings in heavenly places in Christ . . . to the praise of the glory of his grace, wherein he hath made us accepted in the beloved" (Eph. 1:3, 6); "But now in Christ Jesus ye who sometimes were far off are made nigh by the blood of Christ" (Eph. 2:13);

"For in him dwelleth all the fulness of the Godhead bodily. And ye are complete in him, which is the head of all principality and power" (Col. 2:9–10). Added to these Scriptures are all passages which relate acceptance, righteousness, and justification to the act of believing.

In an earlier treatment of the doctrine of imputed righteousness as something secured by the baptism of the Spirit, it has been pointed out that attaining to the righteousness of God is not only realized on the ground of the believer's position in Christ, but that the gift of righteousness is based upon the sweet-savor aspect of Christ's death by which He as Substitute for those without merit offered Himself without spot to God, thus releasing His own merit that it might be available on a righteous ground to all who believe.

4. DUE RECOGNITION OF THE UNION. Having in the first three chapters of the letter to the Ephesians declared the positions and possessions of all who are in Christ Jesus, the Apostle makes it his appeal to those thus blessed that they endeavor "to keep the unity of the Spirit in the bond of peace." They are not told to *make* a union, but rather to keep the union which the Spirit has made. This will be done only as the individual child of God recognizes and loves every other child of God. Such recognition and love does not create a unity but does tend to keep the unity that exists. This unity is manifested in seven factors which the Apostle himself names: "There is one body, and one Spirit, even as ye are called in one hope of your calling; one Lord, one faith, one baptism, one God and Father of all, who is above all, and through all, and in you all" (Eph. 4:4–6). All these features are unifying in their character and none more so than the "one baptism" by the Spirit by which individual believers become members of one spiritual Body. Ritual baptism, as before indicated, has no power in itself to form a unity, but, on the contrary, has served more than other issues to break up observance of the unity which God has made.

When reproving the Corinthian Christians respecting the sins or failures which were present because tolerated in their assembly, the Apostle placed as first on his list of things subject to reproof their divisions and sectarian spirit. Such divisions are the very opposite of the Christian grace of keeping the unity of the Spirit in the bond of peace. This correction by the Apostle stands first in the Corinthian correspondence since in the divine estimation the keeping of the unity of the Spirit is of primary importance. Sectarianism is thus seen to be most displeasing to God and a violent disregard for that which God has wrought. As the keeping of the unity of the Spirit is a personal responsibility, in like manner the correction becomes a personal consideration.

5. THE GROUND OF APPEAL FOR A HOLY LIFE. There is an immeasurable difference between what God may do for the believer and what the believer may do for God. The order of truth in the great doctrinal epistles as they reflect the revelation under grace is first to declare what God has done for those who believe to the saving of their souls and then to appeal to such to walk worthy, or as it becomes those thus saved. This order cannot be reversed or disregarded without great confusion and injury. To attempt to be good in order that one may be accepted of God is not only hopeless but is legal in character and, as to the results obtained, will prove to be as weak as the flesh to which the appeal is made. On the other hand, to beseech men to walk worthy of a completeness and perfection in Christ to which the Spirit has brought them, is to place before them the highest of all activating motives. The new problem in every Christian's life is not how good one must be to be accepted of God, but how good should one be who is accepted of God. Such conformity to the highest heavenly ideals becomes gracious in its character since its demands are the voluntary expressions of a grateful heart and not a forced compliance to law as the basis of any relation to God whatsoever. No enablement is ever offered from God under law, but a God-honoring life is possible under the provisions of grace.

## IV. THE DISTINCTIVENESS

As a consummation of that which has gone before and been implied in previous discussion, the several aspects of truth which are peculiar to this theme may now be presented in order. The primary facts that this ministry—unlike the works of regeneration, indwelling, and filling—is not mentioned in the Old Testament, that it was not in operation before the Day of Pentecost, and that there is no anticipation of it in the age to come restrict it to the present age and its benefits are seen to be exclusively the portion of the Church, the New Creation; in fact, that which the Church represents in her exalted heavenly glory is almost wholly due to this specific ministry of the Holy Spirit. That a company should be called out one by one from both Jews and Gentiles, each individual of which is perfected in the absolute fullness or πλήρωμα of Christ, who is Himself the πλήρωμα of the Godhead bodily (cf. John 1:16; Col. 1:19; 2:9–10), thus in every respect to be fitted for the highest glory, is an innovation which Covenantism cannot admit. On the baptism with the Holy Spirit each member in the Body of Christ depends for every qualification by which he is "made meet to be" a partaker "of the inheritance of the saints in light" (Col. 1:12). It is tragic, indeed, when these great realities are neglected, if not rejected, only because some man-made system cannot make a place for them. What privation both in the knowledge of the truth and its sanctifying power has been suffered by those who have been thus dispossessed of the revelation! Thanks should be given to God that those who are saved, of whatever system of theology they may be a part, do possess these blessings whether they realize it or not; for such is the character of their salvation. In mercy God has never limited His blessings to that which the believer understands. In explaining the distinctiveness of real baptism, then, certain salient truths should be emphasized once more.

1. NOT REGENERATION. The Holy Spirit's work in regenerating results in the impartation of the divine nature which is "Christ in you, the hope of glory" (Col. 1:27), while the Spirit's baptism results in the believer's being placed in Christ. As already asserted, there is the widest distinction to be drawn between that which Christ expressed when He said "Ye in me"—the result of the Spirit's baptism, and "I in you"—the result of the Spirit's regeneration.

2. NOT INDWELLING. The indwelling Spirit, the gift of Christ to every believer, is, in the strict though secondary meaning of *βαπτίζω*, a form of baptism. Christ thus baptizes every believer by the gift of the Holy Spirit when the believer is saved. Six passages have been cited in this connection: Matthew 3:11; Mark 1:8; Luke 3:16; John 1:33; Acts 1:5; 11:16. Each of these passages distinctly asserts that Christ is the baptizing Agent and by His baptism the individual believer is brought under the influence which the presence of the Holy Spirit engenders. The gift of the Holy Spirit to indwell, which gift is universal and is bestowed at the moment of salvation and then as an integral part of salvation, should not be misconstrued because of a very common error, namely, that of supposing the Spirit is received subsequent to salvation and by a restricted number of people who "tarry" or "seek" a second blessing. The benefits which the indwelling Spirit secures are the portion of all believers and are not the manifestations which result from the Spirit's filling. Over against this misinterpretation, there is a group of passages already cited—notably 1 Corinthians 12:13; Galatians 3:27; Romans 6:3–4; Colossians 2:11–13; Ephesians 4:5; 1 Peter 3:21; Mark 16:16—which represent or suggest the Spirit as the

baptizer and Christ, or His Body, as the receiving element. This is that which is termed real baptism because wrought by the Holy Spirit, placing the believer in Christ and thus securing for him the merit and standing of the Son of God.

3. NOT FILLING. It will be observed that the Spirit's baptism is more confused with the Spirit's filling than it is with any other of the Spirit's ministries. Though the examination of the ministry of the Spirit's filling has not yet been undertaken, it being the next and final main division of this volume, certain obvious contrasts between the Spirit's baptism and filling may well be designated. First, as for permanence, the baptism by the Spirit into Christ is wrought but once, when the believer is saved (and remains an unchangeable reality for time and eternity), while the Spirit's filling may be subsequent to salvation and often repeated. Second, there is no experience or feeling related to the Spirit's baptism of the believer into Christ, but all spiritual manifestations of blessing and power are directly related and due to the Spirit's filling. Third, Christians are never enjoined to be baptized by the Spirit into Christ since that is the portion of all who believe, but every child of God is exhorted to be getting filled constantly by the Holy Spirit. Fourth, as declared above, every believer is baptized by the Spirit into Christ, but not every believer is necessarily filled with the Holy Spirit. Fifth, the Spirit's baptism into Christ results in the believer's being vitally joined to Christ for all eternity, while the filling of the Spirit results in outward manifestations and blessings for the present. The baptism establishes the Christian's standing, therefore, while the filling tends to improve the Christian's state. The baptism is a feature of salvation, while the filling is related to service and rewards. Sixth, the Spirit's baptism into Christ is wrought when the terms of salvation are met, while the terms governing the filling of Christians are such as enter into the believer's right relation to the One who has saved him, day by day.

## CONCLUSION

Both the word of introduction and the concluding portion of Dr. Merrill Frederick Unger's article *The Baptism with the Holy Spirit*, already cited, may serve as the closing of this discussion relative to the Spirit's baptism of the believer to place him into Christ. Dr. Unger writes:

The baptism with the Holy Spirit is one of the most vital and important of Scriptural doctrines. Its vast significance can readily be appreciated when it is realized that it is that divine operation of God's Spirit which places the believer "in Christ," in His mystical Body, the Church, and which makes him one with all other believers in Christ, one in life, the very life of the Son of God Himself, one in Him, a common Head, one in sharing His common salvation, hope, and destiny. Indeed, but a cursory consideration will reveal the paramount import and the sweeping ramifications of this vital Bible theme, affecting, as it does, so intimately and vitally the believer's position and experience, his standing and state. The astonishing thing, however, is that a subject of such momentous importance, with such far-reaching effects upon Christian position and practice, should suffer so woefully at the hands of both its enemies and friends. From its enemies it has suffered not so much from open hostility or opposition, as from chronic neglect. It is simply ignored, or at most treated superficially. Those who reject dispensational teaching, who posit an "all-time grace covenant," who make no adequate distinction between the "assembly" of Israel in the wilderness in the Old Testament and the Church as the Body of Christ in the New Testament, simply do not know what to do with it. It remains, and must continue to remain, a Scriptural conundrum to all such. If this doctrine has suffered at the hands of its enemies, it has especially been wounded in the house of its friends. Large groups of earnest and well-meaning, but poorly-taught, Christians, in evident reaction against the neglect and omissions which have attended this truth, have taken it to heart, according to it great emphasis and prominence. In their zeal and enthusiasm, however, they have not always confined themselves to clear and accurate Scriptural statement. Indeed, it would be difficult to find a Biblical theme used at once to teach deeper spiritual living, and yet at the same time subject to more misconception, misstatement, and confusion than this one. Nowhere in the whole range of Biblical theology is there greater need for precise and correct statement of vital truth than in the field of this doctrine. . . .

Having traced in detail the doctrine of the baptism with the Spirit as presented in the Scripture from all the material at hand, put in orderly arrangement, the following results and conclusions are offered: (1) The baptism with the Holy Spirit is a theme of paramount import, vitally affecting the believer's life and walk, his standing and state, his positions and possessions in Christ. (2) The baptism with the Spirit is one of the most abused and confused subjects in the whole range of Biblical theology. (3) The cause of the confusion is centered in confounding this doctrine with regeneration, with the receiving of the Spirit, with the indwelling, with the sealing, with a "second blessing," with the filling, and with water baptism. (4) The dire results of the confusion are: divisions, misunderstandings, disunity in the Body of Christ, obscuration of the gospel of grace, perversion of the truth of the believer's union with Christ, and sad hindrances to holiness of walk and life. (5) Careful study of *all* scriptures bearing on the subject has disclosed that the baptism with the Holy Spirit is merely one of the various ministries performed by the Holy Spirit since He came into the world: that *every* believer the moment he believes in Christ is regenerated, baptized, indwelt, and sealed for all eternity, and has the duty and privilege of continually being filled for life and service. (6) No instance in the Gospels or the Acts, when seen in proper dispensational perspective, is at variance with this truth. That there is no ground in all the Word of God for the error of the baptism with the Holy Spirit being considered as a "second experience" after regeneration becomes patent. (7) Water baptism is not in view at all in Romans 6:3, 4; Galatians 3:27; Ephesians 4:5; Colossians 2:12, and to read it into these passages is to becloud the truth, and to increase the confusion.

With these various truths given their proper emphasis, the doctrine of the baptism with the Holy Spirit is at once lifted out of the haze and fog of error that have so obscured it, and, in its majestic purity and grand simplicity, becomes one of the most precious and vital factors in Christian unity. No wonder the great Apostle cries out for the "one baptism" as one of the indispensable sevenfold unities to be kept in realizing the "unity of the Spirit in the bond of peace" (Eph. 4:3–6)! Who can begin to imagine the mighty transformation that would take place in poor, distraught, divided Christendom, if suddenly all the confusion and obscuration were torn away, and the full blaze and full-orbed glory of the truth of every Christian's oneness in Christ by the baptizing work of the Spirit burst upon the consciousness of all God's people? Blessing, revival, fellowship, and power such as the Church has never experienced, perhaps since Apostolic days, would be the inevitable result. Is it to be thought of, then, as amazing that this vital doctrine should always have been the special target of the most subtle Satanic *assaults?* That this is the case now should inspire to intrepid boldness and uncompromising fidelity in its proclamation and defense, in view of the sublime glory of the imperishable truth it represents.—*Op. cit.*, CI, 232–33, 497–99

# THE BELIEVER'S RESPONSIBILITY

## CHAPTER XII

## INTRODUCTION TO THE BELIEVER'S RESPONSIBILITY

SINCE THEY are void of experimental features, the ministries of the Spirit to the believer already cited—regeneration, indwelling, sealing, and baptizing—have served to establish the truth related to the Christian's positions and possessions. This body of truth may well be termed that which is fundamental and primary in all doctrine respecting the Christian; but there is also that which is rightfully termed *practical* features of truth. These comprehend the believer's responsibility in thought and action toward God, toward his fellow men, and toward self. With regard to importance, there could be no comparison between these two aspects of doctrine though in the one instance all is accomplished completely when one believes and in the other instance there is ceaseless obligation resting upon the convert; yet the situation, all the same, which every pastor confronts in the individual life to which he ministers is within the sphere of the less important, practical phase of doctrine. It may well be called *life truth* since it concerns the outliving of that which is infinitely true and certain in the sphere of *positional truth.* How helpless the would-be soul doctor must be who in his courses of training has never heard even one intimation of the specific instruction which God addresses to the believer, or of the divine plan so extensively taught in the New Testament whereby the Christian may be more than conqueror over evil forces through the power of the indwelling Spirit! Seminary instructors, however, cannot be expected to teach subjects and courses—no matter how important—of which they in turn had never heard in the days of their own education and which they have consistently ignored thereafter.

### I. INTELLIGENT MOTIVES

The Christian who is perfected forever, being in Christ, has, nevertheless, a life of imperfection to live so long as he is in this world. The new problem which he confronts, as several times before stated, is not one of how he should live that he might be accepted and perfected before God, but rather of how he, an accepted and perfected person, should live after these stupendous realities are accomplished by the grace and power of God. Until this vital distinction is comprehended and received, there will be no progress made in the extensive field of truth which directs the Christian's life and service. Until positional truth is recognized and received to the extent that the saved one acknowledges that he is saved and perfected in the sight of God on no other ground than that, on his part, he has believed on Christ to the saving of his soul, and, on God's part, he is justified, being both forgiven and constituted righteous through the immeasurable twofold substitution of Christ—bearing condemnation because of the believer's demerit and offering Himself as the source of merit—there can be only confusion and misunderstanding about the true motivating principle in the Christian's daily life. It could not be denied truthfully that the mass of professing Christians have been deprived of the knowledge of positional truth and because of this have never conceived of any other idea of Christian conduct than that they are obligated to make themselves acceptable to God by their own works of righteousness. Naturally, being so deprived of the knowledge of positional truth they are correspondingly ignorant of the true basis and motive for life truth. This one distinction between positional truth and life truth constitutes one of the most vital contrasts between law and grace. It is declared that the Jew failed because he sought his righteous standing before God by means of the works of the law, being "ignorant" of the truth that God has provided all the standing and merit in and through Christ that His holiness could ever require. Because of this ignorance, the Jew went about "to establish his own righteousness" and did not "submit" or come under the bestowed righteousness of God, Christ being "the end of the law for righteousness to every one that believeth." Over against this, some Gentiles—to whom the law was never addressed and who had therefore never attempted to be owned of God through law-works of righteousness—attained instantly to the bestowed righteousness of God when they received Christ as Savior through faith in Him (Rom. 9:30—10:4). The question of motive in the Christian's daily life is paramount in this discussion. The body of truth now to be considered concerns the daily life of the believer, and no issue is more determining than that of the reason or principle which actuates the one who would attain to a God-honoring life in the way God appoints through the power of the indwelling Spirit. The Holy Spirit cannot cooperate or engender any reality of experience when the very basis of a grace relationship to God is ignored. How, indeed, could the Holy Spirit empower a life which is wholly misguided and wrong in its objectives, methods, and motives? His benefits, of necessity, have significance only for those who recognize and believe that they are perfected once-for-all by simple faith in Christ as Savior and that their new obligation is not to make themselves accepted but rather to walk worthy of the One in whom they are accepted. In John 15:1–16 the words of Christ relative to abiding in Him are recorded. In this context a fundamental distinction must be drawn between the believer's *union* with Christ and his *communion* with Christ. Too often it is supposed that in this passage Christ is teaching that the branch, which represents the Christian, must maintain its union with the vine, which represents Christ. That communion, however, is in view throughout the passage is clearly indicated. In verse 2 it is written: "Every branch in me that beareth not fruit," and the words *in me* declare the perfect union of the fruitless branch to Christ. The obligation upon the branch is to continue in the relation to Christ which makes communion possible, whereby the divine life or energy may flow into the branch so that fruit may be borne. Salvation, which is union with Christ, and the perfect standing which it secures continue always, since such benefits depend only on the believer's position in Christ. However, the believer is ever facing the facts of his own weakness and of the masterful foes which are against him; and only by keeping Christ's commandments, which means adjustment to His perfect will (cf. John 15:10), is the way kept clear for the needed divine power to flow into the believer as sap flows into the branch. This passage illustrates the importance of a right objective and method in the Christian's life if he is to be made spiritual through the imparted divine energy. Though in perfect and unalterable union with Christ, the believer will be fruitless except he remains in that obedient relation to Christ wherein the power of the Spirit may be realized in and through him. Christ declared in verse 10 that He kept His Father's commandments and abode in His love, and this is asserted as the pattern for the believer thus to abide in Him. Certainly, Christ was not striving to keep saved by doing anything required to that end; He did, however, keep in perfect communion with His Father through obedience to His will. Union with Christ is God's undertaking and is wrought for, and continues as the portion of, the one who merely believes; communion is the believer's undertaking—a specific plan of life which calls for an intelligent purpose and method of life, adapted to the precise will of God, on the part of the one who is saved.

## II. PRESCRIBED OBLIGATIONS

Because of the superhuman requirements which rest upon the believer, the Spirit's filling unto supernatural power is demanded. This anticipates the right and true understanding of the Scriptures as well as the needed adjustments which secure divine power.

Three times the Apostle has divided the human family into threefold classification. (1) As respects their essential character in relation to God, he identifies the unsaved Gentiles as the "Uncircumcision," and declares of them, "That at that time ye were without Christ, being aliens from the commonwealth of Israel, and strangers from the covenants of promise, having no hope, and without God in the world" (Eph. 2:12). In the same context (Eph. 2:11–12), the Apostle distinguishes the Jew as one who has received the "Circumcision in the flesh made by hands," which physical change sealed to the Jew the covenant promises of Jehovah (cf. Gen. 17:11). But in addition the same Apostle states that the Christian is set apart with a "circumcision made without hands" (Col. 2:11), which Scripture, as before noted, recognizes his vital union with Christ whereby he is partaking of all heavenly blessings, having been identified with Christ in His death, burial, and resurrection. The same threefold division is set forth in 1 Corinthians 10:32, which reads: "Give none offence, neither to the Jews, nor to the Gentiles, nor to the church of God." (2) As respects their supernatural relationships they are classified according to their attitude toward the written Word of God. In this, as earlier pointed out, they are *natural* men, which is a reference to the unsaved of this age whether Jew or Gentile, *carnal* men, which term identifies the saved man, Jew or Gentile, who is living or walking after the flesh, and *spiritual* men, which terminology indicates the Jew or Gentile who is walking with God in subjection to His revealed will and in dependence upon His power. (3) Finally, the Apostle divides men into three classes in respect to the exercise of divine law or authority over them. In 1 Corinthians 9:20–21 this is disclosed, which passage reads: "And unto the Jews I became as a Jew, that I might gain the Jews; to them that are under the law, as under the law, that I might gain them that are under the law; to them that are without law, as without law, (being not without law to God, but under the law to Christ,) that I might gain them that are without law." In this grouping, first the unsaved Gentiles of all ages and unsaved Jews of the present age are to be recognized as ones who are not under the Mosaic Law; but then at the time of the writing of the Scriptures in previous centuries all Jews had, and indeed until nearly that time when apostolic or Christian Scripture began to be formulated, their rightful place under the law. This, the old classification of Jews under the law, constitutes the second division here—men under the law. In the present age, to be sure, in which the Jew is recognized along with the Gentile as one without merit before God, all mankind is equally without law. The third division of men is that of Christians, whether Jew or Gentile, in which group the Apostle places himself as one who is neither under the law nor without the law but the rather *inlawed to Christ*. "The law of Christ" (cf. Gal. 6:2) is contained in His teachings of Christians about their responsibility as having been perfected through the saving grace of God. The phrase "my commandments," significantly enough, was not used by Christ until His Upper Room Discourse. The body of truth included therein is augmented by that which is presented in the epistles of the New Testament, written as they were by men commissioned unto the very task by Christ. All together there is presented a peculiar obligation adjusted in character to the perfection which the believer sustains in Christ. Never by one exception is this ground of appeal ignored. Full recognition is taken of the revelation that the least of believers is partaking of the πλήρωμα of the Godhead (cf. John 1:16; Col. 1:19; 2:9–10). The directing of the life of one already complete in Christ is technical to the last degree; yet all this has been unobserved to a distressing extent by theologians of past generations. These grace teachings are clear and apparent, and their neglect or the persistent confusion of them with other relationships cannot easily be explained.

The Holy Spirit in enabling the child of God to fulfill all the will of the Father for him in his daily life can be expected to work advantageously only within the range of that which God requires of the believer. If through misguided ignorance the Christian sets himself to keep the Mosaic order when God has faithfully warned him that the keeping of the law is not His will for him and that God has saved him from the law, he must not expect any cooperation of the Holy Spirit in pursuing such a course of error. Naturally, the Bible does not address itself to people who lived and whose obligations were completed before its text was written; however, it does address itself to the people of the age of law which began with Moses and ended with the death of Christ, it does address itself to people of the present age, and it also contemplates an age to come. Thus altogether three great rules of life are written down and each corresponds perfectly with the character of the divine purpose in the age to which it is related. Covenantism, which has molded the major theological conceptions for many generations, recognizes no distinctions as to ages, therefore can allow for no distinctions between law and grace. This dominating attitude of Covenantism must account for the utter neglect of life truth in all their works on theology. No more representative theological dictum from the Covenant viewpoint has been formed than the Westminster Confession of Faith, which valuable and important document recognizes life truth only to the point of imposing the Ten Commandments on Christians as their sole obligation, and in spite of the teachings of the New Testament which assert that the law was never given to Gentile or Christian and that, as said before, the latter has been saved and delivered from it (cf. John 1:16–17; Acts 15:23–29; Rom. 6:14; 7:1–6; 2 Cor. 3:11, 13; Gal. 3:23–25). Let it be restated that the Holy Spirit can be depended upon to enable the believer only as the believer's life and effort are conformed to God's will and plan for him in this age.

## III. DEPENDENCE UPON THE SPIRIT

Yet again it needs to be emphasized that the divine plan for the believer's daily life incorporates the issue of method by which that life shall be lived. Two procedures are possible, namely, dependence upon one's own ability and dependence upon the power of the indwelling Spirit. These two methods are wholly incompatible, or, to use the Apostle's language, they are "contrary the one to the other" (Gal. 5:17). Any attempt to combine two opposing principles will end in failure. Certainly any attempt to live by heavenly standards when depending upon human resources will be a disappointment even though motivated by the greatest sincerity. It is the work of the Holy Spirit to empower the believer, not only in choosing an intelligent manner of life which does not attempt to establish union with Christ but rather understands the need to maintain communion with Christ, never attempting other rules of life than that addressed to the heavenly citizen, but also in confronting the vicissitudes of daily life as he commits it all to Him with the consciousness of man's inability and of His infinite ability. Thus is set forth the fundamental truth that the faith method of life, which stands wholly apart from human strength, is that alone which secures or realizes the Spirit's power and achievement.

## IV. WORD OF GOD

The attitude of any person toward the Word of God is a certain indication of the innermost character and reality of that person's spiritual state. Recognizing this basic truth the Apostle states that all men of this age are divided, as before indicated, into three classes, namely, (a) the natural man—the *ψυχικός* man who is unregenerate, (b) the spiritual man—the *πνευματικός* man who is saved and empowered by the Holy Spirit, and (c) the carnal man—the *σαρκικός* man who is regenerated as being in Christ, but who is living in the sphere of the flesh. So vital is this grouping of all men that the Scriptures bearing on these distinctions should be given specific attention. The natural man, it will be seen, cannot know the things of the Spirit of God, the spiritual man discerns all things, and the carnal man can have only the milk of the Word and cannot have the "strong meat." The central passage reads, "But the natural man receiveth not the things of the Spirit of God: for they are foolishness unto him: neither can he know them, because they are spiritually discerned. But he that is spiritual judgeth all things, yet he himself is judged of no man. For who hath known the mind of the Lord, that he may instruct him? But we have the mind of Christ. And I, brethren, could not speak unto you as unto spiritual, but as unto carnal, even as unto babes in Christ. I have fed you with milk, and not with meat: for hitherto ye were not able to bear it, neither yet now are ye able. For ye are yet carnal: for whereas there is among you envying, and strife, and divisions, are ye not carnal, and walk as men?" (1 Cor. 2:14—3:3). The declaration respecting the natural man regarding his incapacity to know the things of God is of great import as an explanation of the religious situation in the modern world. No injury to the effect of God's truth is more harmful in its extent than that wrought by unregenerate men who, on the ground of human scholarship, are allowed to interpret and define the things of God. Men can hardly be saved who deny the only ground upon which any soul may be redeemed. That great denominations, once known as Christian, are under the direction of educated men who renounce the very ground of salvation by grace through the death of Christ is obvious. Instructors in colleges and universities are almost without exception committed to an unproved hypothesis which brands God's Word as untrue and attempts an inane solution of the problem of origin only because of the basic incapacity of the natural, unregenerate man to receive the things of the Spirit of God. These things are "foolishness" to the unsaved, yet highly educated, man and he cannot—not being in vital relation to the Spirit of God—know them. It still remains true that salvation with all the light it imparts is gained only through faith in a crucified and risen Savior, and no amount of education or ecclesiastical prominence will serve to dispel the spiritual darkness of unregenerateness. On all spiritual themes the opinion and dictum of the unsaved are not only as nugatory as the prattle of a child, but become as injurious as the stand and influence of the false teacher can make them. The basic need of unregenerate man is not education or culture—of great value as they are in their place—but salvation. A sincere student will judge the opinions and utterances of a man on the ground of his primary consideration—is he saved and thus entitled to speak as one enlightened by the Holy Spirit?

The spiritual man is the theme of the remainder of this volume. Suffice it to say at this point that he is called spiritual because he manifests a right adjustment to the Holy Spirit who indwells him. This manifestation includes the enlightenment given to such by which the spiritual man may come to know the Word of God.

The carnal man, to whom a more extended consideration will yet be given, is such because he, though perfectly saved and safe in Christ, is, nevertheless, walking after the flesh. In the portion of the context now under contemplation which describes him (1 Cor. 3:1–3) he is addressed as a *brother*. When this title is used of a spiritual relationship it refers only to one who is definitely a child of God by a birth from above. In the same context it is asserted also that a carnal man is in Christ. These determining words must not go unobserved, because they afford the strongest possible evidence that he is saved and safe. His union with Christ is established, and since it depends on the imputed merit of Christ it can never be broken. The communion of the carnal believer, however, is disturbed by the fleshly manner of his life. More serious than all else, since he receives only the "milk of the word" he is deprived of the sanctifying power of the Scriptures and thus yields to envying, strife, and divisions. Whereas the spiritual man "walks in the Spirit," those who are carnal "walk as men," that is, as the unsaved walk. Instead of a "walk in love," they prefer divisions and separations, violating the essential command that they "keep the unity of the Spirit in the bond of peace." Of all the various evils in the Corinthian church against which the Apostle lifts his voice, the sin of sectarianism is first to be mentioned. The intense sinfulness of sin is indicated here as fully as everywhere else in the New Testament. The sectarian, then, if saved at all, is a babe in his spiritual development. Every discourse which glories in his separate grouping of professed believers is properly classed as *baby talk*. There is but one Body and one Spirit. Each Christian is called upon to love every other Christian on the basis of the unity of the one Body and the kinship in the one family of God. The fact of divisions and the promotion of them are an outward expression of the deeper sin of loveless carnality. One outstanding feature of carnality as here depicted by the Apostle is the separation of one believer from another. This is usually precipitated by the one of the two who deems himself holier than the other, being to that degree void of humility or consciousness of his own unspiritual manner of life. Aside from those specific instances when the church must exercise discipline over erring ones of their number, the carnal man may well be left confidently in the hands of God. As the Apostle warns, "Who art thou that judgest another man's servant? to his own master he standeth or falleth. Yea, he shall be holden up: for God is able to make him stand" (Rom. 14:4). A charitable attitude toward erring believers is sure to be engendered in the heart of the one who deals faithfully and truly before God with his own spiritual condition. By various terms the Bible teaches thus that there are two classes of Christians: those who "abide in Christ" and those who "abide not," those who are "walking in the light" and those who "walk in darkness," those who "walk by the Spirit" and those who "walk as men," those who "walk in newness of life" and those who "walk after the flesh," those who have the Spirit *in* and *upon* them and those who have the Spirit *in* them but not *upon* them, those who are "spiritual" and those who are "carnal," those who are "filled with the Spirit" and those who are not. All this has to do with the quality of daily life in saved people, and is in no way a contrast between the saved and the unsaved. Where there is such an emphasis in the Bible as is indicated by these distinctions there must be a corresponding reality. There is, then, the possibility of a great transition for those who are carnal into the reality of true spiritual living. The revelation concerning this possible transition, with all of its experiences and blessings, is taken seriously only by earnest believers who are faithfully seeking a God-honoring daily life. To such there is boundless joy and consolation in this gospel of deliverance, power, and victory.

It is probable that there are grades of differences within the group known as *spiritual* and within the group known as *carnal*. Some who are classed as spiritual may be more spiritual than others in their group, while some who are classed as carnal may be more carnal than others within their company; but into these shades of distinction the New Testament does not enter. This silence is reasonable. Any relationship to God which is less than a complete adjustment must of necessity be classed as carnal to some extent. It might be more accurate to state that carnality extends over a very wide range of human experience, while spirituality, though latitude be allowed for varied personalities, for varied degrees of educational discipline, and for varied environments, is, nevertheless, standardized to the extent that the experience of the Spirit's filling is accorded to all within that group. It will be remembered, however, that the aspect of the Spirit's manifestation which enters the field of Christian service must be, and is, adapted to the peculiar individual requirements that are appointed by the Holy Spirit. The believer is not an automaton, but exhibits all the seemingly infinite variations found in human characteristics and personality. Nor is he sustaining relations to a God who is no more than the embodiment of inflexible laws. As an earthly parent may recognize the peculiar temperament of an individual child, so God, but to an infinite degree of effectiveness, recognizes the whole field of issues which a particular person presents. What better interpretation can be made of the text "But if ye be led of the Spirit, ye are not under the law" (Gal. 5:18) than that the life is not only personally directed by the Holy Spirit to its last detail, but is contact with a living Person rather than mere conformity to a set of rules? No attainment in Christian experience is more effective or far-reaching in its instructive value than that of coming to know God—not merely to know about Him, but to experience the rest to the soul which such intimate acquaintance with God engenders. In this connection, the importance of not separating Matthew 11:27 from 11:28 may be seen. The passage when connected reads, "All things are delivered unto me of my Father: and no man knoweth the Son, but the Father; neither knoweth any man the Father, save the Son, and he to whomsoever the Son will reveal him. Come unto me, all ye that labour and are heavy laden, and I will give you rest." Spirituality cannot be defined properly as conformity to a set of rules; it is communion, cooperation, and compliance with a sovereign Person. The principle of law may easily become a major hindrance to the spiritual life. God does indicate in His Word that particular manner of life which becomes the spiritual believer and God recognizes the believer's limitations in understanding; but it may be noted too that all such directions for proper conduct may be observed by the Christian rather unwillingly, or out of a sense of necessity, or without the slightest consciousness of a relation to God as His child. To be a spiritual Christian, however, is to walk with God in unbroken, vital companionship and communion in the enabling power of the Holy Spirit.

## V. A SPIRITUAL TRANSFORMATION

As there is a great transition from the estate of the unsaved to that of the saved, there is also a transition for the Christian from the carnal to the spiritual state. The former change is wrought by God in answer to saving faith in Christ, while the latter is brought about by a natural release of the Spirit's power in the believer when needed adjustments are made, which power has all been possessed though not necessarily experienced from the moment of salvation. It is possible that the one saved through faith may, at the same time, be yielded to God and thus enter at once upon a true spiritual experience; but a spiritual state is not a once-for-all achievement: it must be sustained by the Spirit's renewal. It would seem that the Apostle Paul entered into a Spirit-filled experience three days after he was saved and in connection with the visit of Ananias (Acts 9:17–18); yet the Apostle did not fully understand the conditions upon which he might be spiritual, from all appearances, since at a later time he passed through the experience recorded in Romans, chapter 7. There he states, "But how to perform that which is good I find not."

A serious distortion of doctrine has been promoted by zealous but unthinking persons to the effect that the terms of salvation must include, in addition to faith in Christ, a complete surrender to His authority. As important as it is in its place, however, surrender is an issue which belongs only to the child of God. Advocates of this idealism should consider that the demand for surrender—as is true of every other human obligation which men are wont to add to simple faith—does not once appear in the upwards of one hundred and fifty passages in which salvation is said to depend on faith or belief alone. If surrender, or any other condition, is added, these passages become not only wholly inadequate but actually misleading. John 3:16 does not read "For God so loved the world, that he gave his only begotten Son, that whosoever believeth in him *and surrenders to him* should not perish, but have everlasting life," yet those words or their equivalent must be added there as in all other similar Scriptures if any such text is to be depended upon for directions concerning the way of salvation. It remains true, consequently, that there are well-defined conditions upon which the carnal believer may become spiritual and that these are wholly unrelated to the one requirement by which those who are lost may be saved. The fact that Christians are too often carnal is recognized and deplored, and sermonic exhortations are many times addressed to them; but there is little teaching to show *how* the carnal believer may become spiritual. The Apostle surely did not lack for ideals or for desire to realize them when he said, "But how to perform that which is good I find not." Still, he had not at the time gained the knowledge of God's plan and provision for the spiritual life. This, indeed, was later revealed to him since he, above all others, has set forth the spiritual life in all its marvelous reality and declared the precise conditions upon which it may be experienced.

## VI. THE TERMINOLOGY USED

Three phrases are used in the Word of God to represent the Spirit-filled life, namely, *the Spirit upon you, he that is spiritual,* and *filled with the Spirit.* In the first instance—the Spirit upon you—a distinction is to be made between the Spirit dwelling in the believer and His coming upon the Christian. Anticipating the relationship that would obtain between the Holy Spirit and the believer after His coming into the world on Pentecost and declaring the relationship which the Holy Spirit then sustained to the disciples throughout the dispensation in which He was speaking, Christ said: "And I will pray the Father, and he shall give you another Comforter, that he may abide with you for ever; even the Spirit of truth; whom the world cannot receive, because it seeth him not, neither knoweth him: but ye know him; for he dwelleth with you, and shall be in you" (John 14:16–17). To this is to be added the further instructions given the disciples after He had breathed on them and said "Receive ye the Holy Ghost" (John 20:22), namely, that they were to tarry in Jerusalem—that is, undertake no mission or service—until the Spirit came *upon* them (Luke 24:49). Later, He said that, the Spirit coming *upon* them, they would be His witnesses unto the uttermost part of the earth (Acts 1:8). The reference to the Spirit descending *upon* the believer is thus seen to be identical with His filling. In the second instance—he that is spiritual—reference is made to the estate of the one who is Spirit-filled. He alone is to be esteemed spiritual (1 Cor. 2:15). In the third instance—filled with the Spirit—the phrase indicates a full and unrestrained manifestation of the indwelling Spirit. The Spirit's filling is not a receiving of the Holy Spirit since that was accomplished as a part of salvation, nor is it a receiving of more of the Spirit. He is a Person and no person is subject to subdivision, nor could a person be more or less present in any given location. By a more complete release to Him of the believer's life and being, however, the Holy Spirit who indwells the believer may secure a larger sphere of manifestation. To be filled with the Spirit is to have the Spirit fulfilling all that He came into the heart to do. This truth is far removed from the notion that the Holy Spirit is to be received as "a second work of grace" or "a second blessing." The Spirit-filled life is a realization in actual experience of what has been possessed from the moment one is saved. Ephesians 1:3 reveals the truth that every spiritual blessing is secured when one is saved. That verse reads: "Blessed be the God and Father of our Lord Jesus Christ, who hath blessed us with all spiritual blessings in heavenly places in Christ." Of all the five ministries of the Spirit to the believer—regenerating, indwelling, sealing, baptizing, and filling—the last-named is alone commanded and expected of the believer. The implication is that this ministry, quite unlike the other four, depends upon human cooperation and adjustment. It is clear that beyond the one responsibility of believing on Christ unto salvation, no obligation rests upon the Christian respecting the first four ministries named. The command to be filled with the Spirit (Eph. 5:18), being addressed to the child of God, not only indicates that it is an experience subsequent to salvation, but that the Christian's own faithfulness determines the degree of filling. In the preceding chapter of this volume the filling of the Spirit has been contrasted with the baptism with the Spirit. Because of the prevalent confusion of these ministries of the Holy Spirit, especial emphasis has been laid upon the distinction. Little more need be added to what has already been presented other than to point out again the facts that the Spirit's baptism is wrought of God for all believers when they believe, that it engenders no corresponding experience by which its reality may be identified, and that it is in no way related to Christian service or action. Over against this set of facts are the truths that the filling of the Spirit depends upon human faithfulness, that not all believers are so yielded to God as to be filled, that it is the source of all right Christian experience, and that it is the sufficient force behind all Christian life and service. Here it should be noted that in His filling the Holy Spirit causes the one whom He rules to manifest the individual's own personality, to exercise the gifts for service possessed by him—divinely bestowed as they are, and to achieve the work and to fill the place which God has designed for him. Too often it has been supposed that the Spirit-filled life would cause one to conform to some standardized experience, manner of life, or service. Yet there is nothing related to the believer more vital or more to be cherished than individuality. It is not the Spirit's procedure in and through the believer to disannul individuality, but to work through individuality to the glory of God. The Spirit-filled believer is God's normal, though he may not be God's usual, Christian. To be Spirit-filled is not to have gained some extraordinary concession from God; it is to be enabled normally to fulfill the will of God in the sphere of that which is divinely intended for each individual. It could not itself be extraordinary since it is enjoined upon every Christian and, apart from it, all must remain carnal. It is everywhere to be seen in the New Testament that God expects all who witness for Him to be empowered for this service by the filling of the Spirit. And so while there may be sacrifice in the path, the prevailing note for Spirit-filled men is that of joyous experience and overflowing peace. According to Romans 12:2 the yielded life makes full proof of the good, acceptable, and perfect will of God. God's dealing with the early church is certainly the pattern for all believers since the records have been incorporated into the Sacred Text with that obvious purpose. From these records it will be seen that it is the divine ideal for each individual believer to be filled with the Spirit before beginning any Christian service; and as the early Christians were refilled in preparation for each mission, in like manner it should be true with believers today. As before noted, the disciples were bidden to tarry in Jerusalem until they be endued with power from on high (Luke 24:49). It was a waiting until the Spirit came *upon* them. To them the Savior said: "Ye shall receive power, after that the Holy Ghost is come upon you" (Acts 1:8). The significant words, "They were all filled with the Holy Ghost," precede the record of each important service they rendered. The entire family—Zacharias, Elisabeth, and John the Baptist—are all said to have been filled with the Spirit; and unto Christ in the sphere of His humanity—which humanity is the most definite example left for the believer—the Spirit was given without measure (John 3:34), and the phrase, He "being full of the Holy Ghost" (Luke 4:1), qualifies all the things that He did.

In the light of examples which are set before the Christian and of the heaven-high calling he has respecting the character of his daily life, it is not strange that all without exception are commanded to be filled with the Spirit.

In concluding this extended introduction to the more detailed consideration of the Spirit-filled life to follow, it is important to note that three times in the New Testament the effect of strong drink is put over against the Spirit-filled life (Luke 1:15; Acts 2:12–21; Eph. 5:18). As strong drink stimulates the body's physical forces and men are prone to turn to it for help over the difficult places, so the child of God, facing what seems like an impossible responsibility in his heavenly walk and service, is directed to the Spirit as the source of all sufficiency. Every moment in a spiritual life is one of unmeasured need and superhuman demands, and the supply of enabling power or grace must be constantly received and employed. "As thy days, so shall thy strength be." To be filled with the Spirit is to have the Spirit fulfilling in us all that God intended Him to do when God placed Him there. To be filled is not the problem of getting *more* of the Spirit: it is rather the problem of the Spirit getting *more* of Christians. None shall ever have *more* of the Spirit than the anointing which every true Christian has received. On the other hand, the Spirit may get control of all of the believer and thus be able to manifest in him the life and character of Christ. A spiritual person, then, is one who experiences the divine purpose and plan in his daily life through the power of the indwelling Spirit. The character of that life will be such as to manifest Christ. The root cause of that life will be nothing less than the unhindered indwelling Spirit (Eph. 3:16–21; 2 Cor. 3:18). The New Testament is clear respecting just what the Spirit would produce in a fully adjusted life, and all of this revelation taken together forms the Bible definition of spirituality. These undertakings in a believer's life are distinctly assigned to the Spirit, and so are His manifestations in and through the Christian.

There is a twofold development to the Spirit's work in and through the Christian, namely, the negative aspect and the positive aspect. Following the present introduction without more delay, these two aspects will be considered in successive chapters.

## CHAPTER XIII

# POWER TO OVERCOME EVIL

THE INDIVIDUAL is a Christian when rightly related to Christ; the Christian is spiritual when rightly related to the Spirit. Spirituality contemplates two achievements, namely, overcoming evil and promoting that which is good in the believer's life and experience. The one is negative—a disannulling of evil, the other is positive—a realization of the supernatural qualities and accomplishments which belong to a superhuman manner of life. Though so widely different in their immediate aim, both lines of work are essential and to some extent inseparable, though it is quite conceivable that a deliverance from evil might be attained without also a manifestation of the Spirit's power in the sphere of vital achievements for good. The reverse surely could not be true, that is, the experience of the Spirit's power for good would not be enjoyed if evil were not overcome to some degree. But on the other hand it is hardly to be expected that the Holy Spirit, when free to work in the child of God, would not do all that He desires; and both aspects of spirituality, to be sure, belong to His undertaking. Here arises what seems to be a paradox: Evil cannot be overcome apart from the energizing power of the Spirit, yet all this latent power cannot be experienced where evil is not being overcome. The answer to this problem is found in the truth that the Holy Spirit who indwells, when trusted to do so, will accomplish both ends of spirituality and in such relation to Himself as may be necessary. No burden, therefore, is placed upon the Christian to order or arrange respecting the Spirit's undertakings; the Christian is rather enjoined to maintain nothing but a right dependence upon the Spirit regarding all His work in the individual heart. Since evil is ever arising in the heart because of the active power of the sin nature, the power of the Holy Spirit is ever needed to overcome it; and since the obligation to live and serve to the glory of God is always present, the same enabling power of the Spirit is unceasingly required. A poorly thought-out and eccentric notion obtains, namely, that spirituality is achieved when there is a cessation of some outward forms of evil, that spirituality consists in what one does *not* do. Spirituality, however, is not suppression alone; it is also expression. It is not only restraining self; it is the outliving of Christ who indwells. The unregenerate man would not be saved if he ceased sinning; he would still be without the new birth. The Christian would not become spiritual should he abstain from worldliness; he would lack the positive manifestations of the Spirit. Spirituality is primarily an output, a vital living, and a fruitful service for God. However, both the negative and the positive aspects of the spiritual life are essential and each must be given due consideration here. The central passage, to which reference must often be made, is Galatians 5:16–23. In this Scripture there is first an unfolding of the Spirit's work toward the evil flesh and in spite of all the opposition that the flesh engenders. This portion reads, "This I say then, Walk in the Spirit, and ye shall not fulfil the lust of the flesh. For the flesh lusteth against the Spirit, and the Spirit against the flesh: and these are contrary the one to the other: so that ye cannot do the things that ye would. But if ye be led of the Spirit, ye are not under the law. Now the works of the flesh are manifest, which are these; Adultery, fornication, uncleanness, lasciviousness, idolatry, witchcraft, hatred, variance, emulations, wrath, strife, seditions, heresies, envyings, murders, drunkenness, revellings, and such like: of the which I tell you before, as I have also told you in time past, that they which do such things shall not inherit the kingdom of God" (Gal. 5:16–21). Over against this, the portion which records a positive, constructive, spiritual output from the believer's life wrought by the Spirit reads: "But the fruit of the Spirit is love, joy, peace, longsuffering, gentleness, goodness, faith, meekness, temperance: against such there is no law" (Gal. 5:22–23). Attention may now be given to one of these features of a spiritual life.

The Christian experiences an unceasing, simultaneous, threefold conflict—with the world, the flesh, and the devil. The Christian's life is likened to a race, a walk, and a warfare. In the race (Heb. 12:1–2) the weights which the world would impose must be laid aside, in the walk (Rom. 8:4; Gal. 5:16–17) the power of the flesh is to be overcome, and in the warfare (Eph. 6:10–12) Satan and his hosts are to be vanquished. The conflict with the world is outward and calls for drastic separation therefrom, the conflict with the flesh is inward and calls for a complete reliance upon divine strength and for an intelligent and worthy understanding of the innermost forces of human life, the conflict with Satan is largely in spiritual realms and involves the same utter dependence upon the sufficient power of the indwelling Spirit. Satan is the most powerful, the most iniquitous, the most despotic, the most delusive, and the most deadly foe. Conflict with the world is against influences, conflict with the flesh is against inward desires, but conflict with Satan is against a person, unrelenting and cruel, a person who, were he not compelled to gain permission from God for all that he does toward the saints (cf. Job 1:11–12), would destroy every Christian in a moment of time. It is no meaningless figure of speech which declares that Satan as a roaring lion goes about seeking whom he may devour. At no moment of life is the child of God free from anyone of these foes, at no moment of life is he able to face even one of these foes, and at no moment of life is he without the infinite enablement of the indwelling Holy Spirit who is given to him as his resource in this immeasurable impact against evil. Christ said, "Without me ye can do nothing" (John 15:5). Over against this, as the other side of the picture, the Apostle declares, "I can do all things through Christ which strengtheneth me" (Phil. 4:13). Again, he declares, "For the law of the Spirit of life in Christ Jesus hath made me free from the law of sin and death" (Rom. 8:2). Not one of these foes is superior to the Holy Spirit. To discover this, to believe this, and to claim His sufficiency by an attitude of faith is the key to a victorious, God-honoring life. It is an *attitude* of faith and not one act either of faith or crisis experience. Fighting "the good fight of faith" means to maintain a reliance upon the Spirit to fight the foe. This conflict continues as long as there is a foe. Never in this life is the influence of the world eradicated, never is that of the flesh, and never is that of Satan. These foes may well be given an individual and more comprehensive examination.

## I. THE WORLD

Second in scope only to the revealed truth regarding Satan is the confusion, ignorance, and misunderstanding which obtain relative to the facts disclosed in the New Testament about the Satan-ruled, *cosmos* world system. The truth respecting Satan and his *cosmos* system is clearly set forth in the Scriptures; in spite of this, far more than a normal neglect and perversion of these doctrines exists. By this distortion of truth much danger is engendered for the believer lest he himself, reflecting the ignorance of his day, be unaware of the nature, power, and design of these foes. The truth respecting Satan and his world system has been examined at length under Satanology, a subdivision of Angelology. A return to the contemplation of these doctrines is required in the order and course of this chapter.

In the New Testament, the English word *world* is a translation, for the most part, of three widely different Greek terms: *αἰών*, used forty-one times when referring to time, denotes an age; *οἰκουμένη*, used fourteen times, denotes the inhabited earth; and *κόσμος*, used one hundred and eighty-six times, indicates a vast world system. The word *cosmos* (its opposite is chaos) means an order, system, and arrangement which is such because it is so determined by a master mind. Over this system is the one whom Christ three times designated "the prince of this world" (John 12:31; 14:30; 16:11). As before set forth at length, the world system is that project the realization of which actuated Satan in the beginning when he departed from the will of God (John 8:44; Isa. 14:12–14), which world system God has permitted Satan to realize to the end that it may be judged, along with its prince, for what it will have demonstrated itself to be. Beyond and aside from the evident divine permission for this system to run its course, including the evil which it incorporates, God is exercising His own undiminished authority over His creation. Strictly speaking, Satan has created nothing. All that he utilizes, he has appropriated from that which is in no way his own. The precise knowledge of all that enters into the satanic *cosmos* system will be gained only as the contexts are examined in which the word *cosmos* occurs. It is this, the specific study of what is one of the greatest doctrines of the New Testament, which many worthy men have failed to pursue; and, because this body of truth is so little apprehended, the great company of believers are unaware of the enmity which the world system sustains toward God and His people. James writes: "Ye adulterers and adulteresses, know ye not that the friendship of the world is enmity with God? whosoever therefore will be a friend of the world is the enemy of God" (James 4:4). This reference to adultery is tied in here with a spiritual usage and therefore means a forsaking of right love and loyalty toward God, substituting in their place the things of this Satan-ruled world. James says again that Christian responsibility is a call to keep oneself "unspotted" from the world (1:27). It is of great advantage to the Christian to know the nature and extent of the *cosmos* world system. It includes governments ruled by force and motivated by greed (Matt. 4:8–9; Luke 4:5–6); yet the believer must live under, and to a large extent share in, and pray for these governments. Their laws are said to be ordained of God. This satanic system has its educational standards and ideals which resist and ignore every fact and feature of revelation. "The world by wisdom knew not God" (1 Cor. 1:21); yet the child of

God must sustain a relation to the world system and its education in various ways. This world system professes to defend, or at least to tolerate, its own religious ideals, which ideals are no more than a recognition of ethics coupled with a denial of every feature of the saving grace of God made possible through the sacrificial blood of Christ; yet the believer is called upon to associate with men who thus interpret the Christian faith and to keep in such relation to them that he can testify to them. Similarly, the world system presents its own sort of entertainment. The world and "worldly" Christians turn to so-called "worldly" things because they discover in them an anesthetic to deaden the pain of an empty heart and life. The anesthetic, which is often quite innocent in itself, is not so serious a matter as the empty heart and life. Little is gained toward true spirituality when would-be soul doctors have succeeded in persuading the afflicted to get on without the anesthetic. If these instructors do not present the reality of such consolation and filling for heart and life as God has provided, the condition will not be improved. How misleading is the theory that to be spiritual one must abandon play, diversion, and helpful amusement! Such a conception of spirituality is born of a morbid human conscience. It is foreign to the Word of God. It is a device of Satan to make the blessings of God seem abhorrent to young people who are overflowing with physical life and energy. It is to be regretted that there are those who in blindness are so emphasizing the negatives of Christian truth as to create the impression that spirituality is opposed to joy, liberty, and naturalness of expression in thought and life when such are in the Spirit. Spirituality is not a pious pose. It is not merely a "Thou shalt not," "Thou shalt." It flings open the doors into the eternal blessedness, energies, and resources of God. It is a serious thing to remove the element of relaxation and play from any life. We cannot be normal physically, mentally, or spiritually, if we neglect this vital factor in human life. God has provided so well that our joy can be full. It is also to be noted that one of the characteristics of true spirituality calls for it to supersede lesser desires and issues. The Biblical, as well as practical, cure for "worldliness" among Christians is so to fill the heart and life with the eternal blessings of God that there will be a joyous preoccupation and absentmindedness relative to unspiritual things. A dead leaf that may have clung to the twig through the external, raging storms of winter will silently fall to the ground when the new flow of sap from within has begun in the spring. The leaf falls because there is a new manifestation of life pressing from within outward. A dead leaf cannot remain where a new bud is springing, nor can worldliness remain where the blessings of the Spirit are flowing. The preacher is not called upon to preach against "dead leaves." He has a message of the imperishable spring. It is of the outflow of the limitless life of God. When by the Spirit ye are walking, ye *cannot* do the things that ye otherwise would.

The line of demarcation between the things of God and the things of the *cosmos* world is not always easily discerned. At this point, it is imperative that the Christian should be led of the Spirit. However, the conflict with the world, with its glitter, tinsel, and delusions, is very real. The Apostle John writes: "Love not the world, neither the things that are in the world. If any man love the world, the love of the Father is not in him. For all that is in the world, the lust of the flesh, and the lust of the eyes, and the pride of life, is not of the Father, but is of the world. And the world passeth away, and the lust thereof: but he that doeth the will of God abideth for ever" (1 John 2:15–17). The child of God is not of this sort of world. Twice in His last prayer connected with the upper room Christ said: "They are not of the world, even as I am not of the world" (John 17:14, 16). So, again: "We know that we are of God, and the whole world lieth in the evil one" (1 John 5:19, R.V.). It therefore becomes the Christian to live in separation from the world. This he can do only through being empowered and directed constantly by the Holy Spirit. John again declares in his first epistle, "For whatsoever is born of God overcometh the world: and this is the victory that overcometh the world, even our faith. Who is he that overcometh the world, but he that believeth that Jesus is the Son of God?" (5:4–5). It is evident from the fact John refers in verse 5 to faith in the Son of God as the way to victory over the world that he is there contemplating the Christian's deliverance from the *cosmos* world system, which deliverance is wrought when the Christian is saved (cf. Col. 1:13); but it is equally true to say it is by faith or confidence in the power of God that he is delivered from the influence of the *cosmos* world from day to day. The latter deliverance from the world day by day seems to be that to which reference is made in the last half of verse 4, "and this is the victory that overcometh the world, even our faith." Since the line of demarcation between the believer's spiritual walk and the choice of the *cosmos* world often is so difficult to draw, and because the world's attractions and demands are so impelling if not prevailing, divine sufficiency must be claimed at all times and under all circumstances.

## II. THE FLESH

In some instances the word σάρξ, translated *flesh,* is synonymous with the word σῶμα, translated *body;* the word *flesh* is more often employed with reference to the whole of the unregenerate man—spirit, soul, and body. It thus assumes an ethical and psychological meaning which does not inhere in the word *body.* A physical body is denominated *flesh* whether dead or alive, whereas the term *flesh* in its ethical meaning includes not only the body but also that which makes it a living thing—the unseen reality which expresses and manifests itself through the body. A very complex situation is thus confronted wherein the living factors of human existence—spirit, soul, Adamic nature, heart, kidneys, mind, sensibility, will, and conscience—are all integral parts. This complexity, which in some features of it defies human analysis, has had the required treatment under Anthropology previously. Thus —to repeat briefly from Volume II—as a feature of the immaterial part of man is included a nature which is prone to sin. It is in reality the original human nature which has been injured, and as such has been reproduced throughout all succeeding generations. By his first sin the first man became at once a different order of being than that which he was made by creation, and the law of procreation obtained, which is to the effect that the species reproduces after its kind. That Adam's offspring was fallen is confirmed and demonstrated by the act of murder on the part of his first-born. Being derived from Adam, this fallen nature is rightfully termed *the Adamic nature.* Failure to recognize this nature as an unalterable and universal feature in all human existence does not change the fact, and it is the part of wisdom to acknowledge it and should be the plan of one's life to be adjusted to it. Four more or less common errors should be identified and avoided: (1) that man is not evil by nature, (2) that children are born into the world unfallen, (3) that the Adamic nature may be eradicated, and (4) that the Adamic nature may be controlled by the power of the human determination and will. Being an integral part of a human being, this evil nature cannot and will not be dismissed until the body itself in which it functions is redeemed, or until the separation between the body and the immaterial elements of soul and spirit is achieved by death. The Adamic nature is the dominating factor in all that enters into the flesh. That nature remains undiminished and unimpaired in each believer after he is saved and becomes one of the three great foes of the spiritual life.

With the reception of the divine nature which is imparted through regeneration, the Christian becomes a complex being, possessing two natures—not, two personalities—with a corresponding complexity of life, for unless the evil nature is controlled by more than human competency it will assert itself to the dishonor of God. It is not within the range of human will power, even when fortified by the best resolutions, to control the Adamic nature. The conflict must be turned over to the indwelling Holy Spirit with constant and unrelenting faithfulness. To gain the victory the believer must maintain an *attitude* of faith to the end that he may be saved from the reigning power of sin, just as he was saved by an *act* of faith from the guilt and penalty of sin. In every aspect of the situation it is plain that one must live by faith. The life which a justified person should live is, because of his superior foes and because of his own impotency, an impossibility apart from the divine enablement which is realized in answer to faith. Salvation into safety from eternal judgment and salvation into sanctity are both a work of God. Human determination can avail no more in the one than in the other. The fact that the unregenerate possess a fallen nature is generally admitted. The misunderstanding is with regard to the Christian. The Bible teaching is clear, and yet some professing Christians are misled into assuming that they do not any longer possess the tendency to sin. This question may be discussed both from the experimental and from the Biblical standpoint. Experimentally, the most saintly of God's children have been conscious of the presence and power of a fallen nature. This may be called the normal consciousness of the devout believer. Such a consciousness is not an evidence of immaturity: it is rather the evidence of a true humility and clear vision of one's own heart. It does not imply a lack of fellowship with God occasioned by grieving of the Holy Spirit through sin. Who can hate sin more than the one who is *aware* of its presence and power? And who is in greater danger of its havoc in his spiritual life than the one who in unwarranted presumption has assumed that the disposition to sin has been removed? The contention that one has no disposition to sin must be based upon a shocking lack of self-knowledge respecting the motives and impulses of the heart, or, if not, such an assumption is made through failure to comprehend the true character of sin itself. If an individual can convince himself that sin is something different from *anything* he ever does or is inclined to do, beyond indeed anything he ever thinks, feels, or undertakes, he can doubtless convince himself that he has not sinned at all. If, in his own mind, one can modify the character of sin, he can, by that very process, relieve himself from the *consciousness* of sin. There are not a few such people in the world today. Truth of a spiritual nature cannot stand when based upon human experience. It must be based upon revelation. Sin is not what some prejudiced, misguided person *claims* it to be; it is what God has *revealed* it to be. Sin has been well defined, from a study of the whole testimony in the Word of God, as "any violation of, or want of conformity to, the revealed will of God." It is *missing the mark*. But what mark? Surely the *divine* standard. The believer may ask, Have I done *all* and *only* His will with motives as pure as heaven and in the unchanging faithfulness of manner characterizing the Infinite? God has provided the possibility of a perfect victory; but Christians have all too often failed in its realization. If possessed with any degree of the knowledge of God and self-knowledge, they are aware that too often they are far from sinless in the eyes of God. The consciousness of sinfulness at times in their life has been the testimony of the most spiritual believers of all generations, as they have been enabled to see the Person of God in contrast to themselves. Job, the upright in heart, abhorred himself before God. Daniel, against whom no sin is recorded, said "My comeliness was turned in me into corruption."

The central passage bearing upon the truth that the believer possesses two natures and that one of these, the sin nature, cannot be governed even by the will power of a regenerate person is found in Romans 7:15—8:4; but before the passage is quoted some general introductory words are in order. This Scripture presents a conflict between two aspects of the ego which the believer represents. The word *I* appears in two quite different and conflicting uses, but all within the one personality of the Apostle whose experience is here recorded. The controversy is real, being waged as it is between two natures—the original fallen nature which is prone to evil and which for convenience may be styled *the old,* and that which in the same person answers to his saved self and which may be called *the new*. For the time being and for the best of reasons, the saved self is hypothetically contemplated apart from the indwelling Holy Spirit. The vital question is whether a Christian, of himself and merely because he is saved, has power to contend victoriously with his sin nature. No more subtle or deceptive battle is possible. In this conflict between the saved man possessed of a new nature and his fallen nature, the saved man with his holy aims is utterly defeated. Being saved, now he has high and holy ideals, and yet because of his inability to realize these he becomes a "wretched man." Quite in contrast to this sort of battle is the conflict described in Galatians 5:16–17, which passage reads: "This I say then, Walk in the Spirit [lit., by means of the Spirit], and ye shall not fulfil the lust of the flesh. For the flesh lusteth against the Spirit, and the Spirit against the flesh: and these are contrary the one to the other: so that ye cannot do the things that ye would." Here victory over the flesh is assured if it is fought in reliance upon the Holy Spirit. In this passage it is also disclosed that the believer's old nature and the Holy Spirit are always "contrary" the one to the other. These two can never by any self-discipline of the old nature be brought into the slightest agreement. What is true respecting the disagreement between the Holy Spirit and the old nature according to Galatians 5:16–17 is equally true of the disagreement between the new nature or saved self and the old nature according to the Romans passage under consideration. Of the two passages, it should be observed that the one records a total failure and the other a total victory, the essential and impressive difference between them being that in the one instance the limited strength of the saved self has wrought in conflict with the old nature unto total defeat and that in the other instance the Holy Spirit when followed has wrought in conflict with the old nature unto total victory.

Various interpretations of Romans 7:15–25 have been advanced, all of which fail in a greater or less degree to account for the situation which the context sets forth. The more common and more erroneous type is one advanced, for example, by Philip Mauro which contends that the Scripture records here an experience of the great Apostle before he was saved. The fallacy of this interpretation is evident. No such experience could really have occurred in the Apostle's life, nor could it happen in the experience of any unregenerate person. On the contrary, the Apostle declares that before he was saved he lived in all good conscience and before the law as one blameless (Phil. 3:6). Beyond the dictation of a feeble conscience the unsaved entertain no such ideals or purposes as these of Romans 7 to walk well-pleasing to God. God is not in all their thoughts. Finally and conclusively, the same ego of Romans, chapter 7, is continued unaltered into chapter 8 and its Christian emphasis. The difference being indicated between chapters 7 and 8 is not one of salvation, but deliverance from the power of sin and death which is ever the legitimate fruit of the sin nature.

This record is plainly that of the experience of the Apostle Paul. It describes that through which he passed when with less understanding of his own self he had attempted to realize heavenly ideals in life by relying on his own strength of purpose and will. It would be inconsistent for those who have never striven by any means, false or true, to reach such ideals to look down with pity on one who is at least on the way to discover his own limitations and the limitless resources which are resident in the indwelling Spirit.

Having determined that this passage records the struggle of a child of God, it is of real value to note that he, though saved, possesses a fallen nature, and his deliverance is not by eradication but by the overcoming power of the Holy Spirit (Rom. 8:2). From each reference to the old "I" as well as from the parallel phraseology which is found in the passage, namely, "sin [nature] that dwelleth in me" (vss. 17, 20), "In me (that is, in my flesh,) dwelleth no good thing" (vs. 18), "Evil is present with me" (vs. 21), "sin which is in my members" (vs. 23), "I myself serve . . . with the flesh the law of sin" (i.e., the nature—vs. 25), it is evident that the writer possessed a fallen nature. The portion of this passage which leads up to the question "Who shall deliver me?" as read with some comment interjected is as follows: "For that which I [because of the old nature] do I [because of the new] allow not: for what I [the new] would, that do I [the old] not; but what I [the new] hate, that do I [the old]. If then I [the old] do that which I [the new] would not, I consent unto the law [or, will of God for me] that it is good. Now then it is no more I [the new] that do it, but sin [the old] that dwelleth in me. For I know that in me [the old] (that is, in my flesh,) dwelleth no good thing: for to will is present with me; but how to perform that which is good I find not. For the good that I [the new] would I [the old] do not: but the evil which I [the new] would not, that I [the old] do. Now if I [the old] do that I [the new] would not, it is no more I [the new] that do it, but sin [the old] that dwelleth in me. I find then a law [not, a law of Moses], that, when I [the new] would do good, evil [the old] is present with me. For I delight in the law of God after the inward man: but I see another law in my members [the old], warring against the law of my mind [the new, that delights in the law of God], and bringing me into captivity to the law of sin [the old] which is in my members. O wretched [Christian] man that I am! who shall deliver me from the body of this death?"

The nature of this conflict is evident as is also the complete failure being recorded. How to perform that which is good is a problem which every serious Christian faces, and while thousands of preachers are occupied with telling their congregations that they should be good, practically none are telling them *how* to be good. This failure is due to the neglect of Christian life truth in institutions where men are trained for the ministry. This neglect is not due to any want of explicit Scripture bearing upon it, or to any lack of provision on the part of God to the end that believers may be victorious in life and service. The great Apostle discovered what uncounted others have discovered, namely, that, when he would do good, evil—the sin nature with its disposition to sin—was present with him. His own efforts to realize those high ideals, which are the natural accompaniments of a regenerate estate, were ineffective. Thus in uttermost distress he cried, "O wretched man that I am! who shall deliver me from the body of this death?" By a gruesome, yet meaningful, figure the Apostle likens his fallen nature to a corpse lashed to him which he must carry wherever he goes.

The answer to the problem is twofold: he will be delivered *through* the saving work of the Lord Jesus Christ (7:25) and *by* the personal intervention of the Holy Spirit (8:2). The actual or experimental deliverance is by the Holy Spirit, but such a deliverance is made possible only through that which Christ has wrought in His death as a veritable judgment of the sin nature. Though considered earlier, this theme arises at the present point again and for careful examination, since it is a major factor in all Spirit-empowered living and service. Inasmuch as this aspect of Christ's death has constituted the central theme of the preceding chapter in the Roman letter, the Apostle is justified in building his argument upon it and that without further analysis of it. As before stated, the Holy Spirit, being holy, could not be free to do anything with the sin nature unless first it be judged by God and in a manner all-satisfying to Him. Every barrier to infinite holiness must be removed. In this connection it may be observed that the Holy Spirit is free to regenerate the unsaved without judgments or the infliction of a single blow, and on the ground of the truth that Christ died for the sins of the one whom the Spirit would save. The regenerating work of the Spirit is thus seen to be "through Jesus Christ our Lord." In like manner, Christ having died a judgment death unto the sin nature, the Spirit is free to deliver unceasingly "through Jesus Christ our Lord." Christ's death unto sin, meaning the nature, is described in Romans 6:1–10 and consists in the believer's cocrucifixion, codeath, coburial, and coresurrection with Christ. All that the believer is, even to his sin nature, came under that substitution, which substitution has become a perfect judgmental satisfaction secured on the part of God against that nature. Since the entire structure of the divinely arranged plan whereby the believer may live above the power of the flesh to the glory of God is grounded absolutely and solely on the truth that Christ died unto the sin nature as an all-satisfying judgment of it, this fact becomes at once the primary issue, the gospel of deliverance, the good news respecting a finished work for the believer which in point of importance and scope of achievement is second only to that saving work of the Holy Spirit which is based on the finished work of Christ for the unsaved. For his own sake and for the sake of others to whom he may be called to minister, the student should be aware of four immeasurable realities: (1) that every Christian being possessed as he still is of the flesh is called upon to wage a ceaseless warfare against the old nature, (2) that every Christian is indwelt by the Spirit and is thus equipped with power to be victorious over the flesh, (3) that Christ has died the judgment death required against the sin nature, and (4) that the deliverance from the power of the flesh is wrought on the principle of faith or dependence upon the Spirit rather than on the basis of any supposed resources of his own. These four truths which are so closely related are probably more misunderstood and neglected than any others within the range of Bible doctrine. Who, indeed, could estimate what would have been the history of believers as respects their character and faithfulness had these truths been given the elucidating emphasis that belongs to them! How important it is in the progress of each believer that he shall come to a right comprehension and recognition of himself, that is, of the fact and dominating force of the flesh with which he contends! Earlier in this volume, when examining the doctrine of the Spirit's baptism, the truth was presented that by such a baptism Christ is "put on" (cf. Gal. 3:27), and this upon the righteous ground of the sweet savor aspect of Christ's death. Under the present discussion the complementary truth is being contemplated, which reveals that by the death of Christ unto the judgment of the sin nature the "old man" is "put off" for Christ to be "put on." Experimentally, by means of the power of the Holy Spirit the believer may realize the negative aspect of the spiritual life, which means deliverance and preservation from evil; and positionally, by means of the Spirit he may realize the positive aspect of the spiritual life, which is the outliving of the inliving Christ (cf. Gal. 2:20).

Several major passages establish the truth that the believer's flesh with its sin nature was judged by Christ in His death, and show how it was a complete substitution to the extent that the flesh with its sin nature was as perfectly dealt with as it would have been had these features been judged in the believer himself. In truth, since there was nothing of a sin nature in Christ which related Him to a judgment death, the only explanation of His death possible in this aspect of it makes it out a substitution for others; the souls for whom He died this death (cf. Gal. 5:24), upon believing, are reckoned by God to be wholly and eternally in possession of every value of that death. Certain passages may well be considered:

*Galatians 5:24*. "And they that are Christ's have crucified the flesh with the affections and lusts."

Unlike some other references in the New Testament to the death of Christ as a judgment of the sin nature residing in the believer, the tense of the verb as translated in this verse is properly represented. In a past and completed sense the Christian's flesh, with its affections and lusts, was crucified when Christ was crucified. Far, indeed, is this removed from the idea that the believer is to attempt self-crucifixion by any means whatever; rather the great transaction is done and the responsibility resting on the Christian is to *believe* it and to *reckon* it to be true. Complete assurance can thus be gained that the way is also clear for the Holy Spirit to accomplish a full experimental deliverance from the reigning power of sin. The declaration of the passage is direct and conclusive. All that are Christ's *have* crucified the flesh. This is the divine achievement in and through the death of Christ. It is most evident that this refers to a positional rather than an experimental reality; yet how limitless is the value to the believer of the fact that the judgment is accomplished and the victory is possible! There need be no wonder if this fact is not generally understood and recognized. Even the death of Christ as the righteous basis for forgiveness and justification is slighted and misunderstood by the great mass of people; and it is probable that where a hundred have come to comprehend their dependence upon Christ's death for their salvation, there is no more than one that apprehends his dependence upon Christ's death for his sanctification as well.

*Romans 6:1–10*. Though not again quoted here, this Scripture portion should be read with care considering the fact that it is a record—the most extended and exhaustive in the New Testament—of the thing Christ did in judgment of the believer's sin nature. The context continues on, with reference to the presence and power of the sin nature and the possible victory over it, into chapter 8. Having in 6:1–10 declared the truth that a judgment has been gained against the sin nature, the Apostle in 6:11–23 urges the appropriation of this limitless benefit. In 7:1–14 he declares the merit system to be removed, so that the life now in immediate relation to Christ may actually be realized. In 7:15—8:2 the inability of the saved man in himself to overcome the sin nature is declared. The oft-repeated reference to what is described once as "sin which is in my members" indicates the presence of the sin nature in the believer: something which, though identified, is incapable of being governed by any power other than that of the indwelling Spirit. However, the way to victory is prepared since Christ has died unto the sin nature (8:3–13). The victory must be "through Jesus Christ our Lord," but will be wrought out in experience, even a freedom from the power of sin and death, by the Spirit of Life-in-Christ-Jesus. In the one verse, 8:3, a most determining declaration is made. The verse reads: "For what the law could not do, in that it was weak through the flesh, God sending his own Son in the likeness of sinful flesh, and for sin, condemned sin in the flesh." The merit system in itself is holy, just, and good. Its failure must therefore be due to the fact that it was addressed to weak flesh, which could in no wise respond to its demands. Since the merit system fails, as it always does, God moved in the direction of a new principle of living (8:4), namely, a walk after the Spirit or in dependence upon the Spirit. In such case, the whole will of God will be fulfilled *in* the believer, but never will it be fulfilled *by* the believer. Back of this achievement by the Spirit is the truth that, to make a new walk possible, God sent His own Son, who came not as One of sinful flesh, but in the likeness of the flesh of sin, and for sin, that is, the nature, thus to condemn, in the sense of bringing to judgment, that sin —the nature—which is in the flesh. Thus, as a climax at the end of so extended a Scripture bearing on the sin nature and its control, the direct statement is made that Christ brought the believer's sin nature into judgment, and on this legal and righteous ground the Holy Spirit can cause the believer to triumph to the extent of the realization of the full will of God.

Second only to salvation itself is this great reality of a God-honoring life and the divinely provided way in which it is to be attained. That the passage under consideration presents only the problem of the sin nature is obvious from the identification thereof which is repeatedly found in this portion of the Scriptures, Romans 6:1–10, and in that which follows to the end of the context, or to 8:13. The sins of the unsaved or the sins of the saved as such are not in view; it is a problem wholly related to the root of all—the sin nature and its judgment. The following expressions in this context, including 7:15–25 and 8:3, attest this: "dead to sin" (6:2), "planted [or, conjoined] together [with Him] in the likeness of his death" (6:5), "Our old man is [better, as in R.V., *was*] crucified with him" (6:6), "if we be dead with Christ" (6:8), "he died unto sin [i.e., the sin nature] once" (6:10), "Reckon ye also yourselves to be dead indeed unto sin" (6:11), "Sin shall not have dominion over you" (6:14), "sin that dwelleth in me" (7:17, 20), "sin which is in my members" (7:23), "sin in the flesh" (8:3). In no sense is this great theme a mere command for the Christian to try to crucify his own flesh, nor is it something he is called upon to enact by use of a mere ordinance. When any of these untrue interpretations are put on this and other passages, it is at the expense of what is vital and valuable beyond all computation.

The Christian is likewise, through the resurrection of Christ in the substitutionary aspect of it, brought judicially upon resurrection ground whereon death as a judgment for the sin nature is wholly past. This is the sublime reality asserted in Romans 6:7–10, which reads: "For he that is dead is freed from sin. Now if we be dead with Christ, we believe that we shall also live with him: knowing that Christ being raised from the dead dieth no more; death hath no more dominion over him. For in that he died, he died unto sin once: but in that he liveth, he liveth unto God." He that is dead, as the believer is reckoned to be in Christ's judgment death, is freed from those demands respecting the sin nature which required the penalty of death; but then one cannot have died in Christ's death without being made alive also with Him in His resurrection. As this judgment death of His hath no more claim over Christ, being accomplished to infinite completeness, Christ dieth no more, nor is there ever again need of such a death. Therefore, the grand reality emerges that, as Christ died unto the sin nature once for all, even so the one for whom it was accomplished possesses the undiminished benefit of His death to the same degree of infinity of completeness, thus to become not only one in whom the sin nature is judged and who stands freed from the penalty of such a judgment death, but one who has judicially entered the limitless sphere of Christ's resurrection life. This position in resurrection is as actual as either the death or the burial with Christ. On this new ground the believer is enjoined respecting daily life: "If ye then be risen with Christ, seek those things which are above, where Christ sitteth on the right hand of God . . . For ye are dead [as all are for whom Christ thus died], and your life is hid with Christ in God" (Col. 3:1–3).

*Colossians 2:11–12.* "In whom also ye are circumcised with the circumcision made without hands, in putting off the body of the sins of the flesh by the circumcision of Christ: buried with him in baptism, wherein also ye are risen with him through the faith of the operation of God, who hath raised him from the dead."

The right understanding of this Scripture depends very largely on recognizing that the reference to Christ's circumcision is a reference to His death—a putting off of the body or substance of the flesh as a formidable hindrance to spirituality, not Christ's physical body as Paul meant earlier in Colossians 1:22, nor the believer's physical body, but an ethical circumcision in which the sin nature which is found in the flesh is judicially deposed from its rule. As before indicated, this, since Christ Himself had no sin nature, is a case of substitution; it is Christ's judgment death in behalf of the sin nature resident in those for whom He thus died, the same threefold undertaking as Romans 6:2–4 announced, namely, codeath, coburial, and coresurrection. The death represents the execution of the demands of infinite holiness against the sin nature and is in all instances presented as a thing wholly accomplished for the believer. The burial represents the disposition of the offense of the sin nature before God, as that same burial, according to 1 Corinthians 15:3–4, is also the disposition of the offense of the sins of the world. Similarly, Romans 6:4 declares the burial to be the judicial disposition of the offense of the sin nature, itself being secured by the union of Christ and believers which the Spirit's baptism has wrought. Again no command, example, or precept concerning an ordinance is incorporated into this lofty passage of Colossians 2. The reference to baptism is a recognition of the Spirit's baptism, which alone engenders that vital union to Christ by which the believer becomes so identified with Him that he has secured unto himself all the value of Christ's crucifixion, death, burial, and resurrection.

*Ephesians 4:20–24; Colossians 3:8–10.* "But ye have not so learned Christ; if so be that ye have heard him, and have been taught by him, as the truth is in Jesus: that ye put off concerning the former conversation the old man, which is corrupt according to the deceitful lusts; and be renewed in the spirit of your mind; and that ye put on the new man, which after God is created in righteousness and true holiness. . . . But now ye also put off all these; anger, wrath, malice, blasphemy, filthy communication out of your mouth. Lie not one to another, seeing that ye have put off the old man with his deeds; and have put on the new man, which is renewed in knowledge after the image of him that created him."

The two expressions *put off* and *put on* are significant when the right form of the verb is introduced into the translation. Again it is allusion to that past, completed achievement of Christ in His death and resurrection. By that death the old man was put off (cf. Rom. 6:6; Gal. 5:24), and by that death and resurrection the provision was made whereby the new man might be put on. All of this, which is so evidently positional in character, leads with all reasonableness to the exhortations which follow immediately, asking for a God-honoring walk.

## III. THE DEVIL

Any serious and attentive reading of the Sacred Text will disclose two facts, namely, (1) that Satan is as real a being as any other character depicted in the Bible, and (2) that, though limited in what he can do because of divine restraint, he wages an unceasing and unrelenting warfare against those who are saved. Ignorance of Satan's devices, even if all but universal, is without much excuse since the Word of God presents the facts as they appear both on the human and divine sides. The general subject of Satanology, as already treated at length, incorporates the salient features of the doctrine of Satan, such as his ways, his influence over the *cosmos* world, and his enmity against believers. There it has been observed that Satan as a roaring lion goeth about seeking whom he may devour (1 Pet. 5:8). Since there is no enmity between Satan and the unsaved inasmuch as they are his subjects (cf. Col. 1:13) whom he energizes (cf. Eph. 2:2), his assault is directed only against the children of God, and, evidently, because of the divine nature which is in them. Possessing that nature, they become at once an opportunity for Satan's fiery darts to be aimed at God, with whom Satan is primarily in conflict. This onslaught against the children of God and because of the fact that they bear the nature of God is described in Ephesians 6:10–17, which reads: "Finally, my brethren, be strong in the Lord, and in the power of his might. Put on the whole armour of God, that ye may be able to stand against the wiles of the devil. For we wrestle not against flesh and blood, but against principalities, against powers, against the rulers of the darkness of this world, against spiritual wickedness in high places. Wherefore take unto you the whole armour of God, that ye may be able to withstand in the evil day, and having done all, to stand. Stand therefore, having your loins girt about with truth, and having on the breastplate of righteousness; and your feet shod with the preparation of the gospel of peace; above all, taking the shield of faith, wherewith ye shall be able to quench all the fiery darts of the wicked. And take the helmet of salvation, and the sword of the Spirit, which is the word of God." Not only, then, is this warfare real and the foe actual, but his strength surpasses the range of human ability or comprehension. Thus in the passage just cited, the Christian is directed to be cast wholly upon God, and to use the weapons and to follow the instructions God has provided. No human situation or combination of circumstances can be as hopeless as that in which the believer is placed when in conflict with Satan, if depending on human resources. As earlier declared, the conflict with the world is outward, calling, as it does, for separation therefrom, the conflict with the flesh is inward and by so much is circumscribed to take in no more than the individual, while the conflict with Satan is with a mighty person of the spirit realms. In each instance the only hope of success is based on that which the Holy Spirit supplies believers. "Greater is he that is in you, than he that is in the world" (1 John 4:4), "Whom resist stedfast in the faith" (1 Pet. 5:9), and "Be strong in the Lord" (Eph. 6:10): these are not only wise instructions, but they present the only way of victory. Neither Satan, nor the world, nor the flesh is ever eradicated, nor is the conflict ever lessened. God's provision is sufficient for a triumphal conquest even when seemingly the foes are unrestrained.

## CONCLUSION

In concluding this chapter respecting the negative aspect of the spiritual life, it may be restated that each of the three foes—the world, the flesh, and the devil—can outmatch all human ability and the victory over them is gained only by the superior power of the Holy Spirit; and this success, if it is to become a reality in daily life, calls for a peculiar and altogether different plan or principle of living. The change from self-sufficiency to dependence upon the Holy Spirit is a comprehensive one; yet at no time, even when believers are fully enabled, does the Spirit work outside the functions of the human will, nor is a consciousness experienced that another than one's own self is acting or determining. The spiritual life does not consist in the withdrawal of self, of initiative, or of the consciousness of responsibility. "It is God," the Apostle declares, "which worketh in you both to will [with your own will] and to do [with your own doing] of his good pleasure" (Phil. 2:13). Thus it is seen that the actual experience into which the believer is brought as a result of dependence upon the Holy Spirit is not a coercion of his will, but a larger and more effective exercise of it. It is not a matter of the Holy Spirit compelling the one whom He empowers to make choice of right ideals whether that one wills to do so or not; it is the deeper, more effective, and more normal achievement by the Spirit of inclining the one who depends upon Him to *will* in the sense of desire, and to *do* in the sense of complete accomplishment of that which constitutes the will of God—the good and acceptable and perfect will of God (Rom. 12:2)—or what is "according to his good pleasure." The point at issue is vitally important if the by-faith principle is to be exercised in the believer's life. It is natural to conclude that, if another than the believer himself undertakes for him the conflict with the world, the flesh, and the devil, the believer must retire from the encounter and become no more than an interested spectator; but there is no retiring from this threefold impact. The trusting Christian remains in the heat of the battle with no immediate consciousness of the presence of the Spirit on whom he depends. However, the presence of the Holy Spirit is made evident by the fact that the will is making choice of that which honors God and by the fact that victory is experienced in place of defeat. The warning should be sounded concerning every conflict related to the spiritual life, to the effect that, so far as the believer's consciousness is concerned, it is not a matter of lazy withdrawal from reality and responsibility, but rather of the zest of victory through a more effective action of the will, moved, as that will must be, by a more vivid appreciation of and vital determination to attain to every divine ideal. The conflict is not a test of physical strength in a match against an outside foe. It is a battle within and the Christian who is defeated discovers that he has no will power sufficient to determine the issues; still, when strengthened by the Holy Spirit he not only has the will power, but sees clearly and with balance of mind all the features of the problem in which he is involved. The parallel of this divine method of dealing with the human will is to be seen in the salvation of those who are lost, in which instance the choice of Christ by the action of the heart is developed by the Spirit to a point of passionate desire, but all the same the human will acts without compulsion and the unalterable truth is preserved that "Whosoever will may come." Thus the spiritual life is the result of a voluntary choice of God's will and consequently it may be said that "Whosoever will may attain to victory over every foe." As the unsaved do not and cannot make choice of Christ until moved to do so by the action of the Holy Spirit working in the heart, in like manner Christians do not and cannot make choice of the things of God which constitute spirituality until moved to do so by the Spirit working in the mind and heart. Living the spiritual life on a faith basis is not in reality a cessation of works, rather it is the gaining of ability to perform "every good work." Just as James emphasizes the fact that justification before men rests on a works basis, there is a sense in which it is true that spirituality must be demonstrated by the fruit that is borne. There is in the whole field of pistology a form of faith which claims from the Spirit power to work the works of God. This theme must yet reappear for exposition in a later chapter.

It still remains true that this the negative side of spiritual living is secondary to the positive side, which is a vital output, a spiritual reality to the glory of God. The positive aspect is to be considered next in Chapter XIV.

## Chapter XIV

# POWER TO DO GOOD

The reasonableness of the command, addressed, as it is, to every believer, to be filled with the Spirit (Eph. 5:18) is sustained both by the fact that Christ instructed His disciples that no service should be undertaken before the Spirit came upon them (cf. Luke 24:49; Acts 1:4, 8) and that in every subsequent major undertaking they are said to have been refilled for that service. The work of the Holy Spirit in and through each believer is, as has been indicated, both negative (a victory over the world, the flesh, and the devil) and positive—an output from within of that which is good; furthermore, the filling of the Spirit, while it does provide for a triumph over what is evil, has as its more important objective a positive, vital life and service which only God the Spirit can achieve. In the larger field of that which is positive, the work of the Spirit during the present age is comprehended in seven ministries of which the filling is but one; admittedly, however, this ministry alone is directly related to Christians as the ground and source of the spiritual life. The other six ministries—restraining, reproving, regenerating, indwelling, sealing, and baptizing—have been considered in the earlier portion of this volume; as for this the seventh ministry of the Spirit, when related to the output of the spiritual life and service it is set forth in the New Testament as the realization of seven of the Spirit's manifestations in this age. That is, the positive expression of the Spirit's power—apart from His mighty work of overcoming evil—is manifested in no less than seven distinct ways. There is cause here for thanksgiving respecting this fact, for by so much the Christian is not left in darkness relative to the precise realities which constitute a positive, worthy spiritual life and service. Only uncertainties and distress would obtain if all that could be discovered regarding the outworking of the spiritual life had to be gained from the experience of those who attempt to live that life. God's norm or pattern is indicated clearly. Whatever untaught minds have supposed the spiritual life to be, it follows a channel which is, apart from the varying exercise of individual gifts and the outworking of personal responsibilities, a standardized expression of the mind of

God in behalf of the believer. A spiritual Christian is God's *normal* child, though in the outworking of daily life with its human weakness and failure he may not be the *usual* type. It would still remain true that the Spirit-filled life with all its wealth of reality is God's standard, normal, and ideal, even though none ever attained to it. The setting forth of these seven manifestations of the Spirit in the New Testament is not to place an ideal before the believer which he is to try in his own strength to realize; rather it is the presentation to him of that blessed life which he may anticipate as the result of the Spirit's operation in and through him. To these God-manifested ideals the Christian should give attention and to them he should yield himself in sympathy and cooperation, but the achievement is definitely the Holy Spirit's own—these are only manifestations of the Spirit. The seven such realities indicated in the New Testament are: (1) the fruit of the Spirit, (2) the gifts which are inwrought by the Spirit, (3) the praise and thanksgiving which are inspired by the Spirit, (4) the teaching of the Spirit, (5) the leading of the Spirit, (6) the life of faith which is actualized by the Spirit, and (7) the intercession of the Spirit.

## I. THE FRUIT OF THE SPIRIT

"But the fruit of the Spirit is love, joy, peace, longsuffering, gentleness, goodness, faith [or, as in R.V., faithfulness], meekness, temperance" (or, as in R.V., self-control—Gal. 5:22–23).

This context—Galatians 5:16–25—follows naturally after a portion of Scripture but recently considered, namely, Romans 6:1—8:4, in which the Apostle has laid the foundation upon which all spiritual living and effective service is based: it is that aspect of Christ's death which is a judgment of the sin nature, and by which the freedom is secured for the Holy Spirit to pursue an unhindered operation within the Christian in spite of the active presence of the sin nature which is in the flesh. Since God in Christ has "condemned sin in the flesh," the whole will of God may "be fulfilled in us," but never *by* us (Rom. 8:3–4). That is, the Spirit is appointed to bring the whole will of God to realization in the believer's life, which experience could never be achieved when depending upon human ability (cf. Rom. 7:15–25). This end result, which is doing the whole will of God, is not accomplished in all Christians or by virtue of the fact that they are saved, but only in those among the saved ones who "walk not after the flesh, but after the Spirit." The contrast is between those Christians who depend on their own human resources—which line of action is compatible with the character of all law-relationship to God—and those Christians who depend upon the power of the indwelling Spirit. One method represents "the works of the flesh," or that which the law anticipates when it makes its appeal to human resources; the other method, since it contemplates the enablement of the Spirit, results in a realization of all that the Holy Spirit may do. That which follows in the context of Romans 8:4 is an important development of the contrast between the law principle and the faith principle; then too, as stated above, the determining walk by dependence upon the Holy Spirit as announced in Romans 8:4 is taken up again in Galatians 5:16–25, with the continuation of the same contrast between the works of the flesh and the inwrought works of the Holy Spirit. In the Galatians passage the flesh and the Spirit are declared to be wholly irreconcilable. The fact that the two cannot ever be reconciled is true without exception in every child of God (cf. Gal. 5:17), and so long as he remains in this body and in this world. No believer has ever reached the place where he does not need to walk by means of the Holy Spirit. The most mature Christian must, if awake to the truth respecting himself, witness to the fact that the flesh with its affections and desires is present with him and will demonstrate its presence through "the works of the flesh" if not held in check by the superior power of the Spirit. Ideals of respectability may deter one from shocking disregard of society's demands, but the full inward victory over the flesh is gained only by the working of the Spirit in response to specific dependence upon Him. Extended and appalling are "the works of the flesh": "For the flesh lusteth against the Spirit, and the Spirit against the flesh: and these are contrary the one to the other: so that ye cannot do the things that ye would. But if ye be led of the Spirit, ye are not under the law. Now the works of the flesh are manifest, which are these; Adultery, fornication, uncleanness, lasciviousness, idolatry, witchcraft, hatred, variance, emulations, wrath, strife, seditions, heresies, envyings, murders, drunkenness, revellings, and such like" (Gal. 5:17–21). But over against the works of the flesh is the fruit of the Spirit.

When walking by faith or in dependence upon the Holy Spirit, two results are secured: (1) the works of the flesh shall not be fulfilled and (2) the fruit of the Spirit shall have its manifestation. Both the negative and the positive aspects of the spiritual life are guaranteed to those who thus depend upon the Spirit. That which constitutes the fruit of the Spirit is precisely named. It is a product of the Spirit operating in and through the believer. As employed in the passage now being considered (Gal. 5:22–23), the nine words which denote the fruit of the Spirit represent superhuman qualities of character; they could under no natural circumstances be produced by human ability; they are divine characteristics. Similarly, these nine graces taken together are constituted the one fruit of the Spirit. The singular form *fruit* being used is explained by the fact that these nine graces form an indivisible whole. The Holy Spirit will not produce a few of these and not all of them. If any are present, all will actually be present. Thus, also, these nine graces constitute the essential elements of Christian character. With little apparent thought for the implications involved, Christian leaders have urged upon believers the idea that Christian character is a thing to be built by strenuous self-effort, when by so much they enter upon a path which is not only characterized by, but ends with, a dependence upon human works as the basis of any acceptance before God. The supposed sequence in character-building is said to be simply that thoughts determine acts, acts determine character, and character determines destiny. Little need, indeed, is there for a Savior or the power of God in such a program of development. Whatever the world may elect to designate as their plan by which man may reach what is supposed to be right character, a unique, immediate, and effective method is assigned to the child of God. Christian character is a divine product which is not to be realized but partially and that at the end of a painful self-effort, as is the case with the world in using its method, but is a product which becomes wholly and instantly available when right relation to the Holy Spirit is unhindered. As has well been said, Galatians 5:22–23 is the shortest life of Christ ever written, for the fruit of the Spirit is the outliving of the inliving Christ. It may well be accepted, then, as the realization of that experience to which the Apostle referred when he said, "For to me to live is Christ" (Phil. 1:21; cf. Gal. 2:20). Respecting the nine graces which together comprise the fruit of the Spirit, Dr. C. I. Scofield has written: "Christian character is not mere moral or legal correctness, but the possession and manifestation of nine graces: love, joy, peace—character as an inward state; longsuffering, gentleness, goodness—character in expression toward man; faith, meekness, temperance—character in expression toward God. Taken together they present a moral portrait of Christ, and may be taken as the apostle's explanation of Gal. 2:20, 'Not I, but Christ,' and as a definition of 'fruit' in John 15:1–8. This character is possible because of the believer's vital union to Christ (John 15:5; 1 Cor. 12:12, 13), and is wholly the fruit of the Spirit in those believers who are yielded to Him (Gal. 5:22, 23)" (*Scofield Reference Bible,* p. 1247).

With these general introductory words in mind, attention should be given to each of these nine words in their order and note should be made of their divine character as well as the desirability of all that they represent.

1. LOVE. Since the Holy Spirit declares, as He does in 1 Corinthians, chapter 13, that love is supreme among all gifts, it is reasonable that it should stand first on the list of the manifold fruit of the Spirit. Love is the pre-eminent feature of human experience both in the Mosaic and the kingdom dispensations, as it is in the Christian. As for the Mosaic, it is declared that "Love is the fulfilling of the law" (Rom. 13:10); and the advance in responsibility respecting love which the coming kingdom anticipates is stated in Matthew 5:43–44, 46, "Ye have heard that it hath been said, thou shalt love thy neighbour, and hate thine enemy. But I say unto you, Love your enemies, bless them that curse you, do good to them that hate you, and pray for them which despitefully use you, and persecute you. . . . For if ye love them which love you, what reward have ye? do not even the publicans the same?" However, that standard of love which Christ enjoins upon believers of this age is supernatural and wholly divine in character. He said: "A new commandment I give unto you, That ye love one another; as I have loved you, that ye also love one another. By this shall all men know that ye are my disciples, if ye have love one to another" (John 13:34–35). When he is called upon to exercise a divine characteristic and when for the task sufficient power is provided whereby it may be realized, it is not asking too much to expect the believer to manifest that characteristic. Having indicated the divine compassion for lost men which led to the sacrifice on the cross and having indicated also the lack of love in the one who makes no sacrifice for others, the Apostle John inquires of all such, "How dwelleth the love of God in him?" (1 John 3:17). Similarly, the same Apostle, after having stated that the *cosmos* world system should not be loved, declares: "If any man love the [*cosmos*] world, the love of the Father is not in him" (1 John 2:15). This, again, is not a reference to the believer's love for God; it is God's love operating through the believer. It was thus, too, in closing His priestly prayer, as Christ spoke of providing that the love wherewith the Father had loved Him might be in those for whom He prayed (John 17:26). Yet even more directly, the Apostle Paul asserts that "the love of God is

shed abroad [or perhaps, gushes forth] in our hearts by [that is, out from] the Holy Ghost which is given unto us" (Rom. 5:5). In the light of these Scriptures, it is not difficult to accept the reality to which the Apostle refers when he says, "The fruit of the Spirit is love." Dr. Norman B. Harrison has spoken of "God's own Love actuating human life!" So, again, he states: "God labelled His Love 'For the World'—John 3:16; 1 John 2:2. God channelled that Love to earth through the person of His Son. He channelled that Love into our hearts through the person of the Holy Spirit. He would channel that Love out to needy men everywhere through the person of His redeemed children. Thus Love is the key to His redemptive program: received, it becomes our Salvation; responded to, it becomes our Sanctification; released to others, it becomes our Service. And—let us remember it well—Love has no substitute" (*His Love,* pp. 6, 32–33).

As certainly as God's own love passes through His child when filled with the Spirit, so certainly that love will continue to be directed toward its own objects and the Christian thus blessed will love what God loves and hate what God hates. It is therefore pertinent to observe what God is said to love and to note its expression in those who are Spirit-filled; but it should be remembered that this is not human love augmented or stimulated, though human love in itself is very real. It is divine love manifested by and arising from the very Person of the Godhead who indwells the believer. These objects of divine love are named in Scripture.

a. INCLUSIVE OF THE WHOLE WORLD. The emphasis in Scripture is full and complete on this fact, namely, that God loves the world of mankind (cf. John 3:16; Heb. 2:9; 1 John 2:2). What is called "the missionary spirit" is none other than the compassion which brought the Son of God from heaven to earth and then to death so that men might be saved. Interest in lost men is not accidental with Christians, nor is it a mere human trait; it is the immediate realization of divine love. Soul-winning passion is not secured by exhortation; it is a normal outflow from within believers of a divine reality.

b. EXCLUSIVE OF THE WORLD SYSTEM. John declares: "Love not the world, neither the things that are in the world. If any man love the world, the love of the Father is not in him. For all that is in the world, the lust of the flesh, and the lust of the eyes, and the pride of life, is not of the Father, but is of the world" (1 John 2:15–16). This seeming contradiction with the point made in the preceding paragraph can be explained easily when it is recognized that, though it is the same *cosmos* world which God both loves and hates, it is the men of that world which He loves and only their institutions and evil which He hates. Thus the Christian must love the world of lost men and strive for their salvation, and at the same time hate the satanic system in which the lost are placed.

c. INCLUSIVE OF THE TRUE CHURCH. "Much more then, being now justified by his blood, we shall be saved from wrath through him. For if, when we were enemies, we were reconciled to God by the death of his Son, much more, being reconciled, we shall be saved by his life" (Rom. 5:9–10); "Christ also loved the church, and gave himself for it" (Eph. 5:25). He loves His own even though they may wander away, as is revealed in the scene connected with return of the "prodigal son." "If we love one another, God dwelleth in us, and his love is perfected in us" (1 John 4:12). By this divine compassion for one another the Christian attests the reality of his profession and that before the world: "A new commandment I give unto you, That ye love one another; as I have loved you, that ye also love one another. By this shall all men know that ye are my disciples, if ye have love one to another" (John 13:34–35). Such divine love is also the test of brotherhood in Christ: "Hereby perceive we the love of God, because he laid down his life for us: and we ought to lay down our lives for the brethren. But whoso hath this world's good, and seeth his brother have need, and shutteth up his bowels of compassion from him, how dwelleth the love of God in him?" (1 John 3:16–17); "We know that we have passed from death unto life, because we love the brethren" (3:14).

d. WITHOUT END. "Having loved his own which were in the world, he loved them unto the end" (and so, *eternally,* John 13:1). The love of God operating in the believer is said to "suffer long" and then after all that is kind (1 Cor. 13:4).

e. TOWARD ISRAEL. To them God has said, "I have loved thee with an everlasting love" (Jer. 31:3). With some knowledge of God's eternal purposes for the elect nation and also on the part of believers with a right relation to God whereby the divine love may flow out unhindered, there will be a very definite love experienced for this people whom God as definitely and eternally loves as He does the Christian himself.

f. SACRIFICIAL. Those who experience divine love will be impelled to sacrifice to the end that others may be saved and built up in Christ. It is written to Christians: "For ye know the grace of our Lord Jesus Christ, that, though he was rich, yet for your sakes he became poor, that ye through his poverty might be rich" (2 Cor. 8:9). Such an attitude on the part of the Son of God toward the eternal riches must, if reproduced in the Christian, affect largely his attitude toward earthly riches. Not only is the love of God sacrificial regarding heavenly riches; it is sacrificial with respect to life itself. "Hereby perceive we the love of God, because he laid down his life for us." It therefore follows: "And we ought to lay down our lives for the brethren" (1 John 3:16). The Apostle Paul testified: "I say the truth in Christ, I lie not, my conscience also bearing me witness in the Holy Spirit, that I have great heaviness and continual sorrow in my heart. For I could wish that myself were accursed from Christ for my brethren, my kinsmen according to the flesh" (Rom. 9:1–3). The Apostle knew full well that there was no occasion for him to be accursed, since his Lord had been made a curse for all; but he could still be *willing* to be made a curse. Such an experience is the direct outworking in a human life of the divine love which gave Jesus to die under the curse and judgments of the sin of the world. When this divine compassion for lost men is reproduced in the believer, it becomes the true and sufficient dynamic for soul-saving work.

g. UNREQUITED AND PURE. God's love seeks no compensation and is as holy in its character as the One from whom it flows. What imperfect human elements may be fused into it would not be easy to define; but in itself it comes forth from the heart of God uncomplicated and infinitely worthy. God is Himself love. This does not mean that He has attained to love or that He maintains it by an effort. He is love by reason of His essential nature and the source of all the true love which is found in the universe. However, love means, among other things, capacity to be indignant and to react in judgment upon that which is opposed to it unlawfully. This, it may be believed, is also one of the divine features of infinite love.

Useless, indeed, is any attempt to imitate the imparted divine love as that may be normally manifested in the spiritual believer. Even human love is not subject to control by the human will. An individual cannot make himself love what he does not love, nor can he by any ability lodged within himself cause whatever love he experiences to cease. Certainly the possibility of a counterfeit of the divine compassion is inconceivable. If affection for the normal objects of human love cannot be governed by human will, how could affection for the divine objectives be engendered or dismissed at will? Thus it is demonstrated that the presence of divine compassion in the believer's heart is none other than the direct exercise by God Himself of His own love through the believer as a channel. When there is some failure to be adjusted or in right relation to God, the divine love will not flow freely; but when right relation is sustained the flow of divine love is unhindered. Such control of the expression of divine love is far removed from mere human willingness to love or not love that which God loves. Divine love is the dynamic, the motivating force in the spiritual life. With it the life is by so much a realization of the divine ideal; without it there is only tragic disappointment and failure.

Likewise, the superhuman character of divine love is readily apparent. Not only is such love beyond human capacity, but it is as far removed from the quality of human affection as heaven is higher than the earth. Consider again the measure of love being required when Christ said: "A new commandment I give unto you, That ye love one another; as I have loved you, that ye also love one another" (John 13:34). No wonder He went on to say that this wholly supernatural love would be the sign or indisputable evidence to the world of what is Christian reality. Thus He spoke: "By this shall all men know that ye are my disciples, if ye have love [like this] one to another" (vs. 35). In His priestly prayer Christ four times requested that believers might be one, even as the Father and the Son are one. This prayer is answered in the unity being achieved by the one Body which the Holy Spirit has formed. The fact of this unity creates an obligation for every believer to love every other believer with no less than the compassion of Christ who died for them. Should such a love actually be manifested among Christians, Christ declared that, as a sure result, the world would come to *know* and to *believe* Him (cf. John 17:21–23). To possess and to manifest the compassion of God is not anything optional; it is commanded of Christ. It is likewise essential for Christians in their lives, else the world will neither know nor believe Christ. In the light of such deplorable disunity among Christians, it may be questioned whether the world has ever had even a passing opportunity either to know or to believe. Immeasurable is the effectiveness and attractiveness to others of a pure Christian love; and to the one who thus loves the joyous satisfaction is beyond expression. Little wonder that the Apostle contends that love is supreme and the gift to be desired above all others; nor is it other than proper that love should be named as the first among the elements which comprise the fruit of the Spirit. He who loves with divine compassion drinks the wine of heaven and enters actually by experience into the ecstasy which constitutes the felicity of God.

2. Joy. In like manner, joy, which is the second-named element in the fruit of the Spirit, is none other than the celestial joy of God passing through, or reproduced in, the child of God. It is not human joy stimulated or augmented by divine influence. It is the Holy Spirit's own joy and that of Christ and the Father, wrought as an experience in the believer. Nehemiah declared: "The joy of the Lord is your strength" (8:10), and his truth abides forever. Of the imparted divine joy, Christ said: ". . . that my joy might remain in you, and that your joy might be full" (John 15:11). The Apostle John, having declared the fact of fellowship between God, Father and Son, and the believer, states: "And these things write we unto you, that your joy may be full" (1 John 1:4). When prayer is realized in all its blessing, joy will be full (John 16:24). So, also, Peter writes: "Whom having not seen, ye love; in whom, though now ye see him not, yet believing, ye rejoice with joy unspeakable and full of glory" (1 Pet. 1:8). Only the divine joy is a *πλήρωμα* or infinitely full. Great misconceptions have been engendered by artists who essay to paint their imaginary portraits of Christ—a daring enterprise in the light of 2 Corinthians 5:16, by which effort they have seemed to vie with each other in depicting sorrow and grief. To them He was only "a man of sorrows, and acquainted with grief" (Isa. 53:3); but the disciples to whom He spoke and who had accompanied Him throughout His three and a half years of ministry knew full well to what He referred when He spoke of His own joy, as their writings bear witness.

Exhibiting the same general characteristics as love, likewise divine joy can neither be increased nor decreased by the command of the human will, and equally certain is the evidence that such joy cannot be imitated. Celestial joy in the heart constitutes an attractiveness more effective than can be told. It is an element in the Christian greatly desired by God, else it would not be provided by Him as it is. It is a spiritual God-given capacity to be able to suffer with Christ as one who shares with Him the burden of a lost world, and yet both celestial joy and divine sorrow—a feature of His love—are to be experienced by the Christian at one and the same time. If this suggests a contradiction in terms, it is only at the dictation of human limitations in understanding. It is of the nature of God to be both glad and sad at the same time, and such must the spiritual believer be as a result of the outworking of the divine characteristics: not to be neutral, because the one feature neutralizes the other, but to be both sad and glad with undiminished divine fullness as these characteristics are engendered by the Holy Spirit. "Rejoice in the Lord alway: and again I say, Rejoice" (Phil. 4:4); "Rejoice evermore" (1 Thess. 5:16).

3. PEACE. As Christ bequeathed His joy, in like manner He bequeathed His peace when He said: "Peace I leave with you, my peace I give unto you: not as the world giveth, give I unto you. Let not your heart be troubled, neither let it be afraid" (John 14:27). Reference is made here to the peace which is divine but which can be nonetheless wrought in the human heart. The Apostle Paul defined it when he said: "And the peace of God, which passeth all understanding, shall keep your hearts and minds through Christ Jesus" (Phil. 4:7). A distinction should be observed between "the peace of God," which is an inwrought subjective experience, and "peace with God" (Rom. 5:1), which latter phrase refers to the truth that, through the completeness of Christ's work, the believer is on a peace footing with God forever. In the latter case Paul describes the perfection of reconciliation. The peace which Christ bequeathed and which is an element in the fruit of the Spirit, however, is an experience of peace felt in the heart. It, like all else included in the fruit of the Spirit, is the direct and constant impartation of that which constitutes the very nature and character of God. It cannot, any more than love or joy, be secured by the force of the human will, nor can it be dismissed. Only the experience of it can ever demonstrate to oneself what the peace of God really is—a sublime tranquility of heart and mind in spite of every disturbing memory, foreboding, circumstance, or condition. Such peace, priceless as it is, honors God before men and thus satisfies God; indeed, only "great peace" becomes those whose lives are "hid with Christ in God" (Col. 3:3).

These three—love, joy, peace—form a group which represent character as an inward state, that which the heart experiences directly from God and especially as looked at as an entity in itself.

4. LONG-SUFFERING. Each element in the fruit of the Spirit is contrary to a corresponding unspiritual feature in the human heart. The cure for the unspiritual feature is not an attempted cessation from the evil thing, but a substitution of the Spirit's fruit or all the virtue which God imparts. Long-suffering, for example, is the divine antidote to impatience. There is no mere enlarging of human patience being contemplated; rather it is the patience of God inwrought. The long-suffering patience of God knows no bounds. This is seen in His agelong dealing with mankind, in His patience with individual Christ-rejectors, and in His patience with those whom He brings to Himself (cf. Luke 18:7).

When Jehovah proclaimed His name to Moses in the fiery mount it is said: "The Lord passed by before him, and proclaimed, The Lord, The Lord God, merciful and gracious, longsuffering, and abundant in goodness and truth" (Ex. 34:6). Thus Moses in an intercessory prayer reminds Jehovah of His own revelation respecting Himself: "The Lord is longsuffering, and of great mercy, forgiving iniquity and transgression, and by no means clearing the guilty, visiting the iniquity of the fathers upon the children unto the third and fourth generation" (Num. 14:18). And the Psalmist declared: "But thou, O Lord, art a God full of compassion, and gracious, longsuffering, and plenteous in mercy and truth" (Ps. 86:15). The Apostle Paul warns those who oppose themselves against God when he asks, "Or despisest thou the riches of his goodness and forbearance and longsuffering; not knowing that the goodness of God leadeth thee to repentance?" (Rom. 2:4). Even "the vessels of wrath fitted to destruction" are objects of God's long-suffering. It is written: "What if God, willing to shew his wrath, and to make his power known, endured with much longsuffering the vessels of wrath fitted to destruction?" (Rom. 9:22). Peter declares: "The Lord is not slack concerning his promise, as some men count slackness; but is longsuffering to us-ward, not willing that any should perish, but that all should come to repentance" (2 Pet. 3:9). And Peter also states that "the longsuffering of our Lord is salvation" (2 Pet. 3:15).

That the divine characteristic of long-suffering is to be communicated directly to the believer and through him manifested to the glory of God is not only declared since it is said to be an element in the fruit of the Spirit, but also it is written concerning him and the Lord he serves: "Strengthened with all might, according to his glorious power, unto all patience and longsuffering with joyfulness" (Col. 1:11). So, again, the believer is enjoined to put on, and by the divinely provided means, "bowels of mercies, kindness, humbleness of mind, meekness, longsuffering" (3:12). But how definite and personal the great Apostle becomes respecting the inwrought long-suffering of Christ when he says: "Howbeit for this cause I obtained mercy, that in me first Jesus Christ might shew forth all longsuffering, for a pattern to them which should hereafter believe on him to life everlasting" (1 Tim. 1:16)!

Long-suffering is one virtue which must be expected to appear in the believer's life. In the midst of the most vital directions about responsibility to "walk worthy," it is written: "With all lowliness and meekness, with longsuffering, forbearing one another in love; endeavouring to keep the unity of the Spirit in the bond of peace" (Eph. 4:2–3).

Likewise says Paul, "Be patient toward all men" (1 Thess. 5:14). It was a practice of Paul's own experience. He therefore testifies to Timothy: "But thou hast fully known my doctrine, manner of life, purpose, faith, longsuffering, charity, patience" (2 Tim. 3:10); indeed, this virtue belongs especially to those who are called to preach. Addressing Timothy again, the same Apostle commands: "Preach the word; be instant in season, out of season; reprove, rebuke, exhort with all longsuffering and doctrine" (2 Tim. 4:2). It was after Abraham "had patiently endured, he obtained the promise" (Heb. 6:15). The delay in the return of Christ calls for patience. So James exhorts: "Be patient therefore, brethren, unto the coming of the Lord. Behold, the husbandman waiteth for the precious fruit of the earth, and hath long patience for it, until he receive the early and latter rain. Be ye also patient; stablish your hearts: for the coming of the Lord draweth nigh" (5:7–8). The fruit of the indwelling Spirit includes this long-suffering. It will be realized definitely, sufficiently, and as a manifestation of God's own infinite patience when the Spirit's fruit is borne in the life of the believer.

5. GENTLENESS. The gentleness of God does not imply weakness. The Lamb *dumb* before its shearers is a demonstration of that in God which is, as occasion demands, nonresisting; but it should not be concluded that other attributes are not in God also which defend His holy Person and His righteous government: nor will the Spirit-filled believer manifest only gentleness. He, too, may know the power of indignation; but likewise he will be gentle. In his song of deliverance David said, "Thou hast also given me the shield of thy salvation: and thy gentleness hath made me great" (2 Sam. 22:36). This revealing testimony David repeats in Psalm 18:35. The Apostle beseeches the Corinthians "by the meekness and gentleness of Christ" (2 Cor. 10:1). In addition to the disclosure in Galatians 5:22 that gentleness is derived from the Spirit to be reproduced by Him in the yielded believer's life, James also asserts: "But the wisdom that is from above is first pure, then peaceable, gentle, and easy to be intreated, full of mercy and good fruits, without partiality, and without hypocrisy" (3:17). This wisdom is the wisdom of God. It is from above. It is manifested in and through the child of God. How fully the great Apostle experiences the direct power of the Spirit productive of gentleness when he could say: "But we were gentle among you, even as a nurse cherisheth her children" (1 Thess. 2:7)! This same virtue, too, is required of all who would manifest the true grace of God in service. It is written: "And the servant of the Lord must not strive;

but be gentle unto all men, apt to teach, patient, in meekness instructing those that oppose themselves; if God peradventure will give them repentance to the acknowledging of the truth; and that they may recover themselves out of the snare of the devil, who are taken captive by him at his will" (2 Tim. 2:24–26). Likewise the Apostle urges "to speak evil of no man, to be no brawlers, but gentle, shewing all meekness unto all men" (Titus 3:2). Again, the longing heart is encouraged to believe that the endearing and Christlike property of gentleness may be gained, not by human effort or by useless imitation, but as a direct fruitage of the Spirit.

6. Goodness. A hidden but nonetheless vital element in goodness distinguishes that special virtue from the related one of righteousness. The Apostle, for instance, writes, "For scarcely for a righteous man will one die: yet peradventure for a good man some would even dare to die" (Rom. 5:7). This distinction may be indicated by the fact that a righteous man could evict a widow with insufficient funds from her home the day her rent is due, when a good man would find a way to avoid doing so. In the Person of God, goodness reaches to infinity, and the Scriptures bear abundant testimony to His unbounded goodness. In truth, though little consciously acknowledged by them, the world clings to the fundamental conviction that God is good. No mind can picture the distress and confusion that would eventuate were the world to be convinced that God is essentially evil in Himself. Even the sovereignty of God, though in itself so little understood, is an expression of His essential goodness. Accordingly, God said to Moses after he had interceded for Israel: "I will make all my goodness pass before thee, and I will proclaim the name of the Lord before thee; and will be gracious to whom I will be gracious, and will shew mercy on whom I will shew mercy" (Ex. 33:19). In defense of God's perfection and sovereign will, the Psalmist wrote: "For the word of the Lord is right; and all his works are done in truth. He loveth righteousness and judgment: the earth is full of the goodness of the Lord" (Ps. 33:4–5). Nehemiah speaks to God of His "great goodness" (Neh. 9:25, 35), and David anticipated that "goodness and mercy" would follow him all the days of his life (Ps. 23:6). So, again, he declared: "I had fainted, unless I had believed to see the goodness of the Lord in the land of the living" (27:13). Likewise, he said, "Oh how great is thy goodness, which thou hast laid up for them that fear thee; which thou hast wrought for them that trust in thee before the sons of men! Thou shalt hide them in the secret of thy presence from the pride of man: thou shalt keep them secretly in

a pavilion from the strife of tongues" (31:19–20). As noted above, it is the goodness of God that achieves repentance in the wayward heart. This principle of divine action should not be overlooked (Rom. 2:4). A warning to Gentiles in the light of God's judgments upon Israel refers to His goodness, "Behold therefore the goodness and severity of God: on them which fell, severity; but toward thee, goodness, if thou continue in his goodness: otherwise thou also shalt be cut off" (Rom. 11:22). Thus it may be seen that God is essential goodness, which characteristic is held in perfect balance with all His other attributes, and that the Spirit is appointed to reproduce divine goodness in the one He Himself empowers.

7. FAITHFULNESS. The virtue word used here by Galatians 5:22 as the seventh element of fruit is not *faith* in the subjective sense, of course. It is true, also, that saving faith is a divine work in the heart, but obviously it is not true that God exercises any such faith; rather He is faithful, trustworthy, and stedfast, and Galatians 5:22 is a record of this divine characteristic being reproduced in the believer by the Holy Spirit. The human trail of unfaithfulness is corrected only by the larger manifestation of the faithfulness of God. God is ever faithful. It is declared in Lamentations 3:22–23: "It is of the LORD's mercies that we are not consumed, because his compassions fail not. They are new every morning: great is thy faithfulness." No stronger word on the subject can be given than that of Psalm 36:5: "Thy mercy, O LORD, is in the heavens; and thy faithfulness reacheth unto the clouds." God had promised in His faithfulness to remember David. He said, "But my faithfulness and my mercy shall be with him: and in my name shall his horn be exalted. . . . Nevertheless my lovingkindness will I not utterly take from him, nor suffer my faithfulness to fail" (Ps. 89:24, 33). The same eighty-ninth Psalm may well be called the Psalm of Jehovah's faithfulness, since this virtue is mentioned at least six times. The Psalm opens with the words, "I will sing of the mercies of the LORD for ever: with my mouth will I make known thy faithfulness to all generations. For I have said, Mercy shall be built up for ever: thy faithfulness shalt thou establish in the very heavens. . . . And the heavens shall praise thy wonders, O LORD: thy faithfulness also in the congregation of the saints" (vss. 1–2, 5). The faithfulness of Jehovah is a right subject for praise. Hence Psalm 92:1–2 reads, "It is a good thing to give thanks unto the LORD, and to sing praises unto thy name, O most High: to shew forth thy lovingkindness in the morning, and thy faithfulness every night." As certainly, then, as this imperative attribute appertains unto God,

so certainly it may be and will be reproduced in the yielded believer by the Spirit. Such faithfulness will be exhibited in the believer's relations with God, with his fellow men, and with himself. Honesty, sincerity, and sacrificial devotion are factors in this outlived divine faithfulness. This imparted grace will be directed toward that to which God Himself is faithful.

8. MEEKNESS. Of all the elements which together form the fruit of the Spirit, none is more elusive or difficult to define than meekness, and none more needed inasmuch as vanity and pride are the most common of human traits. Were one by self-effort to attain to meekness even to a slight degree, of that achievement one would soon be proud. As strange as it may seem and as contradictory as it may appear when the almightiness, the sovereignty, and the essential glory of God are considered, it is nevertheless true that one of the divine characteristics is meekness. Let it be remembered that meekness does not consist in pretending to be less than one really is; it rather is demonstrated when one does not pretend to be more than one really is. Certainly, the truth which God is must demand that He publish all that is true of Himself. Less than this would be untruth and more than this would be vanity and pride added to untruth. In 2 Corinthians 10:1 reference is made to the meekness of Christ, and similarly meekness is enjoined upon the believer at least twelve times in the Word of God. Zephaniah commands: "Seek ye the LORD, all ye meek of the earth, which have wrought his judgment; seek righteousness, seek meekness: it may be ye shall be hid in the day of the LORD's anger" (2:3). In addition to his statement of the striking fact that divine meekness is to be reproduced in the believer as an element in the fruit of the Spirit, the same Apostle writes: "We then as workers together with him, beseech you also that ye receive not the grace of God in vain" (2 Cor. 6:1; cf. 2 Tim. 2:25), and one of the most vital features of a worthy walk like this, as presented in Ephesians 4:2, is meekness. So, likewise, meekness, among other needed virtues, is to be put on—all by the divinely provided means. It is so recorded in Colossians 3:12: "Put on therefore, as the elect of God, holy and beloved, bowels of mercies, kindness, humbleness of mind, meekness, longsuffering." The same virtue is commanded in 1 Timothy 6:11: "But thou, O man of God, flee these things; and follow after righteousness, godliness, faith, love, patience, meekness." Meekness is the right condition of mind to have that the Word of God may be received. James therefore declares: "Wherefore lay apart all filthiness and superfluity of naughtiness, and receive with meekness the engrafted

word, which is able to save your souls" (1:21). James also speaks of the "meekness of wisdom" (3:13). In addition to all this the Apostle Peter gives a final word, "But sanctify the Lord God in your hearts: and be ready always to give an answer to every man that asketh you a reason of the hope that is in you with meekness and fear" (1 Pet. 3:15). That which is so much needed in every human heart and so essential to a right manner of spiritual life is provided for every believer through the ministration of the Holy Spirit.

9. SELF-CONTROL. Again in the ninth element of the fruit to be named the word *temperance* as found in the A.V., because of its present restricted meaning, fails to convey the Apostle's message. This the last-named of the elements which comprise the fruit of the Spirit is really *self-control* (R.V.). That such a reality is true of God need not be declared or defended; but it is anticipated likewise as a virtue in the believer. Furthermore, when it is named among the nine graces under consideration, there may be assurance that it is not only anticipated, but provided for by the power of the Spirit. Peter includes this characteristic among important graces which he names. He writes: "And beside this, giving all diligence, add to your faith virtue; and to virtue knowledge; and to knowledge temperance; and to temperance patience; and to patience godliness; and to godliness brotherly kindness; and to brotherly kindness charity" (2 Pet. 1:5–7). The Apostle Paul asserts that temperance must characterize the one who would contend for a crown: "And every man that striveth for the mastery is temperate in all things. Now they do it to obtain a corruptible crown; but we an incorruptible" (1 Cor. 9:25). Temperance or self-control is required of a bishop or elder in the church (cf. Titus 1:7–9), so, also, of the aged believer (Titus 2:2).

In concluding these word-studies and the consideration of that to which they give assurance, it may be well to emphasize afresh the truth that God not only anticipates a high and holy manner of life on the part of the one He has saved, but has provided every needed resource whereby the life that will satisfy and glorify Him may be experienced as a manifestation of the Spirit. The life which is approved of God has been stated most fully and clearly by the Apostle in 2 Corinthians 6:3–10: "Giving no offence in any thing, that the ministry be not blamed: but in all things approving ourselves as the ministers of God, in much patience, in afflictions, in necessities, in distresses, in stripes, in imprisonments, in tumults, in labours, in watchings, in fastings; by pureness, by knowledge, by longsuffering, by kindness, by the Holy Ghost, by love unfeigned, by the word of truth, by the power of God, by the armour of righteousness on the right hand and on the left, by honour and dishonour, by evil report and good report: as deceivers, and yet true; as unknown, and yet well known; as dying, and, behold, we live; as chastened, and not killed; as sorrowful, yet alway rejoicing; as poor, yet making many rich; as having nothing, and yet possessing all things." The newly provided principle whereby the believer may, by adjustment to the mind and will of God, experience the results of the Spirit's filling is well seen in the revelation concerning the fruit of the Spirit, which revelation is the first in the series of seven manifestations of the Spirit that together set forth what constitutes the Spirit-filled, or spiritual, life. What God is naturally is, of course, what God requires, and indeed His attributes, so far as they may be adapted to human life, are to be wrought directly in the believer by the Spirit. The life to be lived could not be more divine had the believer moved out of his body and the Spirit alone remained as the occupant, but for the fact that the Spirit makes use of all the faculties as He does of the body of the believer. Then, too, direct manifestation of the divine characteristics is not hindered because of the presence of living human faculties. Contemplation of these nine divinely wrought graces will stimulate an appreciation of their desirability and necessity if the Christian's life is to glorify God or to yield the consolation to himself which only inwrought love, joy, and peace can impart. The unregenerate man who in desperation seeks relief from such unceasing distress as only an empty heart and life create would surely, could he realize their experimental value and could such blessings be purchased with gold, give all in his power to enjoy even a brief period of such satisfaction and comfort; yet such is the blindness of carnality that those to whom all the riches are available drift on unwilling to enter the realms of immeasurable reality. Considering what these limitless blessings are, there need be little wonder that God commands through His Apostle that all who are saved by His grace be filled with the Spirit.

## II. THE GIFTS OF THE HOLY SPIRIT

Regardless of the all but universal disregard of it, the doctrine respecting service gifts which are wrought by the Spirit in the believer occupies a large place in the New Testament and demands its full recognition in any work on Pneumatology. The Apostle's thanksgiving for the Corinthian church when he asserted of them, "Ye come behind in no [spiritual] gift," is hardly understood today; yet this great ministry of the Spirit is a present reality, and becomes a challenge to every individual Christian and to every church which proposes to maintain New Testament ideals.

By way of attempting an accurate definition, it may be said that a gift in the spiritual sense means the Holy Spirit doing a particular service through the believer and using the believer to do it. It is not something the believer is doing by the aid of the Holy Spirit, nor is it a mere augmentation of what is termed a native or natural gift. According to 1 Corinthians 12:7, a gift is a "manifestation of the Spirit." It is conceivable that the Spirit might use native gifts, but the gift which is wrought by the Spirit is an expression of His own ability rather than the mere use of human qualities in the one through whom He works. As it was seen earlier regarding the fruit of the Spirit that it is a direct product wrought by the Spirit within the believer, in like manner the exercise of a spiritual gift is a direct achievement of the Holy Spirit. The fruit of the Spirit is inward, it is standardized, and it is uniform in its outworking; but the gifts which are wrought by the Spirit are outward in the realms of service, and are varied to the point that it may be assumed that no two Christians are appointed to exactly the same responsibility since no two are situated in precisely the same way nor have the same obligations. That this important truth may be understood, certain gifts are named in the Sacred Text. These may serve as a general classification of the Spirit's activities in the field of the believer's service. The specific gifts as named are set forth in the following Scriptures:

"For as we have many members in one body, and all members have not the same office: so we, being many, are one body in Christ, and every one members one of another. Having then gifts differing according to the grace that is given to us, whether prophecy, let us prophesy according to the proportion of faith; or ministry, let us wait on our ministering: or he that teacheth, on teaching; or he that exhorteth, on exhortation: he that giveth, let him do it with simplicity; he that ruleth, with diligence; he that sheweth mercy, with cheerfulness" (Rom. 12:4–8); "Now there are diversities of gifts, but the same Spirit. And there are differences of administrations, but the same Lord. And there are diversities of operations, but it is the same God which worketh all in all. But the manifestation of the Spirit is given to every man to profit withal. For to one is given by the Spirit the word of wisdom; to another the word of knowledge by the same Spirit; to another faith by the same Spirit; to another the gifts of healing by the same Spirit; to another the working of miracles; to another prophecy; to another discerning of spirits; to another divers kinds of tongues; to another the interpretation of tongues; but all these worketh that one and the selfsame Spirit, dividing to every man severally as he will" (1 Cor. 12:4–11); "But unto every one of us is given grace according to the measure of the gift of Christ. Wherefore he saith, When he ascended up on high, he led captivity captive, and gave gifts unto men. (Now that he ascended, what is it but that he also descended first into the lower parts of the earth? He that descended is the same also that ascended up far above all heavens, that he might fill all things.) And he gave some, apostles; and some, prophets; and some, evangelists; and some, pastors and teachers" (Eph. 4:7–11); "As every man hath received the gift, even so minister the same one to another, as good stewards of the manifold grace of God. If any man speak, let him speak as the oracles of God; if any man minister, let him do it as of the ability which God giveth: that God in all things may be glorified through Jesus Christ, to whom be praise and dominion for ever and ever. Amen" (1 Pet. 4:10–11).

For the further elucidation of the doctrine of gifts, 1 Corinthians, chapters 12 to 14 inclusive, should be noted with care, and two important truths should be observed: (1) that every Christian is the recipient of some gift, for of this fact it is written: "But the manifestation of the Spirit is given to every man to profit withal. . . . But all these worketh that one and the selfsame Spirit, dividing to every man severally as he will" (1 Cor. 12:7, 11); "But unto every one of us is given grace according to the measure of the gift of Christ" (Eph. 4:7) and (2) that these gifts are always wrought by one and the same Spirit. Five times in 1 Corinthians 12:4–11 it is declared that, regardless of the variety of gifts or the number of believers through whom He works, without exception the gifts are wrought by the same Person, the Holy Spirit.

As an illustration of the functioning of the spiritual gifts in the Body of Christ, the Apostle compares that spiritual Body to the human body with its many members, and as the members of the human body do not serve the same purpose, in like manner those who comprise the Body of Christ serve in various ways and to various ends. The instructions governing the use of gifts in the Church, the comparative value of gifts, and the required recognition, regulation, and co-ordination of gifts, as all this is set forth in the New Testament, should have every student's attentive consideration.

Of the several gifts named in Ephesians 4:11—"And he gave some, apostles; and some, prophets; and some, evangelists; and some, pastors and teachers"—it may be said that these are leadership ministries of divine appointment in the Church. The service of those designated here as *apostle* evidently ceased with the first generation of the Church, for no such qualified ministry is to be recognized in the Church today. The New Testament prophet's service is defined as follows: "But he that prophesieth speaketh unto men to edification, and exhortation, and comfort" (1 Cor. 14:3). The one here named *evangelist* is not the revivalist of modern times, but is rather the missionary to the unevangelized. The *pastor and teacher*—probably reference to two gifts being exercised by one person—both shepherds the flock and instructs the people of God. Under his ministry the saints are perfected unto the work divinely committed to them and are edified. Every pastor is the dean of a Bible training school, which school is composed of those members in the Church of Christ committed unto him. If the pastor has had no preparation to serve as an accurate teacher of the Word of God, this entire responsibility must go unfulfilled (cf. Eph. 4:11–12).

Christian service as designed and represented in the New Testament is far more orderly and effective than the more or less accidental and disarranged efforts which now receive that name. In the early church, none were released to service who were not thought to be Spirit-filled, and the possession of spiritual gifts was recognized and these gifts were intelligently employed. That all this has now become almost lost to view and foreign to present conditions is evident.

This limited treatment of the whole doctrine of gifts will be strengthened by the following quotation from Dr. John F. Walvoord:

> Before turning to the discussion of the gifts themselves, certain general factors relating to gifts may be mentioned. First, spiritual gifts are revealed to be given sovereignly by God, and as such, they are not properly the objects of men's seeking. To the Corinthians, who were exalting minor gifts to the neglect of more important gifts, Paul wrote, "But covet earnestly the best gifts" (1 Cor. 12:31), yet in his other epistles it is clear from his silence on the subject that seeking spiritual gifts is not a proper subject for exhortation. Because their bestowal is sovereign, it follows that it is not a question of spirituality. A Christian unyielded to the Lord may possess great spiritual gifts, while one yielded may have relatively minor spiritual abilities. According to the Scriptures, "All these worketh that one and the selfsame Spirit, dividing to every man severally as he will" (1 Cor. 12:11). It remains true, of course, that proper adjustment in the spiritual life of the believer is essential to proper exercise of his gifts, but spirituality in itself does not bring spiritual gifts. The question has been raised whether spiritual gifts are a part of the original bestowal of grace accompanying salvation, or whether they are a subsequent work. The Scriptures give no clear answer, but from the nature of the baptism of the Holy Spirit, which occurs at the moment of new birth, and the resultant placing into the body of Christ, it would be reasonable to infer that spiritual gifts are bestowed at that time in keeping with the place of the believer in the body of Christ, even if these gifts are not immediately observed or exercised. Accordingly, spiritual gifts probably attend the baptism of the Holy Spirit, even though their bestowal is not included in the act of baptism. In the analogy

of natural gifts as seen in the natural man, it is clear that all the factors of ability and natural gift are latent in the new-born babe. So, also, it may be true for spiritual gifts in the one born again. In both the natural and spiritual spheres, it is a matter of proper use and development of gifts rather than any additional gifts being bestowed. Second, it may be observed that every Christian has some spiritual gifts. According to the Scriptures, "The manifestation of the Spirit is given to every man to profit withal" (1 Cor. 12:7), and "All these worketh that one and the selfsame Spirit, dividing to every man severally as he will" (1 Cor. 12:11). Christians are "members in particular" (1 Cor. 12:27), and "are one body in Christ, and every one members one of another" (Rom. 12:5). However small the gift, or insignificant the place, every Christian is essential to the body of Christ. As the Scripture puts it, "Nay, much more those members of the body, which seem to be more feeble, are necessary" (1 Cor. 12:22). There is divine purpose in the life of every Christian, and spiritual gifts are in keeping with that purpose. It is the challenge of the Scriptures on this subject (cf. 1 Pet. 4:10) that every Christian fulfill the ministry for which he has been equipped by God. Third, it is clear that gifts differ in value. While there is equality of privilege in Christian faith, there is not equality of gift. According to 1 Corinthians 12:28, "God hath set some in the church, first apostles, secondarily prophets, thirdly teachers, after that miracles, then gifts of healings, helps, governments, diversities of tongues." In the nature of the various gifts, some are more effective and essential than others. Paul contrasts the gift of prophecy and the gift of tongues with the words, "I would that ye all spake with tongues, but rather that ye prophesied" (1 Cor. 14:5); and again, "Yet in the church I had rather speak five words with my understanding, that by my voice I might teach others also, than ten thousand words in an unknown tongue" (1 Cor. 14:19). Fourth, as 1 Corinthians 13 bears witness, spiritual gifts to be profitable must be used in love. Spiritual gifts in themselves do not make great Christians. Their use in the proper way motivated by divine love, which is the fruit of the Spirit, is effective and bears fruit to the glory of God. A fifth general feature of spiritual gifts is that certain gifts were temporary in their bestowal and use. It is clear that the great body of Bible-loving Christians does not have all the spiritual gifts manifested in its midst as did the early apostolic church. On the other hand, certain gifts clearly characterize the entire present dispensation. The considerations leading to the classification of each gift will be noted in its individual treatment. A sixth and concluding feature of spiritual gifts which is of great importance is the evident contrast between spiritual gifts and natural gifts. While God may choose men of natural ability, it is clear that spiritual gifts pertain to the spiritual birth of Christians rather than their natural birth. The qualities of the spiritual gifts are not evident in the individual before his salvation. The spiritual gifts pertain to his new nature rather than his old. Spiritual gifts must not be regarded, then, as an enlargement of natural powers, but a supernatural gift bestowed in keeping with the purpose of God in placing that individual in the body of Christ. It may be frequently observed that individuals with little natural talent are often used mightily of God when those with great natural talent, though saved, are never similarly used. The spiritual gift is not, then, a demonstration of what man can do even under favorable circumstances, but rather it reveals what God can bestow in grace.

An examination of the fifteen spiritual gifts revealed in the New Testament will disclose considerable differences in the character of the gifts. Certain gifts are clearly the possession of the Church today as exhibited in their exercise in gifted men throughout the present dispensation. There is little doubt that some men today have (1) the gift of teaching, (2) the gift of helping or ministering, (3) the gift of administration or ruling, (4) the gift of evangelism, (5) the gift of being a pastor, (6) the gift of exhortation, (7) the gift of giving, and (8) the gift of showing mercy. In contrast to these, as their individual exposition will demonstrate, stand other spiritual gifts known by the early Christians, which seem to have passed from the scene with the apostolic period. Some of these are claimed for today by certain sects, whose neglect of the Scriptural instructions for use of these gifts is in itself a testimony to the spurious quality of their affected gifts. Among these temporary gifts the following can be named: (1) the gift of apostleship, (2) the gift of prophecy, (3) the gift of miracles, (4) the gift of healing, (5) the gift of tongues, (6) the gift of interpreting tongues, (7) the gift of discerning spirits.—*The Doctrine of the Holy Spirit,* pp. 182–85

## III. THE OFFERING OF PRAISE AND THANKSGIVING

Closely related to the experience of joy, which comes second in the list of nine graces comprising the fruit of the Spirit, is that of praise and thanksgiving. This additional feature of the spiritual life obtains the distinction of being directly related to, and the normal result of, the command to be filled with the Spirit, the implication being that, in its primary outworking, the Spirit's filling will result in praise and thanksgiving. The whole context under consideration at this point reads: "See then that ye walk circumspectly, not as fools, but as wise, redeeming the time, because the days are evil. Wherefore be ye not unwise, but understanding what the will of the Lord is. And be not drunk with wine, wherein is excess; but be filled with the Spirit; speaking to yourselves in psalms and hymns and spiritual songs, singing and making melody in your heart to the Lord; giving thanks always for all things unto God and the Father in the name of our Lord Jesus Christ; submitting yourselves one to another in the fear of God" (Eph. 5:15–21).

The stupendous obligation to offer worshipful praise to God and to render thanks for never-ceasing benefits is such that it cannot be discharged by any human being if no more than natural resources are drawn upon. Unfallen angels who have ever been in the glorious presence of God since their creation cease not to cry "Holy, holy, holy, is Jehovah of hosts" (Isa. 6:3, R.V.); yet the infinite value of redemption has never reached them nor has it been required for them. They worship God for His intrinsic worthiness; but how much more obligation rests upon those of humankind who not only have the same obligation to acknowledge the infinite worthiness of God but are the recipients of God's saving grace! In truth, an immeasurable obligation rests upon all men to worship God for what He is, and to acknowledge His love expressed in the death of Christ whether it be received as the ground of salvation or not. It is the normal work of the Spirit to inspire God-honoring praise in the believer's heart. This adoration results directly and automatically in the heart when the Spirit is free to work at all. There is great satisfaction to be found in offering up worthy praise to God. Such an exercise stimulates other graces in the heart and not the least of these is humility.

Similarly, as a result of His filling Christians, the Spirit moves the heart to thanksgiving, and to a degree to which no human being could ever attain. It is perhaps within human bounds to give thanks sometimes for some things, but how different is the requirement which the Bible text presents in bidding one to be thankful "always for all things"! Such superhuman gratitude is included, then, in the command to be filled with the Spirit. If all things are "working together for good to them that love God," there is ample reason for giving thanks by faith for the all things. No argument is needed either to demonstrate the reasonableness of praise and thanksgiving on the lips and from the heart of those who are saved, or to convince an unprejudiced mind of the impossibility of a discharge of this obligation when there is drawing only on that which belongs to human ability. A Spirit-filled life alone will be radiant with praise and thanksgiving.

## IV. THE TEACHING OF THE SPIRIT

The Holy Spirit is the Master Teacher, but spiritually this ministry is restricted, in the main, to the Word of God. That Word has been given to men by God in good faith and with the expectation that it would be understood and received by those for whom it is intended. That they need to study to show themselves approved unto God in making the right divisions of doctrine and in arriving at its true meaning does not lessen the obligation; indeed, few apprehend the fact that the Word of God, quite different from other themes of knowledge, cannot be received with understanding other than by personal illumination such as the Holy Spirit alone can achieve. Even the unsaved receive not the Gospel unless it is by the Spirit disclosed to them (cf. John 16:7–11), and similarly truth can come to the believer only as it is revealed to him by the Spirit. Multitudes are "ever learning, and never able to come to the knowledge of the truth" (2 Tim. 3:7)—learning in that restricted sense that they dimly apprehend certain features of truth, but are never fully informed or transformed by it. An evidence of the Spirit's filling —that which He does when free to work effectively at all—is the bringing of one in whom He dwells to an ever increasing understanding of the Scriptures with all their sanctifying power (John 17:17). Thus the only key to attainment in the knowledge of the Word of God, itself a pedagogical law not appearing in general academic training, is suggested by the imperative necessity that right relation be sustained to the Holy Spirit by which alone His teaching ministry may go on unhindered. The student who is not in right relation to God cannot hope to make progress in the study of spiritual truth. It is regrettable, indeed, that in so many instances whole courses are offered in Bible doctrine without so much as one word of warning or instruction regarding this most vital and fundamental feature of all Christian pedagogy. Little seems to be said or implied in the Scriptures on this theme before the Upper Room Discourse. It is then that Christ first presented this great truth in no uncertain terms. In this discourse He said: "I have yet many things to say unto you, but ye cannot bear them now. Howbeit when he, the Spirit of truth, is come, he will guide you into all truth: for he shall not speak of himself; but whatsoever he shall hear, that shall he speak: and he will shew you things to come. He shall glorify me: for he shall receive of mine, and shall shew it unto you. All things that the Father hath are mine: therefore said I, that he shall take of mine, and shall shew it unto you" (John 16:12–15).

Even after three and a half incomparable years in the constant company and instruction of Christ, it was still true for the disciples that He had many things to say unto them. It must ever be so with believers to the end of this life. He will always have more to reveal to the one who can hear and will heed. That there were truths which they could not then bear is recognition of the fact that these men were precluded from receiving any and all truth related to the death and the resurrection of Christ, since up to that time they did not know or rather believe He would die and be raised again. When all the truth belonging to the present dispensation which depends either on the death or the resurrection of Christ is left out of consideration, there will be little remaining, and of course this demonstrates the fact that the twelve disciples had not at any time preached the gospel of divine grace, which gospel is based wholly upon Christ's death, burial, and resurrection (cf. 1 Cor. 15:3–4). As the Scriptures themselves show, these men preached the gospel of the kingdom. However, a new dispensation with all its reality is dawning for them and all these men are to be taught new and wonderful revelations by the direct ministry of the Spirit. Earlier He has told them that the Holy Spirit "shall be in you" (John 14:17), and to this He adds now (16:12–15) the new and momentous truth that the indwelling Spirit is appointed to undertake a measureless ministry of teaching and that from the incomparable vantage ground of the position He occupies within the heart. Direct and effective beyond all that human experience records is this inner approach of the Spirit to the understanding and heart of man. Witness in support of this the fact that impetuous Peter boldly rebuked Christ only a year or less before His death for asserting that He was about to die and rise again; yet that very same Peter some fifty days after Christ's death arose in the midst of a public throng in Jerusalem and preached the greatest sermon ever heard on human lips if results are to be considered, and his whole appeal was based on the death and resurrection of Christ. Very much truth had reached Peter's mind in the meantime and evidently from no other source than the teaching of the Holy Spirit within Peter's own heart. The arrangement thus divinely provided claims attention from every sincere believer. The Holy Spirit from within the heart is to "guide" into "all truth." The scope of this promise should be observed and the lack of all qualifying conditions. No human limitations may hinder. A dull mind is not considered a special problem for the Spirit. It is still true that He will guide into all truth. Yet He, the Spirit, does not speak the message that He imparts as the Author or Originator of it. Whatsoever He hears, that He speaks. If it be asked who originates and passes on the message to the Holy Spirit living within the heart, the answer is given twice in this limited context, namely, He who said "I have yet many things to say unto you" and who said, speaking of the Spirit, "He shall receive of mine, and shall shew it unto you." The first-mentioned theme in the Spirit's teaching ministry is that of unveiling the prophetic Scriptures. "He will shew you things to come." It is also to be observed that the Spirit in the human heart will glorify Christ rather than Himself and that the richest of all treasures of knowledge to be imparted, the things of Christ, are augmented to the point of including the "all things" of the Father.

As the Upper Room Discourse is the seed plot for the doctrine of the epistles, especially those from the Apostle Paul, it is to be expected that so new and vital a theme as the teaching ministry of the Spirit and the manner of it as set forth in the passage just examined will be given a larger and more amplified presentation in the doctrinal epistles. Such a treatment, indeed, is found in 1 Corinthians 2:9–12, which reads: "But as it is written, Eye hath not seen, nor ear heard, neither have entered into the heart of man, the things which God hath prepared for them that love him. But God hath revealed them unto us by his Spirit: for the Spirit searcheth all things, yea, the deep things of God. For what man knoweth the things of a man, save the spirit of man which is in him? even so the things of God knoweth no man, but the Spirit of God. Now we have received, not the spirit of the world, but the spirit which is of God; that we might know the things that are freely given to us of God."

As in John 16:12–15, the subject of the passage again is "things" —the "things to come," the things of Christ, and the "all things" of the Father. Thus the Apostle refers to "things" which reach the heart of man by direct revelation without reference to the natural channels of information proceeding through the eye gate, the ear gate, and the heart or reasoning power of man. Long before modern psychology attempted to stress the three natural channels of approach to human understanding, this portion of the Word of God had identified them, but had added that to which no psychologist or human pedagogue can of himself attain, much less impart, namely, things which are directly revealed by the Holy Spirit to the one in whom He dwells. In this connection, the Apostle asserts: "Now we have received . . . the spirit which is of God" and to the grand consummation "that we might know the things that are freely given to us of God." The infinite qualification of the Spirit in this role as Teacher is stated in the words: "for the Spirit searcheth all things, yea, the deep things of God." Man may know the things belonging to human spheres, but the Spirit alone knows the things which belong to the sphere of God. Such an illuminating work as this was wrought by God's Son, Christ, for example, in the hearts of two disciples on the Emmaus road. Of this it is written: "And they said one to another, Did not our heart burn within us, while he talked with us by the way, and while he opened to us the scriptures? . . . Then opened he their understanding, that they might understand the scriptures" (Luke 24:32, 45). Thus the believer is placed through the teaching ministry of the Holy Spirit in that unique position of one who may be directly and inwardly taught by the Master Teacher of all teachers, the Holy Spirit of God. Of a certainty will the divine Spirit function in the heart which He fills.

## V. THE LEADING OF THE SPIRIT

Being led of God is one of the grand realities even of the Old Testament. Upwards of forty times the directing hand of God is seen hovering over His people of old; and in the sphere of His humanity, Christ was led by the Spirit (cf. Matt. 4:1; Luke 4:1). In this as much as in any feature of Christ's humanity He became and is the example or pattern for the child of God. The extent of the advantage which this ministry of the Holy Spirit provides is beyond all computation. As a patient may be guided back to health by giving heed to the directions of a wise physician, so the Christian may be led by the Holy Spirit into paths chosen by infinite love, infinite power, and infinite wisdom. A human being is so designed by God that he cannot guide himself. Jeremiah therefore states: "O LORD, I know that the way of man is not in himself: it is not in man that walketh to direct his steps" (10:23). One cannot contemplate the expressed helplessness of David without a consciousness of a like need of divine guidance. He said: "Lead me, O LORD, in thy righteousness because of mine enemies; make thy way straight before my face" (Ps. 5:8); "Lead me in thy truth, and teach me: for thou art the God of my salvation; on thee do I wait all the day" (25:5); "Teach me thy way, O LORD, and lead me in a plain path, because of mine enemies" (27:11); "For thou art my rock and my fortress; therefore for thy name's sake lead me, and guide me" (31:3); "Search me, O God, and know my heart: try me, and know my thoughts: and see if there be any wicked way in me, and lead me in the way everlasting" (139:23–24). No command is recorded in the New Testament which directs the believer to be led of the Spirit; however, it is assumed as a foregone conclusion that apart from this ministry none can follow the path of God's own choosing. It is said, for instance, that "as many as are led by the Spirit of God, they are the sons of God" (Rom. 8:14). That is, by the leading of the Spirit they are proved to be mature sons of God. Here seemingly a distinction is drawn between the *child* of God (τέκνον) and the mature *son* (υἱός), the implication being that not all Christians, though uniformly children of God, are manifesting the characteristics of those who have grown to maturity. In other words, not all Christians are spiritual or Spirit-filled; but those led by the Spirit are. Likewise, it is also written: "If ye be led of the Spirit, ye are not under the law" (Gal. 5:18). Thus, again, it may be suggested that not every saved person is led of the Spirit; for those who are led are so supplied with true counsel and guidance that manifestly they need no outward commandments. This wonderful relationship which provides such blessed realities may easily be perverted by sincere persons if they do not know the right relation to God through which true guidance may be secured. Not only is it demanded that a right understanding should obtain relative to the leading of the Spirit, but that there be freedom from fanaticism, undue emotionalism, and superstition. Since the whole course of a life may be misdirected and that in spite of sincerity, it is needful to an imperative degree for the believer to learn for himself—for no other's experience is a pattern—how to be led of the Spirit. No step can be safely taken in this world apart from divine guidance. But little help can be gained by imitating the experience of others or by following rules which men have made. The leading of the Spirit, as the very term used for this ministry implies, is a most intimate and personal experience. To those who by constant attention and prayer are made familiar with the Spirit's ways of guiding them, the leading becomes one of the richest experiences known to the believer's heart. The importance of substituting infinite wisdom for finite guessing can never be overestimated. It is the purpose of God that a child inside a home shall through obedience avail himself of the wisdom of his parents. It is likewise the purpose of God that His own child through being guided by the Spirit shall avail himself of the infinite wisdom of God. It is worse than useless for the believer to depend on his own wisdom and even more useless and dangerous for him to seek the wisdom and counsel of others, even if believers. In matters of which men can know nothing they are rightfully termed *blind*. On this point Christ asked: "Can the blind lead the blind? shall they not both fall into the ditch?" (Luke 6:39).

Considering the manner in which the will of God may now be known, it should be observed that direct leading by the indwelling Spirit has superseded, as something far more advantageous, the Old Testament method of guidance by natural light, by dreams, by voices, and by tests. All of these early methods should be considered ineffective now. The child of God cannot magnify too much the truth that for him under present grace relationships he lives and serves in closest companionship with the Holy Spirit. He in conjunction with the Spirit occupies the same body and as partners they enter into the same enterprises that God the Father may appoint. Of course, this sort of life is in large degree supernatural; still, no child of God should be afraid of things supernatural. It is also true that every instance of the Spirit's leading has to be contemplated under three tenses or time relationships. There is a time before the experience, the time of the experience itself, and a time after it which is characterized by retrospect. Thus one if Spirit-filled is ever preparing for the experience, ever being led, and ever looking back upon God's faithful dealing. In the matter of preparation, two passages may serve to give all the needed instruction: "Trust in the LORD with all thine heart; and lean not unto thine own understanding" (Prov. 3:5); "I beseech you therefore, brethren, by the mercies of God, that ye present your bodies a living sacrifice, holy, acceptable unto God, which is your reasonable service. And be not conformed to this world: but be ye transformed by the renewing of your mind, that ye may prove what is that good, and acceptable, and perfect, will of God" (Rom. 12:1–2). It is needful for the one who would be led not only to be depending definitely on the Spirit for leading but ever to be willing to be led. Relative to the time when one is actually being led the question may be asked, How may one be aware or conscious of the thing God wills? To answer this query involves the most personal realities, those degrees of development and experience concerning which no two would ever be alike. No Scripture is more revealing about the matter than Philippians 2:13, which states: "For it is God which worketh in you both to will and to do of his good pleasure." This revelation brings assurance which is both definite and final. It may be that a delay will be imposed upon the action being considered or God will speak His will through some other providence or circumstance; but one thing can always be counted upon: He will work within, and the leading in the end creates a convinced mind that all influences may have but engendered anyway. God is certainly able to speak loud enough for a willing soul to hear. George Müller taught and testified out of a very rich experience in fellowship with the Holy Spirit that God leads, not by signs or outward things, but by means of the willing, expectant mind. He sways the judgment itself, and then one becomes clear and convinced about the course God would indicate. The voice of men may be heeded only if God has sent them to His child for that purpose. As for the time after one has been led, there is then the need of resting in that which has been determined for him. The guidance must be so convincing it will not be doubted in days that follow when, perchance, times of testing may come. That leading which takes one to his particular field of service must be of such a definite nature that suffering and hardship can be endured without any questioning of the step by which one reached the place of testing.

Finally, one who is yielded to God must account himself in the will of God when he is unreservedly willing to do God's will. If the position one occupies in life or service is not what God desires, surely He can, providing that one is yielded, move him out into the place which He does choose. The will of God indeed is not primarily a matter of a Christian's being in one place or another; it is rather of his being willing to do God's will. All else is then easily adjusted.

A very vital factor, then, in the spiritual life is that of being led by the Holy Spirit, and this necessary experience will be the portion of all who are Spirit-filled.

## VI. THE LIFE OF FAITH

Most vital indeed is the achievement of the Holy Spirit by which He makes supernatural things real to the one in whom He dwells. This undertaking is quite similar in character to that of His teaching work, save that the latter is largely restricted to impartation of knowledge of the Scriptures while the former comprehends a wide field in the believer's experience. What is most to be emphasized in the former is the truth that the Holy Spirit bears witness in the believer's heart, which witness becomes an assurance that the believer is a child of God. The Apostle Paul declares: "The Spirit itself [R.V., himself] beareth witness with our spirit, that we are the children of God" (Rom. 8:16), and the Apostle John likewise writes: "If we receive the witness of men, the witness of God is greater: for this is the witness of God which he hath testified of his Son. He that believeth on the Son of God hath the witness in himself: he that believeth not God hath made him a liar; because he believeth not the record that God gave of his Son" (1 John 5:9–10). Thus, also, the ability to speak to God the Father with the sense of filial relationship is a work of the Holy Spirit performed in the heart, and then, too, it is because of sonship's genuineness that the Holy Spirit is given to the believer where He may with success engender the consciousness of sonship. It is written accordingly: "And because ye are sons, God hath sent forth the Spirit of his Son into your hearts, crying, Abba, Father" (Gal. 4:6). Not only does the Spirit actualize the sonship relation, but He is appointed as well to make real every great fact of relationship the truth of which may have been theoretically acknowledged by faith. The Apostle's prayers bear directly on this specific work of the Holy Spirit. He prayed "that the God of our Lord Jesus Christ, the Father of glory, may give unto you the spirit of wisdom and revelation in the knowledge of him: the eyes of your understanding being enlightened; that ye may know what is the hope of his calling, and what the riches of the glory of his inheritance in the saints, and what is the exceeding greatness of his power to us-ward who believe, according to the working of his mighty power, which he wrought in Christ, when he raised him from the dead, and set him at his own right hand in the heavenly places, far above all principality, and power, and might, and dominion, and every name that is named, not only in this world, but also in that which is to come" (Eph. 1:17–21); and "that he would grant you, according to the riches of his glory, to be strengthened with might by his Spirit in the inner man; that Christ may dwell in your hearts by faith; that ye, being rooted and grounded in love, may be able to comprehend with all saints what is the breadth, and length, and depth, and height; and to know the love of Christ, which passeth knowledge, that ye might be filled with all the fulness of God" (Eph. 3:16–19).

Like the leading of the Spirit, the Spirit's work of actualizing, being so definitely in the realm of experience, can be distorted by those who lack a right instruction and knowledge of God's ways with them; nevertheless, the leading and the true witness of the Spirit must be recognized and maintained regardless of perversions. It is a matter of Scriptural record that a believer will be made aware of his sonship relation to God by the witness to, and with, his human spirit by the indwelling Third Person. It is indeed the usual attitude of those who comprise the great company of spiritual believers to have peace in their hearts about personal salvation. They may have various problems in the sphere of their daily life, but, unless most abnormal, they do not entertain uncertainty about their own acceptance with God. Such peace is foundational, for none will grow in the knowledge of Christ within the sphere of grace who are not at rest respecting their own relation to God (cf. 2 Pet. 3:18).

It may be concluded, then, that the great realities which enter into a believer's relation to God will be made actual to him by the Holy Spirit.

## VII. THE INTERCESSION OF THE SPIRIT

No believer should be uninformed about the divine arrangement in this dispensation respecting prayer. As a new privilege for the child of God (John 16:24), Christ Himself directed that prayer be offered to the Father in the name of the Son (cf. John 16:23). To this the Apostle adds by the same divine authority that prayer be offered in the enabling power of the Holy Spirit. He writes, "Likewise the Spirit also helpeth our infirmities: for we know not what we should pray for as we ought: but the Spirit itself [R.V., himself] maketh intercession for us with groanings which cannot be uttered. And he that searcheth the hearts knoweth what is the mind of the Spirit, because he maketh intercession for the saints according to the will of God" (Rom. 8:26–27); "Praying always with all prayer and supplication in the Spirit, and watching thereunto with all perseverance and supplication for all saints" (Eph. 6:18). And to this testimony Jude, also, adds: "But ye, beloved, building up yourselves on your most holy faith, praying in the Holy Ghost" (Jude 1:20). According to the first of these passages—Romans 8:26–27—it is indicated that in the sphere of that particular form of prayer designated *intercession,* which is the act of standing between God and man on behalf of another, the human instrument does not know that for which he should pray. How could he know what God's purpose in another person's life might be? Or how could he know what relationship exists between God and his fellow man? Because of this obvious limitation, the Spirit indites the prayer of intercession, and furthermore He, as one of the Godhead who Himself knows the need of human hearts and indeed who searches all hearts, is understood by the Father since He knows perfectly the mind or petitions presented by the Holy Spirit when the Spirit makes intercession for the saints according to the Father's will. Of this divine plan for prayer Dean Alford writes, "The Holy Spirit of God dwelling in us, knowing our wants better than we, Himself pleads in our prayers, raising us to higher and holier desires than we can express in words, which can only find utterance in sighings and aspirations" (*New Testament for English Readers,* new ed., at Rom. 8:27). Thus the Spirit-filled man may and does enter a sphere of effective ministry in prayer because of the Spirit's intercession operating within.

### CONCLUSION

It has been the purpose in this chapter of Pneumatology to present and amplify the revealed truth regarding that which is wrought by the Holy Spirit in the heart and life of the believer whom He fills. The filling with the Spirit results in seven manifestations of Himself in and through the child of God. There need be no doubt about what the Spirit's objectives are. Because of the clear presentation in the Sacred Text, all discordant human experience is to be rejected as irrelevant, and the Christian may judge himself in a most practical way with respect to the measure with which he is Spirit-filled. Attention has been called repeatedly to the determining fact that all of these seven effects are wrought in and through the believer so as to be termed properly *manifestations of the Spirit*. These operations are not to be sought as special concessions from God, but are the normal activities of the Spirit within the one whom He fills. This truth leads on to consideration of the problem of what the precise terms or conditions are, as revealed in the New Testament, upon which a Christian may come into the realization of this priceless, God-honoring experience in daily life.

# CHAPTER XV

## CONDITIONS PREREQUISITE TO FILLING

AGAIN THE BELIEVER is to be confronted with the simplest of conditions, and just those which are naturally required on the human side to the end that he may be Spirit-filled. As is too often the case with interpreters, however, the prerequisite adjustments outlined by the Scripture have been increased, demands being added which are foreign to the revelation God has given. Exhibiting the same disposition to add unappointed burdens, which disposition is displayed when anything is added to the one condition of salvation by faith alone, men have stressed beyond measure the supposed human obligations relative to the Spirit's filling. It is commonly urged that the Spirit's filling depends upon asking or praying for it. This error is prompted by the notion that to pray for the filling of the Spirit is reasonable. By some also who confuse the receiving of the Spirit with the filling of the Spirit, it is believed that prayer for the Spirit is commanded in Luke 11:13, where the Savior's words are recorded thus: "If ye then, being evil, know how to give good gifts unto your children: how much more shall your heavenly Father give the Holy Spirit to them that ask him?" Previously it has been demonstrated that the direction Christ gave as stated in this passage does not and could not apply to believers of the present age, and it is equally true that receiving the Spirit is not the same as being filled with the Spirit. Prayer for the Spirit's filling is an error of great proportions and indicates a misunderstanding of the conditions which now obtain. The Spirit's filling does not await the influence of prayer. God is not withholding this blessing until He is prevailed upon or some reluctance on His part is broken down. He awaits the requisite human adjustments. In other words, He is waiting for the believer to yield all to Him. When the revealed conditions, which are most reasonable, are met, the Spirit goes forward in the believer's heart with all the activities which together constitute the Spirit's filling. The Spirit does not need to be implored to do that which He came into the Christian's heart to do; He is rather imploring the Christian to make the way clear for Him to do His gracious work. The results are immediate and the blessing is secured when the conditions are met, but prayer for the filling of the Spirit is not one of those conditions.

Next to the error of supposing that prayer is a condition upon which the believer may be filled is that of assuming, because the disciples waited ten days for the Spirit before the Day of Pentecost was fully come, that all believers must wait for the Spirit. This notion is possible only because the truth is unobserved that the disciples were not waiting for their own filling, but were waiting for the advent of the Spirit into the world. Since the Spirit came as He did on Pentecost, none have ever had the slightest occasion to wait for Him; but how long and with what patience the Spirit has waited for unyielded lives to be surrendered to Him!

Similarly, there are those who, continuing a misunderstanding of two or three generations ago, contend that the Spirit's filling depends upon some crisis experience, at which time the filling is claimed by a supreme effort of faith resulting in what is thought to be a permanent state of spirituality. Men have taught that Christians should receive the Spirit's filling by a specific effort much as they would draw a deep breath into their lungs. All this, however sincere, ignores the simple truth that the Spirit indwells every believer and so the problem before the believer is only one of adjustment to the end that the Spirit's work in the heart and life may be unhindered.

In approaching the theme respecting the terms upon which the child of God may be filled with the Spirit, it should be clear to all that only those instructions which are set forth in the Scriptures are to be considered. One great preacher of the past tabulated eighteen requirements which he declared must be met by those who would be Spirit-filled; however, in his autobiography, when describing his own experience in becoming thus filled, he failed to indicate that he complied with even one of these unfounded requirements. Such unreality must be avoided and only those conditions which God has revealed are to be considered. Three conditions are directly stated in the New Testament. There are no more and there are no less. Since this is true, it is evident that these three represent all that is required. Of these three conditions, two are negative—what the believer should not do, and one is positive—that which the believer should do. The negative directions are: "And grieve not the holy Spirit of God" (Eph. 4:30) and "Quench not the Spirit" (1 Thess. 5:19), while the one positive condition is: "Walk in the Spirit" (Gal. 5:16). These are now to be considered separately and in the same order.

## I. "GRIEVE NOT THE HOLY SPIRIT OF GOD"

The Christian is indwelt by the Holy Spirit with the purpose in view that the divine life should dominate all his thoughts, actions, and feelings rather than sin, which is so foreign to the Holy Spirit, indeed the very opposite and that which is furthest removed from the absolute purity and sanctity of the indwelling One. The presence of sin in the believer's life grieves the Holy Spirit. This is the testimony of the Bible and it is also the abundant witness of reason. When sin is tolerated in the Christian's daily life, of necessity the Spirit must turn from His ministry *through* the Christian unto a pleading ministry *to* him. The Bible lends no sanction to the idea, so often suggested, that the Spirit is ever grieved away. On the contrary, it is assured that, having taken up His residence in the child of God, He abides forever (John 14:16–17; 1 John 2:27). He remains, but is grieved when sin is present. The grieving of the Spirit becomes a very definite experience in the one within whom the Spirit dwells, an experience which bears a close resemblance to that of his own soul or spirit when depressed. David expressed the feeling which came upon him after his great sin accordingly, saying: "When I kept silence, my bones waxed old through my roaring all the day long. For day and night thy hand was heavy upon me: my moisture is turned into the drought of summer" (Ps. 32:3–4). All of this, being a matter of human experience, is liable to misunderstanding and misinterpretation. Physical conditions often engender a depressed mental state, which state has no relation whatever to the grieving of the Spirit. Allowance should always be made when nerves are depleted or when physical vitality is low. Many are the instances when the mind, because of weakness of nerve or body, is prone to imagine separation from God, even suspecting that an unpardonable sin has been committed. However, the test of all this is very simple. That sin which grieves the Spirit becomes at once a known issue. The sin will stand forth as the known and recognized cause of heart burden. The cure is confession to God and the one who has aught to confess will not be left in doubt or uncertainty about what should be confessed. No one can be definite in confessing unknown sins. Known sin may be confessed in harmony with that knowledge of it which the Spirit creates in the mind and heart. Should a believer be depressed with no recognized wrong coming in view, it is certain that the cause is physical rather than spiritual. In the light of the truth that the Holy Spirit is grieved by sin and that this reaction to sin on the part of the Spirit is experienced by the one in whom He dwells, it may well be questioned whether the believer ever lives by the dictates of his conscience after he is saved. The presence of the Holy Spirit creates new standards as high as divine holiness itself, and the Christian's manner of life either does not or does grieve the Spirit on that high and holy plane. The Apostle testified that his conscience bore him witness in the Holy Spirit (Rom. 9:1–3). It is probable that the Holy Spirit employs the human conscience, but He as certainly imparts to it a new standard concerning what is right and what is wrong. The clear command addressed to the believer is that he "grieve not the holy Spirit of God." There will be little argument from any source against the truth that sin in the Christian is the cause of grief to the Holy Spirit; nor is there aught to be said against the fact that the child of God, being possessed of a fallen nature, and being subject to unceasing conflict with the world, the flesh, and the devil, does sin and thus grieve the Holy Spirit. The practical problem is twofold: (a) how to be kept from sinning and (b) how to apply God's provided cure once sin has entered the life.

1. PREVENTION OF THE CHRISTIAN'S SIN. Three major factors enter into the prevention of sin in the life of the Christian.

First, *the Word of God* is itself a protection when cherished in the heart. The Psalmist declared: "Thy word have I hid in mine heart, that I might not sin against thee" (Ps. 119:11). Not only is the Word of God inevitably a power in preserving from sin, but it is a power in detecting sin within the life. Those Christians who are carelessly sinning do not feel comfortable when reading the Scriptures and they naturally avoid such reading. It is written: "For the word of God is quick, and powerful, and sharper than any twoedged sword, piercing even to the dividing asunder of soul and spirit, and of the joints and marrow, and is a discerner of the thoughts and intents of the heart" (Heb. 4:12).

Second, *the indwelling Spirit* is the resource from whom abundant ability to resist sin may be drawn. The fact of the Holy Spirit's presence and power is the immediate basis of all holy living. Related to this feature of divine enablement is the action of the human will, the empowered determination to do that which alone will honor God. The will is motivated by the knowledge of the exalted positions to which one has been brought through grace and is energized by the Holy Spirit to will and to do that which is well-pleasing unto God.

Third, *the Intercession of Christ* is that aspect of His priestly ministry in heaven by which He sustains His own who are in the world. It contemplates their weakness, helplessness, and limitations. It pertains to the shepherdhood of Christ.

2. REMEDY OF THE CHRISTIAN'S SIN. As an approach to the subject named, one point should be made, and indeed it is easily recognized as fundamental that, in addition to the truth of the sinfulness of sin, the believer should not sin inasmuch as sin grieves the Holy Spirit. Much emphasis is given in the New Testament to this latter truth and, as seen above, God has provided vital hindrances to sin; but it yet remains true that, because of failure to claim the protection God has provided, because of the strength of the foes encountered—the world, the flesh, and the devil—though even these are not too great for God to control, and because of human weakness, the Christian does sin to a greater or less degree and is therefore faced with a different problem than the prevention of sin alone: he must be informed in respect to and act in compliance with the divine plan of remedy. In the light of the probability of some sin in his life, the Christian who does not claim the cure of the effect of his sin will of necessity reach the place where all manifestations of the Spirit's presence and power are annulled and the life is lived under the cloud of depression which the unceasing grief of the Spirit creates. It is therefore an important feature in the realization of the spiritual life for the believer to understand the provisions for restoration to right relations with God and to act upon these provisions with unremitting faithfulness. These divinely furnished provisions for the restoration of the sin-injured believer to right relation to the Holy Spirit are set forth in the Bible in certain major passages, and of these provisions it should be said that they lead the Christian who has been injured by sin back to complete fellowship with God. The results secured by pursuing the divinely arranged plan for restoration are *absolute.* Too much emphasis cannot be placed upon this fact, and there is need always for the truth to be restated in the light of the tendency to suppose that the divine forgiveness and restoration are subject to the same limitations which characterize such human forgiveness and restoration as men exercise toward each other on the basis of leniency and generosity. The major passages respecting divine forgiveness and restoration are now to be considered.

*John 13:3–11.* "Jesus knowing that the Father had given all things into his hands, and that he was come from God, and went to God; he riseth from supper, and laid aside his garments; and took a towel, and girded himself. After that he poureth water into a bason, and began to wash the disciples' feet, and to wipe them with the towel wherewith he was girded. Then cometh he to Simon Peter: and Peter saith unto him, Lord, dost thou wash my feet? Jesus answered and said unto him, What I do thou knowest not now; but thou shalt know hereafter, Peter saith unto him, Thou shalt never wash my feet. Jesus answered him, If I wash thee not, thou hast no part with me. Simon Peter saith unto him, Lord, not my feet only, but also my hands and my head. Jesus saith to him, He that is washed needeth not save to wash his feet, but is clean every whit: and ye are clean, but not all. For he knew who should betray him; therefore said he, Ye are not all clean."

Among other important features to be presented in this Scripture passage and which enter into the believer's right relation to God, is one that is most important, namely, that Christ alone can cleanse the believer from the defilement of sin. In the earlier chapters of this Gospel the way of salvation has been presented, but beginning with chapter 13 and continuing through chapter 17 the believer's privilege and responsibility in relation to God are declared. Of the various major issues which are included in this particular passage or discourse, it is important to notice that cleansing from defilement is the first to be mentioned and that apart from cleansing there can be no normal experience of the great realities which this discourse presents. That Christ could say—as He actually did later on (15:3)—"Now ye are clean through the word which I have spoken unto you" is most impressive. Cleansing, however, is contemplated by Christ in two widely different aspects, namely, that which is wrought as a part of salvation and that which avails to cleanse the defiled believer. Thus in verse 10 of the present passage Christ declares to Peter: "He that is washed [λούω—wholly bathed] needeth not [to be bathed again] save to wash his feet, but is clean every whit." This truth is drawn as respects its reality from the custom of the times, when people bathed in public bathhouses and returning home with bare feet or sandals through the filth of sewerless streets needed on arrival, not a whole bath, but a partial bathing—that of the feet. Coming to Peter, a normal resistance is set up on the part of this one who did not understand the symbolism of the bathing of the feet and who had but a few months before said to Christ: "Thou art the Christ, the Son of the living God" (Matt. 16:16). That resistance was introduced by Peter's remark, "Dost thou wash my feet?" To this Christ said, "What I do thou knowest not now; but thou shalt know hereafter," thus indicating that there was a hidden meaning in the act of washing the disciples' feet—a meaning which depends for its understanding upon the blood of

Christ being shed for cleansing, but which no disciple could then understand since they did not believe that Christ was to die (cf. Luke 18:31–34). Peter is little impressed with any hidden meaning. He sees only the unreasonableness of the Son of God washing a sinful man's feet. His blunt reply to Christ is, "Thou shalt never wash my feet." This protest draws out from the Savior a statement which explains very much of what is involved. Christ said, "If I wash thee not, thou hast no part with me." Here two words are met which need to be understood in their real meaning. The word *wash* (*νίπτω*) speaks only of a partial bathing such as Christ was undertaking, and is quite in contrast with the word λούω of verse 10 which refers to a whole bath. The second word to be rightly understood is *μέρος*, translated *part*—"Thou hast no part with me." There is no implication that Peter would sustain no relation whatsoever to Christ; it is rather a matter of communion. Peter would not be in fellowship unless defilement is removed by the cleansing blood of Christ. The priest of Old Testament times is the type of the New Testament priest and every Christian is a New Testament priest. Fulfilling the type, the Old Testament priest was wholly bathed in a ritual once for all when entering upon his priestly office (Ex. 29:4). In like manner, the New Testament priest is, as a part of his salvation, bathed with the washing of regeneration (Titus 3:5). Similarly, the Old Testament priest was required to be bathed partially—hands and feet—at the laver before every service (Ex. 30:17–21). Thus, also, the New Testament priest must be cleansed repeatedly whenever defilement is contracted; but Christ alone can cleanse, and though the disciples were enjoined to wash one another's feet as an evidence of service one for the other, no human being can cleanse spiritual defilement from his fellow man, nor is he in any position even by symbol to enact so great an undertaking. The truth is thus established that Christ alone can cleanse the defilement of the believer, and that because of His death and His blood shed sacrificially for the believer (1 John 2:2).

*1 John 1:5—2:2.* "This then is the message which we have heard of him, and declare unto you, that God is light, and in him is no darkness at all. If we say that we have fellowship with him, and walk in darkness, we lie, and do not the truth: but if we walk in the light, as he is in the light, we have fellowship one with another, and the blood of Jesus Christ his Son cleanseth us from all sin. If we say that we have no sin, we deceive ourselves, and the truth is not in us. If we confess our sins, he is faithful and just to forgive us our sins, and to cleanse us from all unrighteousness. If we say that we have not sinned, we make him a liar, and his word is not in us. My little children, these things write I unto you, that ye sin not. And if any man sin, we have an advocate with the Father, Jesus Christ the righteous: and he is the propitiation for our sins: and not for our's only, but also for the sins of the whole world."

John is the experienced witness in regard to an unbroken fellowship with the Father and with the Son, as indicated by the first verses of 1 John. In the first chapter of this epistle a message is brought forward directly from Christ's earthly ministry which does not appear in any Gospel record. The message has to do with maintaining communion with the Father and with the Son. In contemplating such a relationship it should be remembered that "God is light," which phrase refers to moral or holy perfection, and it is with such a One that the believer is to have fellowship. The bringing of the Christian into communion with God is not achieved by lowering that which pertains to God; it is rather gained by lifting the believer up to the level upon which communion with God is possible. For one to say that he has fellowship with God while at the same time he is walking in darkness is to lie and to do not the truth; but if the Christian walks in the light as God is in the light, it is to experience fellowship with God, the fellowship which is the normal experience of all who are saved. Such fellowship is not a special concession from God, but is rather that which is provided for all who are rightly related to God. All this immeasurable blessing is conditioned on "walking in the light." To walk in the light is not to become the light, which would be sinless perfection; it is to be adjusted to the light. When the searchlight, which God is, reveals needed changes in one's life before God, then in order to walk in the light one must adapt one's self to the will of God thus revealed. When thus adapted, the blood of Jesus Christ goes on continuously cleansing from all sin. Fellowship does not depend upon an impossible sinless perfection, but on the willing compliance with all that God desires and makes known. Thus confession, which is the outward expression of inward repentance, becomes the one condition upon which a child of God who has been injured by sin may be restored to unbroken fellowship again. Not only will that restoration be absolute to the extent of infinity, but the divine grace that forgives and cleanses is accomplished on a basis which is righteous to the degree of infinity. Since it is God's own child that has sinned to whom He is bound with eternal ties, He is "faithful" to those relationships; and since Christ has met all the rightful judgments against the sin which is in question, He is "just" to cleanse and to forgive. It was thus in the Old Testament order and it must ever be thus wherever God the Holy One deals with human sin. The Israelite brought his sacrifice and it was after the priest offered the sacrifice that the comer there-with was forgiven. Leviticus 4:35 declares: "And he shall take away all the fat thereof, as the fat of the lamb is taken away from the sacrifice of the peace-offerings; and the priest shall burn them upon the altar, according to the offerings made by fire unto the LORD: and the priest shall make an atonement for his sin that he hath committed, and it shall be forgiven him." Great emphasis is placed on the fact that the one condition to be met for restoration of a believer to fellowship with God is confession of sin. Too often prayer for forgiveness is substituted; but prayer for forgiveness is not an adjustment to the Light which God is. Prayer for forgiveness really assumes that God Himself needs to be changed in His attitude toward the one who has sinned.

*1 Corinthians 11:31–32.* "For if we would judge ourselves, we should not be judged. But when we are judged, we are chastened of the Lord, that we should not be condemed with the world."

Coming as it does at the close of the extended portion of this epistle, which portion is devoted to the correction of carnalities in the Corinthian church(1:10—11:34), this clear direction relative to the human responsibility in the cure of the effects upon himself of the Christian's sin is most appropriate. The particular contribution which this passage makes to the whole doctrine of the believer's walk with God is seen in the order of events which it discloses. The Father is here seen to be waiting for the self-judgment or confession of His child who has sinned. This period of seeming silence or inattention on God's part that follows the sin which the believer has committed is easily misunderstood, and may be wrongly interpreted by the believer as indicating that God has not observed the sin which has been committed. It is the grace of God which waits thus for the believer to act first in his own behalf respecting his sin. However, if the sinning child of God will not thus judge himself by a full confession, it becomes necessary for the Father, being the perfect disciplinarian that He is, to bring His child into judgment. This is the force of the Apostle's words: "If we would judge ourselves, we should not be judged." The voluntary act of self-judgment satisfies every divine demand and no judgment from the Father will be imposed. It is only when the Christian withholds his confession and by so much assumes the attitude of self-justification concerning his sin, or through love of it refuses to be adjusted to the holy will of God, that the Father must bring him into the place of correction. It will be recognized again that the issue is not one of sustaining a union with the Father, which union, like sonship, when once established can never be broken; it is rather the issue respecting communion or fellowship. Accordingly it is asked: "Can two walk together, except they be agreed?" (Amos 3:3). God cannot walk in the dark with the believer, nor can fellowship be experienced when the believer is calling black white and white black. The Christian must agree with God that white is white and black is black. Having come into agreement with God, there remains no obstacle to hinder and fellowship is restored by the gracious forgiving and cleansing from God. The passage from Paul goes on to say: "But when we are judged, we are chastened of the Lord." A distinction is obvious at this point between chastisement and penalty or satisfaction. Even though the believer is chastened the penalty for his sin is not required of him, since Christ has taken all penalty upon Himself and it is never required again. Too often, Christians do not comprehend the truth that there is not and could not be any penalty. Chastisement has as its purpose to bring the believer to penitence and through the accompanying confession to restoration. That chastisement is not penal is demonstrated by the fact that restoration and forgiveness are secured at once apart even from chastisement, when confession is made without delay. Penalty could not be delayed or remitted if it were designed to fall upon the believer. Having undertaken to save the Christian from all penal judgments (cf. John 3:18; 5:24; Rom. 8:1, R.V.), and having covenanted to forgive and cleanse instantly and perfectly on the one condition of confession, the believer is chastened only when resisting God. Standing in the merit of the Son of God and being sheltered under the efficacy of Christ's blood, the child of God can never be "condemned with the world."

*Hebrews 12:5–11.* "And ye have forgotten the exhortation which speaketh unto you as unto children, My son, despise not thou the chastening of the Lord, nor faint when thou art rebuked of him: for whom the Lord loveth he chasteneth, and scourgeth every son whom he receiveth. If ye endure chastening, God dealeth with you as with sons; for what son is he whom the father chasteneth not? But if ye be without chastisement, whereof all are partakers, then are ye bastards, and not sons. Furthermore we have had fathers of our flesh which corrected us, and we gave them reverence: shall we not much rather be in subjection unto the Father of spirits, and live? For they verily for a few days chastened us after their own pleasure; but he for our profit, that we might be partakers of his holiness. Now no chastening for the present seemeth to be joyous, but grievous: nevertheless afterward it yieldeth the peaceable fruit of righteousness unto them which are exercised thereby."

The importance of the doctrine respecting chastisement warrants the space given to it in the Sacred Text. The passage quoted is central and from this context as from other Scriptures it may be seen that chastisement comprehends more than correction for evil; it may include discipline, development, or instruction as its objective as well. Were it restricted to correction for evil in the children of God, it could hardly be said to be universal in scope. As for its universal character, it is written: "Whom the Lord loveth he chasteneth," and in chastisement "God dealeth with you as with sons," and unless ye are chastened—as all sons are—ye are "not sons" at all. The believer should not "despise" chastisement nor faint under its discipline. As in the case of an earthly son, every advantage accrues to the one who is "exercised thereby." Verse 6 implies a distinction between chastisement and scourging. Chastisement, as broad as it may be in its outreach, may be experienced many times; but scourging, which seems to mean the final conquering of the will of the believer, would need to be experienced but once. Many sad episodes in the life of the unyielded Christian might be avoided were he to surrender his will to the mind of God.

Though some specific forms of chastisement are named in the Scriptures and this divine undertaking is seen at work in many of the lives recorded in the Word of God, it is probable that, since God deals thus with individual sons, His ways and means in chastisement are manifold. They may vary with every individual situation. The length to which chastisement may go is asserted in 1 Corinthians 11:30. Speaking of irregularities in connection with the table of the Lord and of discipline which may attend such wrongdoing, the Apostle says: "For this cause many are weak and sickly among you, and many sleep." It is thus disclosed that the Father may employ physical weakness, physical sickness, or physical death as His means in chastisement. Reference to physical death is made in the same connection in other New Testament texts. The branch in Christ which bears not fruit may be lifted up out of its place (John 15:2), and there is a sin unto death which a brother may commit (1 John 5:16)—in such a case prayer for healing will be unavailing. Even Satan may be used as an instrument in chastisement. The Apostle declares: "Of whom is Hymenaeus and Alexander; whom I have delivered unto Satan, that they may learn not to blaspheme" (1 Tim. 1:20).

Because of the comfort which it secures and because of the fact respecting the character of God which is revealed therein, the truth that love is the divine motive in every instance where chastisement is employed should not be overlooked. No attempt to expound this important doctrine should be made which fails to indicate that divine chastisement arises in the infinite compassion of God and is administered under the influence of infinite, divine affection.

*2 Corinthians 7:8–11.* "For though I made you sorry with a letter, I do not repent, though I did repent: for I perceive that the same epistle hath made you sorry, though it were but for a season. Now I rejoice, not that ye were made sorry, but that ye sorrowed to repentance: for ye were made sorry after a godly manner, that ye might receive damage by us in nothing. For godly sorrow worketh repentance to salvation not to be repented of: but the sorrow of the world worketh death. For behold this selfsame thing, that ye sorrowed after a godly sort, what carefulness it wrought in you, yea, what clearing of yourselves, yea, what indignation, yea, what fear, yea, what vehement desire, yea, what zeal, yea, what revenge! In all things ye have approved yourselves to be clear in this matter."

This passage is cited as an example of a true repentance on the part of believers. The Apostle had written the Corinthian church—the correspondence of his first epistle to Corinth is in view—and in that message, as before observed, he brought up their sins and irregularities with the result that they were convinced of their evil ways, and in repentance—meaning a thoroughgoing change of mind—they cleared themselves wholly before God. A true repentance will not result in a shallow, temporary experience which goes on tolerating and repeating the evil; however, the power to avoid recurrences is not in the degree of repentance, but in a more effective reliance upon the enabling Holy Spirit. Consideration should be given to this passage in the light of the truth that it is a pattern of what God has a right to expect from all whom He chastens.

*Psalm 51:1–19.* This familiar Psalm, which is too extensive for quotation, presents David as an outstanding example of repentance and confession among Old Testament saints. In the Word of God, David's sin is laid bare and with it his broken and contrite heart. He had partaken of that form of salvation which was accorded Old Testament saints, which salvation, being wrought of God as all salvation must be, was not itself injured. David therefore prayed that the joy of his salvation, rather than the salvation itself, might be restored unto him. It is thus indicated that David understood precisely what he had lost through his sin. His testimony also had been hindered. After making request that he might be restored and anticipating its blessedness, he said: "Then will I teach transgressors thy ways; and sinners shall be converted unto thee." To this extent the Old Testament saints were similar in their relation to God to the New Testament saints; however, striking differences must be observed and such as are disclosed in this Psalm. The New Testament believer need never pray, "And take not thy holy Spirit from me," since the Spirit once given is never removed from the heart of the Christian; nor must the New Testament saint ask for forgiveness and restoration. After Christ has died bearing all sin—that of the Christian as well as that of the unsaved—and after that sin-bearing death has rendered God propitious, there are no grounds remaining for the Christian to be asking God to forgive. He forgives, just as He has promised, when sin is confessed (cf. 1 John 1:9). David recognized, as all saints should, that his sin was primarily against God. "Against thee, thee only, have I sinned" was his heart-broken cry. His restoration based on his confession was complete; for it was in spite of David's sin and after his restoration that Jehovah said, "I have found David the son of Jesse, a man after mine own heart" (Acts 13:22; cf. 1 Sam. 13:14). David's sin was not pleasing to God; but, having repented and having confessed his sin, he was restored to God's favor.

*Luke 15:1–32.* The last of the seven major passages bearing on the cure of the effects of sin upon the spiritual life of a saint—whether he is of the Old Testament or the New—is found in Luke 15:1–32. This portion of the Scriptures contains one parable in three parts (cf. vs. 3). It is the threefold story of a lost sheep, a lost piece of silver, and a lost son. Though three incidents are told, there is but one underlying purpose. The particular value of this passage, in the present connection, lies in its revelation of the divine compassion as seen in the restoration of a sinning saint. It is the unveiling of the Father's heart. The emphasis falls upon the shepherd, rather than upon the sheep; upon the woman, rather than upon the lost piece of silver; and upon the father, rather than upon either son of his. In considering this passage, it must be borne in mind that what is here recorded reflects the conditions which obtained before the cross. It, therefore, has to do primarily with Israel. They were the covenant people of the Old Testament, "the sheep of his pasture," and their position as such was unchanged until the new covenant was made in His blood. Being covenant people, they could return to the blessings of their covenant, if those blessings had been lost through sin, on the grounds of repentance and confession. This, according to the Scriptures and as has been seen, is true of all covenant people. Israel's covenants are not the same in character as "the new covenant [made] in his blood"; but the terms of restoration into the blessings of the covenant are the same in the one case as in the other. The *factuality* of the covenant abides through the faithfulness of God, but the *blessing* of the covenant may be lost through the unfaithfulness of the saint. The blessing is regained, too, not by forming another covenant, but by restoration into the unchanging privileges of the original covenant. The threefold parable here is about Israelites and was addressed to them. Whatever application there may be in the parable to Christians under the new covenant is possible only on the ground of the fact that the way of restoration by repentance and confession is common to both old and new covenants. In the parable, therefore, is supplied a picture of the heart of God toward any and all of His covenant people when they sin.

The parable opens thus: "Then drew near unto him all the publicans and sinners for to hear him. And the Pharisees and scribes murmured, saying, This man receiveth sinners, and eateth with them." Here is the key to all that follows. "Publicans and sinners" were not Gentiles. "Publicans" were Israelites under the covenant "made with the fathers" who had turned traitor to their nation to the extent of becoming taxgatherers for Rome. "Sinners" were Israelites under the same covenant who had failed to present the sacrifices for sin as prescribed by the Law of Moses. An Israelite was accounted "blameless" before the law when he had provided the required offerings. Thus Paul could say of himself concerning his former position as no more than a Jew under the law: "touching the righteousness which is in the law, blameless." The Apostle is not claiming sinless perfection; he is testifying to the fact that he had always been faithful in providing the sacrifices prescribed by the Law of Moses. The Pharisees and scribes were Israelites who gave all their energies to the exact fulfillment of the Law of Moses. Paul was once no more than a Pharisee, "an Hebrew of the Hebrews." These men were not Christians and should not be judged as such. There is little in common here with Christians. These Israelites were blameless through the animal sacrifices which anticipated the death of Christ. Christians are blameless through faith in the effectual blood of Christ which has already been shed. One is a justification by works, inadequate because contingent on the human side; the other is a justification by faith concerning a finished work of God. The Pharisees and scribes murmured when they saw that Jesus received publicans and sinners and ate with them. He, therefore, spoke this parable unto *them,* His critics. The parable is explicitly addressed to murmuring Pharisees and scribes rather than to everybody, anywhere. And there can be little understanding of the truth contained in it unless the plain purpose for which it is told is kept in mind. In turning to an interpretation of the parable, some consideration must be given to the well-nigh universal impression that this parable is a picture of salvation. While it is a blessed picture of the heart of God, it most evidently has to do with His work of *restoration* rather than of *regeneration.*

The first division of the parable concerns a man who had a hundred sheep. "What man of you, having an hundred sheep, if he lose one of them, doth not leave the ninety and nine in the wilderness, and go after that which is lost, until he find it?" This is not a picture of ninety-nine sheep and one goat: it is of one hundred sheep and "sheep," according to the Scriptures, are always symbolic of covenant people. Israelites were sheep, so also are the Christians in this dispensation. Jesus, when speaking of those to be saved through His death, said to the Jews: "Other sheep I have, which are not of this fold" (John 10:16). Another important distinction should be noted in this parable: The sheep, the piece of silver, and the son were *lost,* but they were lost only to the point that they needed to be *found.* This is hardly the same as being lost in such an utter way as to need to be *saved.* The Biblical use of the word *lost* has at least these two widely different meanings. "The Son of man is come to seek and to save that which was lost"; but, in all three parts of this parable, it is seeking and finding rather than seeking and saving. The word *save,* it should be observed, does not once appear in this parable. Should this parable be accepted as a teaching in regard to salvation, there is no escaping the error of Universalism; for this Shepherd seeks *until* He finds that which is lost. The passage, on the other hand, presents a blessed revelation of the heart of God toward His wandering child who needs to be found rather than to be saved. "Ninety and nine" who are safe in the fold compared to one that is lost is a poor picture of the proportions which have always existed in this age between the saved and unsaved. Were the parable to teach the salvation of a sinner, far better would it have been had it made the figures ninety and nine who were lost in contrast to one that was safe in the fold. The parable continues: "And when he hath found it, he layeth it on his shoulders, rejoicing. And when he cometh home, he calleth together his friends and neighbours, saying unto them, Rejoice with me; for I have found my sheep which was lost. I say unto you, that likewise joy shall be in heaven over one sinner that repenteth, more than over ninety and nine just persons, which need no repentance."

The sinner here referred to can be none other than one of the covenant "sinners" mentioned in the first verse of the passage and concerning whom the parable was told. He, being a covenant person, is here pictured by the Spirit as returning on the grounds of repentance, rather than as being saved on the grounds of saving faith. So, again, one could hardly find any class of persons within the church corresponding to the "ninety and nine just persons, which need no repentance." Such a case was possible, nevertheless, under the Law of Moses, the Apostle Paul when under Judaism being a good example. The very Pharisees and scribes to whom the parable was addressed were also of that class. Within the outward demands of the Law of Moses, they needed no repentance. Repentance, which means a change of mind, is a vital element in present salvation; but it is now *included* in the one act of believing, for fully one hundred and fifty passages in the New Testament condition our present salvation on believing, or its synonym, faith. The Gospel by John, written especially that we might believe that Jesus is the Christ, the Son of God, and that believing we might have life through His name, does not once use the word *repentance*. The unsaved today are saved through believing, which evidently includes such repentance as can be produced by those who are "dead in trespasses and sins." Repentance means a change of mind and no one can believe on Christ as his Savior and not have changed his mind with respect to his sin, his lost condition, and the placing of his saving trust in the One who is "mighty to save."

The second division of the parable concerns the woman and the lost piece of silver. It is the same story of seeking and finding that which was lost. The special emphasis in this division of the parable falls on the *joy* of the one who finds. It is the joy of the One in whose presence the angels are. The story, again, is of a repenting sinner, rather than of a believing sinner.

The third division of the parable tells of "a certain man." This story is evidently told to reveal the heart of the father. Incidentally, he had two sons, and one of them was typical of a "publican and sinner," and the other of a "Pharisee and scribe." One left the blessings of his father's house (but did not cease to be a son); the other murmured, as did the scribes and Pharisees, when the "sinner" was restored. No greater depths of degradation could be pictured to a Jewish mind than to be found in a field feeding swine. Here we have the Lord declaring, in the terms of His own time and people, that a wandering *son* may return by confession, even from the lowest depths of sin. It was there, in that field with the swine, that the son "came to himself" and purposed to return to his father with a confession, which is only the normal expression of a true heart-repentance. There is no mention of regeneration. Nothing is said of faith, apart from which no soul could hope to be saved into sonship. He was a son and returned to his father as a son. The sentiment that an unsaved person, when turning to Christ, is "returning home," as is sometimes expressed in sermons and gospel songs, is foreign to the teaching of the Word of God. Sons, who have wandered away may return home, and, as being lost in the state of wandering, may be found. This could not apply to one who has never been a child of God. Such are certainly lost, but need rather to be saved. In this dispensation, unsaved people may *turn* to God, but they do not *return* to God. When the returning son was a great way off the father saw him and had compassion on him and ran and fell on his neck and kissed him. The father saw him because he was looking that way. He had not ceased to look since the hour the son departed. Such is the picture of God the Father's heart, expressed, as well, in the searching carried on both by the shepherd and the woman. All righteousness would require that this returning boy be punished most severely. Had he not dishonored the father's name? Had he not squandered his father's substance? Had he not brought himself to ruin? But he was not punished. The fact that he was not punished unfolds to believers of this dispensation the blessed truth that, because of the work of Christ on the cross, the Father can and will receive His child without punishment. The terms of restoration to be met are only a brokenhearted confession. The guilt of the sin has fallen on Another in our stead.

It is important to observe that the father kissed the son even before his confession was made. Reason would dictate that the son be kissed after his confession. So far as this incident may be made to apply rightfully to the present relationships between God the Father and Christians who have sinned, it emphasizes the truth that *God is propitious*, having been rendered propitious by the all-satisfying death of Christ as substitute in judgment due the Christian's sins. In this connection, it is written: "And he [Christ in His death] is the propitiation for our [Christians'] sins" (1 John 2:2). It is the fact that Christ died as substitute which makes it possible for God to receive those for whom He died as though every obligation to divine justice which their sins created is met, as indeed these obligations were met by Christ acting for them. It is not tears, repentance, or pleading on the part of those who have sinned. Both the unsaved and the sinning believer are invited to come to a propitious God. Of great import also is the fact that, without reprimand or punishment, the son was reinstated in the position and blessing of the father's house. The confession which he prepared was not fully repeated to the father. The last words "and make me as one of thy hired servants" were cut off by the vigorous command of the father, "Bring forth . . ." Thus, instantly, when a complete confession is made, regardless of additional words the penitent one would present, the restoration is achieved.

The confession of this son was first toward heaven and then to his father. This is the true order of all confession. It must be first to God and then to those who would be wronged by the withholding of our confession. Great is the power of a brokenhearted confession. No one can believe that the wandering son, after having been restored, and after resting again in the comforts of that fellowship and home, would immediately ask his father for more of his goods that he might return to the life of sin. Such action would be wholly inconsistent with the heartbroken confession he has made. True confession is real and transforming in its power (cf. 2 Cor. 7:11). He was a *son* during all the days of his absence from home. Had he died in the field with the swine, he would have died as a son. So far as this illustrates the estate of a sinning Christian, it may be concluded, from this and all the Scriptures on this subject, that an imperfect Christian, such as we all are, would be received into the heavenly home at death, though he suffer loss of all rewards and much joy, and though, when he meets his Lord face to face, he is called upon there to make his hitherto neglected confession.

From these seven major passages it may be concluded that the cure of the effects of sin on the spiritual life of a child of God is promised to the one who in repentance of heart makes a genuine confession of his sin. Sin is always sin in the sight of God. It is no less sin because it is committed by a Christian, nor can it be cured in any case other than through the redemption which is in Christ. It is because the redemption-price has already been paid in the precious blood of Christ that God can save sinners who only believe and restore saints who only confess. Not one degree of the punishment that fell upon our Substitute can ever fall on saint or sinner. Since Christ bore it all for us, believing or confessing is all that can righteously be demanded. Until confession is made by the one who has sinned, he is contending for that which is evil and thus is in disagreement with the Father. "Can two walk together, except they be agreed?" God cannot agree with sin. The child can agree with the Father, and this is true repentance which is expressed in true confession. Again let it be said: repentance is a change of mind. By it those who have sinned turn unto God from sin. The blessing does not depend upon sinless perfection; it is a matter of not grieving the Spirit. It is not an issue concerning *unknown* sin; it is an attitude of heart that is willing always instantly to confess every *known* sin. "If we confess our sins, he is faithful and just to forgive us our sins, and to cleanse us from all unrighteousness." The Christian who fully confesses all *known* sin will have removed one—if not all—of the hindrances to the fullest manifestation of the Spirit. "And grieve not the holy Spirit of God whereby ye are sealed unto the day of redemption" (Eph. 4:30).

From the foregoing discussion, it may be determined that one of the conditions upon which the believer may be Spirit-filled is met when that which grieves the Holy Spirit is removed by complete confession, which confession is the expression of a contrite heart. The secret by which this aspect of responsibility may best be maintained is to keep short accounts with God. Let the first impression of spiritual depression be a signal to ascertain at once the cause and as readily to apply the remedy—confession to God.

## II. "QUENCH NOT THE SPIRIT"

The second direct command which governs the right relation between the Holy Spirit and the believer is stated in 1 Thessalonians 5:19, "Quench not the Spirit." These are words of solemn import since they imply a most serious possibility in the Christian's attitude toward the Holy Spirit. The thoughtful child of God is thus reminded of the heaven-high responsibility and reality which an unbroken companionship with the Holy Spirit imposes—a responsibility and a reality which cannot be lessened or avoided. Though the demands are superhuman, there is no ground upon which it properly can be considered a burden or bondage to avoid the quenching of the Spirit. Every demand which the presence of the Spirit engenders is in itself a path into untold riches of blessing. In truth, the presence of the Holy Spirit and the riches of His benefits constitute an earnest and foretaste of heaven's immeasurable realities. Spiritual sanity will never shrink from the obligations which life in company with the Holy Spirit creates. Those obligations at best may be but partially discharged, but the ambition to comply with all that they exact should never be lacking. Again attention is directed to the fact that this, like the former issue respecting the grieving of the Spirit, is a direct mandate which suffers no option relative to acquiescence. Both behests are negative, making request respecting specific things which must not be allowed if the full measure of the Spirit's blessing is to be realized. Though somewhat similar since they are addressed alike to the believer's inner life and power to react, they are different. The Spirit is grieved when sin occurs and remains unconfessed. This feature of the truth is altogether within the scope of the negative side of the spiritual life. The Spirit is quenched when the Christian resists or rejects the will of God for him, which body of truth as set forth in the Scriptures is usually within the scope of the positive side of the spiritual life, though it is possible to quench the Spirit by resisting God respecting issues which have to do with victory over sin as well as in issues which pertain to life and service. The three requirements which condition the Spirit's filling—(a) confession of every known sin, (b) yielding to the will of God, and (c) walking in dependence upon the Holy Spirit—are not based upon an irrational caprice in God. They indicate that which is the foundation of communion and fellowship—what is to be sustained between the Holy Spirit and the one in whom the Spirit dwells. Nothing is shrouded with mystery or veiled even from those who are the least capable of understanding. The problem is one of accepting and doing the will of God. This is the central issue in the whole problem of the spiritual life. In the last analysis, the confession of every known sin and the maintaining of the principle of reliance upon the Spirit in the daily walk depend on the action of the human will, but it is equally true and far more consequential that the human will be empowered by the Holy Spirit, else it does not act to God's glory. It is written, "For it is God which worketh [ἐνεργέω—*energize*] in you both to will and to do of his good pleasure" (Phil. 2:13). The initial act is a surrender to the will of God, after which the human will may be depended upon to fulfill its responsibility as empowered by the Holy Spirit. In defense of a theoretical Calvinism and as a criticism of the teaching that the spiritual life depends upon the action of the human will even though energized of God, Dr. B. B. Warfield wrote that by so much it amounted to "subjecting all gracious workings of God to human determinating" (*Princeton Review,* April, 1919, p. 322). No worthy student of Biblical doctrine would question that God has a sovereign purpose or that all things are working toward the realization of that purpose, but it must be acknowledged as well from such passages as Romans 12:1–2; Galatians 5:16; Ephesians 4:30; 1 Thessalonians 5:19;

and 1 John 1:9 that the appeal is to the human will, with every implication present which might establish the truth that, in the divine plan, the human will determines the whole course of the believer's life. The failure at this point with extreme Calvinists arises from the fact that, in their zeal to defend the doctrine of divine sovereignty, they do not recognize how the very sovereignty of God in its outworking utilizes the human will as its instrument, not, however, by any form of coercion, but by that form of persuasion which enlightens and engenders holy desires to which the will may respond and by which it may be motivated. Here, again, it must be asserted with all possible force that when a decision is made regarding some step in the spiritual life, even under the most powerful, impelling inducements which God may impart, the action of the human will is sovereign and free in its own choice. As before demonstrated, this same procedure characterizes the whole undertaking when a soul is saved through faith in Christ. It matters nothing that the human will has no power in itself to accept Christ. The heart must be moved completely by the Holy Spirit or no choice of Christ is made; but just the same when the choice is made it is not due to coercion but to the will acting in its sovereign freedom. None can doubt the implication in the text which avers: "Whosoever will, let him take the water of life freely." It is misleading to assert, as Dr. Warfield was wont to do, that "whosoever God wills may come." It nevertheless is true, but not in the same sense in which extreme Calvinists have presented it, namely, that whosoever God compels will come—rather it should be stated thus: that whosoever God calls with an efficacious call, which call is a persuasion sufficient to guarantee the determined choice, will, of his own sovereign determination, come. Let it not be supposed that this interpretation of an important Biblical doctrine lends any support to the Arminian notion that unregenerate men—because of some hypothetical, universal impartation of "common grace"—may at any time, under any circumstances, and by virtue of their own unaided vision and determination accept Christ as Savior if they will to do so. Only tragic misconceptions have been the fruit of an extreme Calvinism which conceives of the human will as overpowered by God, and of a fallacious Arminianism which makes no place in its reckoning for the inherent, constitutional necessity of immediate divine action upon the human will before the right choice can be made at all. The spiritual life is in all instances presented as the result of the free choice of the believer's will; but this doctrine must not be left to stand alone. Another doctrine of even more vital significance is the truth that the will must be moved by God. This fact may well lead to consideration of the problem concerning the quenching of God's Spirit. Such a theme will be contemplated under five general divisions, namely, (1) resistance of the Spirit, (2) the yielded life, (3) the example of Christ, (4) the will of God, and (5) the sacrificial life.

1. RESISTANCE OF THE SPIRIT. As used in 1 Thessalonians 5:19, the word *quench* does not mean to extinguish in the sense that the Spirit might become extinct or be expelled from the heart. Such an interpretation would come into direct contradiction with other Scriptures which assert that the Holy Spirit abides in the Christian forever. It refers rather to the suppressing of the Spirit's manifestations, or that which results when the divine forces are arrested upon which the spiritual life depends. As intimated above, the Spirit is quenched by an attitude of resistance or indifference toward the known will of God. More simply stated, it is saying No to God.

2. THE YIELDED LIFE. All the responsibility resting on the believer with respect to the quenching of the Spirit, like that resting on him with respect to the grieving of the Spirit, is summed up in the one word *yield.* In the following major division of this chapter it will be seen that the one requirement which secures a cure for a walk after the flesh is summed up in the one word *walk*—in its relation to the Holy Spirit. Thus in the briefest and most vital manner three great responsibilities—the three which condition spirituality—are gathered up in three words, namely, *confess, yield,* and *walk.* The context in which the yielded life may principally be found is Romans 6:1–23. The theme at that point, as before noted, is sanctification in daily life and by the power of the Holy Spirit alone. Daily victory over the flesh by means of the Spirit is made possible on a righteous ground by the fact that Christ has died the judgment death which belonged to the fallen nature of the believer. There follow two vitally essential responsibilities which rest directly and unceasingly upon the child of God: He is to *reckon* the judgment death of Christ which had the believer's fallen nature in view to be achieved wholly, and thus to believe that all deliverance is provided and now made possible even at infinite cost; and he is to *yield* himself unto God as one who has passed through cocrucifixion, codeath, and coburial with Christ as a judgment upon his fallen nature, and thus to believe that now through union with Christ in resurrection he is "alive from the dead." The believer is to count the members of his body to be "instruments of righteousness unto God." Thus, yielding to God is seen to be more than a secondary or isolated responsibility. It is as

essential as the whole doctrine of experimental sanctification which depends upon it. The appeal to live the yielded life as presented in Romans 6 is as follows: "Likewise reckon ye also yourselves to be dead indeed unto sin, but alive unto God through Jesus Christ our Lord. Let not sin therefore reign in your mortal body, that ye should obey it in the lusts thereof. Neither yield ye your members as instruments of unrighteousness unto sin: but yield yourselves unto God, as those that are alive from the dead, and your members as instruments of righteousness unto God" (vs. 11–13). The same appeal is made again in Romans 12:1–2, which states: "I beseech you therefore, brethren, by the mercies of God, that ye present your bodies a living sacrifice, holy, acceptable unto God, which is your reasonable service. And be not conformed to this world: but be ye transformed by the renewing of your mind, that ye may prove what is that good, and acceptable, and perfect, will of God." Presentation of the whole body unto God is termed a "reasonable service," or, perhaps better, "spiritual worship," which is not a sacrifice to be offered in death, but a living sacrifice that continues its dedication throughout all of a lifetime on earth. The life is not to be run into the mold of this age, but to be transfigured by the unhindered manifestation of that divinely renewed mind. The Authorized Version uses the word *transform* as a translation of *μεταμορφόομαι,* which word probably should be translated *transfigure* (cf. Matt. 17:2; Mark 9:2; 2 Cor. 3:18). This distinction is important. A thing may be transformed by a light shining upon it from without, but a thing is transfigured only as release is secured of a light from within. The transfiguration of Christ was not from without, but was rather the outshining of His essential Shekinah glory. The appeal in Romans 12:2 is for the manifestation or outshining of the divine nature which the believer possesses, that is, the manifestation of the Spirit in the realization of a truly spiritual life. Such a yielding as is called for would, it is assured, make full proof of what is that *good,* that *acceptable,* and that *perfect* will of God. No richer experience is conceivable than that depicted by the help of these three words of description. It is the life supreme. The words "I beseech you" with which this passage begins (cf. Eph. 4:1) are far removed from a command; they are a pleading for a specific manner of life which becomes the child of God. It is not a plea for something the believer *must* do to be saved or to continue saved; it is rather something one *should* do because he is saved. The exhortation is for dedication and not, as so frequently misstated, for consecration, since consecration is an act of God alone by which He takes up and applies that which has been dedicated. The Christian surrenders, yields, and dedicates; God must employ what is thus presented. A so-called reconsecration is also terminology open to question, though it has been and is so generally mentioned and undertaken. Dedication, if done at all as God would have it, hardly needs to be done over. In other words, dedication is an all-determining act and not a process.

The question may well be asked, Why in the light of the inherent sovereign right of the Creator over the creature whom He has made should there be any hesitation in the human heart respecting an absolute conformity to the mind and will of God? As has been demonstrated at length under satanology, the first resistance of the Creator's authority was introduced by Lucifer, son of the morning, who is, according to the Scripture, the greatest of all the angels. He it was who led what may have been a third part of the angels of God after him in rebellion against God, and these became the demons and evil powers of supernatural origin who are described and identified in the New Testament. This same great angel entered the Garden of Eden and accomplished the constitutional degeneration of the first man and the first woman, and through them the ruin of the race, from which ruin only a lifeblood-redemption by the Son of God could rescue. That men are fallen and in a state of independence toward God is clearly indicated by the fact that it is so difficult, even for regenerate people, to be conformed to the will of God. Why should any creature find it difficult to be obedient unto God? Not only does God have the inherent, sovereign right over that which He has made, but the highest possible destiny for each individual, whether angel or human, is to be found in fulfilling precisely the thing for which he was created. Nothing is more irrational than to suppose that a creature can better his estate or improve his prospects by keeping the direction of his life in his own hands. Satan himself is the supreme example of this folly. By turning from the exalted position and ever increasing glory that was his by creation over to a *cosmos*-world program in opposition to God, he evidently supposed that he was improving his fortunes; but in place of the eternal honor and glory as the highest of all angels which was once his portion, he must spend eternity in the lake of fire. There is no uncertainty about Satan's destiny. That destined lake was made for "the devil and his angels" (Matt. 25:41) and is God's answer to the creature who rebels against His rightful authority. If men go to the lake of fire, it is because they, too, have adopted the satanic philosophy of independence toward God (cf. Rev. 20:12–15). Lest in such a discussion and in view of the crushing defeat and eternal misery coming to the enemies of God an impression be created that God plays the tyrant who is disposed only to destroy such as resist Him, it should be remembered that only benefits commensurable with the infinite love of God are in store for those who do His will; and, as a message to the unsaved, that to obey the gospel, to conform to God's priceless plan of redeeming grace, is the first step in the doing of His will.

3. THE EXAMPLE OF CHRIST. In the range of His humanity, Christ became the exemplar of that manner of life which alone will please the Father. To the end that He might in all respects represent the perfect divine ideal, Christ apparently drew not at all upon His own resources as a member of the Godhead, but suffered Himself to be wholly dependent, as every believer must do, upon the Holy Spirit. In the same perfection of conformity, He surrendered His human life and mind to the will of His Father. Having entered the human sphere, there was no other course open to the One who was appointed to become the perfection of the divine ideal. Above all else, it becomes one who enters the human sphere to be yielded utterly to the will of God. Anything less than complete yieldedness is anarchy in the household of God. Returning for the moment to the record respecting the insubordination of the highest angel, it will be remembered that his sin consisted in not only rejecting the will of God but substituting something of his own design in place of that will. As a consummation of five "I will's" set against the mind of God, Satan said, "I will be like the most High" (Isa. 14: 13–14)—like God in the only particular in which the creature may resemble Him, namely, acting in independence (of God); and such disobedience is the very essence of sin. It was the same disobedience that Satan prompted in the lives of the first man and the first woman. It was the same disobedience that Satan sought to excite in the humanity of Christ by and through the threefold temptation in the wilderness. As in the case of the first Adam there was no inherent evil in the thing proposed, so in the case of the Last Adam the things suggested were not in themselves evil. As it must always be, the sin consisted in the disobedience of the creature to the Creator. In this His perfect obedience, Christ became, in His humanity, the model of a right relationship to God. It is recorded of Him when about to descend into the world that He said: "Wherefore when he cometh into the world, he saith, Sacrifice and offering thou wouldest not, but a body hast thou prepared me: in burnt-offerings and sacrifices for sin thou hast had no pleasure. Then said I, Lo, I come (in the volume of the book it is written of me,) to

do thy will, O God" (Heb. 10:5–7). As He came near the cross He said: "Nevertheless not my will, but thine, be done" (Luke 22:42). Thus, too, it is recorded of Him that, in the darkest hour of His separation from conscious fellowship with the Father, He said, "But thou art holy" (Ps. 22:3). The Apostle records of Christ that "He became obedient unto death, even the death of the cross" (Phil. 2:8). He who could truthfully say, "I do always those things that please him" (John 8:29), is said Himself, though a Son, to have "learned obedience by the things which he suffered" (Heb. 5:8). The absolute yieldedness of the Great Son to His Father becomes thus the example of that surrender which is the rightful attitude of all those who through the regenerating work of the Spirit have become sons of God. To such the Apostle writes: "Let this mind be in you, which was also in Christ Jesus" (Phil. 2:5). The first word of this injunction, *let,* is especially illuminating. By whatever word the Greek is translated, it suggests that the outworking of the mind of Christ will be produced in the believer by Another, and that the believer's responsibility is that of letting, allowing, or electing the mind of Christ. Such an exalted mind can never be produced by the believer, nor maintained by him; but He who worketh in the child of God "both to will and to do of his good pleasure" (Phil. 2:13) is fully able to accomplish this great end. It is essential that the Christian know what is included in the mind of Christ which is thus to be reproduced in him, otherwise there can be no intelligent cooperation in the undertaking. Hence the essential elements which make up the mind of Christ are enumerated. The passage goes on to record: "Who, being in the form of God, thought it not robbery to be equal with God: but made himself of no reputation, and took upon him the form of a servant, and was made in the likeness of men: and being found in fashion as a man, he humbled himself, and became obedient unto death, even the death of the cross. Wherefore God also hath highly exalted him, and given him a name which is above every name: that at the name of Jesus every knee should bow, of things in heaven, and things in earth, and things under the earth; and that every tongue should confess that Jesus Christ is Lord, to the glory of God the Father" (Phil. 2:6–11). The seven steps downward followed by seven steps upward, which altogether comprise this declaration of the mind of Christ (cf. Heb. 12:1–2), are not listed merely to relate vital facts respecting Christ, but to inform the believer and thus prepare him for the outworking of these great values in his own life. The seven steps downward represent sacrifice, while the seven steps upward represent glory. It is the cross followed by the crown. Not all the elements of the mind of Christ may find an immediate reproduction in the believer; however, three may be considered in particular and as representative of all. (1) The willingness of Christ to leave His native sphere and rightful abode and to come, as the Father chose for Him to do, into this world as an outworking of the saving grace of God, all of which could be expressed by the words: "I'll go where you want me to go." (2) Similarly, also, Christ was willing to become whatever His Father desired Him to become, even to becoming of "no reputation," and in so doing He was saying in effect to His Father: "I'll be what you want me to be." And (3) in His obedience, even unto the death of the cross, He was saying virtually, "I'll do what you want me to do." These and similar words are often sung, and no doubt the singing of them is less demanding than an entry into the direct and immediate experience of all that these phrases delineate. Such, indeed, must be the pattern of the life which is yielded to God.

In another instance the surrendered life is likened by Christ to the branch abiding in the vine (John 15:1–16). As before indicated, abiding in Christ is not a matter of maintaining *union* with Christ, which union is secured rather by the Spirit's baptism and endures as long as the merit of Christ endures, but a matter of maintaining *communion* with Christ. Abiding is continuance in the relationship wherein divine vitality may be imparted and God-honoring fruit may be borne. When thus related to Christ in unbroken communion, prayer is effectual (John 15:7), joy is celestial (John 15:11), and fruit is perpetual (John 15:16). This life—so much to be desired—depends upon abiding, and abiding upon obedience. The Savior said: "If ye keep my commandments, ye shall abide in my love; even as I have kept my Father's commandments, and abide in his love" (John 15:10). Again Christ appears as the supreme example of faithfulness. The object in view with His own abiding or obedience to the Father's commandments was not to maintain union, for that could never be broken; it was to maintain communion between Father and Son in the sphere of the Son's humanity. In like manner, let it be repeated, keeping the commandments of Christ on the part of the believer is not to maintain union, which union could never be broken; it is to maintain unbroken communion—communion which depends upon finding and doing the will of God. Abiding is the result of being yielded to the known will of God, as Christ yielded to His Father's will. In all this, Christ is set forth as the Pattern.

Here it is well to observe that yieldedness to the will of God is not demonstrated by some one particular issue alone; it is rather a matter of having taken the will of God as the rule or dominating principle of one's whole life. To be in the will of God is simply to be willing to do His will without reference to any single distinctive feature of that will. It is electing God's will to be final before any specific problem may have arisen for decision. It is not a willingness to do some one thing; it is the willingness to do anything, when, where, and how it may seem best to the wisdom and love of God. It is taking the normal position of child-like trust which freely consents to the wish of the Father before any detail thereof is discovered. The importance of this distinction is clear. It is too often said: "If he wishes me to do a certain thing, let Him show me what it is and I will determine what I will do about it." To that attitude of heart nothing is revealed. There should and must be a relationship of trust in which the will of God is assented to once for all and without reservations. Why should it not be so? Is it lurking in the mind and heart to say, "Lord, I knew thee that thou art an hard man . . ."? Is He a hard taskmaster? Is there any hope whatsoever that the child of God may of himself choose what is best when keeping all of life in his own hands? No futile promises need be made Him that one will not sin or that the natural desires of the heart will be revolutionized just by human strength. The Father delights only in that which is best for His child and He will never impose upon His child or be careless. On the basis that for every reason God's will is best, the covenant to do that will when it has been revealed is not difficult. From that point on, it is His part to work in the believer both to will and to do of His good pleasure. Long waiting may be endured before His will is revealed, but when it has been revealed there is no room for debate. To hesitate is to say No to God and to quench the Spirit.

4. THE WILL OF GOD. Again this most vital feature of the spiritual life—guidance—must be introduced in a logical approach to all the truth now being considered. Certain general suggestions are in order: (1) The leading of the Spirit is only for those who are already committed to do the will of God. He is able to speak loud enough to make a willing soul hear. (2) The guidance of the Spirit will always be in harmony with the Scriptures which in their primary application direct the life of the believer in this dispensation. The Christian seeking guidance may go to the Scriptures with prayerful expectation; yet the Bible is not a magic lottery. The will of God is not found by opening the Bible to some chance verse and abiding by its message. Such notions disregard the essential truth that leading is from the Holy Spirit who, being the indwelling One, manifests His guidance within the believer's heart and

mind, but not now by signs, dreams, or visions. The Spirit may use outward things, events, or circumstances; nevertheless it is still a matter of His leading and not of the mere instrument which He may employ. A general knowledge of the Word of God as a whole is most to be desired, since leading is in harmony with all that the Bible presents and not usually centralized on one particular text by itself. (3) There are no rules governing the Spirit's leading. No two are led altogether alike and it is equally probable that no one person is ever led twice in quite the same manner. General principles may be announced as are here set forth; the application of these, however, will vary in every instance. In view of the vital importance of the leading of the Holy Spirit in each Christian's life, the ability to be led is one of the most consequential factors in that life. This competency will be gained only through attention and personal experience. Every believer should learn to magnify the reality of the Spirit's indwelling presence and should become familiar with the Spirit's ways in respect to his own life. In the light of the fact that leading by the Spirit proves so individual, it should be obvious that it is most dangerous to seek guidance from even the best of men. God may choose to use men to give the direction the believer needs; still, again, it is not guidance from men, but from the Spirit through such men. To be guided of the Spirit is to be moved through the most delicate relationships the heart can know. To be led by the mere gentle glance of His eye—He said, "I will guide thee with mine eye" (Ps. 32:8)—is far more to be desired than the harsh "bit and bridle" (cf. Ps. 32:9). The appeal of a morbid conscience, mistaken impressions about duty, or a lack of understanding of the Word of God may mislead, but the error may often be detected by the fact that the false leading proves to be irksome, painful, and disagreeable whereas according to Romans 12:2 the will of God is "good, and acceptable, and perfect." God it is who is working in the believer "that which is wellpleasing in his sight" (Heb. 13:21), for He "worketh in you both to will and to do of his good pleasure" (Phil. 2:13).

5. THE SACRIFICIAL LIFE. Doing the will of God must ever be voluntary on the believer's part. He was saved from the bondslavery to sin into the glorious liberty of the children of God. He is commanded to stand fast in that liberty wherewith Christ hath made him free. Christ is no slave owner. His redeeming blood did not purchase the Christian with a view to his being passed from one slavery to another. He may say, however, as a Hebrew servant in the Old Testament was permitted to do: "I love my master . . . I will not go out free" (Ex. 21:5), and

so by dedication, which is wholly voluntary, become the bondslave of Christ. It was thus that Christ became the bondslave in His human relation to the Father. The phrase "Mine ears hast thou opened" (lit., digged or pierced—Ps. 40:6, R.V. margin) doubtless relates the self-dedication of Christ to the type set forth in Exodus 21:5–6. The highest motive for yielding to God is not merely a desire for victory in daily life or for power or for blessing; it is for the Christ life, which is sacrificial, to be realized. Sacrificial does not necessarily mean painful; here it is simply descriptive of doing the will of Another. Some pain may lie in the path, but the prevailing note is one of joy and the experience of the heart is peace.

Every child of God, then, must definitely yield to the will of God, not concerning some one issue of daily life, but concerning all things as an abiding attitude toward God. Apart from such self-dedication, there is no escaping the Father's scourging hand; for the Father cannot, and will not, suffer His child to live on without the priceless blessings which His love longs to bestow and which of necessity are conditioned on a surrendered will. Satan and Christ stand opposed in the matter of doing God's will. Satan by five awful "I will's" repudiated God's will; Christ in as many distinct declarations (and more) committed Himself to the will of His Father. Every unyielded will but perpetuates the crime of Satan. To be spiritual and Spirit-filled, the believer must not say No to God. "Quench not the Spirit."

## III. "WALK IN THE SPIRIT"

Advancing at this point to a contemplation of the third condition upon which the Spirit's filling may be experienced, it should be restated that this condition is positive in character while the two already considered are negative—respecting that which should not be allowed. The positive requirement concerns that which is to be wrought in the life by the Holy Spirit and is far-reaching in what it includes. The Authorized Version translation of a determining verse like Galatians 5:16 is misleading. By this kind of rendering the text seems to impose responsibility upon the believer to maintain a walk in the Holy Spirit, whereas the more accurate rendering of the text assigns such achieving of the walk to the Holy Spirit and enjoins upon the Christian the attitude of dependence upon the Spirit. It is obvious that the Christian has no power within himself, in spite of the new nature, whereby to enter, promote, or maintain a walk in the Spirit. It is because of this native incapacity that the Spirit is given to indwell him. The whole situation is reversed and impossible assumptions are suggested when the believer is urged to walk by his own ability rather than by the Holy Spirit. The responsibility resting upon the Christian is not that of attempting the walk; it is rather the obligation to maintain an attitude of confidence and expectation toward the Holy Spirit, which dependence will make the Spirit's promotion of the walk a blessed reality. One interpretation of this passage in Galatians implies that the believer is to lead or direct the Holy Spirit, while the more defensible viewpoint makes out that the believer is to be led in a path of God's own choosing and to be empowered by the Spirit unto every good work. The immediate promise to the believer is that when walking by means of the Spirit the lust of the flesh will not be fulfilled. In the same context (Gal. 5:16–23) it is declared at verse 18 that they who are led of the Spirit are not under the law. This declaration is more than an assertion that the believer when led by the Spirit is free from the Mosaic system of merit; rather it is implied that the Spirit's leading opens into an entirely different field of responsibility, which field incorporates the whole will of God—one vastly more extended regarding what is included than a mere conformity to standards and rules. In the sphere of the Spirit's leading, every phase of individual life and service is contemplated and its realization is assured. To "walk in the Spirit" means, then, to depend upon the Spirit. The use as a literary figure of the act of walking to represent the continued responsibility of living daily to the glory of God is apt. Every step in the process of physical walking is an incipient fall. In each step the body is thrown out of balance and onward without physical support, depending upon a step of the foot forward to recover balance and support. Thus the walk in the Spirit is not only a constant series of commitments, but a constant casting of one's self upon the Spirit with the confidence and anticipation that all needed support will be realized. All of this suggests personal intimacy with the Holy Spirit. His presence is to be an actuality in experience, and the practice of depending consciously and habitually upon His enabling power must be maintained. This specific manner of life is wholly unlike the natural ways and practices of men. The walk by means of the Spirit is an achievement which calls for unceasing attention and patient advancement, looking to its execution. All who are born into this world must learn to walk as a proper function of the physical body; it should not be deemed strange if it is required of those born of the Spirit that they too learn by experience and practice how to walk by means of the same

Spirit. It is to be expected that a child will creep before it walks and that it will experience many failures and falls before being able to walk freely. It is equally reasonable to expect a certain amount of effort and failure to occur along the path before the walk by the Spirit is perfected. Doubtless it is only an unexperienced theoretical consideration in the minds of the great majority of believers that the Holy Spirit has taken up His abode in their hearts. To such it becomes a day of marvelous discovery when perhaps in feeble faith they rest their weight upon Him and discover by living experience that He is there and ready and willing to accomplish that which is committed to Him. It need not be demonstrated further that if the power of the Spirit is to be actualized one must pass beyond the range of theories, and into the vital tests of a commitment of even the first step in a walk by means of the Spirit to His gracious person to accomplish. No intelligent step can be taken until there is some distinction borne in mind about the difference in method and practice between walking by dependence upon self or the flesh and walking by dependence upon the Spirit. Here, again, rules are of little aid. The walk by the Spirit must be the outworking of personal experience—not the attempted imitation of others, but the result of one's own trial of faith. It is probable that as a general method a definite commitment in the morning of all that awaits one during the day is effective, though often extra and special commitments will be required as the day advances. The important feature is the character of this commitment. It is not merely asking for help during the day—a practice far too common among spiritual believers; it is entering into a definite covenant-understanding with God in which natural ability and resources are renounced and confidence exercised toward the Spirit that He will Himself actuate and motivate the entire life. This exercise of faith should be sufficiently definite that real expectation is engendered and a time of evaluation and thanksgiving be observed at the close of the day. A true confiding in the morning will call for a survey and recounting when the day is done. Then, in the light of the success or failure, lessons may be learned about one's true progress in a spiritual walk.

At this point an added word over that presented earlier respecting the experimental feature of the walk by means of the Spirit is in order, namely, that, within the range of the believer's experience, there is no indication, manifestation, or identification of either the presence or the activity of the Spirit beyond the noticeable results that He achieves. The human mind continues to weigh all issues, the affections and desires are still dominant, and the will acts with normal freedom and responsibility. The point to be noted is that the Spirit, wholly apart from any intrusion of His own faculties, is "working in"—energizing—the believer to the willing and doing of that which is well-pleasing to God (Phil. 2:13). The fact and force of the Spirit's energy will be seen in the quality of the results and not in any recognition of the manner of His working. However, the truly sincere believer will nevertheless, from the heart and because of the actual results, be moved to thanksgiving when a day thus lived is completed. In many instances the spiritual life has been misstated and therefore misunderstood. The impression has been created that the natural functions of human life are to be set aside and the mind and will are rendered dormant, to the end that the Spirit may exercise His own mind and will. Such a notion is foreign to the plan of God as that purpose is revealed in the New Testament. As He did with Gideon, the Spirit clothes Himself with the believer's body and faculties and, without manifestations of Himself, works in and through those faculties. Though thus hidden from observation, it is nonetheless the uncomplicated work of the Spirit. With the tremendous issue of the believer's life in view, it is evident that definiteness in the matter of the believer's attitude of trust is of major importance.

With this introduction to the subject in mind, attention may be given to the disclosure in Scripture that the Christian faces unceasingly on the negative side of his spiritual life three superior foes—the world, the flesh, and the devil—and on the positive side of his spiritual life that he faces the superhuman responsibility of filling to the measure of completeness all that enters into those manifestations which together constitute the Spirit's filling. A large portion of this volume has already been devoted to the contemplation of these far-reaching issues which make up the believer's life and service. To restate fully this body of truth is not necessary. It does remain to be seen, however, that the victory both in the sphere of conflict with foes and in the sphere of a God-honoring manner of life and service depends wholly on a relationship to the Spirit which is unhindered with respect to the presence of evil and actively reliant on Him for the outworking of His perfect will. Thus again the child of God is seen to confront the question of his actual dependence on the indwelling Spirit. It may easily become the beginning of effective spiritual living on the part of a Christian when he believes and heeds God's Word respecting the provisions which are his through the gift to him of the Spirit. Rationalism is directly opposed to faith. There are those who rebel at the teaching that salvation is by faith alone. They rebel either because they do not know, or do not believe, the Word of God. There are those, likewise, who rebel at the teaching that an unbroken victory in the believer's daily life is by faith alone, and this, too, is either because they do not know, or do not believe, the Scriptures. The doctrine concerning a divinely produced sanctity of life does not rest upon one or two proof-texts. It is one of the great themes, if not the most extensive, theme in the epistles; for not only is the doctrine taught at length, but every injunction to the Christian is based upon the exact principles revealed in the doctrine. It is one of the most vital elements in the age-characterizing provisions of grace.

1. THE WORLD. The *cosmos* satanic system which is termed the *world* is defined at length in earlier portions of this work. In this *cosmos* system the Christian must live and yet keep himself unspotted from it (James 1:27). The border line between the world and that which is a rightful sphere of spiritual living cannot well be defined. Naught but the personal leading of the Spirit will determine these problems. It is here that Christians need to learn to be gracious one toward another. The Scriptures assert that those who are strong are free to do what those who are weak may not do with advantage. It becomes those who are weak to avoid judgment of the strong, and it is essential for those who are strong to avoid putting a stumbling block into the path of the weak. The Apostle declares: "Him that is weak in the faith receive ye, but not to doubtful disputations. For one believeth that he may eat all things: another, who is weak, eateth herbs. Let not him that eateth despise him that eateth not; and let not him which eateth not judge him that eateth: for God hath received him" (Rom. 14:1–3). Nothing could be more definite than this teaching, which avers that each man in sincerity is to be persuaded in his own mind. If, perchance, an error is made by anyone under these circumstances, it will be remembered that Christians are accountable to God and not finally to each other (cf. Rom. 14:4). Such indeed is the need, that there is introduced both guidance by the Holy Spirit regarding all that arises as a conflict between the world-system and the believer and also a definite provision whereby the believer may claim on the principle of faith the enabling power of the Holy Spirit to overcome the solicitations of the world-system. In executing a walk by means of the Holy Spirit in its relation to the *cosmos* system, it is required that positive dependence on the Spirit be exercised unremittingly.

2. THE FLESH. That within the Christian which lusts against the

Holy Spirit, creating various problems, is termed in the New Testament *the flesh*. Careless Christians are not concerned with the Person and work of the Holy Spirit, or with the exact distinctions which condition true spirituality; but these distinctions and truths do appeal to those who really desire a life that is well-pleasing to God. Satan has pitfalls and counterfeit doctrines in the realm of the deepest spiritual realities. The majority of these false teachings are based on a misapprehension of the Bible teaching about sin, especially the sin question as this is related to the believer. The Scripture is "profitable for doctrine, for reproof, for correction, for instruction in righteousness: that the man of God may be perfect [full-grown], throughly furnished unto all good works" (2 Tim. 3:16–17); accordingly in the same epistle believers are urged to the end that they might "study" and "rightly divide" the Word of Truth. It should be noted that two out of four of the values of the Scripture in the life of the "man of God," as recorded in the above passage, are "reproof" and "correction"; yet how few, especially of those who are holding an error, are of a teachable spirit! It seems to be one of the characteristics of all satanic errors that those who have embraced them seem never inclined honestly to reconsider their ground. They read only their sectarian or misleading literature and often carefully avoid hearing any corrective teaching from the Word of God. This difficulty is greatly increased when their error has led them to assume some unwarranted position regarding a supposed deliverance from sin, or personal attainments in holiness. A "correction," or "reproof," to such seems to be a suggestion toward "backsliding," and no zealously minded person would easily choose such a course as that. Much error is thriving along these lines with no other dynamic than human zeal, and the Word of God is persistently distorted to maintain human theories. Many of these errors are reproved and corrected when the fundamental distinction is recognized between the Christian's *position* in Christ and his *experience* in daily life. Whatever God has done for believers in Christ is perfect and complete; but such perfection should not be confused with the imperfect conduct of daily life.

3. THE DEVIL. The Bible represents Satan as the enemy of the saints of God, and especially is this seen to be true of the saints in this age. There is no controversy between Satan and unsaved people, for they are a part of his world-system. They have not been delivered from the power of darkness and translated into the kingdom of the Son of God's love. Satan is the energizing power in those who are unsaved (Eph. 2:2), as God is the energizing power in those who are saved (Phil. 2:13).

Every human being is either under the power of Satan or under the power of God. This is not to say that Christians may not be influenced by Satan or the unsaved not influenced by the Spirit of God, but that each man's life as a whole is linked with one domain or the other; and, furthermore, Satan's domain is not at all points characterized by things that are inherently evil as life is estimated by the world. Satan's life-purpose is to be "like the most High" (Isa. 14:14), and he appears as "an angel of light" and his ministers "as the ministers of righteousness" (2 Cor. 11:13–15). His followers, in their role as ministers of righteousness, preach a gospel of reformation and a salvation won by human character, rather than salvation won by grace alone unrelated to any human virtue. Therefore, the world, notwithstanding all its moral standards and culture, is not necessarily free from the power and energizing control of Satan. He it is who would ever promote forms of religion and human excellence apart from the redemption that is in Christ, and the world is evidently being energized to undertake that very thing. He has blinded the unsaved, but only concerning one thing: they are blinded by Satan lest the light of the glorious gospel of Christ should shine unto them (2 Cor. 4:3–4).

The enmity of Satan has always been directed against the Person of God alone and not against humanity as such. It is only when men have been made "partakers of the divine nature" that they are confronted with this mighty foe. The thrusts of his "fiery darts" are aimed really at God who indwells them. However, the conflict is nonetheless real and the foe superhuman. "Finally, my brethren, be strong in the Lord, and in the power of his might. Put on the whole armour of God, that ye may be able to stand against the wiles [or, strategies] of the devil. For we wrestle not against flesh and blood, but against principalities, against powers, against the rulers of the darkness of this world, against spiritual wickedness in high places" (Eph. 6:10–12). These world-rulers of the darkness of this age, the spiritual powers of wickedness who are here said to wage a ceaseless conflict against us, cannot be overcome by human strategy or strength. The Bible lends no sanction to foolish suppositions that the devil will flee at the mere resistance of a determined human will. We are to "resist the devil," but it must be done while "stedfast in the faith" and "submitting" ourselves unto God (James 4:7; 1 Pet. 5:9). Satan, being by reason of creation superior in glory to all other creatures, cannot be conquered by any of them unaided. Even Michael the archangel, it is said, "when contending with the devil . . . durst not bring against him a railing accusation, but said, The Lord rebuke thee." Michael the archangel does not contend unauthorized with Satan. He must depend rather on the power of Another, thus acting on a principle of dependence rather than on a principle of independence. Certainly a Christian, with all his many present limitations, must appeal to the power of God in the conflict with this mighty foe, and he is indeed directed to do this: "Above all, taking the shield of faith, wherewith ye shall be able to quench all the fiery darts of the wicked ['evil one,' R.V.]" (Eph. 6:16).

The believer's conflict with Satan is as fierce and unceasing as that superhuman being can make it. Before him Christians of themselves are as nothing; but God has anticipated this helplessness and provided a perfect victory through the indwelling Spirit: ". . . because greater is he that is in you, than he that is in the world" (1 John 4:4). A Christian, because of the power of his new enemy, must "walk by means of the Spirit" if he would be triumphant over the devil.

# CHAPTER XVI

## RELATED DOCTRINES

SINCE THE PROBLEM of the influence of the flesh in the Christian is inward and ever present, there are altogether three important doctrines involved in this discussion, namely, (1) the doctrine of the believer's share in Christ's death, (2) the doctrine of perfection, and (3) the doctrine of sanctification. These are closely related, especially the latter two, and the first, it will be seen, is the ground upon which the last two are made possible. Many unwarranted assumptions and fanatical notions regarding both perfection and sanctification would be avoided if the Scriptures bearing on these doctrines were heeded. Here, again, reproof and correction (2 Tim. 3:16–17) might take an important place if allowed to do so.

Though considered extensively on earlier pages, attention must be called first of all to the terms "old man"—*παλαιὸς ἄνθρωπος*—and "sin"—*ἁμαρτία*, as referring to the nature. The word *flesh* is broad in its significance, and within its boundaries and pertaining to it are these two factors—the "old man" and "sin." Though these factors are similar to such a degree that few may distinguish between them, it is well to give attention to the Scripture related to each.

The terminology "old man" is used only three times in the New Testament. Once it has to do with the present *position* of the "old man" through the death of Christ (Rom. 6:6). In the other two passages (Eph. 4:22–24; Col. 3:9) the fact that the "old man" has been put off forever is made the basis of appeal for a holy life. In Romans 6:6 it is written: "Knowing this, that our old man is ['was,' R.V.] crucified with him." There can be no reference here to the *experience* of the Christian, but rather to a cocrucifixion "with him" and most evidently at the time and place where Christ was crucified. In the context this passage follows immediately upon the statement concerning the Christian's transfer in federal headship from the first Adam to the Last Adam (Rom. 5:12–21). The first Adam, as perpetuated in the believer, was judged in the crucifixion of Christ. The "old man," the fallen nature received from Adam, *was* "crucified with him." This cocrucifixion, as has been seen, is of the greatest importance, on the divine side, in making possible a true deliverance from the power of the "old man." A righteous judgment must be gained against the sin nature before any divine work can be undertaken toward deliverance. The judgment is now by the cross secured, and the way is open for blessed victory through the Spirit. In the second passage in which the term "old man" is used, the fact that the old man was already crucified with Christ is the basis for an appeal to follow next: "That ye [did, Greek] put off concerning the former conversation the old man, which is corrupt according to the deceitful lusts; and be renewed in the spirit of your mind; and that ye [did, Greek] put on the new man, which after God is created in righteousness and true holiness" (Eph. 4:22–24). In the third passage the position in Christ suggests again a corresponding experience: "Lie not one to another, seeing that ye have put off the old man with his deeds; and have put on the new man, which is renewed in knowledge after the image of him that created him" (Col. 3:9–10). *Positionally* the "old man" has been put off forever. *Experimentally* the "old man" remains as an active force in the life which can be controlled only by the power of God. Christians avail themselves of that divine sufficiency when they renounce entirely the thought of compromise with, or toleration of, the fruit of the old nature and by faith apply the divinely provided counteragency for victory through dependence on the Spirit. The result of "reckoning" as dead and "mortifying your members" will be to make way for the Spirit to work out in the life the manifestations of the "new man," Christ Jesus. The child of God could not of himself judge the "old man." That, however, has been done *for* him by Christ. Nor can he control the "old man." That has to be done *for* him by the Spirit. "Put ye on the Lord Jesus Christ, and make not provision for the flesh, to fulfil the lusts thereof" (Rom. 13:14). The fruit of the "old man" and the fruit of the "new man," it will be remembered, are clearly contrasted in Galatians 5:19–23: "Now the works of the flesh are manifest, which are these; Adultery, fornication, uncleanness, lasciviousness, idolatry, witchcraft, hatred, variance, emulations, wrath, strife, seditions, heresies, envyings, murders, drunkenness, revellings, and such like. . . . But the fruit of the Spirit is love, joy, peace, longsuffering, gentleness, goodness, faith, meekness, temperance" ('self-control,' R.V.). There is no Biblical ground for a distinction between the Adamic nature and "human nature." The unregenerate have but one nature, while the regenerate have two. There is but one fallen nature, which is from Adam, and but one new nature, which is from God. The "old man," then, is the Adamic nature which has been judged in the death of Christ. It still abides with the saved one as an active principle in his life, and his *experimental* victory over it will be realized only through a definite reliance upon the indwelling Spirit. The "old man" is a part, therefore, but not all, of the "flesh."

In certain portions of the Scriptures, notably Romans 6:1—8:13 and 1 John 1:1—2:2, there is also an important distinction between two uses of the word ἁμαρτία, *sin*. The two meanings will be obvious if it is remembered that the word sometimes refers to the Adamic nature, and sometimes to evil resulting from that nature. Sin, as a nature, is the source of sin which is committed. Sin is the root which bears its own fruit in sin which is evil conduct. Sin is the "old man," while sins are the manifestations in daily life. Sin is what the individual is by birth, while sins are the evil he does in life. There is abundant Biblical testimony to the fact that the "flesh," the "old man," or "sin," are the source of evil, and are the possession of the child of God so long as he remains in this earthly body. Believers have a blessed treasure in the possession of the "new man" indwelling them; but they have this treasure "in earthen vessels." The earthenware is the "body of our humiliation" (2 Cor. 4:7; Phil. 3:21, R.V.). Personality—the ego—remains the same individuality through all the operations of grace, though it experiences the greatest possible advancement, transformation, and regeneration from its lost estate in Adam to the positions and possessions of a son of God in Christ. That which was lost is said to be forgiven, justified, saved, and receives the new divine nature which is eternal life. That which was dead is born again and becomes a new creature in Christ Jesus, though it remains the same personality which was born of certain parents after the flesh. Though born of God and possessing a new divine nature, the weakness of the flesh and the dispositions of the sin nature abide until the final change of residence from earth to heaven. In 1 John 1:8, 10 is given clear warning against any presumption concerning sin. First of all, Christians are warned against saying that they have no sin nature: "If we say that we have no sin, we deceive ourselves, and the truth is not in us." This is distinctly a word concerning the sin nature of the Christian and has no application whatever to the unsaved. It is addressed to believers, and to *all* believers. It will not do to suppose that reference is made in the passage to some unfortunate, unenlightened, or unsanctified class of Christians. There is no class distinction whatsoever here. It is the testimony of the Spirit of God with reference to *every* born-again person. For any such to say that he has no sin nature means that the person is self-deceived and the truth not in him. This passage is evidently intended for correction of those Christians who are claiming to be free from the sin nature and who may have made themselves believe that they are free. A self-satisfied mind is not necessarily the mind of God. In the same passage Christians are also warned against saying that they have not sinned as sins are fruit of the old nature: "If we say that we have not sinned, we make him a liar, and his word is not in us" (1 John 1:10). Nothing could be more explicit than this statement. It is possible that a Christian may have been instructed to say that he has not sinned; but here is a word of reproof when he confronts the testimony of the Spirit of God. Again, this is not said concerning some unsanctified class of Christians; it is something concerning all Christians. To depart from the clear teaching of this great corrective passage is to make God a "liar" and to disclose the fact that "his word is not in us." The source of sin is, then, the sin nature, rather than the new divine nature. This important truth is pointed out in the same epistle a bit later in a passage which primarily teaches that the Christian does not now *practice* sin lawlessly as he did before he received the new divine nature, but which also teaches that sin cannot be traced to the divine nature as its source: "Not anyone that has been begotten of God practices sin, because his seed [i.e., the divine nature] abides in him, and he [with particular reference to the 'seed'] is not able to sin, because of God he [with particular reference to the 'seed'] has been begotten" (3:9, Greek). It is evident that the new nature is something which has been begotten of God, and because of the presence of this nature the one in whom it dwells does not now practice sin as he did before he was saved, nor can sin ever be produced by the new nature which is from God. The passage does not teach that Christians do not sin, or even that some Christians do not sin; for there is no one class of Christians in view, and what is here said is true of all who have been "begotten of God." It is further taught in the Scriptures that, since there are two natures in the believer, there is a conflict between the new nature, as operative through the Spirit, and the old nature, as operative through the flesh: "This I say then, Walk in the Spirit, and ye shall not fulfil the lust of the flesh. For the flesh lusteth against the Spirit, and the Spirit against the flesh: and these are contrary the one to the other: so that [when walking by the Spirit] ye cannot do the things that ye [otherwise] would" (Gal. 5:16–17). Another aspect of this truth is taken up at length in Romans 7:15—8:4. In this passage the old "I" is seen to be in active opposition to the new "I." It is sometimes claimed for this passage that it refers to an experience in the Apostle's life before he was saved. This is open to serious question. No such conflict can Biblically be related to the life of Saul of Tarsus, nor for that matter to any other unregenerate man. Saul of Tarsus was not a "wretched man": he was a self-satisfied Pharisee, living "in all good conscience" and "touching the righteousness which is in the law, blameless." It was only when he began to "delight in the law of God after the inward man" that this deeper conflict was experienced. So, also, the claim is sometimes made that this passage had to do only with Paul as once a Jew under the Law of Moses and so could not apply to any Gentile, since the Law of Moses was not addressed to Gentiles. It is quite true that the law was not given to Gentiles. The primary purpose of this passage is not to set forth some distinguishing characteristic of a Jew convicted under the law; it plainly represents a saint of today confronted with the impossibility of living according to the revealed will of God, not only because of human impotence, but because of an active opposing principle to be found in the "flesh." The mind and will of God for the believer under grace, as has been seen, is infinitely more impossible to human strength than the Law of Moses. So much the more are Christians found to be "wretched" men when attempting their present conflict with no more than the "arm of flesh." The law of God, as referred to in the New Testament, sometimes means His present will for His people rather than simply the "law of Moses." It is clear that the conflict in this Romans passage is between *evil* and *good,* in general terms, rather than a matter of the Law of Moses. If believers under grace are not in view in Romans 7, neither are they in Romans 8; for in passing from one chapter to the other there is no break in the development of the doctrine or its application. In combating this viewpoint it has been pointed out that there is a particular crisis being indicated by the words in 7:25, "I thank God through Jesus Christ our Lord." However, this really is not a word of thanksgiving for salvation; it is praise for deliverance from the reigning power of sin. And it is deliverance for the one who could say next: "So then with the mind I myself serve the law of God; but with the flesh the law of sin." This statement scarcely describes the experience of an unregenerate man. Earlier in the context the Law of Moses has been set aside as the believer's rule of life today (6:14; 7:1–6), and the new law of Christ (1 Cor. 9:21; Gal. 6:2; John 15:10), the "life in Christ Jesus" (Rom 8:2), or that which is produced *in* the believer by the Spirit (Rom. 8:4) has come into view. No mention of the Spirit is made in this passage. It is therefore not even a conflict between the Spirit and the "flesh"; it is rather one between the new "I" and the old "I." It is the new "I"—the regenerate man—isolated, for the time being, from the enabling power of the Spirit, and seen as confronting by itself the whole law of God (vs. 16), the unchanging "flesh" (vs. 18), and the capacities of the new man (vss. 22–23, 25). A vital question is raised: Can the regenerate man, apart from the Spirit, fulfill the whole will of God? The answer is clear. Though he "delight" in the law of God (in which no unregenerate man delights; cf. Rom. 3:10–18; 1 Cor. 2:14), he must discover the divinely provided power to live which is released only through the death of Christ (vs. 25), and through the power of the Spirit (8:2). Apart from this there is even for him only continued defeat.

The passage, with some interpretations, as before presented, is as follows: "For that which I [because of the old nature] do I [because of the new] allow not: for what I [the new] would, that do I [the old] not; but what I [the new] hate, that do I [the old]. If then I [the old] do that which I [the new] would not, I consent unto the law [or, will of God for me] that it is good. Now then it is no more I [the new] that do it, but sin [the old] that dwelleth in me. For I know that in me [the old] (that is, in my flesh,) dwelleth no good thing: for to will is present with me; but how to perform that which is good I find not. For the good that I [the new] would I [the old] do not: but the evil which I [the new] would not, that I [the old] do. Now if I [the old] do that I [the new] would not, it is no more I [the new] that do it, but sin [the old] that dwelleth in me. I find then a law [not, a law of Moses], that, when I [the new] would do good, evil [the old] is present with me. For I delight in the law of God after the inward man: but I see another law in my members [the old], warring against the law of my mind [the new that delights in the law of God], and bringing me into captivity to the law of sin [the old] which is in my members. O wretched [Christian] man that I am! who shall deliver me from the body of this death?" (vss. 15–24).

The answer to this great question and cry of distress with which the above passage closes is given in a following verse (8:2): "For the law of the Spirit of life in Christ Jesus hath made me free from the law of sin and death." This is more than a deliverance from the Law of Moses; it is the immediate deliverance from sin (the old) and death (its results; cf. Rom. 6:23). The effect of this deliverance is indicated by the blessedness recorded in the eighth chapter, in contrast to the wretchedness recorded in the seventh chapter. It is all of the helpless and defeated "I" in the one case, and of the sufficient and victorious "I," by enablement of the Spirit, in the other. Christians, then, are to be delivered by the law or power of the Spirit. But attention must be called again to the fact, as stated in 7:25, that it is possible only "through Jesus Christ our Lord." Believers are delivered *by* the Spirit; but it is made righteously possible "through Jesus Christ our Lord" because of their union with Him in His crucifixion, death, and burial.

## I. THE BELIEVER'S SHARE IN CHRIST'S DEATH

The doctrine which discloses the believer's share in Christ's death fills a large place in the Pauline epistles and is the ground upon which the spiritual life is made righteously possible. Nothing could be more explicit or determining than the Apostle's word in Galatians 5:24, which declares: "And they that are Christ's have crucified the flesh with the affections and lusts." Reference is made in this text to that special aspect of Christ's death which was and is a judgment of the believer's sin nature and on the basis of which the Holy Spirit, who indwells the believer, is rendered righteously free to take control of the sin nature. All forms of perfection and sanctification (soon to be considered) which relate to daily experience in the matter of deliverance from the sin nature are wholly dependent upon this substitutionary death of Christ in behalf of the sin nature. Deliverance is wrought by the Spirit alone and the Spirit's freedom to overcome the sin nature depends wholly upon the truth that the sin nature has been judged by Christ on the cross. However, what Christ has wrought is provisional and awaits intelligent appropriation on the part of the believer.

Three verbs are introduced by Romans 6:11–13 which present in logical order the responsibility of the Christian in directing the action of his own will.

First, *reckon*. "Likewise reckon ye also yourselves to be dead indeed unto sin, but alive unto God through Jesus Christ our Lord" (vs. 11). The exhortation presented in this passage means simply to believe these revealed facts of union with Christ as having regard to one's self, and to believe them enough so as to act upon them with confidence.

Second, *let not*. "Let not sin therefore reign in your mortal body, that ye should obey it in the lusts thereof" (vs. 12). *Give no sanction to sin* is the thought here, but the prohibition found in the words "let not" implies that the plan pursued should be according to God's promise of overcoming sin by a dependence upon the Holy Spirit.

Third, *yield*. "Neither yield ye your members as instruments of unrighteousness unto sin: but yield yourselves unto God, as those that are alive from the dead, and your members as instruments of righteousness unto God" (vs. 13). This exhortation lays bare the very essence of the act of dependence on the Spirit: "yield" your members for instruments of righteousness as those who stand on resurrection ground should do.

In a reconsideration of the death of Christ as related to the sin nature—which restatement seems demanded to complete this final declaration of truth respecting the walk by means of the Holy Spirit and to conclude the study of the larger body of Scripture relative to the spiritual life—it may be said that by the death of Christ both the *penalty* of sins committed was borne for all men and the *power* of sin was judged and broken for the children of God. The accomplishment of all this was a problem of infinite dimensions; for sin is primarily against God and He alone can deal with it. The Bible pictures sin as it is seen from the divine standpoint. It also unfolds God's one problem, which was created by sin, and records His exact manner and method of solution.

The theme under consideration is concerned with the death of Christ only as that sacrifice is related to the divine judgment of the sin nature in the child of God. The necessity for such a judgment and the sublime revelation that the work of judgment is now fully accomplished for the believer is unfolded in Romans 6:1–10. This passage is the foundation of as well as the key to the possibility of a "walk in the Spirit." Herein it is declared that Christians need not "continue in sin," but instead may "walk in newness of life." "Sin shall not have dominion over you," it is said, and the child of God need no longer be a bondslave to sin. To this end He hath wrought in the cross. How important in His eyes, then, is the quality of the Christian's daily life; for Christ's death not only contemplated his eternal blessedness in the glory, but his present "walk" as well! The old nature must be judged in order that God may be free to deal with it in the believer's daily life and apart from all judgments. What destruction would fall on the unsaved if God had to judge them for their sins before they could be saved! "O LORD, correct me, but with judgment; not in thine anger, lest thou bring me to nothing" (Jer. 10:24). How great is His mercy! He has already taken up the sin question and solved it for all men in the death of the Substitute. Because of this He now can save from the *penalty* of sin. Even so, to what greater lengths His mercy has gone since He has also entered into righteous judgments of the "old man"! And because of this God is able now to deliver His child from the *power* of sin. The "old man" is said to have been "crucified with him" and "dead with Christ," "buried with him" and partaking as well in His resurrection life. All this, it is revealed, was to serve one great purpose: that "we also should walk in newness of life," even as Christ "was raised up from the dead by the glory of the Father." What a deliverance and walk may be experienced since it is according to the power and glory of the resurrection! Resurrection, it may be added, is not the mere reversal of death; it is introduction into the power and limitless boundaries of eternal life. In that new sphere and by that new power the Christian may now walk.

The passage opens thus: "What shall we say then? Shall we continue in sin, that grace may abound? God forbid. How shall we that are dead to sin ['We who have died to sin,' R.V.; so, also, vss. 7–8, 11; Col. 2:20; 3:3], live any longer therein?" In the preceding chapters of this epistle salvation unto *safety* has been presented. At the beginning of this passage the question of salvation unto *sanctity* of daily life is taken up. This second aspect of salvation is provided only for the one who is already saved unto safety. "Shall we [who are now saved and safe in grace] continue in sin?" It would not *become* them to do so, as the children of God, and it is not *necessary* for them to do so since they are now "dead to sin." But who is "dead to sin"? Is it true that any Christian ever *experienced* a death to sin? Never was there one. But the death which is mentioned in this passage is said to be accomplished for *every* believer. All Christians are here said to have died unto sin. A death which is all-inclusive could not be accounted *experimental*. It is *positional* the rather. God reckons *all* believers, relative to their sin nature, to have died *in* Christ and *with* Christ; for only thus can they "walk in newness of life" as those who are "alive unto God." It is no longer necessary to sin. Christians cannot plead the power of a tendency over which they have no control. They still have the tendency, and it is more than they can control; but God has provided the possibility of a complete victory and freedom both by judging the old nature and by giving them the presence and power of the Spirit. Then follows the important explanation of the believer's present relation to the death of Christ as forming the ground of his deliverance from the power of sin. First an outline is given (Rom. 6:3–4), and then the same truth is repeated, but more in detail (vss. 5–10). It is not within the scope of this discussion to consider the importance of a sacrament that purports to represent the truth of the believer's death with Christ. Such, at best, is but the shadow of the substance. No ordinance performed by man can accomplish what is here described. The Christian's baptism *into* Jesus Christ can be none other than the act of God in placing him *in* Christ (cf. Gal. 3:27). This evidently is a baptism into His Body performed by the Spirit (1 Cor. 12:13); for in no other sense are *all* "baptized into Jesus Christ." Being by the baptism of the Spirit vitally united and placed "in him" those who are saved partake of what He *is* and what He has *done*. He *is* the righteousness of God, and the Scriptures teach that they are *made* the righteousness of God *in Him* (2 Cor. 5:21) and *made* accepted *in the Beloved* (Eph. 1:6). All this is true because they are "in him." So, also, He has substituted for them, and what He has done is reckoned unto them because they are "in him"—or in other words because they are baptized into Jesus Christ.

The argument in this passage of Romans 6 is based on the vital union by which Christians are organically united to Christ through their baptism into His Body: "Know ye not [or 'are ye ignorant,' R.V.], that so many of us as were baptized into Jesus Christ were baptized into his death?" As certainly as believers are "in him" do they partake of the *value* of His death. So, also, the passage states: "Therefore we are buried with him by baptism into death" (cf. Col. 2:12). Then too Christians are declared to be actually partakers of His crucifixion (vs. 6), death (vs. 8), burial (vs. 4), and resurrection (vss. 4–5, 8) and as essentially as they would partake in this union had they been crucified, dead, buried, and raised themselves. Being baptized into Jesus Christ is the *substance* of which cocrucifixion, codeath, coburial, and coresurrection are *attributes*. One is the *cause*, while the several others are the *effects*. All this uniting is unto the realization of one great divine purpose, namely, "that like as Christ was raised up from the dead by the glory of the Father, even so we also should walk in newness of life," or by a new life-principle. The Christian's "walk," then, is the divine objective. Christ died in the believer's stead. The judgment belonged to the believer, but Christ became his Substitute. He is thus counted as a copartner in all that his Substitute did. What He did forever satisfied the righteous demands of God against the "old man" and opened the way for a "walk" well-pleasing to God (cf. 2 Cor. 5:15). As the passage proceeds, this truth of the believer's copartnership in Christ is presented again and with greater detail: "For if [or 'as'] we have been planted [conjoined, united, grown together; the word is used but this once in the New Testament] together in the likeness [i.e., oneness, cf. Rom. 8:3; Phil. 2:7] of his death, we shall be [now, and forever] also in the likeness of his resurrection." The Christian is already conjoined to Christ by the baptism of the Spirit (1 Cor. 12:12–13), which places him positionally beyond the judgments of sin, and he is therefore free to enter the experience of the eternal power and victory of His resurrection. "Knowing this [or, because we know this], that our old man is ['was,' R.V.] crucified with him [and for the same divine purpose as stated before], that the body of sin might be destroyed [our power of expression is through the body. This well-known fact is used as a figure concerning the manifestation of sin. The body is not destroyed; but sin's power and means of expression may be annulled. Cf. vs. 12], that henceforth we should not serve [be bondslaves to] sin [i.e., the *old man*]. For he that is dead is freed ['justified,' R.V.] from sin [i.e., they who have once died to sin, as the believer has in his Substitute, now stand free from its legal claims]. Now if we be dead with Christ [or, since we died with Christ], we believe we shall also live with him [not only in heaven, but *now*. There is as much certainty for the *life* in Him as there is certainty for the *death* in Him]: knowing ['For we know,' R.S.V.] that Christ being raised from the dead dieth no more; death hath no more dominion over him [the Christian is thereby encouraged to believe as much concerning himself]. For in that he died, he died unto sin [i.e., the nature] once: but in that he liveth, he liveth unto God" (and hence so may the believer live unto God). Such facts are recorded in the Scriptures concerning the meaning and value of the death of Christ and the Christian's present position in Him, that he may be led to believe that it is all a blessing for him and is actually true of him now. Believing this, he can fearlessly claim a position in His boundless grace and dare to enter the life of victory. So far in this passage nothing has been said touching any human obligation, nor has reference even been made to any work of man. It is all the work of God for the child of God, indeed, and the conclusion of this great passage is to the effect that it is His plan and provision that he should know that God has already provided for him a deliverance from bondservitude to sin. Based on this knowledge gained from the Word concerning all that God has done in Christ, an injunction immediately follows the passage being discussed which presents the Christian's responsibility: "Likewise reckon ye also yourselves to be dead indeed unto sin, but alive unto God through Jesus Christ our Lord." He is not exhorted to reckon the sin nature to be dead; but he is exhorted to reckon himself to be dead unto it.

Did the death of Christ literally destroy the power of the "old man" so that the believer can have no disposition to sin? No, for the passage goes on to state: "Let not sin therefore reign in your mortal body, that ye should obey it in the lusts thereof." Evidently, then, the "old man" will remain active, apart from sufficient control. The union with Christ has provided a possible deliverance; but it must be entered into and claimed by acts of faith like those expressed in the words "reckon," "let not," and the additional words which follow in the passage: "But yield yourselves unto God, as those that are alive from the dead, and your members as instruments of righteousness unto God. For sin [i.e., the nature] shall not have dominion over you: for ye are not under the law [which provides no power for its fulfillment], but under grace" (which provides for its fulfillment the sufficient Substitute and the limitless enablement of the Spirit of God). Every provision has been made. "Let not sin therefore reign in your mortal body, that ye should obey it in the lusts thereof." Who can measure the truth that is compressed into the one word heading this plea, "therefore"? It refers to all of the divine undertakings in the death of Christ by which the Christian has been conjoined to Him in order that he may receive the eternal values of Christ's crucifixion, death, burial, and resurrection. All this was accomplished for him before he was born. "Therefore," because of all this which is now accomplished and provided, the believer has limitless encouragement to enter into God's plan and purpose for his deliverance. Faith, which believes the victory to be possible because it reckons the "old man" to have been judged, is the normal result of such a revelation. Christians are nowhere enjoined to *re-enact* His crucifixion, death, burial, and resurrection; but they are encouraged by the revelation of what has been done to *reckon* the divine requirements for their deliverance from the "old man" to have been met perfectly and to believe that, because of this, they can now "walk in newness of life."

Would any Scripture justify the claim of some Christians that they have died to sin as a personal experience? Several New Testament passages refer to the believer as being already dead. None of these, however, point to an *experience;* they refer rather to a *position* into which the believer has been brought through his union with Jesus Christ in His cross death. "Wherefore if ye be dead with Christ" (Col. 2:20); "For ye are dead ['ye died,' R.V.], and your life is hid with Christ in God" (Col.

3:3); "I am crucified with Christ" (Gal. 2:20); "But God forbid that I should glory, save in the cross of our Lord Jesus Christ, by whom the world is crucified unto me, and I unto the world" (Gal. 6:14); "And they that are Christ's have crucified the flesh with the affections and lusts" (Gal. 5:24). In the last passage, as in the others, reference is made to something that is accomplished in all those who are Christ's. It could not, therefore, refer to some experience, the result of a special or particular sanctity on the part of a few. These passages, since they refer to all believers, can have but one meaning: in their union with Christ the "flesh with the affections and lusts" has *positionally* been crucified. The word "crucify" as related to believers is always dated in the past, implying the judicial fact and not a spiritual experience. The believer may "mortify," which means to reckon to be dead; but he is never called upon to crucify. Even mortifying is possible only by the enabling power of the Spirit: "But if ye through the Spirit do mortify the deeds of the body, ye shall live" (Rom. 8:13). It is plainly stated in Scripture that crucifixion is accomplished once-for-all. In view of this basic divine accomplishment, the child of God is exhorted to "reckon; yield; mortify [count to the dead]; put off; let not; put away; take unto you the whole armour of God; set your affection on things above; put on the new man, which is renewed in knowledge after the image of him that created him; deny himself; abide in Christ; fight; run the race; walk in love; walk in the Spirit; walk in the light; walk in newness of life." Such is the human responsibility toward the deliverance which God has provided through the death of His Son and proposes now to accomplish by the Spirit. The divine objective, then, in all that is recorded in Romans 6:1–10 is a "walk in newness of life." God has met every demand of His holiness in accomplishing for the believer, through Christ, all the judgment against the sin nature that He could ever demand. It is recorded now for him to understand and believe. "Knowing this," or, "because he knows this," he is justified in possessing confidence that he may "walk in newness of life" by the enabling power of the Spirit. What rest, peace, and victory would be the portion of the children of God if they really did know that the "old man" was crucified with Christ and so, on the divine side, it is made possible for them to live where sin's power and manifestation may be constantly annulled!

The whole doctrinal statement concerning a possible deliverance from bond-servitude to sin, as contained in Romans 6:1—8:4, is summarized and concluded in the last two verses of the context (8:3–4). In these two verses seven factors which enter into the revelation concerning a possible victory over sin, and which have been the subjects of discussion in the whole context, are mentioned again as a consummation of all that has gone before. The seven factors are: (1) "the law" (8:3), which represents here the righteous will of God because not limited to the Law of Moses (cf. 6:14; 7:4, 25) which passed away as a rule of life (7:1–6; 2 Cor. 3:7–18; Gal. 3:24–25). It rather includes that which the Spirit produces in the one who is spiritual (8:4; Gal. 5:22–23). The attempt, in mere human strength, to secure perfect righteousness through obedience to any precepts will always fail. Grace provides well enough that its heaven-high standards may be realized through the energizing power of the Spirit. (2) Being "weak through the flesh" (8:3), or the utter inability of human resources in the presence of heavenly requirements (7:14–23; John 15:5). (3) "Sin in the flesh" (8:3), or that in the flesh which is different from "weakness"; now it is something opposed to the Spirit (7:14–23; Gal. 5:17). (4) Christ came "in the likeness of sinful flesh" (8:3). He took the place of vital union with the sinner (6:5, 10–11); but did not become a sinner, or partake of the sin nature (Heb. 4:15; 7:26). (5) "And for sin, condemned [or 'judged'] sin in the flesh" (8:3). Thus He met every claim of the righteousness of God against the "old man" (6:10; 7:25). (6) "That the righteousness of the law might be fulfilled in us" (8:4; cf. 7:4, 22, 25), though never fulfilled *by* us (6:4, 14; 7:4, 6). It is therefore the "fruit of the Spirit." (7) "Who walk not after the flesh, but after the Spirit" (8:4). Such is the human condition for a victorious "walk." It must be wrought by the Spirit (6:11–22). Full provisions are made through the divine judgment of the flesh and the old man for the spiritual life of every Christian, even the fulfilling of the whole will of God in him by the Spirit. But these provisions become effective only to those who "walk not after the flesh, but after the Spirit." The believer has clear revelation and instruction from God, and it is perilous to neglect or confuse these or to fail in the exact responsibilities committed to him.

## II. PERFECTION

Closely related to the doctrine of the spiritual life and especially the death of Christ as a part of it are the two kindred doctrines of perfection and sanctification. A brief reference to each of these is necessary here.

In the Word of God, perfection is presented under seven aspects: (1) the Old Testament use of the word as applied to persons. The word in the Old Testament has the meaning of "sincere" and "upright." Noah was "perfect" (Gen. 6:9); Job was "perfect" (Job 1:1, 8); through avoiding the sins of the Gentile nations, Israel was bidden to be "perfect" (Deut. 18:13); the end of the "perfect" man was said to be peace (Ps. 37:37); so, also, the saints of the Old Testament order will appear in the heavenly city as "the spirits of just men made perfect" (Heb. 12:23). The Bible does not teach that such people were sinless.

(2) Positional perfection in Christ. "For by one offering he hath perfected for ever them that are sanctified" (Heb. 10:14), i.e., those set apart unto God by their salvation. The extent and force of this passage will be seen if the word *saved* is substituted for the word *sanctified.* This is clearly a verse on the perfection of the work of Christ for the believer and so must not be related to the Christian's daily life.

(3) Spiritual maturity and understanding. "Howbeit we speak wisdom among them that are perfect" (i.e., full-grown, 1 Cor. 2:6; cf. 14:20; see, also, 2 Cor. 13:11; Phil. 3:15; 2 Tim. 3:17).

(4) Perfection which is progressive. "Are ye so foolish? having begun in the Spirit, are ye now made [or, to be made] perfect by the flesh?" (Gal. 3:3).

(5) Perfection in some one particular. (a) In the will of God: "That ye may stand perfect and complete in all the will of God" (Col. 4:12). (b) In imitating one aspect of the fullness of God: "Be ye therefore perfect, even as your Father which is in heaven is perfect" (Matt. 5:48). The context is of the Father's love for His enemies and so the injunction is to the effect that this aspect of the Father's goodness should be reproduced. (c) In service: "Make you perfect in every good work" (Heb. 13:21). (d) In patience: "But let patience have her perfect work, that ye may be perfect [or, mature] and entire, wanting nothing" (James 1:4).

(6) The ultimate perfection of the individual in heaven. "Whom we preach, warning every man, and teaching every man in all wisdom; that we may present every man perfect in Christ Jesus" (Col. 1:28; cf. 1:22; Phil. 3:12; 1 Thess. 3:13; 1 Pet. 5:10).

(7) The ultimate perfection of the corporate body of believers in heaven. "Till we all come in the unity of the faith, and of the knowledge of the Son of God, unto a perfect man, unto the measure of the stature

of the fulness of Christ" (Eph. 4:13; see also 5:27; John 17:23; Jude 1:24; Rev. 14:5).

The noun *perfection* as found in the New Testament is a translation of two Greek roots, τέλειος meaning *mature* and καταρτίζω meaning *adjust*. And it is obvious that neither of these words, etymologically considered, has any reference to sinlessness. These facts should be estimated most carefully by any who have attempted the formation of a doctrine on the somewhat misleading use of the English word, *perfect*. There is a complete deliverance by the Spirit for every child of God, but this should not be confused with any use of the word *perfect* when the incapacity to sin is implied by that word.

## III. SANCTIFICATION

Again the doctrine must not be made to exceed that which is actually expressed by the Biblical use of its fundamental word, *sanctify*. To discover the full scope and meaning of this word it is necessary to include all passages in the Old and New Testament where it is used, and add to these as well all passages where the words *saint* and *holy* are used, since these three words ordinarily are all translations both in Hebrew and Greek of the same root word. The basic meaning of *sanctify, saint,* and *holy* is such that a person or thing is thereby said to be set apart, or classified, usually as pertaining unto God. Though these words and the truth they express are found throughout the whole Bible, the discussion now is concerned only with that aspect of the teaching which applies to the child of God under grace. Here it will be found that believers are the objects of a threefold sanctification.

First, positional sanctification. "But of him are ye in Christ Jesus, who of God is made unto us . . . sanctification" (1 Cor. 1:30); "By the which will we are sanctified through the offering of the body of Jesus Christ once for all" (Heb. 10:10). Thus, also, the Apostle addresses all believers as *saints,* and in the Scriptures reference is made to "holy prophets, holy brethren, a holy priesthood, holy women, a holy nation." Such they are by their position in Christ. Paul addressed even the Corinthian believers as *saints* and as already *sanctified* (1 Cor. 1:2; 6:11); yet his very letter for Corinth was written to correct those Christians because of sin (1 Cor. 5:1–2; 6:1, 7–8). They were saints and sanctified as in Christ, but were far from being such in daily life.

Second, experimental sanctification. This second aspect of the sanctifying work of God for the believer is *progressive* in some of its aspects, so is quite in contrast to the *positional* sanctification which is "once for all." It is accomplished by the power of God through the Spirit and through the Word: "Sanctify them through thy truth: thy word is truth" (John 17:17; see also 2 Cor. 3:18; Eph. 5:25–26; 1 Thess. 5:23; 2 Pet. 3:18). Experimental sanctification is advanced according to various relationships. (1) In relation to the believer's yieldedness to God. In virtue of presenting his body a living sacrifice, the child of God thereby is set apart unto God and so is experimentally sanctified. The presentation may be absolute and thus admit of no progression, or it may be partial and so require a further development. In either case it is a work of experimental sanctification. (2) In relation to sin. The child of God may so comply with every condition for true spirituality as to be experiencing all the provided deliverance and victory from the power of sin, or, on the other hand, he may be experiencing but a partial deliverance from the power of sin. In either case, he is set apart and thus is experimentally sanctified. (3) In relation to Christian growth. This aspect of experimental sanctification is progressive in every case. It therefore should in no way be confused with incomplete yieldedness to God or incomplete victory over sin. Its meaning is that the knowledge of truth, devotion, and Christian experience are naturally subject to development. In accord with their present state of development as Christians, believers experimentally are set apart unto God. That development should be advanced with each passing day. And thus, again, the Christian is subject to an experimental sanctification which is progressive.

Third, ultimate sanctification. Even *experimental* sanctification will be perfected when the saints are gathered into the Savior's presence in glory. "When he shall appear, we shall be like him" and "conformed to the image of his Son" (1 John 3:2; Rom. 8:29).

The Bible teaching in regard to sanctification, then, is (1) that all believers are *positionally* sanctified in Christ "once for all" at the moment they are saved. This sanctification is as perfect as He is perfect. (2) All believers are *being* sanctified by the power of God through the Word, and this sanctification is as perfect as the believer is perfect. So, also, (3) all believers *will be* sanctified and perfected in glory into the very image of the Son of God. The Bible, therefore, does not teach that any child of God is altogether sanctified experimentally in daily life before that final consummation of all things.

## IV. ERADICATION TEACHING

That there is a sin nature in the Christian which God recognizes as such and for which He has made complete provision to the end that it may be dealt with in a manner satisfying to His infinite holiness is an apparent and solemn truth that revelation discloses, and with that truth every right and real Christian experience must of necessity be in harmony. Revelation is equally as explicit regarding the divine plan to be followed for sanctification as regarding the divine provisions to be employed if this nature is to be brought into the place of control God has designed for it. On the other hand, rationalism in a veiled and pious form and passing as that which is superspiritual has advanced a theory respecting the disposition of the sin nature. No Scripture, when rightly interpreted, teaches this rationalistic theory, and no human experience has ever conformed to it actually. The whole subject is metaphysical to an advanced degree and in its consideration human opinion or supposed experience can prove or establish nothing. It is the plain, direct testimony and instruction to be found in the New Testament which must be accepted. The theory assumes that it is God's purpose to eradicate the sin nature and for this every believer should be seeking. Hence strange human ideas and requirements are introduced which are foreign to Scripture. Truths and doctrines are distorted or wholly misstated to sustain an unfounded human notion. This statement of criticism is not merely one person's opinion ranged against another person's opinion. But those who teach eradication of the old nature cannot and therefore do not base their claims upon the Word of God. They not only ignore the Scripture teaching that the sin nature abides in its active power in spite of the fact that it is judged for the believer by Christ in His death, but they ignore as well the extended body of Scripture which directs the believer to gain constant deliverance through the power of the indwelling Spirit. In fact, if eradication is God's way of dealing with the fallen nature, there is practically no need for the present work of the Holy Spirit. All of this divine work, then, is damaging to the theory, while the theory is itself dangerous to sincere souls. Being without Biblical ground upon which to stand, this theory is stated in as many ways as there are teachers to promote it. The present discussion can concern itself only with the principles involved and the conclusions therefrom which are to be drawn. A sincere determination to be well-pleasing unto God doubtless actuates many who promote the eradication idea; however, the Biblical doctrine of an unceasing overcoming of evil by the power of the Spirit in answer to a definite dependence upon the Spirit is diametrically opposed and contrary to the eradication theory. If one is true the other cannot be. Consideration of some definite issues involved may serve to make these assertions of criticism conclusive.

First, eradication is not the divine method of dealing with the believer's three great foes. These, as before indicated, are the world, the flesh, and the devil. No one has ever suggested a plan for becoming free from the influence of the world that would get the world eradicated. As truly, the flesh in its larger sphere of reality, which includes the sin nature, is never said to be eradicated, but is definitely said to be held in subjection by the Spirit when the daily walk is committed to Him (Gal. 5:16–17). Nor has any person been relieved from satanic influence by the eradication of Satan. Why, then, and to what great advantage in itself if standing alone, would be the eradication of the sin nature, which is only an integral part of one of these mighty foes none of which can ever be eradicated?

Second, eradication is not according to human experience. Though some boldly claim the eradication of their sin nature, few have ever demonstrated very successfully a sinless life. The acid test of these assumptions would be taken if a man and a woman, each of whom believed themselves—and upon the best evidence known to such claims—to have experienced eradication of the sin nature, married and had a child. Would that child be born without a sin nature? It would not, and simply because of the fact that the sin nature, regardless of suppositions, had not been eradicated in the case of either parent. Some have claimed that eradication returned them to the estate of innocence from which Adam fell; but that estate, if ever regained, would not be maintained for a moment under the present stress of life. The first lapse necessarily would return the supposed unfallen one to the fallen estate. Scripture, however, knows nothing of a fall on the part of any human being other than the first parents, but it does assert that redemption is wrought for all and that a way of deliverance from the inherited fallen nature has been secured for the child of God through Christ's death and through the power of the Holy Spirit.

Third, Eradicationists ignore the great body of truth which presents the overcoming work of the Holy Spirit in the believer and the deeper aspect of Christ's death that serves as the ground of all deliverance. That death to sin which is positional and which includes every believer, on the other hand, is interpreted as being experimental and limited to a few who have claimed some estate that the New Testament knows noththing of. Nevertheless, all that has been wrought by God is to the end that the believer may "walk" upon a new life-principle (Rom. 6:4). The human responsibility in this walk is far removed, indeed, from what it would be if perchance the sin nature were actually removed. No place could be made under such circumstances for the words "reckon, yield, let not sin reign, put off, mortify, or abide." The nature is not so much to be reckoned dead as that the believer is dead to it.

Fourth, Eradicationists magnify human experience to the point that they disregard any revelation which disagrees with their experience. Of what value is revelation, think such, when one has had an experience, especially if the revelation tends to correct or contradict the experience?

Fifth, the New Testament warns specifically against the eradication error. In 1 John 1:8 it is said: "If we say that we have no sin, we deceive ourselves, and the truth is not in us." Reference here is to a sin nature, whereas in verse 10 reference is to sin which is the fruit of the evil nature. To say as an assumption that one does not have a sin nature may be due to self-deception; nevertheless, to any such it is declared: "The truth is not in him." The basic claim of the Eradicationist is well stated in the words: "Because my sin nature is eradicated, I am not able to sin," whereas the testimony of the one who follows the divine provision and pattern is: "Because of the death of Christ and the immediate power of the Spirit, I am able not to sin." The two theories, then, are not to be reconciled. For believers are, according to a rationalistic theory, to be relieved from stress by an abrupt removal of the disposition to sin, which removal terminates all future conflict with a sin nature and exalts the beneficiaries to the supposed high level of existence wherein the Word of God respecting deliverance by the Holy Spirit through the death of Christ does not apply to them. On the other hand, the New Testament teaches a perfect victory over all evil—the world, the flesh with all its component parts, and the devil—by the constant enabling power of the Holy Spirit. There is not even room for discussion to determine which of these two propositions is taught in the Bible.

## CONCLUSION

The third condition, then, upon which one may be spiritual, is a definite reliance upon the Spirit, which means a "walk by means of the Spirit." Such a reliance upon the Spirit is imperative because of the impossible (humanly speaking) heavenly calling, the unspiritual power of the world, the opposing power of Satan, and the continued presence of the "flesh" with its Adamic nature. The child of God cannot meet tomorrow's issues today. The walk is something undertaken step by step and this demands a constant appropriation of the power of God. The Christian life is never likened to an ascension in which one might go up spiritually above the earth-level once-for-all and have no trouble or temptation here again. It rather is "a walk, a race, a fight." All this speaks of continuation. The good fight of faith is that of continuing an attitude of reliance upon the Spirit. To those who thus walk with God, there is opened a door into "fellowship with the Father, and with his Son Jesus Christ" and into a life of fruit-bearing and service with every spiritual manifestation of power, to the glory of God. What, then, is true spirituality? It is the unhindered manifestation of the indwelling Spirit. There are, in all, seven aspects of manifestation. These blessed realities are all provided for in the presence and power of the Spirit and will normally be produced by the Spirit in the Christian who is not grieving the Spirit, but has confessed every known sin; who is not quenching the Spirit, but is yielded to God; and who is walking in the Spirit by an attitude of dependence upon His power alone (Gal. 5:22–23). Such a one is spiritual because he is Spirit-filled. The Spirit is free to fulfill in him all the purpose and desire of God for his life. There is nothing in daily life and service to be desired beyond this. "Thanks be to God, which giveth us the victory through our Lord Jesus Christ."

"Our blest Redeemer, ere He breathed
His tender last farewell
A Guide, a Comforter, bequeathed
With us to dwell . . .

"And every virtue we possess,
And every victory won,
And every thought of holiness,
Are His alone."

## CHAPTER XVII

# AN ANALOGY

THOUGH WITHIN the positive aspect of the spiritual life a comparison may be drawn between those things which are bestowed or imparted when one is saved and the manifestation of the Spirit in the daily life of the Spirit-filled Christian, there also are various well-defined features of comparison which suggest an analogy between deliverance from the *penalty* of sin in the salvation of those who are out of Christ and deliverance from the *power* of sin on the part of those who among believers comply with the conditions governing the spiritual life. Without doubt, the positive benefits received when God saves are of primary import; yet the analogy now to be pursued, as suggested above, contemplates nothing other than two forms of salvation—one from the penalty and one from the power of sin. It is perhaps needful to point out the fact that the Bible treats the believer's deliverance from bond-servitude to sin as a distinct form of salvation. As would be expected from the Epistle to the Romans, which epistle declares the whole scope of salvation from both the penalty and the power of sin unto absolute security forever, there appears as itself the main structure of the book this differentiation between salvation from the penalty of sin unto forgiveness, imputed righteousness, and justification through Christ's death (Rom. 1:1—5:21), on the one hand, and salvation from the power of sin unto sanctification, which is both positional and experimental, as made possible through the same death of Christ (Rom. 6:1—8:27), on the other hand. This very structure of the doctrinal portion of the Epistle to the Romans will serve to emphasize the force of the fivefold analogy which follows.

### I. THE LOST ESTATE

The Word of God presents an extended description of the estate of all the unregenerate in their need of salvation from the guilt and penalty of sin. They are said to be "lost, condemned, and [spiritually] dead"; "there is none righteous, no, not one"; "all have sinned, and come short of the glory of God." But back of all this is the revelation that in themselves they are helpless and without power to alter or improve their condition. Their only hope is to depend completely on Another for His saving power and grace. "Believe on the Lord Jesus Christ, and thou shalt be saved."

In like manner, the Scriptures reveal the estate of the regenerate in relation to the power of the sin nature to be one of impotence and helplessness: "For I know that in me (that is, in my flesh,) dwelleth no good thing"; "I find then a law, that, when I would do good, evil is present with me." The hope of the child of God in his salvation from the power of sin is also linked with a complete dependence upon the power and grace of Another. "For the law of the Spirit of life in Christ Jesus hath made me free from the law of sin and death"; "Ye are of God, little children, and have overcome them: because greater is he that is in you, than he that is in the world"; "If by the Spirit ye are walking, ye shall not fulfil the lust of the flesh."

## II. THE DIVINE OBJECTIVE AND IDEAL

The greatest of all contrasts exists between the estate of the unregenerate person and the estate of that same individual after he is saved. Eternity alone can measure this transformation. Forgiveness is infinitely perfect for him, even unto such purification as will qualify the child of God to be void of even a shadow of sin in the presence of God forever; likewise, sonship to God actual and eternal, the divine righteousness which is imputed, perfection once-for-all, justification without a cause, reception of the very πλήρωμα or fullness of the Godhead whereby he is being "conformed to the image" of the Greater Son, to name a few blessings of position.

With no less of a perfect divine ideal in view, the Christian is called to a heaven-high manner of life and victory, through Christ's death unto the sin nature and the limitless enabling power of the Holy Spirit. The believer is besought to "walk worthy" of the glorious positions which are his through infinite grace and power. He is bidden to "walk in the light."

## III. THE GIFT OF GOD

Salvation must be of God alone, for every aspect of it is beyond human power and strength. Of the many great miracles which taken together constitute salvation from the guilt and penalty of sin, not one of them could even be understood, let alone be accomplished, by man. "It [the gospel of Christ] is the power of God unto salvation"; ". . . that he might be the justifier of him which believeth."

It is equally true that the believer is helpless to deliver himself from the power of sin. God alone can do it, and He proposes to do it according to the revelation contained in His Word. There is no power in man whatsoever to deliver from "the world, the flesh, and the devil." "If by the Spirit ye are walking, ye shall not fulfil the lust of the flesh"; "It is God which worketh in you both to will and to do of his good pleasure"; "The law of the Spirit of life in Christ Jesus hath made me free from the law of sin and death"; "Finally, my brethren, be strong in the Lord, and in the power of his might"; "Who shall deliver me? . . . I thank God through Jesus Christ our Lord."

## IV. THE WORK OF THE CROSS

Were the sinner unsheltered and should God judge his sins in the man himself, there would be nothing left to save. It is only as God has already judged the sinner's life in a Substitute that He can save him from consuming judgments; indeed, since that substitution was perfect and complete, the sinner is now saved from every punishment or penalty and unto infinite perfection in Christ. Such a salvation both satisfies the love of God for the one He saves and glorifies God forever. Because no moral obstacle remains to hinder divine love from its utmost expression, God proceeds to do all that infinity can do—He causes the one who is saved to become like Jesus Christ, His Son. A marvel of divine grace like this can be wrought by God on no other ground than the substitution that Christ has accomplished. It is essential, too, that the sinner take cognizance of the ground upon which he is saved. He then must come voluntarily and intelligently to God through the provided Savior. By the death of His Son, God has rendered Himself free to save the chief of sinners, i.e., to do it in such a way that He is righteous and just.

In like case there could be no salvation for the Christian from the power of sin had not God first taken the flesh with its sin nature, its "old man," into judgment. The believer's condition would be hopeless indeed if Christ had not first thus brought the sin nature into judgment. As in the case of the penalty for sin, the judgment work on the cross is done now and God is rendered propitious toward both sinner and saint. The "old man" was judged in a cocrucifixion, a codeath, and a coburial with Christ. ". . . knowing this, that our old man is ['was, R.V.] crucified with him." Since Christ has died unto the sin nature, perfecting all divine judgments against it, God is now infinitely free to take direct control of the flesh and its sin nature to the end that He may achieve deliverance for the saint from bond-servitude to sin. All this is something for the believer to "reckon" to be true and on the accepted ground of Christ's judgment of the "old man" to "yield himself unto God."

## V. THE PLACE OF FAITH

Since salvation is always and only a work of God, the only relation man can sustain to it is that of expectation toward the One who alone can undertake and accomplish it. Salvation from the guilt and penalty of sin is wrought for the unsaved the very *moment* he believes. It is conditioned on a solitary *act* of faith. Men are not saved, or kept saved, from the consequences of sins because they *continue* in their faith. Saving faith, as related to this the first aspect of salvation, is a completed transaction. "For God so loved the world, that he gave his only begotten Son, that whosoever believeth in him should not perish, but have everlasting life" (John 3:16); "Verily, verily, I say unto you, He that heareth my word, and believeth on him that sent me, hath everlasting life, and shall not come into condemnation; but is passed from death unto life" (John 5:24); "Believe on the Lord Jesus Christ, and thou shalt be saved, and thy house" (Acts 16:31).

Salvation unto sanctity of daily life is equally a work of God, and the only relation the child of God can sustain to it is an *attitude* of expectation toward the One who alone is able. There should be an adjustment of the life and will to God, and this salvation must then be claimed by faith; but in this case it is still only an attitude of faith. Believers are saved from the power of sin as they believe. The one who has been justified by an *act* of faith must now henceforth *live* by faith. There are a multitude of sinners for whom Christ has died who are not now saved. On the divine side, everything has been provided and they have only to enter by faith into His saving grace as it is available for them in Jesus Christ. Just so, there are a multitude of saints whose sin nature has been perfectly judged and every provision made on the divine side for a life of victory and glory to God who are not now realizing a life of victory. They have only to enter by faith into the saving grace available to deliver from the power and dominion of sin. This step would introduce them to the reality of "a walk, a race, a warfare." All of this signifies a constant attitude. Christians are told to "fight the good fight of faith." Sinners are not saved until they trust the Savior, and saints are not victorious until they trust the Deliverer from the reigning power of sin. God has made this rescue possible through the cross of His Son. Salvation from the power of sin must be claimed by faith. Discussing this fifth aspect of the analogy, Bishop H. C. G. Moule of Durham, England, writes:

> The first case is in its nature one and single: an admission, an incorporation. The second is in its nature progressive and developing: the discovery, advancing with the occasion for it, of the greatness of the resources of Christ for life. The latter *may,* not *must,* thus include one great crisis in consciousness, one particular spiritual act. It is much more certain to include many starting-points, critical developments, marked advances. The act of self-surrendering faith in the power of Christ for inward cleansing of the will and affections may be, and often indeed it is, *as it were* a new conversion, a new "effectual calling." But it is sure, if the man knows himself in the light of Christ, to be followed by echoes and reiterations to the end; not mere returns to and beginnings from the old level (certainly it is not the plan of God that it should be so), but definite out-growths due to new discovery of personal need and sin, and of more than corresponding "riches" in Christ. With each such advance the sacred promise of the *fulness of the Spirit* will be received with a holy and happy realization.—*Outlines of Christian Doctrine,* 2nd rev. ed., p. 199

The Spirit, when saving from the reigning power of sin, does not set aside the personality of the one He saves. He merely takes possession of the faculties and powers of the individual. It is the power of God acting through the human faculties of the will, emotions, desires, and disposition. The experience of the believer who is being empowered is only that of a consciousness of his own power of choice, his own feelings, desires, and disposition as related to self. The strength which he possesses, however, is "in the Lord, and in the power of his might."

### CONCLUSION

Because so far this discussion has dealt primarily with the theory or doctrine of the spiritual life, the addition of a few practical suggestions may not be amiss. Since a life in the power of the Spirit depends upon a continuous attitude of reckoning and appropriation, it is important for most Christians to have a time of definite dealing with God in which they may examine their hearts in the matter of sin and their need of yieldedness, and in which they may acknowledge both their insufficiency and His sufficiency as revealed by the Spirit. Then, at that particular time, they may claim His power and strength to supplant their weakness. The Bible makes no rules about the time or conditions. It is a case of the individual child, in all the latitude of his own personality, dealing with his Father.

Spirituality is not a future ideal; it is to be experienced *now*. The vital question is, "Am I walking in the Spirit now?" The answer to this question should not depend on the presence or absence of some unusual manifestation of the supernatural. Much of everyone's life will be lived in the uneventful commonplace; but even there the believer should have conviction that he is right with God and in His unbroken fellowship. "Beloved, if our heart condemn us not, then have we confidence toward God" (1 John 3:21). Likewise, the child of God should not mistake worn nerves, physical weakness, or depression for unspirituality. Many times sleep is more needed than prayer, and physical recreation than heart-searching.

Be it remembered, too, that His provisions are always perfect, but that the Christian's entrance into these provisions is often imperfect. There is doubtless too glib a reference to human attitudes and actions in relation to God as if they were absolute, such as absolute surrender, absolute consecration, and absolute devotion. If there are well-defined conditions upon which the believer may become spiritual, let him remember that, from the standpoint of the infinite God, his compliance with those conditions is often imperfect. What God provides and bestows is in accord with the fullest divine perfection, but the Christian's adjustment is human and therefore usually subject to improvement. The fact nevertheless of the believer's possible deliverance, which depends upon the Spirit alone, does not change. The child of God will have as much at any time as he makes it possible for the Spirit to bestow.

Normally, the spiritual Christian will be occupied with effective service for his Lord. This, however, is not a rule. Christians need only to take care that they are yielded and ready to do whatever He may choose. To "rest in the LORD" is one of the essential victories in a spiritual life. "Come ye yourselves apart . . . and rest a while." A child of God is just as spiritual when resting, playing, sleeping, or incapacitated, if it is His will for him, as he is when serving.

The spiritual life is not passive. Too often it is thus misjudged and because of the fact that one, to be spiritual, must cease from self-effort in the direction of spiritual attainments and learn to live and serve by the power God has provided. True spirituality knows little of quietism.

It rather is life much more active, enlarged, and vital because it is energized by the limitless power of God. Spirit-filled Christians are quite apt to be exhausted physically at the close of day. They are weary *in* the work, but not weary *of* it.

The Spirit-filled life is never free from temptations; but "God is faithful, who will not suffer you to be tempted above that ye are able; but will with the temptation also make a way to escape, that ye may be able to bear it." The plain teaching of this promise, in harmony with all Scripture on the subject, is that temptations as phenomena which are "common to man" attack all Christians, but that withal there is a divinely provided way of escape. The child of God does not need to yield unto temptation. There is always the *possibility* of sin, but never the *necessity*. It has been well said that spiritual believers are honored with warfare in the front-line trenches. There the fiercest pressure of the enemy is felt. But they are also privileged to witness the enemy's crushing defeat, so abundant is the power of God; and thus the spiritual believer is highly honored.

Living in unrealities is a source of hindrance to spirituality. Anything that savors of a "religious pose" is harmful. In a very particular sense the one who has been changed from the natural to the spiritual sometimes needs to be changed back to a naturalness again—meaning, of course, a naturalness of manner and life. The true spiritual life presents a latitude sufficient to allow the believer to live very close to all classes of people without ever drawing him from God. Spirituality hinders sin, but should never hinder the friendship and confidence of sinners (Luke 15:1). Who can see the failure of others more than the one who has spiritual vision? And because of this fact, who needs more the divine power to keep him from becoming critical, with all that follows therefrom? Christians need to study most carefully the adaptation practiced by the Apostle Paul as he revealed it in 1 Corinthians 9:19–22. If one's kind of spirituality makes Christ unattractive to others, it needs some drastic changes. May God save His children from assuming a holy tone of voice, a holy somberness of spirit, a holy expression of face, or a holy garb (if by the garb they wish to appear holy)! True spirituality is an inward adorning. It is most simple and natural and should be a delight and attraction to all.

It will not do to *impersonate* ideals or to *imitate* others. Just here is the great danger in analyzing experiences. Some are so easily induced to try to imitate someone else. That which gives a believer priceless distinctiveness is his own personality, and he cannot please God more than by being what He designed him to be. Some Christians are disposed to traffic in unlived truth, repeating pious phrases the truth of which they have never really experienced. This must always grieve the Spirit.

Children of God are dealing always with their Father. Too often the walk in the Spirit is thought to be a mechanical thing. The believer is not dealing with a machine: he is dealing with the most loving and tenderhearted Father in all the universe. The deepest secret of his walk is just to know Him, and so to believe in His Father-heart that he can cry out his failures on His loving breast if need be, or speak plainly to Him in thanksgiving for every victory. When Christians know the consolation and relief of such communion, they will have less occasion to appeal to anyone else. It is theirs to tell Him just what they feel, just how bad they are at heart—and even their darkest unbelief. To do this only opens the heart to Him for His blessed light and strength. Separation from close-up communion is the first thing that one should fear, and the first aid in every spiritual accident is the simple act of telling Him everything repentantly. Having made confession, the believer should reckon his forgiveness and restoration fully accomplished and immediately return to His fellowship and grace.

The teaching that "the bird with broken pinion never soars so high again" is most unscriptural. Through the sacrifice of Christ, no penalty because of sin remains today for saint or sinner (if the latter will receive Him). Rather "the bird with broken pinion may higher soar"; but of course there should be no complacency with failure and defeat for that reason.

Christians are never wonderful saints of whom God may justly be proud; they are His little children, immature and filled with foolishness, with whom He is endlessly patient and on whom He has been pleased to set all His infinite heart of love. He is wonderful: Christians are not.

Believe what is written. Remember the vital words of Romans 6:6, 9: "Knowing this . . ." or, "because we know this." One is always justified in acting on good evidence. Where, then, is there a safer word of testimony than the imperishable Word of our God? From that very Word believers *know* that God has provided a finished judgment for their sins and for their sin, and that the way is open for an overflowing life in the power of the blessed Spirit. The believer should know that such a life is His loving purpose for him. He is to believe His unfailing promise. So far from imposing on Him if he claims this grace, to fail to claim *all* that His love would bestow will hurt Him more than all else.

True spirituality is a great reality. It is *all* of the manifestations of the Spirit in and through the one within whom He dwells. He manifests in the believer the life which is Christ. He came not to reveal Himself but to make Christ real *to* the heart, and *through* the heart, of man. Thus the Apostle Paul could write: "For this cause I bow my knees unto the Father of our Lord Jesus Christ, of whom the whole family in heaven and earth is named, that he would grant you, according to the riches of his glory, to be strengthened with might by his Spirit in the inner man; that Christ may dwell in your hearts by faith; that ye, being rooted and grounded in love, may be able to comprehend with all saints what is the breadth, and length, and depth, and height; and to know the love of Christ, which passeth knowledge, that ye might be filled with all the fulness of God. Now unto him that is able to do exceeding abundantly above all that we ask or think, according to the power that worketh in us, unto him be glory in the church by Christ Jesus throughout all ages, world without end. Amen."